AI-Driven Knowledge Management Assets, Volume 2

AI-Driven Knowledge Management Assets, Volume 2: Strategies for the Modern Business Landscape

EDITED BY

MILTIADIS D. LYTRAS

The American College of Greece, Greece

AND

MEIR RUSS

University of Wisconsin–Green Bay, USA

Stellenbosch University, South Africa

emerald PUBLISHING

United Kingdom – North America – Japan – India – Malaysia – China

Emerald Publishing Limited
Emerald Publishing, Floor 5, Northspring, 21-23 Wellington Street, Leeds LS1 4DL

First edition 2026

British Library Cataloguing in Publication Data
A catalogue record for this book is available from the British Library

ISBN: 978-1-83662-779-1 (Print)
ISBN: 978-1-83662-778-4 (Online)
ISBN: 978-1-83662-780-7 (Epub)

INVESTOR IN PEOPLE

To Fay, that keeps me grounded every day, with all my love.

Contents

About the Editors *xi*

About the Contributors *xiii*

Introduction

Chapter 1 Unveiling the AI-Driven Knowledge Asset Landscape: Foundations, Innovations, and Integration Strategies *3*
Miltiadis D. Lytras and Meir Russ

AI-Driven Decision Support Systems in Business

Chapter 2 How Artificial Intelligence Affects the Decision-Making Process in Business: AI-Driven Decision Support Systems *17*
Cem Ufuk Baytar

Chapter 3 AI-Driven Decision Support Systems for Transforming Employee Engagement and Training in Business *37*
Jill Courtney

Case Studies on AI-Driven Knowledge Management Systems

Chapter 4 Implementing Artificial Intelligence for Knowledge Management in Small and Medium Enterprises *63*
Kabiru Ishola Genty, Godwin Kaisara, Sulaiman Olusegun Atiku and Hylton James Villet

Chapter 5 Technology Using Artificial Intelligence (AI) to Enhance Productivity and Sustainability in Atlantic Salmon Production and Challenges From Knowledge Management *81*
Per Harald Rødvei, Knut Ingar Westeren and Martin Munkeby

Chapter 6 Transforming Knowledge Management Through Synergistic Artificial Intelligence–Human Collaboration *105*
Viraj Dawarka and Geshwaree Huzooree

Chapter 7 Architectural Artificial Intelligence Design Patterns for Knowledge Management Processes *133*
Giovanna Di Marzo Serugendo and Lamia Friha

Chapter 8 Cooperation Between Artificial Intelligence and Lateral Transshipment: Qualitative Study *153*
Elleuch Fadoi

The Role of AI and KM in Enhancing Employee Relationship and Talent Management

Chapter 9 How Artificial Intelligence Influences Employees' Organisational Behaviour in Workplaces *169*
Mandy Mok Kim Man, Wong Wan Ting, Lebene Soga and Maria Fernandez-Muiños

Chapter 10 AI in Action: Decoding the Employee Experience Connection to Boost Engagement *195*
Puneet Kumar and Nayantara Padhi

Chapter 11 Reimagining Talent Management Through the AI-Knowledge Nexus *221*
Unnar Theodorsson

The Future of AI in Knowledge Management: Challenges and Opportunities

Chapter 12 The Prospective Developments of Artificial Intelligence in the Domain of Knowledge Management: Challenges and Opportunities *239*
Viraj Dawarka, Alisha Hingun Goolam Gukan and Aisha Bibi Idoo

Chapter 13 Artificial Intelligence–Driven Knowledge Management for Development in the Global South: Bridging Digital Divides Through Localized Innovation *265*
Nanette Y. Saes, Bruce W. Watson and Liam R. Watson

Chapter 14 Artificial Intelligence and Knowledge Management Systems: Transforming the Future of Business Operations in the Fourth Industrial Revolution *285*
Rashmi Kumari, Sujata Priyambada Dash and Rajeshwari Chatterjee

Conclusion

Chapter 15 Safeguarding the Future: Addressing Fraud, Misuse, and Ethical Vulnerabilities in AI-Driven Knowledge Management *307*
Meir Russ and Miltiadis D. Lytras

About the Editors

Miltiadis D. Lytras is a Professor (Full) at The American College of Greece and a Visiting Research Professor at Effat University in Saudi Arabia. Dr Lytras is a world-class expert in the fields of digital transformation and technology-enabled learning. He is an expert in advanced computer science and management, an editor, a lecturer and a research consultant, with extensive experience in academia and the business sector in Europe, the Middle East and Asia.

Prof. Meir Russ earned his PhD in Strategy, Entrepreneurship and International Business from The Ohio State University in 1993 and holds a BSc in Electronic Engineering and an MBA from Tel Aviv University. A founder of a high-tech company and international consultant in strategy and knowledge management, he was named Professor Emeritus at the University of Wisconsin–Green Bay in 2020. He is also a Research Fellow at Stellenbosch University (South Africa) and a Visiting Professor at the University of Łódź (Poland). Prof. Russ is the Chief Editor of the *Online Journal of Applied Knowledge Management* (OJAKM) and was the founding Chief Editor of the *International Journal of Management and Business* (IJMB). He was the author of over 45 peer-reviewed publications and editor of nine books; he has taught and delivered seminars globally, including in China, Italy, Spain, Norway, France, Mexico and the Semester at Sea program.

About the Contributors

Sulaiman Olusegun Atiku (PhD) is a Professor of Human Resources Management. He has published articles on human resources and knowledge management and has delivered keynote addresses at various academic forums. Sulaiman is also an Adjunct Professor at Walter Sisulu University in South Africa.

Cem Ufuk Baytar is a researcher, an educator and a consultant specializing in management information systems, system analysis and design, e-commerce and data analytics. He earned his PhD in business administration from Beykent University, Istanbul. He has participated in various IT projects related to e-commerce, ERP, digital archiving and document management systems at both international and national levels. Currently, Cem Ufuk is a member of the Management Information Systems Department at İstanbul Topkapı University, Turkey.

Rajeshwari Chatterjee worked as a Research Fellow in the Department of Environmental Science at the Indian Institute of Social Welfare and Business Management, Kolkata, India. She worked as an Assistant Professor in the Department of HMCT from 2007 to 2023. Currently, she is an Assistant Professor at the Department of Chemical Engineering, Birla Institute of Technology, Mesra, Ranchi. She has completed her PhD in Management BIT, Mesra and PhD in Science from IIT-ISM, Dhanbad. She has published about 30 papers in international/national journals and proceedings of international conferences.

Jill Courtney is a senior engineer, multimedia producer, educator, and instructional designer specializing in traditional and AI-supported training systems, workforce development, and educational leadership. Currently supporting advanced learning initiatives as a government contractor, Courtney has extensive experience across K-12, higher education, government, and entertainment sectors. She holds a Bachelor's in Music Education from St. Olaf College, a Musical Theatre degree from AMDA-NY, a Master's in Audio Engineering from New York University, an Education Specialist degree in Educational Leadership and Administration from Lipscomb University, and a Doctorate in Instructional Design Leadership from Franklin University. An active member of IEEE, SWE, WiCyS and AES, Courtney serves on the Strategic AI Advisory Board at the University of Colorado-Colorado Springs. She is certified in Agile Project Management, Strategic AI, and Prompt Engineering. Her methodology integrates instructional design, applied AI, multimedia production and systems thinking to optimize learning performance within complex, high-accountability environments.

Sujata Priyambada Dash is currently working as an Assistant Professor in the Department of Management, Birla Institute of Technology, Mesra, Ranchi, Jharkhand, INDIA. Her research interests include Human Capital Management, Emotional Intelligence, Blockchain and AI in HRM. She has published her research work in many National and International Journals (Scopus and ABDC indexed) and attended various National and International Conferences, Workshops and Faculty Development Programmes. She has published book chapters in Scopus indexed Edited Book volumes in International Publication houses such as Springer, CRC Press, Taylor and Francis and Wiley. Her professional affiliation is AIMS-Associations of Management Scholar.

Viraj Dawarka is a Senior Lecturer and a researcher in Computer Science at the University of Staffordshire, London Campus, UK, where he leads the BSc (Hons) Cloud and Network Computing programme, teaches and leads modules in the BSc and MSc computing programmes. He also mentors all the third-year computing students from different programmes. He holds a PhD in Computer Science specializing in Energy Efficiency and Cloud Robotics from the Open University of Mauritius, a Postgraduate Certificate in Higher and Professional Education from the University of Staffordshire, an MSc in Software Engineering from the University of Greenwich and a BSc (Hons) in Computer Science with Network Security from the University of Technology, Mauritius. A Fellow and Senior of the Higher Education Academy (FHEA) (SFHEA), Dr Dawarka has taught 30+ computing modules within his 10+ years in academia, served as an External Examiner for UK universities and published journal articles, book chapters, and conference papers in IEEE, Elsevier and other platforms. He also reviews academic publications and has chaired international conferences, contributing significantly to the field.

Giovanna Di Marzo Serugendo is a full Professor at the University of Geneva, Switzerland since 2010. From 2016 to 2024, she was the Director of the Computer Science Center of the University of Geneva. She was nominated in 2018 among the 100 digital shapers in Switzerland. Her research interests relate to decentralized AI software with self-organizing and emergent behaviour, semantic AI and digital twins. This involves studying natural systems, modelling their behaviour, designing and developing artificial collective systems. Her domain of research encompasses smart cities, smart grids, management of underground objects, GLAMs and urban structures. Giovanna co-founded the IEEE International Conference on Self-Adaptive and Self-Organizing Systems (SASO) and the ACM Transactions on Autonomous Adaptive Systems (TAAS), for which she served as Editor in Chief from 2005 to 2011.

Elleuch Fadoi is a Senior Lecturer at the University of Economic Science and Management of Sfax and an active researcher in the Governance, Finance and Accounting Laboratory. With over 5 years of academic experience, she dedicates most of her time to scientific research and is passionate about expanding her contributions across a range of interdisciplinary fields.

María Fernández-Muiños is an early-career academic with a strong research and teaching background in the field of business and organizational studies. Currently serving as an Assistant Professor at the University of León (Spain), she was awarded the Extraordinary Doctorate Prize at the University of Salamanca (Spain) for her outstanding academic achievements. Her scholarly work includes publications in peer-reviewed international journals and book chapters with leading academic publishers. Dr Fernández-Muiños has presented her research at several renowned international conferences and has actively contributed to multidisciplinary research projects. Her research interests encompass strategic management, corporate social responsibility (CSR), leadership and business ethics. More recently, her work has explored the intersection of AI and entrepreneurship, as well as mindfulness and spiritual leadership in organizational contexts. She has undertaken international research and training stays at the University of Reading (Henley Business School, UK) and has participated in various teaching innovation initiatives at the University of Salamanca. Her research has received competitive funding from both European and national sources, enabling her to continue her contributions to high-impact research in the field.

Lamia Friha holds a PhD in Computer Science, in Artificial Intelligence (AI), from the University of Geneva. She was in 1998 at the International Telecommunication Union (ITU), then in 2000 at Kudelski, and since 2003, she has been the Senior Project Manager at the Information Systems Division of the University of Geneva. She is also a lecturer at both the University of Geneva and Haute École de Gestion (HEG, Geneva). Lamia oversees the R&D cell.

Kabiru Ishola Genty holds a PhD in Human Resource Development from the University Putra Malaysia. He is a Senior Lecturer in the Department of Industrial Relations and Human Resource Management (HRM) at Lagos State University in Nigeria. Currently, he is attached to the Harold Pupkewitz Graduate School of Business at the Namibia University of Science and Technology as a Senior Postdoctoral Research Fellow.

Alisha Hingun Goolam Gukan has a sound background in marketing research and analytics. She currently serves as a Senior Lecturer at Nottingham Trent University, UK. Known for her passion for students and dedication to fostering a caring learning environment, she works with a team of academics and marketing practitioners, assisting in the academic and professional growth of higher education students. Her skills have been shaped over more than 15 years of working experience, particularly in research design and consultancy. This extensive experience has culminated in a recent book publication that explores the dynamic intersection of branding and the self-concept. Other projects include papers that underline her commitment to elevating brand communication strategies through AI, reflecting an integration of academic rigour and practical consultancy experience.

Geshwaree Huzooree is the programme leader for the BA Business Management programme at Edinburgh Napier University, where she also lectures in Strategy and Project Management in the MBA Programme. She is a Senior Fellow of the Higher Education Academy and served as a Senior Lecturer at Curtin Mauritius for eight years. With 7 years of IT industry experience in software development and project management, she holds a PhD in Computer Science (2020), an MSc in Software Engineering Projects and Management (2014) and a BSc in Computer Science and Engineering (2007) from the University of Mauritius. Her research focuses on project management, remote working, higher education, health informatics, AI and digital technologies. Dr Geshwaree received the Best Oral Presenter Award (2018) for her work on diabetes sensor technologies. She has authored journal articles, book chapters and edited books and has published extensively in reputable platforms such as IEEE and Springer, addressing real-world challenges through impactful research.

Aisha Bibi Idoo is a Senior Graduate Teaching Assistant at Middlesex University Mauritius, specializing in Information Technology. She holds both a Bachelor of Science and a Master of Science in Information Technology from Curtin University Mauritius, where she also served as a Teaching Assistant during her undergraduate studies. Aisha's research interests focus on Web Development, particularly in creating dynamic and user-friendly web applications. In addition to her teaching role, she supervises final-year projects involving emerging technologies like Robotics, Augmented Reality/Virtual Reality and AI, aiming to solve contemporary challenges with innovative solutions. Passionate about mentoring, Aisha strives to design projects that challenge students and benefit both the university and the wider computing community. Her dedication to pedagogy and practical, impactful projects reflects her commitment to student growth and the advancement of computing.

Godwin Kaisara holds a PhD in Information Management. A Research Fellow at the Namibia University of Science and Technology's in Harold Pupkewitz Graduate School of Business, he is the author of several book chapters and journal articles on Information and Communication Technologies.

Puneet Kumar is a lecturer in the Directorate of Education, GNCT of Delhi, India. He has expertise in the management discipline and specializes in employee engagement, employee experience, HR analytics and workplace spirituality. Holding a PhD in Management focusing on Employee Engagement, Dr Kumar has established himself as a thought leader. With industry experience working with Thomas Assessment, a leading provider of behavioural assessments, Dr Kumar has developed a unique understanding of human behaviour and its impact on organizational performance. A prolific researcher, Dr Kumar has published articles in national and international refereed journals, contributing significantly to the body of knowledge in his field.

Rashmi Kumari received her B.Tech degree in Computer Science & Engineering from BIT Sindri, Dhanbad, India, in 2018 and her MBA degree in HRM from BIT Mesra, Ranchi, India, in 2020. She is currently working toward the PhD degree with the Department of Management, Birla Institute of Technology Mesra, Ranchi, India. Her research interest includes HRM and Organizational Behaviour. She has authored or co-authored various research articles in prestigious journals, book chapters and conference proceedings.

Mandy Mok Kim Man is a highly respected academic with extensive experience in tertiary education. She is deeply committed to fostering academic excellence and promoting student development. Her research contributions are considerable, including 65 scholarly papers and conference proceedings, along with eight book chapters published by reputable publishers, including Emerald, US, UK and reputable local publishers. Beyond her academic publications, she actively engages in public scholarship, contributing articles to various social media platforms, newspapers and magazines. She has also been invited to deliver numerous talks and conduct workshops at prestigious academic and professional conferences. Her dedication and excellence have been recognized through numerous prestigious awards and accolades. She has held the position of visiting scholar at Kobe Gakuin University in Japan. She has collaborated on cross-national research projects with scholars from both local and international universities, with her research findings published in reputable international journals.

Martin Munkeby is a serial entrepreneur and a technologist. He is currently serving as the COO of CageEye, a high-tech company doing hydroacoustics for fish farming. He is the former co-founder of NorseAqua AS and nowHow AS.

Nayantara Padhi is a distinguished academic in the management field, currently serving as a Professor at the School of Management Studies, Indira Gandhi National Open University (IGNOU), New Delhi, India. Prof Padhi's academic career spans over two decades, which has been marked by significant contributions to education and research. Her work includes coordinating and developing MBA programmes, MOOCs, skill development workshops and translating educational materials into regional languages under various national projects. An accomplished author, Prof Padhi has published 9 books, 35 articles and 40 book chapters, with notable works in HRM, Organizational Behaviour and Corporate Governance.

Per Harald Rødvei holds a PhD in Political Science and is an Associate Professor of Organization and Management at Nord University. His research interests include HRM, wage policy and incentive systems and organizational sustainability. Rødvei has extensive experience as a manager, a consultant in both the public and private sectors and a member of governmental committees, including the Norwegian Parliament's Wage Commission.

Nanette Y. Saes is a Senior International Business Communication strategist, a facilitator and a sworn translator, specializing in ICT and AI-driven innovation in communication and language solutions. As a former Research Fellow at Stellenbosch University's Centre for Knowledge Dynamics & Decision Making, she explored the application of emerging technologies to enhance Group

Decision Support Systems, receiving Best Research Idea Awards at the Knowledge Management Conferences (2021, 2017). Nanette played a key role in launching the South Africa Netherlands Cyber Security School (SANCS), leading local PR and engagement in Southern Africa. She also contributed to AI-focused initiatives, including a special issue of *Quest* magazine, shedding light on AI's opportunities and challenges in Africa. Her recent projects include leading the UX and engagement strategy for a mobile-first AI app tailored to the Global South, along with developing the associated branding and communications. Nanette holds a Master of International Business Communication from Radboud University and has led digital communication initiatives for clients like Nestlé and the Boston Consulting Group.

Lebene Soga is a Professor of Entrepreneurship and Management Practice at Leeds Business School, Leeds Beckett University, UK. His research explores technology-mediated managerial practices, entrepreneurship ecosystems and leadership. His research seeks to progress the understanding of various organizational challenges and the implications of new technologies for management practice. His insights are featured in the *Wall Street Journal, Financial Times, Forbes*, etc. He has published in leading journals including *Organizational Research Methods, Information Technology and People, Technological Forecasting and Social Change, Harvard Business Review, MIT Sloan Management Review, European Journal of Work and Organizational Psychology, Journal of Business Research*, etc.

Unnar Theodorsson is an accomplished scholar and an educator specializing in talent management, knowledge management and organizational behaviour. He holds a postdoctoral position at the Department of Organization (IOA) at Copenhagen Business School and is also an Assistant Professor at the Department of Business Administration at the University of Iceland. Dr Theódórsson earned his PhD in Business Administration from the University of Iceland and has conducted international research at institutions including the Wharton School at the University of Pennsylvania and Hanyang University in South Korea. His current research explores the integration of AI into talent and knowledge management, as well as the relationship between regulatory compliance and innovation in the banking sector.

Wong Wan Ting is an undergraduate student at the University of Reading Malaysia, pursuing a Bachelor of Science in Business and Management. She has demonstrated exceptional academic performance and has actively participated in various student activities, for which she was awarded the prestigious Best Student Award in 2024. Her research interests encompass the domains of AI, digital marketing, innovation and organizational behaviour. She has established a robust academic foundation in these areas, which has motivated her to investigate the transformative potential of AI in shaping workplace dynamics. Her research endeavours aim to provide insightful analysis into the influence of AI on employee engagement and productivity. Ms Wong is deeply committed to research that explores the integration of technology within organizational structures and its broader implications for business practices. With her academic background and strong interest in innovation, she aspires to contribute to the development of effective strategies that address the evolving challenges of today's dynamic business environment.

Hylton James Villet (PhD) is the Director of Harold Pupkewitz Graduate School of Business. Hylton has vast experience in academia, and he has provided consultancy services to various organizations and government agencies in Namibia and beyond.

Bruce W. Watson is a leading expert in AI, cybersecurity, algorithmics and silicon chip fabrication, with a multi-decade career spanning Microsoft, Cisco, academia and startups. An Honorary Full Professor at the University of KwaZulu-Natal's School of Management, IT and Public Governance, he is a Global Commissioner for Responsible AI in the Military Domain, contributing to correctness-by-construction and African perspectives. Bruce holds two PhDs – one in Computing Science & Engineering (Eindhoven University) and one in Computer Science (University of Pretoria) – and a Mathematics/C&O degree from the University of Waterloo. He founded AI for Computational Thinking at the Centre for AI Research (Stellenbosch) and has supervised dozens of postgraduate students. His research underpins developments in cybersecurity, computational genetics and knowledge graph algorithms. A frequent keynote speaker and active contributor to the UN's AI Advisory Board, Bruce is committed to developing responsible AI solutions that advance knowledge management and innovation across Africa and globally.

Liam R. Watson is the Founder and CEO of Watcode AI, where he leads the development of cutting-edge AI software solutions addressing critical challenges across Africa and beyond. A pioneering force in applied AI and machine learning, Liam began programming at age 11 in Cape Town and now brings over a decade of experience, including six years specializing in AI and deep learning. As a Computer Science student at the University of Waterloo, he has earned recognition for his academic excellence, impactful research and awards such as the "Best Research Idea Award" at the IIAKM Knowledge Management Conference. His work spans cybersecurity compliance tools, autonomous AI systems and large language models. Beyond technical innovation, Liam mentors young developers and champions wider access to transformative technologies, believing deeply in AI's power to drive socio-economic growth. His leadership style emphasizes collaboration, innovation and unlocking diverse talent for transformative impact.

Knut Ingar Westeren has been a Professor of Economics at Nord University since 2001. He has his PhD from the University of Minnesota/NTNU(Norway). He teaches HRM and Knowledge and Competitiveness and has written numerous articles and books dealing with different aspects of competitiveness and human resources linked to the knowledge economy. He has been working with several companies in Norway, Denmark, Brazil and Chile and has been linked to several universities like UNIOESTE in Brazil and the University of Wisconsin in the United States.

Introduction

Chapter 1

Unveiling the AI-Driven Knowledge Asset Landscape: Foundations, Innovations, and Integration Strategies

Miltiadis D. Lytras[a] *and Meir Russ*[b]

[a]The American College of Greece, Greece
[b]University of Wisconsin - Green Bay, USA; Stellenbosch University, South Africa

Abstract

Artificial Intelligence (AI) is reshaping the nature, value, and dynamics of knowledge assets in organizations. This chapter offers a foundational exploration of AI-driven knowledge management assets, emphasizing how emerging technologies create, enhance, and transform these assets across industries. We begin by classifying core types of knowledge assets, including human, structural, and relational assets, and then examine the emergence of AI-generated content, codified intelligence, and autonomous process insights as new forms of digital capital. Particular focus is given to AI's role in business process automation, where algorithmic knowledge increasingly serves as a central asset. We also present a framework for integrating AI-generated knowledge into traditional enterprise systems and human workflows, emphasizing the balance between augmentation and automation. This chapter positions AI-enhanced knowledge assets not as replacements for human contribution but as catalysts that elevate decision-making, innovation, and organizational adaptability.

Keywords: AI-driven knowledge management; knowledge assets; KM ecosystem; innovations; integration strategies

AI-Driven Knowledge Management Assets, Volume 2, 3–13

Published under exclusive licence by Emerald Publishing Limited
doi:10.1108/978-1-83662-778-420261001

Introduction: Redefining Knowledge Assets in the Age of Artificial Intelligence

The concept of knowledge as a strategic asset has long been established in management literature (Edvinsson & Sullivan, 1996; Russ, 2021; Sarirete et al., 2022; Chui et al., 2020; Visvizi et al., 2020). Traditionally, organizations have invested heavily in capturing explicit knowledge (manuals, reports, systems) and fostering tacit knowledge (expertise, intuition, experience). In the digital era, these assets became structured in enterprise platforms, knowledge bases, and learning ecosystems. However, with the exponential rise of artificial intelligence—especially natural language processing (NLP), machine learning (ML), and generative AI—a new class of *AI-driven knowledge assets* has emerged, challenging the traditional taxonomy of organizational capital (Böhm & Durst, 2025; Rezaei, 2025; Wang et al., 2025; Zhang, Zhang, et al., 2025).

In this new paradigm, knowledge is not only consumed and shared—it is generated, structured, and autonomously created by intelligent systems. AI can now create new product ideas, generate workflows, summarize vast datasets, optimize decisions, and even derive abstract conceptualizations from real-time data. These capabilities are not simply tools—they are assets in their own right, possessing informational, strategic, business, and financial value.

At the same time, the rise of AI-generated knowledge creates a dual imperative: how to *integrate these new assets* effectively into organizational infrastructure, and how to ensure that *human intelligence is not displaced, but empowered and enhanced* in the process. Businesses must now manage not only what people know but also what machines know—and ensure the synergistic alignment between the two (Kloth & Jonathan, 2025; Zhang, Zhang, et al., 2025; Liu et al., 2024; Olan et al., 2024; Chen, 2024; Iaia et al., 2024; He & Burger-Helmchen, 2024).

In this chapter, we explore:

- The *types of knowledge assets* evolving under AI's influence;
- The emergence of *AI-generated assets* as core to business process automation;
- The *enhancement pillars* that support AI integration into traditional systems and workflows.

Through this lens, we aim to provide a conceptual and strategic grounding for the rest of the volume, which will explore sector-specific applications, managerial implications, and advanced deployment strategies.

Mapping the New Landscape of Knowledge Assets in the AI Era

The digital transformation era has long expanded our understanding of knowledge assets beyond simple documentation and expertise. However, with the rise of AI—particularly generative AI, intelligent automation, and advanced analytics—organizations are now seeing the formation of entirely new *asset classes* that blend human cognition with machine intelligence.

This section outlines the foundational knowledge asset types in modern business and explores how AI technologies are generating, reshaping, and/or augmenting them. We propose a layered structure that distinguishes between *traditional*, *digitally enhanced*, and *AI-driven* knowledge assets (c.f., Russ, 2021, Fig. 3), all of which must be strategically managed for competitive advantage.

Traditional Knowledge Asset Categories

Drawing from classical knowledge management theory (Edvinsson & Sullivan, 1996; Nonaka & Takeuchi, 1995; Sveiby, 1997), knowledge assets typically fall into the following categories:

a. Human Capital
   - Expertise, skills, creativity, experience, intuition
   - Carried by individuals; hard to codify but critical for innovation
   - Traditionally developed through training, mentorship, and job rotation

b. Structural Capital
   - Documented procedures, databases, manuals, software code, and patents
   - Owned by the organization; easier to standardize and replicate
   - Embedded in processes, IT systems, and organizational routines

c. Relational Capital
   - Knowledge embedded in customer relationships, networks, and partnerships
   - Includes client insights, market intelligence, feedback loops, and co-creation knowledge

These assets are *context-bound* and evolve over time. Their management relies on cultural, managerial, and infrastructural support to capture, store, and disseminate value-adding knowledge.

Digitally Enhanced Knowledge Assets

With digitization, many traditional assets have become big-data enabled, *data-rich, and system-integrated.* Examples include:

- Enterprise knowledge bases integrated with ERP and CRM platforms
- Cloud-based documentation and versioning tools (e.g., SharePoint, Confluence)
- Learning management systems (LMS) track competence development
- Searchable repositories of structured and unstructured data (e.g., customer support histories, R&D insights)

These tools enable knowledge scalability and faster retrieval, but they still rely heavily on *human input and structuring*.

Emergence of AI-Driven Knowledge Assets

Artificial intelligence brings an entirely new dimension: *knowledge that is generated, inferred, or autonomously maintained by intelligent systems*. As shown in Table 1.1, this includes:

These assets *do not exist statically*—they are continuously refreshed and refined based on incoming data, interactions, and environmental triggers. They represent a new form of *intangible digital capital* that is often:

- Context-aware
- Predictive
- Personalizable
- Dynamic

New Ownership and Value Considerations

AI-generated knowledge assets raise *complex questions of ownership, validity, and lifecycle management*:

- Who owns the insights generated by AI trained on employee behavior?
- How do we validate the correctness of continuously updating algorithmic knowledge?

Table 1.1. AI-Driven Assets.

Type of AI-Driven Asset	**Description**
Algorithmic knowledge	Insights derived from ML models (e.g., churn predictions, fraud detection)
Generated content assets	Summaries, reports, articles, or solutions created by GenAI tools
Behavioral and intent inference models	Knowledge based on analysis of user behavior, decision paths, and preferences
AI-enhanced ontologies and taxonomies	Dynamically evolving classification systems using AI and NLP
Cognitive process maps	Knowledge flow maps created through an AI-driven process mining
Multimodal knowledge objects	Integrated content combining text, voice, image, and video (e.g., AI-created training simulations)

- Can AI-generated knowledge be patented, licensed, or sold?
- Organizations must now build *governance frameworks* not just for knowledge protection, but also for *knowledge ethics, explainability, and traceability.*

Toward an Integrated Asset Architecture

To move forward, businesses should treat *AI-generated knowledge* not as a parallel stream but as a *complementary layer* on top of human-created and system-stored assets. This requires:

- Blended repositories that capture both human and machine outputs
- Version control systems for AI-generated content
- Metadata standards for AI-inferred knowledge (e.g., confidence level, data source)
- Transparent tagging of AI-augmented decision inputs in workflows

By combining *traditional, digitally enhanced,* and *AI-driven knowledge assets,* organizations can create a resilient and intelligent *knowledge architecture* that supports innovation, decision-making, and agility at scale.

Integrating AI into Traditional Systems and Human Efforts: Pillars and Prerequisites

As organizations begin leveraging artificial intelligence to extend or reimagine their knowledge management capabilities, they face a complex yet essential challenge: *how to integrate AI-driven assets into existing systems, workflows, and human-centered processes.* This integration is not simply technical—it is conceptual, operational, and cultural.

While much of the excitement around AI centers on disruption and transformation, the *most effective deployments are those that enhance,* rather than replace, traditional systems and human intelligence. In this section, we introduce the *four strategic pillars* for such integration and highlight the *organizational conditions* required for success.

Four Enhancement Pillars for AI–KM Integration

The proposed pillars framework includes four foundational strategies that guide the effective integration of artificial intelligence into knowledge management systems. These pillars—*Augmentation over Automation, Embedding AI into Existing Enterprise Infrastructure, Orchestrating Human-Machine Collaboration,* and *Dynamic Knowledge Lifecycle Management*—serve as a roadmap for organizations aiming to enhance the value of their knowledge assets while maintaining human-centric decision-making and adaptability.

Pillar 1: Augmentation over Automation.

Contrary to the dystopian fear that AI will replace humans, most successful AI-KM implementations aim to *augment human intelligence* rather than eliminate it. This means designing systems that:

- Provide *recommendations*, not commands;
- Suggest *next-best-actions*, not replacements;
- Support *exploratory learning*, not rigid prescriptions.

AI-generated knowledge (e.g., a suggested course of action, a synthesized report) should be positioned as a *second opinion* to be validated, contextualized, and refined by humans. This ensures trust, accountability, and adaptability—especially in complex, ambiguous decision-making environments.

Pillar 2: Embedding AI into Existing Enterprise (Data/Information/Knowledge) Infrastructure.

Rather than discarding traditional KM systems, organizations must embed AI functionality within them. This includes:

- Adding *semantic search* and *automated tagging* to document repositories;
- Integrating *chatbots or copilots* into internal platforms like SharePoint, Confluence, or Teams;
- Using *process mining tools* within ERP systems to uncover and streamline tacit knowledge workflows.

This embedded approach not only preserves prior investments but also ensures that users continue to work within familiar environments, reducing friction and increasing adoption.

Pillar 3: Orchestrating Human-Machine Collaboration.

AI integration demands new forms of *collaboration between humans and digital agents*. Knowledge workers are no longer just consumers of AI output—they are co-creators, trainers, and evaluators of AI-driven knowledge. Organizations must establish:

- *Feedback loops* where employees flag incorrect or irrelevant AI suggestions;
- *AI training protocols* based on internal knowledge models;
- *Decision checkpoints* where human judgment overrides automated conclusions in sensitive contexts.

Such structures foster a culture of shared intelligence, where machines amplify human insight rather than operate in parallel silos.

Pillar 4: Dynamic Knowledge Lifecycle Management.

AI-generated knowledge is *non-static*—it evolves with data streams, user behavior, and environmental inputs. As a result, knowledge lifecycles must become:

- *Shorter* (from creation to obsolescence);
- *More flexible* (real-time updates, adaptive schemas);
- *More transparent* (metadata tracking confidence scores, source data, revision history).

Traditional KM lifecycles—collection, storage, retrieval, reuse—must be redesigned to accommodate AI's pace and scope.

Organizational Conditions for Sustainable Integration

Embedding AI-driven knowledge assets into business systems and processes requires more than infrastructure upgrades. It demands *alignment of strategic goals, capabilities, and reward systems* across the organization. Key enabling conditions include:

- *Leadership Commitment*: Senior executives must champion the shift from knowledge storage to knowledge activation, making AI-KM a strategic priority.
- *Governance Structures*: Establishing AI-KM steering committees to oversee ethical use, security, data access, and accountability for AI-generated content.
- *Cultural Preparedness*: Encouraging experimentation, reducing fear of automation, and promoting digital curiosity among knowledge workers.
- *Technical Interoperability*: Ensuring that AI modules can interface with legacy systems, data lakes, and collaborative platforms through APIs and middleware.
- *Investment in Human Capital*: Supporting upskilling and capacity-building programs that prepare employees to work with AI tools effectively and responsibly.

Building Human-Centric Human Capital: Skills and Competencies for the AI-KM Era

While technology enables the infrastructure for AI-driven knowledge management, it is the *people* who shape how knowledge is interpreted, contextualized, and turned into action. As AI becomes embedded in enterprise knowledge ecosystems, the *human role does not disappear—it evolves*.

The next generation of knowledge workers and leaders must possess a *blended set of technical, cognitive, and interpersonal skills* that allow them to collaborate with intelligent systems, guide ethical implementations, and navigate dynamic organizational change. In this section, we articulate the *core competencies* required and offer guidance for how businesses can prepare their workforce for the future of knowledge.

Managerial Skills and Leadership Adaptation

For managers and leaders, AI in knowledge management presents *a strategic opportunity and a cultural challenge*. Leading in this space requires a *new mindset*—one that moves beyond control and delegation to facilitation, alignment, and capability-building.

a. AI-KM Strategy Alignment

- Defining strategic goals for AI-KM implementations (e.g., accelerating onboarding, reducing time-to-insight, supporting innovation).
- Prioritizing use cases with measurable ROI and scalable value.

b. Ethical Oversight and Trust Management

- Ensuring AI tools used in KM comply with ethical guidelines and promote fairness, transparency, and data protection.
- Guiding organizational discussions around trust, autonomy, and decision rights.

c. Change Enablement and Capacity Building

- Designing programs to upskill employees, shift mindsets, and reduce resistance to AI adoption.
- Leading cross-functional AI-KM initiatives with stakeholders from IT, HR, operations, and knowledge services.

Technical and Cognitive Skills for Knowledge Workers

At the foundation of the AI-KM workforce are *knowledge professionals* who engage with information, derive insights, and support decision-making. Their success increasingly depends on fluency with digital tools and a critical understanding of AI-generated content.

a. AI Literacy

- Understanding how algorithms generate knowledge, including limitations, bias, and confidence thresholds.
- Knowing how to prompt, interpret, and critically assess outputs from GenAI, NLP tools, and recommender systems.

b. Digital Content Curation

- Using AI tools to synthesize, structure, and personalize knowledge artifacts (e.g., executive briefings, learning modules, customer support scripts).
- Managing metadata, versioning, and relevance scoring in AI-augmented repositories.

c. Analytical Thinking

- Interpreting AI-driven dashboards and predictive models in the context of business strategy.
- Asking critical questions about data sources, assumptions, and organizational implications.

d. Collaboration with Digital Agents

- Navigating workflows that involve conversational AI, copilots, and intelligent automation tools.
- Understanding the handoff between human and machine contributions in co-creative environments.

Workforce Transformation Strategies

To future-proof their KM capabilities, organizations must design workforce development programs that align with both *AI maturity* and *KM strategic goals.* As shown in Table 1.2, suggested approaches include:

Ultimately, the shift to AI-enhanced knowledge work is not a threat to human talent—but a *call to elevate it.* Human-centered AI-KM strategies empower workers to focus on judgment, creativity, and insight while offloading repetitive cognitive burdens to machines.

Table 1.2. Workforce Development Program Strategy.

Strategy	**Description**
AI-KM competency frameworks (first 12 Months)	Mapping roles to required technical, analytical, and strategic skills
Microlearning and modular training (next 36 months and continuous update)	Offering short, targeted learning on GenAI, prompt engineering, and NLP use cases
AI-KM labs and sandboxes (next 36 months and continuous update)	Creating safe spaces for employees to experiment with AI-driven knowledge tools
Peer learning and knowledge exchange (next 36 months and continuous update)	Facilitating cross-team sharing of AI experiences, use cases, and challenges
Rotational programs across functions (next 36 months and continuous update)	Building interdisciplinary literacy in both business and AI domains

Conclusion: Toward a Strategic and Inclusive Vision of AI-Driven Knowledge Assets

The integration of artificial intelligence into knowledge management is not simply a technological upgrade—it represents a *fundamental redefinition of what constitutes organizational knowledge* and how that knowledge is created, distributed, and applied. In this chapter, we have laid the foundation for understanding the *emerging ecosystem of AI-driven knowledge assets*—a landscape that merges human expertise, digital structure, and machine-generated insights.

We began by exploring how knowledge assets, long conceptualized as human, structural, and relational capital, are being reconfigured by the rise of AI. We introduced the notion of *AI-generated assets*—dynamic, predictive, and self-evolving—and positioned them not as replacements for traditional knowledge systems but as *enhancements to the enterprise cognitive infrastructure.*

The chapter then presented four pillars for the effective *integration of AI into traditional systems and human workflows*, emphasizing augmentation over automation, and stressing the importance of ethical collaboration between humans and machines. We also examined the organizational and technological conditions that must be met for AI-KM adoption to succeed at scale.

Equally important, we highlighted the *human side of transformation.* Without the right talent and leadership capabilities, even the most powerful AI tools will fail to deliver lasting value. As such, we identified key technical, analytical, and managerial competencies and proposed workforce transformation strategies aimed at building an *AI-KM-ready organization.*

The message is clear: AI is no longer a future vision—it is already embedded in how businesses process, interpret, and act on knowledge. However, *technology alone is not the asset—intelligent deployment is.* The most valuable organizations will be those that treat AI as a strategic enabler of learning, innovation, and sustainable performance.

As the rest of this volume will show, each business domain—from supply chain and human resources to customer experience and innovation—can benefit from the thoughtful deployment of AI-driven knowledge strategies. But the journey must begin with a *holistic understanding of assets*, a clear integration roadmap, and a commitment to ethical and human-centered innovation.

The chapters that follow will dive into specific applications, case studies, and sector-based insights. Together, they form a practical and forward-looking guide to transforming knowledge into a *living asset*—one that grows, learns, and empowers in real time.

References

Böhm, K., & Durst, S. (2025). Knowledge management in the age of generative artificial intelligence – from SECI to GRAI. *VINE Journal of Information and Knowledge Management Systems.* https://doi.org/10.1108/VJIKMS-10-2024-0357

Chen, E. (2024). Empowering artificial intelligence for knowledge management augmentation. *Issues in Information Systems, 25*(4), 409–416. https://doi.org/10.48009/4_iis_2024_132

Chui, K. T., Lytras, D. M., & Vasant, P. (2020). Combined generative adversarial network and fuzzy C-means clustering for multi-class voice disorder detection with an imbalanced dataset. *Applied Sciences (Switzerland)*, *10*(13). https://doi.org/10.3390/app10134571

Edvinsson, L., & Sullivan, P. (1996). Developing a model for managing intellectual capital. *European Management Journal*, *14*(4), 356–364.

He, X., & Burger-Helmchen, T. (2024). Evolving knowledge management: Artificial intelligence and the dynamics of social interactions. *IEEE Engineering Management Review*. https://doi.org/10.1109/EMR.2024.3519342

Iaia, L., Nespoli, C., Vicentini, F., Pironti, M., & Genovino, C. (2024). Supporting the implementation of AI in business communication: The role of knowledge management. *Journal of Knowledge Management*, *28*(1), 85–95. https://doi.org/10.1108/JKM-12-2022-0944

Kloth, R., & Jonathan, G. M. (2025). The missing link: Knowledge management and the social dimension of business-IT alignment. *Complex Systems Informatics and Modeling Quarterly*, *2025*(42), 63–82. https://doi.org/10.7250/csimq.2025-42.04

Liu, Y., Ying, Z., Ying, Y., Wang, D., & Chen, J. (2024). Artificial intelligence orientation and internationalization speed: A knowledge management perspective. *Technological Forecasting and Social Change*, *205*. https://doi.org/10.1016/j.techfore.2024.123517

Nonaka, I., & Takeuchi, H. (1995). *The knowledge creating company*. Oxford University Press.

Olan, F., Nyuur, R. B., & Arakpogun, E. O. (2024). AI: A knowledge sharing tool for improving employees' performance. *Journal of Decision Systems*, *33*(4), 700–720. https://doi.org/10.1080/12460125.2023.2263687

Rezaei, M. (2025). Artificial intelligence in knowledge management: Identifying and addressing the key implementation challenges. *Technological Forecasting and Social Change*, *217*. https://doi.org/10.1016/j.techfore.2025.124183

Russ, M. (2021). Knowledge management for sustainable development in the era of continuously accelerating technological revolutions: A framework and models. *Sustainability*, *13*(6), 3353.

Sarirete, A., Balfagih, Z., Lytras, Brahimi, T., & Visvizi, A. (2022). Artificial intelligence and machine learning research: Towards digital transformation at a global scale. *Journal of Ambient Intelligence and Humanized Computing*, *13*(7), 3319–3321. https://doi.org/10.1007/s12652-021-03168-y

Sveiby, K. E. (1997). *The new organizational wealth: Managing & measuring knowledge-based assets*. Berrett-Koehler Publishers.

Visvizi, A., Jussila, J., Lytras, M. D., & Ijäs, M. (2020). Tweeting and mining OECD-related microcontent in the post-truth era: A cloud-based app. *Computers in Human Behavior*, *107*, 105958.

Wang, M., Yang, Y., & Zhong, P. (2025). How does AI affect the self-actualization of content creators in dynamic environments? A knowledge management perspective. *Technology in Society*, *81*. https://doi.org/10.1016/j.techsoc.2025.102855

Zhang, Q., Zuo, J., & Yang, S. (2025). Research on the impact of generative artificial intelligence (GenAI) on enterprise innovation performance: A knowledge management perspective. *Journal of Knowledge Management*. https://doi.org/10.1108/JKM-10-2024-1198

Zhang, W., Zhang, W., Daim, T., & Yalçın, H. (2025). AI challenges conventional knowledge management: Light the way for reframing SECI model and Ba theory. *Journal of Knowledge Management*, *29*(5), 1618–1654. https://doi.org/10.1108/JKM-02-2024-0203

AI-Driven Decision Support Systems in Business

Chapter 2

How Artificial Intelligence Affects the Decision-Making Process in Business: AI-Driven Decision Support Systems

Cem Ufuk Baytar

İstanbul Topkapi University, Turkey

Abstract

Businesses require data-driven insights to gain a competitive advantage because of digital transformation. Companies must manage vast amounts of data to make timely and accurate decisions. AI (Artificial Intelligence) technologies are integrated with decision support systems (DSSs) to enhance the speed and effectiveness of decision-making processes. This integration is referred to as AI-driven DSS. Top management must make strategic decisions to shape their organizations' futures, and AI-driven DSSs support this need. An AI-driven DSS includes technologies, such as data mining, predictive analytics, and machine learning. Organizations should invest in DSSs integrated with AI to improve decision quality. This chapter is designed to provide an understanding of how AI-integrated DSSs influence the decision-making processes. Its objectives are to (a) detail AI-driven DSSs and differentiate them from traditional decision support models, (b) explain core AI technologies used in DSSs and how they enhance decision-making, (c) evaluate real-life applications of AI-powered DSSs across various industries, and (d) offer perspectives on the future of AI in decision support. This chapter is intended for readers seeking to understand how AI-driven DSSs have transformed business practices. The expanding literature on AI in business will benefit from this chapter's inclusion of practical examples, future insights, and guidance on leveraging AI for competitive advantage.

Keywords: Artificial intelligence; decision-making; decision support systems; knowledge management; expert systems; digital transformation

AI-Driven Knowledge Management Assets, Volume 2, 17–36

doi:10.1108/978-1-83662-778-420261002

Introduction to AI in Business Decision-Making

Business decision-making has become a key application domain for AI technologies. The combination of data analysis algorithms and human oversight creates a robust DSS, where automated analytical processes generate recommendations for human decision-makers, who ultimately retain the authority to determine the final course of action (Abrokwah-Larbi & Awuku-Larbi, 2024; Perifanis & Kitsios, 2023; Rajagopal et al., 2022; Reis et al., 2024).

The term AI refers to the ability of computerized systems, robots, and other programmable devices to perform tasks typically associated with intelligent entities. The goal of AI is to replicate human-like intelligence in machines by imitating human characteristics such as cognitive processes, learning capabilities, logical reasoning, and environmental interactions. AI-enabled decision-making systems are expected to excel at analyzing complex, multidimensional data sets, applying domain-specific knowledge for reasoning and decision prioritization, and autonomously enhancing future decisions by learning from past experiences (Bharadiya, 2023; Enholm et al., 2022).

Decision-makers increasingly turn to AI to automate decision-making because complex business environments often exceed human cognitive capacities. AI technologies can present complex analyses and relevant decisions in a comprehensible manner, significantly transforming how businesses and economies operate. This shift necessitates a careful examination of the broader impacts of AI technologies (de Bruijn et al., 2022; Ivanov, 2023).

The adoption of AI currently faces challenges because of unforeseen consequences that affect both the initial and ongoing management of AI-powered DSSs. These effects complicate the oversight of AI tools before deployment and implementation. On one hand, decision-critical AI mechanisms may lead to outcomes that are difficult to control. On the other hand, systems that use AI merely to enhance human decision-making remain manageable. The overarching aim of developing AI-enhanced systems is to improve decision quality by learning from successful past decisions rather than simply replicating fixed rules. To avoid biased outcomes, AI technologies must be investigated independently of specific business decision contexts (Allioui & Mourdi, 2023).

AI is being increasingly integrated into business operations, significantly influencing decision-making processes. AI-driven DSSs improve the quality of business decisions by reducing irrational judgments and emphasizing data-driven insights. These systems use algorithms for data collection, processing, and retrieval to assist managers in decision-making (Soori et al., 2024). The business environment is rapidly evolving because of globalization, market competition, technological advances, and diverse customer demand. As a result, the need for timely and accurate decision-making presents considerable challenges. For instance, reactive decisions can hinder strategic implementation and operational problem-solving, whereas proactive approaches can support opportunity identification, problem detection, and strategy development. Understanding AI's critical role in business decision-making highlights its importance in helping organizations adapt to contemporary demands (Ahmad et al., 2022; Allioui & Mourdi, 2023).

Evolution of DSSs

This section provides an overview of the characteristics of traditional DSSs and intelligent DSSs (IDSSs).

Traditional Decision Support Systems

A decision support system is a special-purpose computer-based information system that assists decision-makers in using data and models to solve problems. The main components of a DSS include a database, a model base, a knowledge base, and a user interface (Mannina et al., 2019; Stanek et al., 2022; Tariq & Rafi, 2012). Models play a vital role in representing real-world phenomena. Decision models are developed to describe, understand, and analyze decision problems. In addition, DSSs serve as communication platforms that facilitate the exchange of ideas between users and experts (Talari et al., 2022; Tariq & Rafi, 2012; Yun et al., 2021).

The primary objective of a traditional DSS is to manipulate and analyze data. These systems lack the capability for intelligence augmentation. Users are responsible for manually creating and analyzing various scenarios, datasets, and models, as well as running the corresponding analyses (Talari et al., 2022; Yun et al., 2021). The types of DSS can be summarized as follows (Olavsrud, 2024; Ponomarev & Mustafin, 2021):

- Data-Driven DSS: These systems focus on analyzing large volumes of data from various sources. Common applications include querying databases and data warehouses to generate reports or dashboards using business intelligence tools.
- Model-Driven DSS: These systems use mathematical and analytical models to assist in decision-making. They help evaluate different scenarios and the impacts of various decisions, such as systems used for financial modeling or forecasting demand.
- Knowledge-Driven DSS: These systems provide specialized knowledge to support decision-making. They often encompass expert systems that offer recommendations based on a knowledge base. Examples include systems used in medical diagnosis or product recommendation.
- Document-Driven DSS: These systems manage and retrieve documents, supporting decision-making by providing access to unstructured data such as text documents, reports, and articles. They are commonly used to search large databases of research papers or internal company documents.
- Communication-Driven DSS and Group DSS: Designed to enhance communication and collaboration among team members, these systems support

group decision-making through platforms that facilitate virtual meetings and discussions, such as Microsoft Teams or Zoom.

- Hybrid DSS: These systems integrate elements of various DSS types to meet diverse decision-making needs. A comprehensive business planning tool that incorporates data analysis, modeling, and document management functionalities serves as an example.

Intelligent Decision Support Systems

An IDSS enhances decision-making through the integration of AI technologies. When a DSS incorporates AI, it simulates human capabilities such as reasoning and common sense. An IDSS is an interactive system that uses data, expert knowledge, and models to help solve complex and poorly structured problems (Bharadiya, 2023; Soori et al., 2024; Tariq & Rafi, 2012). Key features of an IDSS include the following (Soori et al., 2024):

- Data Integration: IDSSs can consolidate data from multiple sources, providing a comprehensive view for analysis and decision-making.
- Real-Time Analysis: These systems often support real-time data processing, allowing users to make decisions based on the most current information available.
- Predictive Analytics: By using historical data, IDSS can forecast future trends, helping organizations anticipate both challenges and opportunities.
- User Interactivity: These systems typically feature user-friendly interfaces that allow users to interact intuitively, adjust parameters, and explore various scenarios.
- Knowledge Management: IDSSs often incorporate knowledge bases containing rules, heuristics, and best practices relevant to the decision-making context, enhancing the system's ability to deliver intelligent recommendations.

There is a growing need for IDSSs that assist operators and decision-makers in planning, controlling, and optimizing complex systems involving numerous variables and parameters that evolve over time. AI has the capacity to process large volumes of information and identify patterns, trends, and relationships that support strategic decision-making. AI algorithms can develop predictive models for various decisions and their potential outcomes, enabling risk and benefit analysis. Routine decision-making processes can be managed by AI, thereby allowing human managers to focus on more complex and challenging issues (Bharadiya, 2023; Tariq & Rafi, 2012). The groups of IDSS can be summarized as follows (Kaklauskas, 2015).

- Text Analytics and Mining-Based DSSs: These systems use text mining techniques to extract valuable information from unstructured data sources, supporting decision-making through the analysis of large text datasets.

- Recommender Systems: These systems apply various techniques to generate recommendations, including collaborative, content-based, demographic, knowledge-based, suggestions, community-based, and hybrid approaches.
- Advisory Systems: These systems provide guidance without making final decisions for users. They support unstructured decision-making scenarios by synthesizing expert knowledge.
- Expert Systems: These systems encapsulate expert knowledge to evaluate and determine solutions to well-structured problems. Unlike advisory systems, they are rule-based and focused on structured decision-making.
- Biometrics-Based DSSs: These systems use biometric data for decision-making purposes.
- Data Mining and Analytics: These systems identify patterns and relationships within data to support informed decisions.
- Neural Networks and AI-Based Systems: These systems integrate machine learning techniques to enhance decision-making capabilities.
- Process Mining Integration: These systems analyze business processes and optimize decisions based on workflow data.
- Adaptive DSS: These systems evolve based on user interactions and feedback.
- Robotic and Sensory DSS: These systems incorporate robotics and sensory data to support real-time decision-making in dynamic environments.

Recent advances in AI have enabled the integration of intelligent agent technologies into various systems, including DSSs. Intelligent agents possess the capability to act independently, allowing them to analyze situations, adapt models, explore possibilities, and make decisions to achieve specific goals (Kühl et al., 2022).

AI and Knowledge Management

Knowledge management (KM) involves several key processes, including knowledge creation, storage and retrieval, sharing, and application. AI capabilities can support each of these dimensions. In other words, AI tools enhance knowledge creation by identifying patterns in data and generating new insights. They also improve information storage and retrieval through better organization and classification, while facilitating knowledge sharing across organizational boundaries (Jarrahi et al., 2023).

The successful integration of AI in KM requires more than just technological adoption—it also demands significant organizational transformation. These changes center on three main components: people, infrastructure, and processes.

People

- Elevating Humans in KM: Rather than viewing workers as obstacles to automation, organizations should recognize their essential role. Reskilling and upskilling knowledge workers are necessary to align their competencies with future demands and to ensure effective integration with AI systems (Caine & Firth-Butterfield, 2020).

- Training Knowledge Scientists: New roles such as knowledge scientists and data scientists are becoming increasingly important. These professionals are essential for preparing training datasets used in machine learning and for ensuring AI systems perform effectively and explain their decisions (Blumauer, 2019; Doran et al., 2017).
- Seeking AI Champions: AI champions act as internal advocates who promote the idea that AI is intended to augment—not replace—human efforts. They help connect AI capabilities with KM objectives, ensuring alignment between technology and organizational objectives (Brown et al., 2021).

Infrastructure

- Preparing Data: A strong data infrastructure is crucial for AI applications in KM. Emphasis must be placed on data quality and volume, collected and structured through collaborative, cross-functional efforts (Joshi & Wade, 2020).
- Facilitating Interpretability and Accountability: AI systems must be user-friendly and accountable, enabling users to understand how decisions are made. Supervised learning models and well-prepared datasets are critical to building trust in AI outputs (Davenport & Seseri, 2020).
- Developing Knowledge Graphs: Knowledge graphs help manage and enhance relationships among data points, enabling more meaningful analysis powered by AI technologies (Elnagar & Weistroffer, 2019).

Processes

- Pursuing Mutual Learning: Organizational processes can be redesigned to foster ongoing mutual learning between AI systems and human workers, creating a collaborative environment that enhances decision-making (Jarrahi et al., 2023).
- Forming Cross-Functional Teams: Diverse teams are vital to successful AI implementation. Collaboration between AI experts and domain professionals ensures AI applications effectively support KM (Malone, 2018).
- Redesigning for Automation and Augmentation: Automation should not be seen as a replacement for humans, but as a way to enhance their contributions. Automated systems can handle repetitive tasks, allowing knowledge workers to focus on strategic decision-making (Dan et al., 2017).

Integration of AI Into Decision-Making Processes

AI simulates human thought by using algorithms to build systems that can think similarly to human beings. As a subfield of AI, machine learning (ML) opens new possibilities for creating intelligent computers. Deep learning (DL), a subset of ML, represents data abstraction through model architectures. DL mimics the functioning of the human brain. ML, as a type of AI technology, is used to automate complex decision-making processes. Various ML algorithms include case-based reasoning (CBR), artificial neural networks (ANNs), genetic algorithms, natural language processing (NLP), inductive learning, and others (Bharadiya, 2023).

AI's influence on organizational decision-making is a common source of concern. Organizations operate across multiple hierarchical levels where decisions are made, and resources are allocated to subunits, projects, or employees (Booyse & Scheepers, 2024; Cao et al., 2021; Rajagopal et al., 2022; Zhao & Gómez Fariñas, 2023). These decisions shape the organization's progress, competitiveness, productivity, and profitability. Corporate culture is often reflected in how decisions are made—ranging from formalized procedures with prescribed rules to informal methods based on judgment and experience (Cao et al., 2021; Zhao & Gómez Fariñas, 2023).

AI-powered decision support systems are transforming how decisions are made in businesses. This discussion focuses on the significant effects of AI on corporate decision-making frameworks, particularly regarding the functionalities and capabilities of AI-driven DSSs designed for internal organizational decisions (Rajagopal et al., 2022).

AI's superior data processing and analytical capabilities improve decision-making efficiency compared to traditional manual approaches. Innovations in AI technology will increasingly influence how enterprise managers make decisions (Aldoseri et al., 2023; Ara et al., 2024; Tabesh, 2022; Zdravković et al., 2022).

Change Management and Organizational Culture

Integrating intelligent algorithms into ongoing business processes presents challenges. AI systems are unlikely to gain universal acceptance. Individuals may resist algorithmic decisions, particularly in societies where people expect to make choices for themselves. Users must first understand IDSS and build trust in the algorithms.

A strategy is needed to manage both the transition to AI and its inevitable consequences. One way to ease this transition is to democratize complex AI algorithms, ensuring everyone can comprehend the principles behind their decisions.

Transparency and accountability throughout the decision-making process are essential. Public discourse should foster a culture in which employees critically engage with AI systems to prevent the reinforcement of biases that may exist in training data or society at large (Kerzel, 2020; Raj Shrestha et al., 2020; Zhao & Gómez Fariñas, 2023).

Training and Upskilling Employees

To remain competitive in a rapidly evolving environment, companies are compelled to adopt AI innovations. However, integrating AI into business operations brings challenges—especially regarding how this new paradigm fits within the organization's values and culture. Additionally, understanding AI's influence on decision-making remains in its early stages, even as more businesses begin outsourcing decisions to AI (Chen, 2022; Schemmer et al., 2022).

Chen (2022) proposed a framework for AI-based training, exploring the integration of AI in organizational training and development. This framework has the potential to transform traditional training into personalized, effective learning experiences. It can convert individual knowledge into group knowledge, recommend customized training programs, and deliver content tailored to employees' learning preferences and needs. However, implementing AI in training also presents challenges, such as high operational costs, data security and legal risks, potential job displacement, equity concerns, negative employee attitudes toward AI, and difficulties in evaluating training outcomes (Chen, 2022).

Business Cases on AI-Driven Decision-Making

The real-world business cases below illustrate how AI-driven solutions influence decision-making processes (Bosc Tech Labs, 2024).

Case: NVIDIA—Using AI to Evolve Gaming Graphics

- Challenge: The gaming industry demands increasingly realistic and high-performance graphics, which pose technical challenges.
- AI Solution: NVIDIA employs AI-driven technologies like Deep Learning Super Sampling (DLSS) to enhance graphics rendering.
- Impact: Raised industry standards and delivered a more immersive, realistic gaming experience for players.

Case: Amazon—Revolutionizing Supply Chain Management

- Challenge: Managing a global supply chain while meeting customer demands, controlling inventory, streamlining shipping, and reducing costs.
- AI Solution: AI algorithms for predictive inventory management assess market trends and customer behavior to forecast product demand.
- Impact: Reduced operational costs, improved delivery efficiency, and enhanced customer satisfaction.

Case: IBM Watson Health

- Challenge: Processing large volumes of patient data in health care to support disease progression analysis and personalized treatment.
- AI Solution: IBM Watson uses cognitive computing and NLP to analyze medical records, patient data, and research literature.
- Impact: Improved efficiency and accuracy in diagnoses and laid the foundation for personalized health care.

Case: Zara—Retail Fashion With AI

- Challenge: The fast-paced fashion industry requires real-time management of trends and inventory to avoid overstocking.
- AI Solution: Zara uses AI algorithms to analyze sales and trend data, optimizing inventory based on customer preferences.
- Impact: Increased customer satisfaction and profits through trend alignment and inventory.

Case: JP Morgan—Legal Documents Analysis With AI

- Challenge: High time consumption and potential errors in the analysis of legal documents hinder efficiency.
- AI Solution: JP Morgan's Contract Intelligence (COIN) uses NLP to analyze and extract information from legal documents.
- Impact: Significant time savings and reduced errors in contract interpretation.

Applications of AI-Driven DSSs

The integration of AI technologies into conventional DSSs has led to the emergence of IDSSs. An IDSS is a decision-support technology that incorporates AI techniques to help decision-makers address complex, imprecise, and ill-structured problems (Tariq & Rafi, 2012).

An increasing number of DSSs now include domain knowledge, modeling, and analysis components to provide intelligent assistance to decision-makers. A knowledge-based DSS includes a knowledge base subsystem that provides domain-specific expertise. This knowledge is used to formulate and model problems and to validate and analyze results (Psarommatis & Kiritsis, 2022). A knowledge-based intelligent DSS (KIDSS) features a knowledge management subsystem that captures, stores, and utilizes knowledge. Emerging AI tools such as case-based reasoning and machine learning are used within this subsystem. These tools allow DSS to extract knowledge from historical data and previous decisions, supporting real-time decision-making that is complex, repetitive, and time-sensitive (Gaman et al., 2023; Meski et al., 2021).

Health Care Sector

AI-assisted DSS applications have gained prominence in the health care industry due to increasing demand for improved solutions to a wide range of health care problems (Khosravi et al., 2024). There is a general consensus that AI can enhance diagnostic accuracy, with the expectation that its implementation will lead to better patient outcomes, fewer invasive procedures, and reduced instances of misdiagnosis. AI can also improve treatment decision-making by analyzing clinical data records.

AI technology can enhance health care decision-making by supporting workflow redesigns in dental professions. Many AI tools aim to improve patient–clinician interactions by increasing the reliability of diagnostics and treatment decisions, thereby impacting the overall decision-making process (Khosravi et al., 2024). Studies have shown that AI can improve organizational decision-making by tracking and predicting outcomes and the effectiveness of health care activities, such as patient satisfaction, safety, care quality, cost control, and protocol adherence.

Machine learning (ML) algorithms are applied to clinical data stored in health information systems to evaluate health care process performance. These algorithms also predict future outcomes and performance levels. In addition, AI can identify best practices across clinical departments, monitor progress toward goals, and provide feedback and recommendations for improvement (Khosravi et al., 2024).

Various AI-based digital platforms have attracted significant attention from both service providers and users because they offer opportunities to implement patient-centered care within health care systems. With the advancement of AI, decision-making in health care is undergoing substantial transformation, especially in diagnostic prediction, classification, and offering valuable recommendations and insights (Elhaddad & Hamam, 2024).

As new technologies evolve and data volumes increase, standard and mechanistic functions will increasingly be automated. AI will take on many tasks traditionally requiring expert judgment. For example, in cancer therapy treatment planning, AI can assist with calculating dose distributions that meet required conditions for both target areas and healthy issues (Shegai et al., 2021).

Recent advancements in AI-based planning systems have led to dose distribution prediction models that generate plans based on simple input parameters. These models draw on prior planning experience, functioning as representations of the planner's intelligence (Mashayekhi et al., 2023).

Supply Chain Industry

AI is expected to become one of the most influential technologies in the future of supply chain (SC) management. AI and ML play vital roles in SC digital transformation. Research has identified trends and developments in the field by analyzing SC subdomains, key publications, institutions, and geographic distribution (Rana & Daultani, 2022).

ML for predictive maintenance involves monitoring machine health and predicting future timelines. This allows timely maintenance actions, avoiding both excessive servicing and unexpected downtime (Guillaume et al., 2020). In sectors where failures have critical consequences, interpretability is essential. Human decision-makers must understand the basis of predictions before acting on them. This has led to increased interest in explainable machine learning models in predictive maintenance (Paraschos et al., 2021).

AI has also transformed SC demand forecasting. ML models are used to detect nonlinear demand patterns. However, ML models often exhibit black-box behavior, which can result in biases. XAI methods can address this by helping users understand the rationale behind model outputs (Reis et al., 2024).

The Sector of Law

AI models contribute to legal operations, particularly through natural language processing tools used to automatically generate business contracts. These tools reduce the time required for manual drafting. However, recent studies have identified various vulnerabilities in such models, emphasizing the need for human supervision to minimize misinformation or bias. XAI methods help stakeholders understand how AI models generate contractual information (Reis et al., 2024).

E-Commerce: B2B

Papagiannidis et al. (2023) conducted a study aimed at exploring the negative aspects of AI deployment in a B2B context—specifically within energy trading—and how these factors influence relationships between traders and AI developers. Data were collected through semi-structured interviews with AI managers, traders, and developers, along with the use of secondary data sources. The study analyzed the experiences and narratives of employees regarding AI's impact on their work and interactions.

This study revealed important findings as follows (Papagiannidis et al., 2023):

- Nature of Work: Employees expressed mixed feelings toward AI integration. While AI increased efficiency and scalability, it also raised concerns about job security and deskilling, as traders became increasingly reliant on AI systems for trading operations.
- Responsibility: Debates emerged regarding accountability for AI-generated decisions. It was often unclear whether responsibility for failures should rest with AI developers or traders—especially when the AI outputs resulted in financial or reputational risk.
- Conflicts and Effects: The introduction of AI created tensions between traders and AI developers. Disagreements arose concerning the effectiveness and reliability of AI systems when compared to traditional methods. Trust in AI outputs remained a major concern.

The study concludes that although AI presents opportunities for increased efficiency and improved decision-making, it also introduces significant risks and challenges. These must be addressed through better training, clearly defined accountability structures, and consistent communication among stakeholders. Table 2.1 summarizes some of the AI-driven DSS-related studies in the literature from 2021 to 2025.

Table 2.1. The Summary of the Related Works.

Work	Subject/Related to	Concepts/Tools/ Algorithm	Business Context/Field
Zhang et al. (2025)	Developing a system for ship collision and grounding prevention	AI-enabled predictive analytics and multiphysics systems	Maritime transport
Barbieri et al. (2025)	Systems-based framework for clinical DSS integration	Theoretical application of the SEIPS model	Health care
Ahmad and Sohel (2025)	Evaluating DSS effectiveness in water consumption	DSSAT, APSIM, CropWat, AquaCrop, GesCoN, and VegSyst	Water systems
Yalçın et al. (2025)	Hybrid DSS for transport policy selection	IF-SIWEC-ARLON hybrid method	Transportation
Kierner et al. (2025)	Developing a clinical decision system	Machine learning, clinical rule-based engine	Health care
Reis et al. (2024)	Selecting XAI methods	Context-aware DSS with ML algorithms	Supply chain management
Mustofa et al. (2024)	AI-driven model for student dropout risk	Logistic regression, neural network, XAI	Education
Pinto et al. (2024)	Conceptual framework for integrating conversational AI with DSS	Natural Language	Supply chain management
Caballero et al. (2024)	Pilot candidate selection	Interpretable and explainable ML techniques	Army
En-Naaoui et al. (2024)	Proactive risk management	Fuzzy inference, neural network, and support vector machine	Health care
Nakhaei et al. (2023)	Water management in power plants	Adaptive neuro-fuzzy inference system, multicriteria	Power Plants

Table 2.1. *(Continued)*

Work	Subject/Related to	Concepts/Tools/ Algorithm	Business Context/Field
		decision-making techniques	
Rosati et al. (2023)	Predictive maintenance	Feature extraction strategy and ML prediction model	Manufacturing
Jia et al. (2022)	Financial DSS	Deep learning algorithms for decision-making	Finance
Psarommatis and Kiritsis (2022)	Zero defect manufacturing	Data-driven and knowledge-based approaches	Manufacturing
Yun et al. (2021)	Human–computer interaction-based DSS	Data-mining techniques	Industrial applications

Future Trends and Developments in AI-Driven Decision Support Systems

AI technology has become a widely adopted approach for addressing enterprise-level problems. AI-driven DSSs have gained increasing attention from both practitioners and scholars. Technologies such as ML, DL, expert systems, big data techniques, natural language processing, computer vision, and robotics have been applied to DSS across various domains. These smart systems support decision-making at different management levels, including strategic, tactical, and operational decisions (Elgendy et al., 2022; Rajagopal et al., 2022).

AI-driven DSS research has been applied across industries such as finance, production, supply chain, transportation, and health care. New AI-based DSSs have been developed, and existing ones have been upgraded by integrating different AI technologies. Applications of AI-driven DSSs include areas such as risk management, anomaly detection, credit scoring, finance, production, health care, and manufacturing (Aldoseri et al., 2023).

As AI-driven DSSs become increasingly prevalent in industries such as finance, health care, and energy, there is a growing trend toward incorporating "explainability" into AI models that inform or automate business decisions. XAI refers to model-agnostic or model-specific methods that provide post hoc explanations of AI decision outcomes. These explanations can be presented in textual, graphical, or tabular formats. Providing automated explanations helps users understand the reasoning behind AI decisions, fostering trust in AI models and reducing the risk of adverse consequences (Alufaisan et al., 2021).

AI is an important field in terms of research and practice. It enables intelligent behavior through high-performing, cost-efficient applications. ML approaches, such as deep learning, are central to supporting data-driven decision-making. Many organizations and executives recognize that AI presents vital business opportunities for long-term success. However, rapid changes in AI make it difficult for companies to develop appropriate governance mechanisms to fully capitalize on its economic potential (Schneider et al., 2020; Shepherd & Majchrzak, 2022).

Nonetheless, companies may face unexpected consequences from AI applications that are outside of their control. These include issues of fairness, safety, security, and ethics. AI systems may produce biased decisions. This could ultimately lead to legal consequences for the organization. ML models—the core of many AI systems—are often optimized for a single performance metric, ignoring other considerations. For example, credit-scoring models may prioritize accuracy while neglecting fairness across different social groups (Schneider et al., 2020).

Conclusion

AI-driven decision-making can enhance operational efficiency, optimize resource optimization, and support integrated plications, leading to the development of a framework-based system for business use cases. However, unstructured business data can hinder effective data mining. Algorithmic extraction processes can optimize data modeling and increase the intelligence of automated decision-making architectures. The proliferation of AI tools is transforming decision processes—making processes across industries—from finance to marketing. A multi-layered, AI-enabled architecture enhances traditional decision-making frameworks.

Interest in incorporating AI into business operations has grown significantly, driven by resource constraints and the need for higher-quality decisions. This work addresses the influence of AI on decision-making in business, with a focus on DSSs. It also reflects current academic discussions around AI in DSSs and presents insights from interviews with early AI adopters in business. With technologies such as the internet, mobile devices, and data analytics tools becoming widespread, data-driven decision-making continues to expand. AI represents the next step in the data-driven decision-making trend. Although academic research on AI as a DSS remains relatively nascent, it is a prominent theme among business leaders. This study bridges the gap between academic theory and real-world practice, providing valuable insights from both perspectives.

In response to the growing use of AI in business decision-making, this work offers a foundational framework for future academic exploration of AI-driven DSS. For practitioners, it highlights the characteristics, boundaries, and best practices for deploying AI in decision support, aiding decision-makers in developing their AI strategy. It is therefore critical to further explore the use of

AI-driven DSSs in everyday business areas such as finance, marketing, operations, and human resources—domains where managerial positions have a direct effect on business outcomes. Because such decisions influence company-wide efficiency, revenue, costs, and profitability, implementing AI-driven DSSs in these areas can be especially beneficial and impactful.

References

Abrokwah-Larbi, K., & Awuku-Larbi, Y. (2024). The impact of artificial intelligence in marketing on the performance of business organizations: Evidence from SMEs in an emerging economy. *Journal of Entrepreneurship in Emerging Economies*, *16* (4), 1090–1117. https://doi.org/10.1108/JEEE-07-2022-0207

Ahmad, T., Madonski, R., Zhang, D., Huang, C., & Mujeeb, A. (2022). Data-driven probabilistic machine learning in sustainable smart energy/smart energy systems: Key developments, challenges, and future research opportunities in the context of smart grid paradigm. *Renewable and Sustainable Energy Reviews*, *160*, 112128. https://doi.org/10.1016/j.rser.2022.112128

Ahmad, U., & Sohel, F. (2025). Evaluating decision support systems for precision irrigation and water use efficiency. *Digital Engineering*, *4*, 100038. https://doi.org/10.1016/j.dte.2025.100038

Aldoseri, A., Al-Khalifa, K. N., & Hamouda, A. M. (2023). Re-thinking data strategy and integration for artificial intelligence: Concepts, opportunities, and challenges. *Applied Sciences*, *13*(12), 7082. https://doi.org/10.3390/app13127082

Allioui, H., & Mourdi, Y. (2023). Unleashing the potential of AI: Investigating cutting-edge technologies that are transforming businesses. *International Journal of Computer Engineering and Data Science*, *3*(2), 1–12.

Alufaisan, Y., Marusich, L. R., Bakdash, J. Z., Zhou, Y., & Kantarcioglu, M. (2021). Does explainable artificial intelligence improve human decision-making? *Proceedings of the AAAI Conference on Artificial Intelligence*, *35*(8), 6618–6626. https://doi.org/10.1609/aaai.v35i8.16819

Ara, A., Maraj, M. A. A., Rahman, M. A., & Bari, M. H. (2024). The impact of machine learning on prescriptive analytics for optimized business decision-making. *International Journal of Management Information Systems and Data Science*, *1* (1), 7–18. https://doi.org/10.62304/ijmisds.v1i1.112

Barbieri, D. F., Srinivasan, D., Ulrich, J., Ranganathan, S., Chang, C., Gerac, J. A., & Cha, J. S. (2025). Systems-based framework for clinical decision-support system integration for patient sepsis management: A theoretical application of the SEIPS model. *Human Factors in Healthcare*, *7*, 100098. https://doi.org/10.1016/j.hfh.2025.100098

Bharadiya, J. P. (2023). A comparative study of business intelligence and artificial intelligence with big data analytics. *American Journal of Artificial Intelligence*, *7* (1), 24–30. https://doi.org/10.11648/j.ajai.20230701.14

Blumauer, A. (2019, December 30). Explainable AI: The rising role of knowledge scientists. *Forbes*. https://www.forbes.com/sites/forbestechcouncil/2019/12/30/explainable-ai-the-rising-role-of-knowledge-scientists/#428c9b8603f0

Booyse, D., & Scheepers, C. B. (2024). Barriers to adopting automated organisational decision-making through the use of artificial intelligence. *Management Research Review*, *47*(1), 64–85. https://doi.org/10.1108/MRR-09-2021-0701

Bosc Tech Labs. (2024, July 23). 10 detailed artificial intelligence case studies 2024. *The Medium*. https://medium.com/@bosctechlabs/10-detailed-artificial-intelligence-case-studies-2024-1fb26ea63aa8

Brown, S., Davidovic, J., & Hasan, A. (2021). The algorithm audit: Scoring the algorithms that score us. *Big Data and Society*, *8*(1). https://doi.org/10.1177/2053951720983865

Caballero, W. N., Wasilefsky, D., Johnstone, C., Gaw, N., & Jenkins, P. R. (2024). Responsible machine learning for United States Air Force pilot candidate selection. *Decision Support Systems*, *180*, 114198. https://doi.org/10.1016/j.dss.2024.114198

Caine, M., & Firth-Butterfield, K. (2020, October 22). How AI can train workers for the jobs of the future. *World Economic Forum*. https://www.weforum.org/agenda/2020/10/ai-jobs/

Cao, G., Duan, Y., Edwards, J. S., & Dwivedi, Y. K. (2021). Understanding managers' attitudes and behavioral intentions towards using artificial intelligence for organizational decision-making. *Technovation*, *106*, 102312. https://doi.org/10.1016/j.technovation.2021.102312

Chen, Z. (2022). Artificial intelligence—Virtual trainer: Innovative didactics aimed at personalized training needs. *Journal of the Knowledge Economy*, *14*, 2007–2025. https://doi.org/10.1007/s13132-022-00985-0

Dan, W., Elliott, T., & Noga, M. (2017, May 31). Eight ways machine learning is improving companies' work processes. *Harvard Business Review*. https://hbr.org/2017/05/8-ways-machine-learning-is-improving-companies-work-processes

Davenport, T., & Seseri, R. (2020, December 15). What is a minimum viable AI product? *MIT Sloan Management Review*. https://sloanreview.mit.edu/article/what-is-a-minimum-viable-ai-product/

de Bruijn, H., Warnier, M., & Janssen, M. (2022). The perils and pitfalls of explainable AI: Strategies for explaining algorithmic decision-making. *Government Information Quarterly*, *39*(2), 101666. https://doi.org/10.1016/j.giq.2021.101666

Doran, D., Schulz, S., & Besold, T. R. (2017). *What does explainable AI really mean? A new conceptualization of perspectives*. https://arxiv.org/pdf/1710.00794.pdf

Elgendy, N., Elragal, A., & Päivärinta, T. (2022). DECAS: A modern data-driven decision theory for big data and analytics. *Journal of Decision Systems*, *31*(4), 337–373. https://doi.org/10.1080/12460125.2021.1894674

Elhaddad, M., & Hamam, S. (2024). AI-driven clinical decision support systems: An ongoing pursuit of potential. *Cureus*, *16*(4). https://doi.org/10.7759/cureus.57728

Elnagar, S., & Weistroffer, H. R. (2019). Introducing knowledge graphs to decision support systems design. In *Information systems: Research, development, applications* (pp. 3–11). Springer. https://doi.org/10.1007/978-3-030-29608-7_1

En-Naaoui, A., Kaicer, M., & Aguezzoul, A. (2024). A novel decision support system for proactive risk management in healthcare based on fuzzy inference, neural network and support vector machine. *International Journal of Medical Informatics*, *186*, 105442. https://doi.org/10.1016/j.ijmedinf.2024.105442

Enholm, I. M., Papagiannidis, E., Mikalef, P., & Krogstie, J. (2022). Artificial intelligence and business value: A literature review. *Information Systems Frontiers*, *24*(5), 1709–1734. https://doi.org/10.1007/s10796-021-10186-w

Gaman, O., Shyshatskyi, A., Babenko, V., Pluhina, T., Degtyareva, L., Shaposhnikova, O., Pronin, S., Protas, N., Stasiuk, T., & Kutsenko, I. (2023). An analysis of knowledge representation methods in intelligent decision-making support systems. *Technology Audit and Production Reserves*, *5*, 22–26. https://doi.org/10.15587/2706-5448.2023.289747

Guillaume, A., Vrain, C., & Wael, E. (2020). Predictive maintenance on event logs: Application on an ATM fleet. *Semantic Scholar*. https://api.semanticscholar.org/CorpusID:244478735

Ivanov, S. H. (2023). Automated decision-making. *Foresight*, *25*(1), 4–19. https://doi.org/10.1108/FS-09-2021-0183

Jarrahi, M. H., Askay, D., Eshraghi, A., & Smith, P. (2023). Artificial intelligence and knowledge management: A partnership between human and AI. *Business Horizons*, *66*, 87–99. https://doi.org/10.1016/j.bushor.2022.03.002

Jia, T., Wang, C., Tian, Z., Wang, B., & Tian, F. (2022). Design of digital and intelligent financial decision support system based on artificial intelligence. *Computational Intelligence and Neuroscience*, *2022*, 962937. https://doi.org/10.1155/2022/1962937

Joshi, A., & Wade, M. (2020, August 10). The building blocks of an AI strategy. *MIT Sloan Management Review*. https://sloanreview.mit.edu/article/the-building-blocks-of-an-ai-strategy/

Kaklauskas, A. (2015). Intelligent decision support systems. In *Biometric and intelligent decision making support* (Vol. 81, pp. 25–50). Springer. https://doi.org/10.1007/978-3-319-13659-2_2

Kerzel, U. (2020). Enterprise AI canvas - Integrating artificial intelligence into business. *Applied Artificial Intelligence*, *35*(1), 1–12. https://doi.org/10.1080/08839514.2020.1826146

Khosravi, M., Zare, Z., Morteza Mojtabaeian, S., & Izadi, R. (2024). Artificial intelligence and decision-making in healthcare: A thematic analysis of a systematic review of reviews. *Health Services Research and Managerial Epidemiology*, *11*. https://doi.org/10.1177/23333928241234863

Kierner, S., Kierner, P., & Kucharski, J. (2025). Combining machine learning models and rule engines in clinical decision systems: Exploring optimal aggregation methods for vaccine hesitancy prediction. *Computers in Biology and Medicine*, *188*, 109749. https://doi.org/10.1016/j.compbiomed.2025.109749

Kühl, N., Schemmer, M., Goutier, M., & Satzger, G. (2022). Artificial intelligence and machine learning. *Electronic Markets*, *32*, 2235–2244. https://doi.org/10.1007/s12525-022-00598-0

Malone, T. W. (2018). How human-computer "superminds" are redefining the future of work. *MIT Sloan Management Review*, *59*(4), 34–41.

Mannina, G., Rebouças, T. F., Cosenza, A., Sànchez-Marrè, M., & Gibert, K. (2019). Decision support systems (DSS) for wastewater treatment plants – A review of the state of the art. *Bioresource Technology*, *290*(2019), 121814. https://doi.org/10.1016/j.biortech.2019.121814

Mashayekhi, M., McBeth, R., Nguyen, D., Yen, A., Trivedi, Z., Moon, D., Avkshtol, V., Vo, D., Sher, D., Jiang, S., & Lin, M. H. (2023). Artificial intelligence guided physician directive improves head and neck planning quality and practice uniformity: A prospective study. *Clinical and Translational Radiation Oncology*, *40*, 100616. https://doi.org/10.1016/j.ctro.2023.100616

Meski, O., Belkadi, F., Laroche, F., Ritou, M., & Furet, B. (2021). A generic knowledge management approach towards the development of a decision support system. *International Journal of Production Research*, *59*(22), 6659–6676.

Mustofa, S., Emon, Y. R., Mamun, S. B., Akhy, S. A., & Ahad, Md. T. (2024). A novel AI-driven model for student dropout risk analysis with explainable AI insights. *Computers and Education: Artificial Intelligence*, *8*(2025), 100352. https://doi.org/10.1016/j.caeai.2024.100352

Nakhaei, M., Ahmadi, A., Gheibi, M., Chahkandi, B., Hajiaghaei-Keshteli, M., & Behzadian, K. (2023). A smart sustainable decision support system for water management of power plants in water stress regions. *Expert Systems with Applications*, *230*, 120752. https://doi.org/10.1016/j.eswa.2023.120752

Olavsrud, T. (2024, January 29). *Decision support systems: Drive better decision-making with data*. CIO. https://www.cio.com/article/193521/decision-support-systems-sifting-data-for-better-business-decisions.html

Papagiannidis, E., Mikalef, P., Conboy, K., & Van de Wetering, R. (2023). Uncovering the dark side of AI-based decision-making: A case study in a B2B context. *Industrial Marketing Management*, *115*(2023), 253–265. https://doi.org/10.1016/j.indmarman.2023.10.003

Paraschos, S., Mollas, I., Bassiliades, N., & Tsoumakas, G. (2021, August 19–26). VisioRed: Visualisation tool for interpretable predictive maintenance [Conference presentation]. In *Proceedings of the 30th international joint conference on artificial intelligence (IJCAI-21), Montreal, Canada*. https://doi.org/10.24963/ijcai.2021/713

Perifanis, N.-A., & Kitsios, F. (2023). Investigating the influence of artificial intelligence on business value in the digital era of strategy: A literature review. *Information*, *14*(2), 85. https://doi.org/10.3390/info14020085

Pinto, R., Lagorio, A., Ciceri, C., Mangano, G., Zenezini, G., & Rafele, C. (2024). A conversationally enabled decision support system for supply chain management: A conceptual framework. *IFAC-PapersOnLine*, *58*(19), 801–806. https://doi.org/10.1016/j.ifacol.2024.09.198

Ponomarev, A., & Mustafin, N. (2021). Decision support systems configuration based on knowledge-driven automated service composition: Requirements and conceptual model. *Procedia Computer Science*, *186*(2021), 654–660. https://doi.org/10.1016/j.procs.2021.04.213

Psarommatis, F., & Kiritsis, D. (2022). A hybrid decision support system for automating decision making in the event of defects in the era of zero defect manufacturing. *Journal of Industrial Information Integration*, *26*, 100263. https://doi.org/10.1016/j.jii.2021.100263

Raj Shrestha, Y., Krishna, V., & von Krogh, G. (2020). Augmenting organizational decision-making with deep learning algorithms: Principles, promises, and challenges. *Journal of Business Research*, *123*(2021), 588–603. https://doi.org/10.1016/j.jbusres.2020.09.068

Rajagopal, N. K., Qureshi, N. I., Durga, S., Ramirez Asis, E. H., Huerta Soto, R. M., Gupta, S. K., & Deepak, S. (2022). Future of business culture: An artificial intelligence-driven digital framework for organization decision-making process. *Complexity*, *2022*(1), 1–14. https://doi.org/10.1155/2022/7796507

Rana, J., & Daultani, Y. (2022). Mapping the role and impact of artificial intelligence and machine learning applications in supply chain digital transformation: A bibliometric analysis. *Operations Management Research*, *16*, 1641–1666. https://doi.org/10.1007/s12063-022-00335-y

Reis, M. I., Gonçalves, J. N. C., Cortez, P., Carvalho, M. S., & Fernandes, J. M. (2024). A context-aware decision support system for selecting explainable artificial intelligence methods in business organizations. *Computers in Industry*, *165*(2025), 104233. https://doi.org/10.1016/j.compind.2024.104233

Rosati, R., Romeo, L., Cecchini, G., Tonetto, F., Viti, P., Mancini, A., & Frontoni, E. (2023). From knowledge-based to big data analytic model: A novel IoT and machine learning based decision support system for predictive maintenance in Industry 4.0. *Journal of Intelligent Manufacturing*, *34*(1), 107–121. https://doi.org/10.1007/s10845-022-01960-x

Schemmer, M., Kühl, N., & Satzger, G. (2022, January 3–7). Intelligent decision assistance versus automated decision-making: Enhancing knowledge work through explainable artificial intelligence [Conference presentation]. In *Proceedings of the 55th Hawaii international conference on system sciences, Honolulu, HI, United States*. https://doi.org/10.24251/hicss.2022.185

Schneider, J., Abraham, R., Meske, C., & vom Brocke, J. (2020). AI governance for businesses. *Information Systems Management*, *40*(3), 229–249. https://doi.org/10.1080/10580530.2022.2085825

Shegai, P. V., Shatalov, P. A., Zabolotneva, A. A., Falaleeva, N. A., Ivanov, S. A., & Kaprin, A. D. (2021). Challenges faced by clinicians in the personalized treatment planning: A literature review and the first results of the Russian national cancer program. *Critical Care Research and Practice*, *2021*, 6649771. https://doi.org/10.1155/2021/6649771

Shepherd, D. A., & Majchrzak, A. (2022). Machines augmenting entrepreneurs: Opportunities (and threats) at the nexus of artificial intelligence and entrepreneurship. *Journal of Business Venturing*, *37*(4), 106227. https://doi.org/10.1016/j.jbusvent.2022.106227

Soori, M., Jough, F. K. G., Dastres, R., & Arezoo, B. (2024). AI-based decision support systems in Industry 4.0: A review. *Journal of Economy and Technology*. https://doi.org/10.1016/j.ject.2024.08.005

Stanek, S., Sołtysik-Piorunkiewicz, A., & Szary, M. (2022). The knowledge components in DDMKCC model as the catalyst of a hybrid DSS-The IT company case study. *Journal of Organizational Knowledge Management*, *2022*(2022). https://ibimapublishing.com/articles/JOKM/2022/965062/

Tabesh, P. (2022). Who's making the decisions? How managers can harness artificial intelligence and remain in charge. *Journal of Business Strategy*, *43*(6), 373–380. https://doi.org/10.1108/JBS-05-2021-0090

Talari, G., Cummins, E., McNamara, C., & O'Brien, J. (2022). State of the art review of big data and web-based decision support systems (DSS) for food safety risk assessment with respect to climate change. *Trends in Food Science & Technology*, *126*, 192–204. https://doi.org/10.1016/j.tifs.2021.08.032

Tariq, A., & Rafi, K. (2012). Intelligent decision support systems - A framework. *Information and Knowledge Management*, *2*(6), 1–6.

Yalçın, G. C., Limon, E. G., Kara, K., Limon, O., Gürol, P., Deveci, M., Demirayak, Ö., & Tomaskova, H. (2025). A hybrid decision support system for transport policy selection: A case study on Russia's Northern Sea route in Artic region. *Socio-Economic Planning Sciences*, *98*(2025), 102171. https://doi.org/10.1016/j.seps.2025.102171

Yun, Y., Ma, D., & Yang, M. (2021). Human–computer interaction-based decision support system with applications in data mining. *Future Generation Computer Systems*, *114*, 285–289. https://doi.org/10.1016/j.future.2020.07.048

Zdravković, M., Panetto, H., & Weichhart, G. (2022). AI-enabled enterprise information systems for manufacturing. *Enterprise Information Systems*, *16*(4), 668–720. https://doi.org/10.1080/17517575.2021.1941275

Zhang, M., Taimuri, G., Zhang, J., Zhang, Di., Yan, X., Kujala, P., & Hirdaris, S. (2025). Systems driven intelligent decision support methods for ship collision and grounding prevention: Present status, possible solutions, and challenges. *Reliability Engineering & System Safety*, *253*, 110489. https://doi.org/10.1016/j.ress.2024.110489

Zhao, J., & Gómez Fariñas, B. (2023). Artificial intelligence and sustainable decisions. *European Business Organization Law Review*, *24*, 1–39. https://doi.org/10.1007/s40804-022-00262-2

Chapter 3

AI-Driven Decision Support Systems for Transforming Employee Engagement and Training in Business

Jill Courtney

JCreative Multimedia, USA

Abstract

As organizations navigate increasing digital complexity, engaging, training, and retaining employees has become critical for competitive advantage. Traditional training and decision-making tools often fall short in providing personalized, data-informed support for modern workforces. In response, artificial intelligence-driven decision support systems (AI-DSS) have emerged as strategic tools, leverage predictive analytics, automation, and real-time feedback to enhance employee engagement and skill outcomes.

This chapter explores AI-DSS applications that personalize learning paths, automate performance diagnostics, and enhance adaptive training. Examples explored include Amazon's predictive AI, utilized for onboarding, Microsoft's AI-driven skilling initiative, UPS's AI-integrated logistics training, and Harbinger Group's agentic AI for executive coaching.

Beyond operational benefits, AI-DSS tools are increasingly assessed for their capacity to foster trust, ethical governance, and cognitive balance. Research emphasizes the importance of transparency, feedback loops, and human-AI collaboration in maintaining long-term learning retention and critical thinking integrations. By integrating agentic AI, RAG, and behavioral analytics, organizations can reframe employee engagement beyond a static HR function; rather it can be viewed as a dynamic, decision-informed business strategy. The chapter highlights AI-DSS's role in enhancing workforce satisfaction, skill retention, and organizational agility, establishing adaptive learning as a central artery to enterprise resilience in the AI era.

AI-Driven Knowledge Management Assets, Volume 2, 37–60

Published under exclusive licence by Emerald Publishing Limited
doi:10.1108/978-1-83662-778-420261003

Keywords: AI-driven decision support systems (AI-DSS); employee engagement and workforce development; agentic AI and autonomous learning systems; predictive analytics for training and retention; ethical AI governance in workforce systems; adaptive learning and real-time performance feedback

Introduction

As organizations face rapid technological advancement and evolving employee expectations, workforce engagement and training have become central to long-term business sustainability. In today's data-intensive environment, traditional training systems and top-down decision-making processes increasingly fail to meet the needs of modern learners or support adaptive talent development. In response, artificial intelligence–driven decision support systems (AI-DSS) have emerged as a strategic solution for personalizing learning, enhancing employee engagement, and enabling evidence-based development pathways (Basnet, 2024; Compugen, 2025; Gerlich, 2025; Soori et al., 2024).

Unlike static knowledge management (KM) repositories, modern AI-DSS platforms continuously process real-time behavioral, operational, and performance data to support informed decisions across the employee lifecycle, from onboarding and skills-tracking to targeted upskilling and retention strategies. For example, Amazon leverages predictive analytics to identify skill gaps and improve onboarding efficiency (DigitalDefynd, 2025a), while a Microsoft AI skilling initiative integrates DSS to reskill more than one million workers through adaptive content and capability mapping (Boltt, 2025). At UPS, AI-DSS enhances training by embedding machine learning into logistics operations, enabling smarter delivery planning and faster workforce performance optimization (DigitalDefynd, 2025b).

Beyond technical implementation, AI-DSS platforms are actively reshaping organizational engagement by enabling context-aware collaboration, identifying latent expertise, and structuring knowledge flow. These systems act as intelligent co-pilots, detecting engagement gaps, dynamically recommending interventions, and supporting development pathways tuned to the individual. Emerging systems like case studies analyzed by Moveworks and Harbinger Group exemplify this transformation through the use of agentic AI; autonomous digital agents that respond to real-time behavior and guide learning experiences through personalized feedback loops (Acharya et al., 2025; Brennen, 2025; Harbinger Group, 2025; Marr, 2025; Purdy, 2024).

Yet the success of AI-DSS depends on more than functionality. As employees engage with AI-generated feedback, ethical integration, explainability, and transparency are essential to maintain trust and safeguard cognitive development (Dasari, 2023; Gerlich, 2025; Hardman, 2025b; Yu et al., 2023). When AI systems are opaque or overly prescriptive, they can erode critical thinking, reduce learning autonomy, and undercut long-term knowledge retention, especially among early-career professionals (Hardman, 2025a; Heung & Chiu, 2025; Jošt et al., 2024).

This chapter examines how organizations are deploying AI-DSS to transition from fragmented, compliance-based training to intelligent, scalable ecosystems for engagement and learning. Drawing on enterprise case studies, emerging research, and the evolution of agentic architectures, the sections that follow explore how AI-DSS tools can foster a workforce that is not only digitally fluent but resilient, empowered, and decision-ready in an increasingly AI-driven business landscape.

The Evolution of AI-DSS in the Workforce

From Legacy Systems to Adaptive Workforce Decision Tools

Decision support systems (DSS) have evolved significantly since their early development as rule-based models in the 1960s. Originally used to support structured decision-making through statistical calculations and rigid logic, contemporary DSS have matured into dynamic, AI-enabled platforms that adapt to real-time user data. Fueled by predictive analytics, machine learning (ML), and natural language processing (NLP), these systems now play an integral role in workforce training and engagement, enabling organizations to assess, respond to, and anticipate employee development needs (Basnet, 2024; Compugen, 2025; Gerlich, 2025; Soori et al., 2024).

Today's AI-DSS ingest data from across the employee lifecycle, including HR records, learning logs, feedback loops, and performance metrics. The goal is to detect skill gaps, monitor engagement trends, and recommend personalized development pathways (Basnet, 2024; Compugen, 2025). Unlike legacy knowledge management systems, which emphasize documentation and storage, AI-DSS transform data into real-time learning interventions, making workforce decision-making both contextualized and adaptive.

Enterprise Applications in Training and Development

Organizations such as Amazon, Microsoft, and UPS have emerged as early leaders in operationalizing AI-DSS within employee development pipelines. At Amazon, predictive analytics inform onboarding processes and skill gap detection, enabling the delivery of targeted training based on employee role, location, and experience level (DigitalDefynd, 2025a). A Microsoft skilling initiative used AI-DSS to align learning experiences with projected workforce demands, offering real-time course recommendations across sectors (Boltt, 2025). UPS, by contrast, integrates AI into its logistics training ecosystem, dynamically adjusting employee assignments, route planning, and upskilling activities to optimize field-based performance (DigitalDefynd, 2025b).

These use cases show that AI-DSS do more than streamline internal workflows. They actively influence development trajectories by embedding feedback loops, surfacing engagement metrics, and tailoring learning experiences to both individual and organizational goals (Compugen, 2025; Taylor, 2025).

Transforming Knowledge Into Action

AI-DSS also represent a pivotal evolution in enterprise knowledge management. Rather than requiring employees to manually locate information, modern systems surface just-in-time recommendations, contextualized to the learner's current role, progress, and engagement phase (Leyden & Hart-Davis, 2025; SnapLogic, 2025; Soori et al., 2024). With retrieval-augmented generation (RAG), conversational interfaces, and knowledge graphs, learning platforms now function as interactive environments that deliver actionable insight precisely when needed (Liang et al., 2023).

Agentic AI further extends these capabilities. Systems like Harbinger Group's coaching platform autonomously generate development strategies by interpreting behavioral data and adjusting interventions in real time (Acharya et al., 2025; Compugen, 2025; Harbinger Group, 2025; Leyden & Hart-Davis, 2025). This shift from static content delivery to collaborative decision-making represents a broader movement from human-led instruction toward shared autonomy in professional development.

Decision-Making at the Speed of Change

AI-DSS platforms provide the responsiveness necessary to meet fast-changing workforce demands. They help organizations forecast disengagement, anticipate reskilling needs, and deploy early interventions using predictive modeling and continuous data ingestion (Basnet, 2024; Jošt et al., 2024; Taylor, 2023). The result is a more agile and evidence-based approach to employee development, where insights are acted upon in time to influence outcomes, not just report on them after the fact.

As these tools become more embedded in decision-making workflows, ethical design becomes essential. Features such as explainable AI, opt-in personalization, and data transparency are necessary to build employee trust and preserve learning autonomy (Dasari, 2023; Gerlich, 2025; SnapLogic, 2025; Yu et al., 2023).

The evolution of AI-DSS thus represents not just a technical transformation, but a cultural one. These systems empower employees to thrive in dynamic roles while helping organizations align training with broader strategic goals. The sections that follow will examine the components and case studies that illustrate how AI-DSS is redefining the future of workforce engagement and training.

Core Components of AI-DSS for Engagement and Training

AI-DSS function through the integration of multiple technological layers and organizational practices that enable adaptive, ethically grounded decision-making. In doing so, AI-DSS transforms knowledge management from a static repository model into a dynamic, behavior-driven flow system, capturing, adapting, and redistributing organizational knowledge in real time. In the context of employee engagement and training, these systems form the foundation of intelligent learning environments that continuously assess needs, deliver tailored interventions, and support long-term workforce development (Hardman, 2025a, 2025b; Soori et al., 2024; Yu et al., 2023). The following components define the architecture and operational logic of effective AI-DSS platforms.

Data Aggregation and Integration

A foundational step in AI-DSS implementation is the consolidation of data from across the employee experience. Traditional training ecosystems often operate in silos; isolated human resource information systems (HRIS), learning management systems (LMS), communication tools, and performance logs are not linked. AI-DSS overcome this fragmentation by integrating multiple data sources into a unified framework that provides a comprehensive profile of each employee's skills, learning history, collaboration behavior, and engagement indicators (AI Expert Network, 2024; Compugen, 2025; Heung & Chiu, 2025).

Data Processing and Validation

Once data is aggregated, it must be cleaned, standardized, and validated to ensure accurate downstream analytics. AI platforms use normalization and anomaly detection to address missing or outdated information and to resolve conflicting records. For example, if LMS records and HR evaluations are misaligned, the system flags discrepancies to avoid generating misleading recommendations (Brennen, 2025; Soori et al., 2024; Taylor, 2023; Undru, 2025). This improves both the fairness and reliability of AI-informed decision-making.

Predictive and Behavioral Analytics

AI-DSS do more than report; they forecast. Using behavioral signals such as participation rates, learning velocity, and team collaboration metrics, AI-DSS can identify disengagement risks or impending skill gaps. Predictive analytics tools model these trends, while prescriptive analytics suggest tailored interventions, such as new training modules, workload redistribution, or mentorship matching (Basnet, 2024; Dasari, 2023; DigitalDefynd, 2025a, 2025b). These systems transform passive data into proactive strategy (see Fig. 3.1).

Agentic AI and Autonomous Delivery

Advancements in agentic AI enable AI-DSS to autonomously generate personalized learning recommendations, coaching prompts, and developmental plans without continuous human direction. Platforms like Harbinger Group's executive coaching system exemplify this by combining RAG, pattern recognition, and reinforcement learning to adjust coaching pathways based on behavioral feedback (Acharya et al., 2025; Harbinger Group, 2025; Layden & Hart-David, 2025;

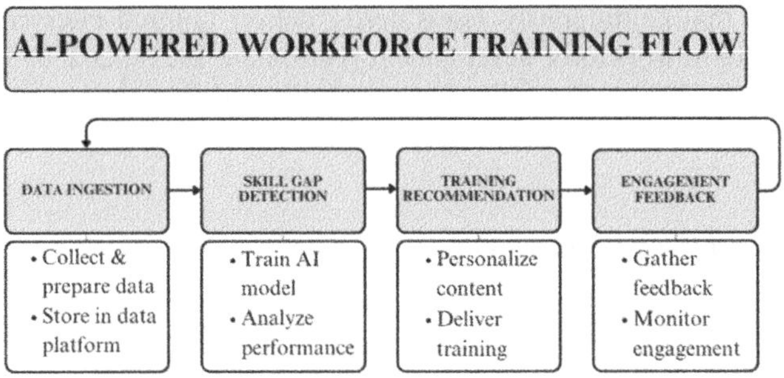

Fig. 3.1. AI-Powered Workforce Training Flowchart. *Note.* This diagram illustrates the full decision-making cycle of an AI-DSS applied to workforce development. It begins with data ingestion and model training, proceeds through personalized training delivery, and completes the loop with performance feedback and model recalibration, supporting continuous learning and adaptive engagement strategies. *Source:* Data collected by author.

Marr, 2025). This capacity allows AI to act not as a content curator, but as a dynamic collaborator.

Real-Time Adaptability

Modern AI-DSS platforms continuously adapt as new information is received. When a user's engagement drops in a course or collaborative behavior changes, AI can automatically generate real-time suggestions, ranging from content delivery pacing to team reconfiguration. This agility ensures responsiveness to emerging trends rather than reliance on lagging indicators (Basnet, 2024; Compugen, 2025; Liang et al., 2023; Taylor, 2025).

Transparent Governance and Ethical Safeguards

As AI-DSS increasingly influence career pathways, performance evaluation, and leadership development, ethical governance becomes critical. Core safeguards include fairness audits, explainable AI models, opt-in personalization controls, and transparent logic pathways. Transparency allows users to understand how and why recommendations are generated, strengthening trust and promoting adoption (Dasari, 2023; SnapLogic, 2025; Soori et al., 2024; Yu et al., 2023).

Organizational Alignment and Culture of Use

The efficacy of AI-DSS does not rest on technology alone. Organizations must foster a culture that encourages data-literate decision-making and AI fluency. Leaders should champion ethical AI use, while employees must feel empowered to challenge or interpret AI-generated insights. Studies show that user engagement and knowledge retention increase when employees collaborate with, rather than defer to, AI systems (Basnet, 2024; Compugen, 2025; Gerlich, 2025; Jošt et al., 2024; Undru, 2025).

In summary, the successful implementation of AI-DSS requires attention to infrastructure, ethics, and organizational culture. When thoughtfully deployed, these systems serve not only as technological tools but as enablers of workforce growth, adaptive learning, and strategic engagement.

Real-World Use Cases: AI-DSS in Employee Engagement and Training

This section explores real-world implementations of AI-DSS with a focus on enhancing employee engagement, personalized learning, and performance-driven workforce strategies.

Use Cases in Employee Training and Engagement

The adoption of AI-DSS is redefining how organizations support employee development, retention, and engagement. These systems replace traditional, static training programs with intelligent, adaptive learning ecosystems that evolve in response to individual needs and organizational strategy (Basnet, 2024; Gerlich, 2025; Heung & Chiu, 2025; Leyden & Hart-Davis, 2025; Soori et al., 2024).

Amazon: Predictive Analytics for Workforce Optimization

Amazon implements AI-DSS to personalize workforce onboarding, forecast training needs, and adapt development strategies based on real-time employee data. Its platforms synthesize human resources records, learning behaviors, and sentiment data to guide targeted learning journeys and improve role alignment (DigitalDefynd, 2025a).

These systems operate across several employee development domains. AI-driven onboarding recommendations reduce time-to-productivity by suggesting tailored training plans for new hires. Predictive models assess performance gaps, prompting interventions through leadership development programs or technical skills modules. In logistics training, adaptive delivery frameworks guide warehouse staff through role-specific learning, contributing to performance optimization. In all cases, AI recommendations are context-aware, adapting to location, job function, and departmental goals.

The results of these applications are substantial. Amazon attributes over 35% of its total revenue to personalized AI recommendations, demonstrating the value of tailored user experiences (DigitalDefynd, 2025a). In workforce training, this same personalization model supports measurable improvements in retention, onboarding speed, and development pacing. In fulfillment environments, predictive maintenance and performance analytics reduce downtime and operational inefficiencies, indirectly benefiting employee experience and enabling higher throughput without increasing labor strain.

Taken together, Amazon's approach demonstrates how AI-DSS can enable enterprise-scale personalization of learning and performance support, aligning individual growth with strategic business outcomes while strengthening knowledge continuity and retention.

Microsoft: Skilling and AI-Powered Career Pathways

Microsoft's AI-DSS are embedded across global employee development and national workforce training initiatives. In South Africa, Microsoft launched a major AI skilling program aimed at empowering one million individuals with in-demand digital and AI capabilities by 2026 (Boltt, 2025). The initiative combines competency mapping, adaptive learning tools, and data-informed feedback loops to deliver scalable, inclusive training aligned with national economic goals.

Microsoft also deploys AI-DSS within its enterprise ecosystem, using tools like Microsoft Copilot, Power BI, and Viva to personalize onboarding, monitor engagement, and optimize employee learning outcomes. According to a joint study with IDC, companies deploying Microsoft AI solutions reported a return of $3.50 for every $1 invested, with 92% of implementations completed in under a year and ROI typically realized in 14 months (Taylor, 2023, 2024). These systems also enhance decision support through predictive analytics, enabling managers to detect skill gaps and burnout signals in real time.

As of 2024, Microsoft had reached over six million learners globally through AI-enhanced skilling programs. Case-specific data includes Noventiq saving 989 hours in four weeks through Microsoft Copilot and SPAR Group reporting a 93% productivity boost after deployment (Taylor, 2023, 2025). Additionally, a Canadian financial institution using Microsoft's AI tools reported a 25% drop in turnover and a 40% productivity lift in under six months (Compugen, 2025). These outcomes validate Microsoft's AI-DSS approach as both scalable and strategic, delivering tangible improvements in engagement, retention, and adaptive workforce development.

UPS: Logistics, Onboarding, and AI-Facilitated Performance Support

UPS implements AI-DSS to support real-time employee enablement, reduce operational inefficiencies, and scale onboarding across its global logistics network. Key systems include the On-Road Integrated Optimization and

Navigation (ORION) platform, which personalizes delivery routes using predictive data, and the MeRA tool, a large language model (LLM)-driven system that automates customer service responses while augmenting agent training (AI Expert Network, 2024; Krause, 2025).

AI-DSS tools also support UPS's multilingual workforce training through the Languages Across Logistics (LAL) platform, which enhances onboarding and collaborative engagement across 20 countries. Predictive maintenance systems extend the performance of fleet assets, minimizing downtime and improving delivery consistency (DigitalDefynd, 2025b).

As a result, UPS reports that the ORION platform has reduced driver mileage by over 100 million miles per year, saving $300 million and cutting 100,000 metric tons of carbon emissions (Krause, 2025). The MeRA tool reduced customer email response times by 50%, allowing agents to shift focus toward complex interactions and training (AI Expert Network, 2024). Multilingual AI training systems have enabled consistent performance development across diverse global teams, supporting higher engagement, faster upskilling, and more efficient route learning (DigitalDefynd, 2025b).

Harbinger Group: Personalized Leadership Coaching With Agentic AI

Harbinger Group implemented an agentic AI-DSS to automate and scale personalized leadership coaching. Developed for a global skilling platform, the system combines RAG, natural language processing, and behavioral pattern recognition to deliver adaptive training plans tailored to individual development trajectories (Harbinger Group, 2025).

The platform classifies leaders by behavioral signals and communication styles, delivering just-in-time coaching content aligned with specific role requirements. Unlike rule-based mentoring programs, Harbinger Group's agentic AI retrieves relevant content from an extensive knowledge base and dynamically refines learning pathways based on user feedback. This represents a shift from static course delivery to real-time, decision-informed development.

Organizations using the platform reported a 50% reduction in content discovery time, a 30% reduction in manual plan creation, and an average monthly savings of 20 hours per manager through automated content retrieval (Harbinger Group, 2025). The approach also improves the transfer of behavioral data into structured leadership insights, allowing organizations to embed coaching patterns into reusable knowledge systems and extend decision support beyond performance management into long-term leadership development.

Moveworks: Context-Aware Learning Assistance With Agentic AI

Moveworks reported on several different use cases of utilizing agentic AI assistance in different business domains. For IT, Power Design deployed an agentic artificial intelligence solution through what they have called H elpBot. Using natural language processing (NLP), it delivers real-time, autonomous assistance across enterprise systems. Built on an agentic automation engine, HelpBot functions as a conversational AI assistant that responds to employee IT requests. Unlike standard AI chatbots, HelpBot integrates data across systems to proactively identify learning gaps, resolve issues autonomously, and adapt its recommendations over time. Over 1,000 hours of complex tasks have been automated by using HelpBot (Brennen, 2025).

For the HR team, Palo Alto Networks built an agentic AI program for hybrid workers in need of personalized support, called FLEXWORK. It uses Natural Language Understanding to have conversations with employees in real-time. But the decision-making programming sets it apart from typical AI with an agentic AI solution giving responses using a blend of reasoning and judgment which allows reactive adaption to different situations and provides problem-solving (Brennen, 2025).

For the financial industry, Bud Financial has become a banking technology leader on the consumer side through an agentic AI experience that can learn about each customer's financial history, position, and goals, then execute tasks on their behalf to help improve their finances, save on overdraft fees, or take advantage of higher interest rates through internal account transfers (Brennen, 2025).

For cybersecurity, Darktrace uses agentic AI algorithms modeled on the human immune system.

It continuously monitors network traffic, detects complex cyber threats, autonomously identifies and responds to previously unseen cyber-attacks in realtime, hunts for anomalies within the network, and applies advanced machine learning techniques to decide the best course of action. This allows human security teams to focus on high-level tasks and more complex organizational issues (Brennen, 2025).

SnapLogic: Predictive Burnout Detection and Personalized Microlearning

SnapLogic applies AI-DSS to improve employee engagement, retention, and well-being by automating burnout detection and scaling learning interventions. The company's agentic AI agents use real-time behavioral data and workforce sentiment analysis to flag disengagement risks and recommend proactive support strategies. These agents integrate with HR systems and productivity tools to assess workload imbalance, task completion rates, and digital fatigue (SnapLogic, 2025).

The system recommends personalized microlearning modules, short-form content, or workflow adjustments based on employee context. These interventions are timed to prevent productivity drops, support mental health, and foster skill development without overwhelming learners. SnapLogic's platform also allows HR leaders to track learning engagement across departments, assess the impact of interventions, and align training with team-level KPIs, embedding knowledge flow into the daily work experience.

Companies using SnapLogic's workforce intelligence agents have reported reduced attrition rates, improved training completion rates, and higher engagement with just-in-time learning resources (SnapLogic, 2025). Organizations also saw measurable reductions in burnout risk profiles over 90-day windows, with increased utilization of learning libraries and increased manager confidence in using AI dashboards for talent planning. These results demonstrate how AI-DSS can proactively shape workforce development while supporting knowledge continuity and emotional well-being.

ThoughtSpot: Transparent Analytics Through Conversational Interfaces

ThoughtSpot highlights the Spotter platform, which integrates agentic AI into business intelligence environments, allowing employees to query enterprise data using natural language. Unlike traditional dashboards that require advanced data literacy, Spotter enables self-service insight discovery, bridging the gap between business users and data teams by eliminating the need for ticketing systems or technical mediation (Undru, 2025).

The agentic AI engine powering Spotter proactively surfaces real-time insights based on behavior, context, and role. Employees can ask complex, multi-variable questions such as, "Which departments show declining engagement metrics among new hires over the past two quarters?" and receive immediate, visual answers within their workflow. By shifting analytics from static to interactive, the system supports data-driven decisions at the point of action.

Organizations using Spotter reported reduced analytics response time, improved adoption of workforce dashboards, and greater transparency in performance reviews and training decisions (Undru, 2025). Spotter's role-based personalization and conversational interface democratize data access across the enterprise, enhancing knowledge flow, strengthening trust in AI-generated insights, and encouraging active engagement with learning and performance data.

While most current implementations are concentrated in large-scale enterprises, small and mid-sized organizations are also beginning to pilot AI-DSS for tasks such as performance tracking, onboarding optimization, and scalable training delivery.

Table 3.1. Use Case Comparison Table.

Organization	AI Strategy	Use Case Type	Measurable Outcomes
Amazon	Predictive analytics for onboarding and workforce allocation	Personalized training and logistics learning	35% of revenue via personalization; reduced onboarding time; improved fulfillment accuracy; reduced downtime (DigitalDefynd, 2025a)

(Continued)

Table 3.1. *(Continued)*

Organization	AI Strategy	Use Case Type	Measurable Outcomes
Microsoft	Adaptive skilling at national scale; LLMs for productivity	Enterprise and public workforce upskilling	6M+ trained; $3.5:1 ROI; 40% productivity gain; 25% turnover reduction (Boltt, 2025; Compugen, 2025; Taylor, 2025)
UPS	Real-time AI route optimization and multilingual training systems	Onboarding, field learning, and LLM support	Saved $300M/year; 50% faster email response; improved global upskilling (AI Expert Network, 2024; Krause, 2025)
Harbinger Group	Agentic AI coaching platform with RAG and behavior tracking	Executive training and development	50% less content search time; 30% fewer manual workflows; 20 hours/month saved per manager (Harbinger Group, 2025)
Moveworks	HelpBot with agentic automation engine	Knowledge navigation and 24/7 internal support	1,000+ hours automated; reduced ticket load; increased engagement (Brennen, 2025)
SnapLogic	Predictive analytics for burnout and disengagement	Microlearning and emotional well-being	Reduced attrition; improved training completion; 90-day burnout risk drop (SnapLogic, 2025)
ThoughtSpot	Conversational analytics and insight delivery	Performance dashboards and workforce transparency	Faster insights; increased training engagement; stronger trust in AI outputs (Undru, 2025)

Source: Data collected by author.

Note. This matrix (Table 3.1) compares organizations profiled in the chapter, outlining their AI strategies, workforce training applications, and measurable outcomes. It enables cross-case synthesis and illustrates how AI-DSS platforms are being applied to enhance employee engagement and knowledge development across industries.

Implications of AI-DSS Adoption

The real-world cases examined in this chapter demonstrate that AI-DSS are not only optimizing individual business processes; they are also reshaping how organizations approach workforce development, knowledge transfer, and engagement at scale. The diversity of applications reveals common patterns in how AI-DSS accelerate learning, reduce administrative burdens, and support behavior-based performance strategies.

Amazon and UPS exemplify the operational value of real-time, AI-informed training and onboarding. Their AI-DSS tools improve responsiveness, align learning with logistics performance, and help distribute contextual knowledge across globally dispersed workforces. Microsoft and Harbinger Group case studies show that scalable personalization, whether for public-sector skilling or executive coaching, requires decision systems that combine predictive modeling with adaptive feedback loops. Meanwhile, Moveworks, SnapLogic, and ThoughtSpot illustrate how conversational interfaces, agentic agents, and embedded analytics increase learning access, improve self-service resolution, and enhance trust in AI systems.

Taken together, these implementations highlight a set of cross-case implications. First, the most effective AI-DSS deployments shift training from a content-centered activity to a decision-enabled process; one in which insight, feedback, and learning occur simultaneously. Second, organizations that integrate AI-DSS into broader knowledge management frameworks improve their ability to preserve, surface, and transfer knowledge as both a learning asset and an operational resource. Finally, these systems demonstrate that personalization, automation, and trust are not mutually exclusive; in fact, they work best in tandem when deployed transparently and aligned with business objectives.

As AI-DSS adoption continues to expand, future success will depend not only on the quality of the technology itself, but on an organization's readiness to embed these systems into cultural, cognitive, and ethical infrastructure.

Benefits and Challenges of Implementing AI-Driven DSS in Engagement and Training

AI-DSS offer organizations a strategic opportunity to rethink how they approach employee development, engagement, and retention. By combining predictive analytics, adaptive learning delivery, and real-time feedback mechanisms, AI-DSS platforms help align training efforts with business needs while fostering personalization at scale (Basnet, 2024; Gerlich, 2025; Hardman, 2025a; Jošt et al., 2024; Soori et al., 2024). Yet, the transformative potential of these systems also introduces implementation risks, particularly in areas such as ethics, infrastructure, and workforce trust.

Benefits of AI-DSS in Workforce Development

When implemented effectively, AI-DSS can enhance multiple dimensions of workforce strategy:

- *Personalized Learning and Adaptive Training* By analyzing employee performance data, behavioral insights, and skills maps, AI-DSS platforms deliver personalized learning paths. For example, Amazon's predictive systems align technical training recommendations with evolving job demands, improving engagement and role alignment (DigitalDefynd, 2025a).
- *Enhanced Knowledge Flow and Collaboration* AI tools support knowledge management by identifying internal expertise, automating content recommendations, and facilitating mentorship connections. SnapLogic and Moveworks demonstrate how real-time learning prompts and conversational AI agents break down silos and improve knowledge sharing across distributed teams (Brennen, 2025; SnapLogic, 2025).
- *Predictive Insights for Engagement and Retention* Microsoft's AI-DSS -enabled skilling programs integrate workforce capability mapping and burnout risk analytics to support succession planning and proactive L&D interventions (Boltt, 2025; Compugen, 2025; Taylor, 2023, 2025).
- *Efficiency and Cost Savings* AI systems automate training development, delivery, and evaluation, reducing repetitive content, accelerating upskilling, and increasing return on learning investment (Basnet, 2024; Gerlich, 2025; Hardman, 2025a, 2025b; Jošt et al., 2024; Soori et al., 2024).

Challenges in Implementation and Adoption

Despite the benefits, AI-DSS deployments face a range of barriers that must be addressed to ensure long-term viability:

- *Data Privacy, Security, and Compliance* AI-DSS depend on continuous access to employee data. Without clear safeguards such as encryption, access controls, and compliance with global privacy regulations like GDPR and CCPA, these systems can erode workforce trust (Leyden & Hart-Davis, 2025; Yu et al., 2023).
- *Bias and Fairness* AI models can reproduce historical biases in promotion, training, and evaluation data. Ongoing auditing, fairness metrics, and dataset diversification are essential to prevent structural inequities from being encoded into system logic (Dasari, 2023; Leyden & Hart-Davis, 2025;Soori et al., 2024).
- *Workforce Adoption and Trust* Employee skepticism may emerge around job displacement, surveillance, or lack of control. Organizations must emphasize explainable AI, participatory design, and transparent framing to position AI-DSS as a developmental ally, not a judgment engine (Dasari, 2023; Gerlich, 2025; Soori et al., 2024).
- *Technical Integration and Resourcing* Legacy infrastructure can hinder AI-DSS integration. Many systems require cloud-native environments, skilled data

teams, and new cross-functional governance models to function effectively (Basnet, 2024; Dasari, 2023; Leyden & Hart-Davis, 2025; Soori et al., 2024).

- *Strategic Alignment and ROI Measurement* Without clear benchmarks, AI-DSS can be deployed in ways that fail to produce measurable outcomes. Organizations should launch pilot programs with built-in feedback loops and link performance metrics to real workforce objectives (Compugen, 2025).

Organizations that approach these challenges strategically by grounding AI-DSS in ethical design, clear governance, and cultural alignment will greatly benefit; they will be positioned to unlock not just automation, but transformation in workforce engagement, learning, and long-term talent development.

Ethical AI Governance and Human-AI Collaboration

As AI-DSS become embedded in employee development, their governance must extend beyond technological oversight. These tools now shape employee learning trajectories, training access, performance feedback, and advancement opportunities. In doing so, they exert significant influence on workforce outcomes and must therefore be deployed with clear ethical frameworks, human oversight, and trust-centered design principles (Dasari, 2023; Gerlich, 2025; Leyden & Hart-Davis, 2025; Yu et al., 2023).

Transparency and Explainability in AI Systems

A major challenge in responsible AI-DSS adoption is making system logic interpretable to non-technical users. In training and development contexts, especially those involving high-stakes leadership coaching or career advancement, opacity often undermines trust. Explainable AI (XAI) techniques surface the rationale behind training recommendations, model decisions, and performance assessments, ensuring that employees and leaders can engage critically with AI-generated insights (Gerlich, 2025).

Real-world implementations such as ThoughtSpot's Spotter platform and Moveworks' HelpBot illustrate this principle. Spotter allows employees to ask natural language queries about engagement trends or training outcomes and receive real-time visualizations (Undru, 2025). HelpBot similarly enables conversational access to policy, role-based learning resources, and performance data, reducing the barrier to insight while preserving transparency (Brennen, 2025).

Balancing Automation With Human Judgment

While AI-DSS can dramatically increase efficiency, over-reliance can displace essential human nuance. The most effective systems augment, rather than replace, human decision-making. In hybrid frameworks, AI generates recommendations and performance projections, but humans apply context and judgment. This ensures that learning and promotion decisions remain adaptive and individualized (Basnet, 2024; Jošt et al., 2024).

For example, Harbinger Group's agentic coaching platform surfaces personalized feedback in real time, but leaves control of action planning and coaching direction in the hands of human mentors. The system acts as a collaborator, not a substitute, reinforcing autonomy while enhancing consistency and accessibility (Harbinger Group, 2025).

Designing for Fairness and Accessibility in Learning Systems

AI-DSS models trained on historical workforce data risk perpetuating inequities unless continuously audited for bias and representative coverage. Fairness requires more than removing biases, where possible; it demands design strategies that accommodate learning differences, will support equal access, and promote adaptability across various skill levels (Soori et al., 2024). This includes developing flexible training pathways for early-career professionals, nontraditional learners, and individuals with unique developmental needs.

Embedding ethical governance also requires participatory design. Feedback loops, opt-in customization, and AI literacy programs empower employees to shape how AI systems support their learning. These design features ensure that systems remain adaptive not only to business goals but also to workforce diversity and input (Hardman, 2025a, 2025b; Heung & Chiu, 2025; Jošt et al., 2024).

Ethical AI governance and human-AI collaboration are not just regulatory concerns; they are strategic imperatives. Organizations that embed transparency, preserve human agency, and design for accessibility will foster long-term trust and sustain learning cultures built for adaptation, equity, and engagement (see Fig. 3.2).

Impacts on Learning Design, Motivation, and Cognitive Development

Personalized Learning vs Metacognitive Erosion

AI-DSS are reshaping how employees experience learning and skill development. These platforms do more than deliver content; they actively mediate how learners engage with material, build cognitive strategies, and sustain motivation in complex work environments. One core advantage of AI-DSS is their ability to align instructional delivery with principles from learning science, particularly in areas such as pacing, modality, and challenge level.

Rather than defaulting to one-size-fits-all models, AI-DSS adjust content delivery in real time based on learner signals, including performance data, completion patterns, and behavioral cues. This approach improves learner retention, supports differentiated learning styles, and fosters more effective knowledge transfer Hardman, 2025a, 2025b; Heung & Chiu, 2025; Jošt et al.,

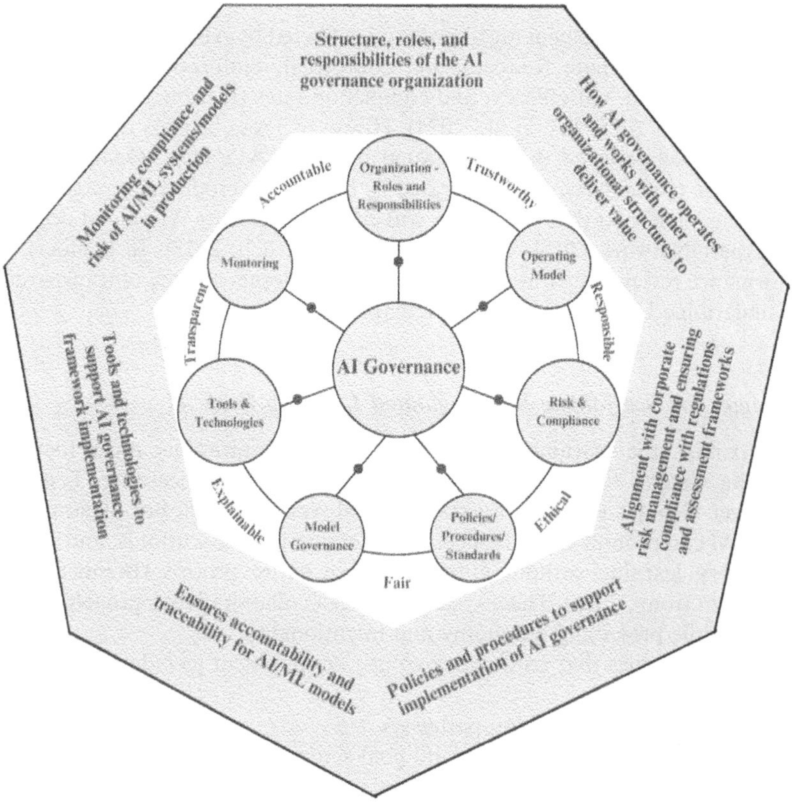

Fig. 3.2. AI Governance Framework. *Note.* This diagram illustrates layered governance dimensions surrounding AI deployment in workforce contexts. It includes operational safeguards such as model monitoring, ethical policies, tools and technologies, and oversight structures. These layers reinforce core principles of trust, transparency, and accountability across decision support systems. *Source:* Adapted from Dasari (2023).

2024). However, research also warns of the risks associated with over-personalization. Hardman (2025b) and Jošt et al. (2024) caution that excessive reliance on generative tools can reduce metacognitive effort, encouraging surface-level completion over deeper understanding. When AI removes too much cognitive load, learners may fail to build the critical thinking strategies needed for long-term problem solving.

LLMs and the Risks of Overreliance in Skill Development

Motivation and engagement are also directly affected by AI-DSS design. Systems that provide immediate feedback and contextual reinforcement can increase learner motivation, self-efficacy, and completion rates (Hardman, 2025a, 2025b; Heung & Chiu, 2025; Jošt et al., 2024). However, these benefits diminish when users feel disempowered or disconnected from the AI's logic. Opaque recommendations, particularly those generated by LLMs, can erode learner agency and reduce the likelihood that employees will critically evaluate AI-guided decisions (AI Expert Network, 2024; Compugen, 2025; Gerlich, 2025). In contexts like performance review preparation or leadership development, lack of transparency can undermine both confidence and engagement.

Strategies for Scaffolding Self-Regulated Learning With AI

To maximize the learning value of AI-DSS, organizations must focus on designing systems that support, not replace, self-regulated learning. Tools like Harbinger Group's coaching assistant and Moveworks' HelpBot illustrate how agentic AI can prompt critical reflection, offer just-in-time scaffolds, and support exploratory learning without automating the entire process (Brennen, 2025; Harbinger Group, 2025). These systems model a collaborative approach, guiding learners while preserving autonomy and intentionality.

Design strategies that reinforce cognitive development include:

- Transparency in AI decision pathways
- Opportunities for learner input and goal-setting
- Challenge calibration to prevent over-scaffolding
- Feedback that reinforces process thinking rather than just correctness

Ultimately, AI-DSS platforms have the potential to transform workplace learning into a more resilient, personalized, and cognitively supportive experience. But this potential depends on ethical, pedagogically sound design; where human learning remains central, and AI acts as a flexible collaborator rather than a substitute for effort or judgment.

Current and Emerging Directions in AI-Driven Workforce Development

The evolution of AI-DSS is moving beyond automation and analytics into new territory; one defined by agentic intelligence, human-centered design, and lifelong learning ecosystems. These emerging models do not simply deliver insights; they collaborate with learners, adapt to dynamic conditions, and recalibrate training in real time. This section explores the most impactful innovations shaping the future of employee engagement and workforce development through AI-DSS.

Agentic AI as the New Standard in Decision Support

Agentic AI is no longer an experimental model. It is becoming the default architecture for DSS designed to enable continuous, adaptive learning. Unlike earlier automation tools, agentic AI operates in goal-directed ways, interpreting behavior, detecting context, and generating next-best actions without requiring constant human configuration (Acharya et al., 2025; Brennen, 2025; Leyden & Hart-Davis, 2025; Marr, 2025; Purdy, 2024).

This shift is especially impactful in workforce training and development. Traditional AI-DSS platforms recommend static learning modules based on predefined rules or historic performance. In contrast, agentic systems monitor in-the-moment learning signals, updating training content dynamically via analyzing engagement patterns, knowledge gaps, and communication shifts.

Harbinger Group's executive coaching assistant exemplifies this transformation. By combining RAG and reinforcement learning, the platform identifies leadership development needs and recalibrates training plans based on behavioral feedback (Harbinger Group, 2025; Leyden & Hart-Davis, 2025). Rather than delivering generic content, it builds tailored coaching sequences aligned with role-specific performance trajectories.

Moveworks' HelpBot applies similar logic in the enterprise support space. It interprets help requests across IT and knowledge management systems, routing users not only to answers, but to contextual learning resources. This enhances task completion while reinforcing knowledge retention (Brennen, 2025).

Together, these applications show that agentic AI is not just improving training; it is changing the nature of decision-making itself. By enabling AI systems to act as collaborators, not just recommenders, organizations are beginning to operationalize AI-DSS as a core part of how people learn, develop, and lead.

Scaling RAG, LLMs, and Adaptive Microlearning Systems

The ability of AI-DSS to personalize learning and scale engagement across a distributed workforce increasingly depends on the integration of three interlocking technologies: RAG, LLMs, and adaptive microlearning platforms. Together, these tools enable organizations to convert static training modules into living knowledge ecosystems; those that evolve in response to learner behavior, business priorities, and cognitive feedback.

RAG combines pretrained generative AI with internal knowledge sources to produce grounded, contextual answers. Rather than offering generic recommendations, RAG-equipped AI-DSS platforms pull from curated data repositories to generate learning materials, performance insights, and skill assessments tailored to the user's current goals and role. This capability significantly enhances knowledge accessibility, especially in dynamic roles where employees must navigate rapidly changing information landscapes (Acharaya et al., 2025; Compugen, 2025; DigitalDefynd, 2025a; Harbinger Group, 2025; Leyden & Hart-Davis, 2025). In enterprise examples featured in case studies through

ThoughtSpot and Moveworks, RAG agents are used to surface actionable content within Slack, email, and workflow systems, minimizing friction and expanding the reach of knowledge assets (Brennen, 2025; Leyden & Hart-Davis, 2025; Undru, 2025).

LLMs further extend this functionality by interpreting natural language prompts, automating content creation, and enabling hyper-personalized learning delivery. They also help democratize access to information, lowering barriers for employees who may not have strong digital literacy or traditional academic training. However, the deployment of LLMs must be carefully designed: when used without clear transparency or quality control, these models can overwhelm learners, propagate inaccuracies, or reduce learner agency by offering overly deterministic pathways (AI Expert Network, 2024; Gerlich, 2025; Heung & Chiu, 2025; Jošt et al., 2024).

Adaptive microlearning systems are critical for breaking knowledge into flexible, bite-sized modules that can be served contextually as needed. These systems use behavioral data to adjust content pacing, re-sequence learning tasks, and identify knowledge decay. This approach supports retention, especially in frontline roles where learning must occur in short bursts and often under time constraints. Adaptive microlearning has also been linked to reduced training drop-off and improved learner satisfaction (Basnet, 2024; Compugen, 2025; Hardman, 2025a, 2025b; Leyden & Hart-Davis, 2025).

Collectively, these technologies enable AI-DSS platforms to function not only as learning delivery tools but as knowledge infrastructure. They reinforce feedback loops between data, behavior, and insight, helping organizations retain institutional knowledge while delivering more relevant and engaging learning experiences. For knowledge management professionals, this represents a powerful evolution: one in which content is no longer stored and retrieved manually, but curated, adapted, and optimized in real time.

By scaling these technologies responsibly (grounded in transparency, feedback, and user empowerment), organizations can transform their training systems into self-renewing, AI-enhanced environments that support both workforce development and long-term retention.

Designing for Cognitive Resilience and Lifelong Learning

As AI-DSS become central to training and workforce development, organizations must not only consider what these tools can do, but also how they shape learning over time. A growing body of research warns that while generative AI may boost short-term knowledge access, it can also compromise metacognition, reflective practice, and long-term retention if poorly implemented (Hardman, 2025a, 2025b; Heung & Chiu, 2025; Jošt et al., 2024).

Designing AI-DSS for cognitive resilience requires a clear philosophical stance: one that treats the learner not as a passive recipient of optimized content, but as an active agent in meaning-making. Instructional systems must prioritize the learning process over efficiency, offering structured guidance while preserving the space for exploration, challenge, and goal setting. This includes:

- Making decision pathways transparent and editable
- Embedding metacognitive prompts within learning sequences
- Supporting error recovery and reflection, not just task completion
- Calibrating difficulty dynamically, based on learner progress and fatigue

Agentic AI systems provide a powerful framework for achieving this balance. Tools like Harbinger Group's coaching assistant and Moveworks' HelpBot promote learning-by-doing, allowing learners to explore decisions and access just-in-time content without being locked into rigid pathways (Brennen, 2025; Harbinger Group, 2025; Leyden & Hart-Davis, 2025). These systems act as co-pilots, suggesting, adapting, and recalibrating based on behavioral data, rather than automating learning into a one-click experience.

Importantly, instructional intentionality must extend beyond platform design. To lead this shift, learning professionals must interpret AI outputs, create adaptive content, and cultivate cultures that prioritize lifelong learning over mere compliance. Ethical learning design becomes a strategic asset, not just to prevent cognitive harm, but to elevate organizational learning capacity.

When implemented with care, AI-DSS can support not only personalization, but neurocognitive sustainability. They can help learners stretch, recover, reflect, and grow, developing the internal scaffolding needed to thrive in environments of constant change. But achieving this requires an enduring commitment to pedagogy, human agency, and the cultivation of learning that lasts. This same commitment must extend to how organizations manage knowledge itself; AI-enhanced KM systems must not only enable access, but also reinforce durability, contextual recall, and transferability over time.

Conclusion

The emergence of AI-DSS marks a pivotal shift in how organizations engage, train, and empower their workforce. These platforms have evolved from passive analytics tools into dynamic ecosystems capable of real-time personalization, predictive insight, and autonomous guidance. As demonstrated throughout this chapter, AI-DSS are not hypothetical; they are actively reshaping learning, development, and knowledge strategies across industries (Basnet, 2024; DigitalDefynd, 2025a, 2025b; Leyden & Hart-Davis, 2025; Soori et al., 2024).

Case studies from Amazon, Microsoft, UPS, Harbinger Group, SnapLogic, Moveworks, and ThoughtSpot illustrate how AI-DSS platforms enable proactive learning journeys, detect disengagement signals, and support executive coaching through agentic AI. These systems not only optimize performance and retention; they redefine what it means to engage and develop talent in the flow of work (Boltt, 2025; Brennen, 2025; Harbinger Group, 2025).

Yet the value of AI-DSS lies not only in automation, but in alignment with cognitive science, ethical governance, and strategic workforce goals. As Gerlich (2025), Hardman (2025a, 2025b), Heung and Chiu (2025), and Jošt et al. (2024) proclaim, the most effective learning systems are those that prioritize transparency, autonomy, and the preservation of deep thinking. When AI-DSS are implemented without these anchors, they risk accelerating learning without enriching it.

This chapter has explored the dual nature of AI-DSS; both their promise and their complexity. To succeed, organizations must move beyond tools and tactics to build ethical infrastructures. Fairness audits, knowledge feedback loops, and explainable interfaces will support both organizational agility and learner resilience. Technologies such as RAG, LLMs, and agentic AI must be grounded in human-centered design and long-term talent strategy (Dasari, 2023; Leyden & Hart-Davis, 2025; Liang et al., 2023; Marr, 2025; Purdy, 2024).

Looking ahead, AI-DSS will serve as foundational infrastructure for business resilience and competitive advantage. When deployed with clarity, care, and cultural alignment, they can elevate knowledge management from static documentation to a living system, turning data into development and insight into innovation.

But the real imperative is this: instructional designers, L&D leaders, and digital strategists must step forward now. The future of workforce learning will not be written by algorithms alone. It will be shaped by the intentional choices we make about how technology serves human growth. Organizations that embed ethical, pedagogically grounded AI into the fabric of work will not only future-proof their learning ecosystems; they will also build workplaces that are smarter, fairer, and profoundly more human.

References

Acharya, D. B., Kuppan, K., & Divya, B. (2025). Agentic AI: Autonomous intelligence for complex goals – A comprehensive survey. *IEEE Access*, *13*, 18912–18936. https://doi.org/10.1109/ACCESS.2025.3532853

AI Expert Network. (2024). *Case study: UPS leverages AI to transform operations.* AIX. https://aiexpert.network/ai-at-ups/

Basnet, S. (2024). The impact of AI-driven predictive analytics on employee retention strategies. *International Journal of Research and Review*, *11*(9), 50–65. https://www.ijrrjournal.com/IJRR_Vol.11_Issue.9_Sep2024/IJRR06.pdf

Boltt, J. (2025). *Microsoft commits to skilling one million people for digital skills through artificial intelligence skilling initiative in South Africa.* Microsoft News. https://news.microsoft.com/source/emea/features/microsoft-south-africa-launches-ai-skilling-initiative-to-train-1-million-people-by-2026/

Brennen, A. (2025). *The power of agentic AI: 6 real-world examples and business use cases.* Moveworks. https://www.moveworks.com/us/en/resources/blog/agentic-ai-examples-use-cases. Accessed on April 12, 2025.

Compugen. (2025). *Boosting productivity and retaining talent: How Microsoft AI supercharges your workforce.* https://resources.compugen.com/en-ca/blog/boosting-productivity-and-retaining-talent-how-microsoft-ai-supercharges-your-workforce. Accessed on November 12, 2025.

Dasari, P. (2023). *A quick guide to ethical and responsible AI governance*. TechCrunch. https://techcrunch.com/2023/12/18/a-quick-guide-to-ethical-and-responsible-ai-governance/. Accessed on April 12, 2025.

DigitalDefynd. (2025a). *10 ways Amazon is using AI: Case study*. https://digitaldefynd.com/IQ/amazon-using-ai-case-study/. Accessed on November 12, 2025.

DigitalDefynd. (2025b). *5 ways UPS is using AI: Case study*. https://digitaldefynd.com/IQ/ups-use-ai-case-study/. Accessed on April 12, 2025.

Gerlich, M. (2025). AI tools in society: Impacts on cognitive offloading and the future of critical thinking. *Societies*, *15*(1), 6. https://doi.org/10.3390/soc15010006

Harbinger Group. (2025). *Agentic AI for automated custom leadership coaching and analysis*. https://www.harbingergroup.com/case-studies/agentic-ai-for-automated-custom-leadership-coaching-and-analysis/. Accessed on April 12, 2025.

Hardman, P. (2025a). *The great online learning reset? How agentic AI is forcing us to reimagine online learning – for the better*. https://drphilippahardman.substack.com/p/the-great-online-learning-reset. Accessed on April 12, 2025.

Hardman, P. (2025b). *The impact of Gen AI on human learning: A research summary*. https://drphilippahardman.substack.com/p/the-impact-of-gen-ai-on-human-learning. Accessed on April 12, 2025.

Heung, Y. M. E., & Chiu, T. K. F. (2025). How ChatGPT impacts student engagement from a systematic review and meta-analysis. *Computers and Education: Artificial Intelligence*, *8*, 100361. https://doi.org/10.1016/j.caeai.2025.100361

Jošt, G., Taneski, V., & Karakatič, S. (2024). The impact of large language models on programming education and student learning outcomes. *Applied Sciences*, *14*(10), 4115. https://doi.org/10.3390/app14104115

Krause, C. (2025). *UPS and agentic AI: A case study in logistics innovation*. The CDO TIMES. https://cdotimes.com/2025/01/06/ups-and-agentic-ai-a-case-study-in-logistics-innovation/. Accessed on April 12, 2025.

Leyden, T., & Hart-Davis, G. (2025). *Agentic AI for dummies: Integrail special edition*. John Wiley & Sons.

Liang, Z., Yu, W., Rajpurohit, T., Clark, P., Zhang, X., & Kaylan, A. (2023). Let GPT be a math tutor: Teaching math word problem solvers with customized exercise generation. *arXiv Preprint*. https://doi.org/10.48550/arXiv.2305.14386

Marr, B. (2025). *Leadership at warp speed: How to drive success in the era of agentic AI*. Bernard Marr & Co. https://bernardmarr.com/leadership-at-warp-speed-how-to-drive-success-in-the-era-of-agentic-ai/. Accessed on April 12, 2025.

Purdy, M. (2024). *What is agentic AI, and how will it change work?* Harvard Business Review. https://hbr.org/2024/12/what-is-agentic-ai-and-how-will-it-change-work. Accessed on April 12, 2025.

SnapLogic. (2025). *AI agents: The final frontier of the enterprise*. SnapLogic, Inc. https://www.snaplogic.com/wp-content/uploads/2025/02/AI-Agents-The-Final-Frontier-of-the-Enterprise.pdf. Accessed on April 12, 2025.

Soori, M., Ghaleh Jough, F. K., Dastres, R., & Arezoo, B. (2024). AI-based decision support systems in Industry 4.0: A review. *Journal of Economy and Technology*. https://www.sciencedirect.com/science/article/pii/S2949948824000374. Accessed on April 12, 2025.

Taylor, A. (2023). *New study validates the business value and opportunity of AI*. Microsoft News. https://blogs.microsoft.com/blog/2023/11/02/new-study-validates-the-business-value-and-opportunity-of-ai/. Accessed on April 12, 2025.

Taylor, A. (2025). *AI business impact: Microsoft AI use cases*. Microsoft News. https://www.microsoft.com/en-us/microsoft-cloud/blog/2025/07/24/ai-powered-success-with-1000-stories-of-customer-transformation-and-innovation/. Accessed on November 12, 2025.

Undru, A. (2025). *Agentic AI examples: Real-world use cases for modern teams*. ThoughtSpot. https://www.thoughtspot.com/data-trends/ai/agentic-ai-examples. Accessed on November 12, 2025.

Yu, L., Li, Y., & Fan, F. (2023). Employees' appraisals and trust of artificial intelligence's transparency and opacity. *Behavioral Sciences*, *13*(4), 344. https://www.mdpi.com/2076-328X/13/4/344

Case Studies on AI-Driven Knowledge Management Systems

Chapter 4

Implementing Artificial Intelligence for Knowledge Management in Small and Medium Enterprises

Kabiru Ishola Genty[a, c], *Godwin Kaisara*[a], *Sulaiman Olusegun Atiku*[a, b] *and Hylton James Villet*[a]

[a]Namibia University of Science and Technology, Windhoek, Namibia
[b]Walter Sisulu University, South Africa
[c]Lagos State University, Lagos, Nigeria

Abstract

This chapter explores the implementation of artificial intelligence (AI) for knowledge management (KM) in small and medium enterprises (SMEs). Compared with larger corporations, SMEs frequently encounter limits to their capacity to adopt comprehensive KM strategies due to limited access to resources. The chapter argues that the deficit in KM is an obstacle to operational efficiency and SMEs' sustainability. It thus proposes a comprehensive framework for understanding, implementing and optimising the integration of AI in SMEs from the lens of an effective KM system. A desk review approach was adopted to scan the extant literature on AI applications for KM in SMEs, including the analysis of selected secondary case studies. The chapter concluded that AI applications for KM are fundamental for knowledge sharing capabilities in SMEs. Therefore, a continuous learning and adaptability culture should be cultivated to promote a collaborative learning environment.

Keywords: Artificial intelligence; continuous learning; digital platforms; knowledge management; machine learning; SMEs

AI-Driven Knowledge Management Assets, Volume 2, 63–80

Published under exclusive licence by Emerald Publishing Limited
doi:10.1108/978-1-83662-778-420261004

Introduction

The recent proliferation of Artificial Intelligence (AI) applications has transformed organisational processes and procedures, triggering hopes for greater efficiency and increased productivity (Anane-Simon & Atiku, 2024). Conversely, there are fears that humans will be replaced by smart machines in production systems, leading to job losses and higher unemployment (Chiarini et al., 2024). AI can be referred to as intelligent machines that can perform tasks such as problem-solving, speech recognition and decision-making like humans (Anane-Simon & Atiku, 2024).

Knowledge management (KM) is the systematic process of capturing, organising, sharing and utilising knowledge and information in organisations to enhance performance and decision-making capabilities (Abubakar et al., 2019; Atiku, 2020; Intezari & Gressel, 2017; Russ, 2021). The KM deficit in small and medium enterprise (SME) hinders operational efficiency and sustainability (Ghofrani, 2024). Accordingly, SMEs encounter challenges due to limited access to resources, which hinders their capacity to adopt KM strategies relative to larger corporations. This deficiency is evident in several areas, such as insufficient knowledge retention and the absence of KM policies. As a result, many SMEs depend heavily on tacit knowledge, which can lead to 'business amnesia' due to their inability to document or codify essential tacit knowledge, exacerbated by the high employee turnover (Ajibade, 2016).

AI is instrumental in addressing the KM gap in SMEs by offering tools that improve knowledge acquisition, sharing and utilisation (Anane-Simon & Atiku, 2024). AI can automate routine tasks, enhance data analysis capabilities and support decision-making processes for SMEs to concentrate on strategic initiatives rather than daily operational concerns (Anane-Simon & Atiku, 2024). Moreover, AI empowers SMEs to leverage big data for insights that promote innovation and enhance operational performance. With proper AI applications in developing KM strategies, SMEs can develop more effective frameworks for knowledge sharing and fostering a collaborative learning environment to develop products and services that are environmentally friendly (Atiku et al., 2024).

Furthermore, AI helps to stimulate deep learning, which enhances human capabilities in image recognition, voice recognition and analytical processing (Dai & Ke, 2022; Jarrahi et al., 2022). Hence, AI can support the fundamental dimensions of KM, namely, creation, storage and retrieval, sharing and application of knowledge (Jarrahi et al., 2022). This emphasises the necessity of human–AI collaboration for decision-making processes in SMEs and also underlines the effects of incorporating AI applications for KM in SMES, to enhance workforce creativity and innovative performance.

This chapter illuminates opportunities that are associated with the implementation of AI for KM activities in SMEs. Recent advances in AI can provide new foundations for the transformation of KM in SMEs (Sanzogni et al., 2017). The chapter explores the link between KM and AI in supporting business activities, especially among SMEs. It proposes a framework that integrates KM dimensions with AI adoption phases. This framework serves as a tool to promote

AI applications as solutions tailored to SMEs' priorities. These include business process improvement, eco-friendly efficiency and eco-innovation in developing products and services. The chapter is structured into subsections to explicitly discuss the link between AI and KM within the context of SMEs. It points out the evolution and phases of AI-KM; the applications, benefits, opportunities and challenges, as well as AI implementation strategies in the digital age.

Knowledge Management Capabilities in SMEs

KM capabilities are necessary for the growth and competitiveness of SMEs. It is expected that SMEs should manage their knowledge assets and choice of technologies by adopting an organisational level innovation openness approach to encourage intra- and inter-organisational collaboration, experimentation and risk-taking capabilities (Khan et al., 2024). SMEs need to gain the knowledge and capabilities that reinforce innovation and value creation for customers (Khan et al., 2024). The extent to which they are willing and able to engage in innovative practices, including collaborating and knowledge sharing internally or externally, is known as 'organisational-level open innovation'. As a result of innovation openness, SMEs cultivate an innovative culture in which employees are encouraged and rewarded for learning, sharing and fostering new technologies, such as AI in business operations.

While SMEs can play a crucial role in driving economic growth, the effective integration of AI technologies is essential for their success and sustainability. Baabdullah et al. (2021) assert that AI is a new generation of technologies that can facilitate SMEs' competitive advantage and sustainability. Furthermore, the implementation and acceptance of AI technologies can result in enhanced market share, increased revenue, improved efficiency, greater productivity and superior decision-making capabilities in SMEs.

SMEs are constrained by their small scale, which limits their ability to reap the benefits of AI (Ghofrani, 2024). Nevertheless, SMEs can optimise their production by adopting these new technologies through learning by doing, innovating and continuously interacting with them. There should be human–AI collaboration in SMEs to achieve better outcomes, including improved customer satisfaction. For example, AI applications that could bolster customer engagement include chatbots, Motion and Akiflow. SMEs should invest in training managers and workers on the use of such platforms. The exposition of AI and its applications in SMEs is presented in the next section.

Understanding AI and Its Applications in SMEs

The adoption of AI applications such as process automation, analytics, optimisation and predictive modelling is essential for effective KM in SMEs. Factors such as perceived benefits, organisational resources, governance structures, supporting services and environmental pressures should be considered for effective implementation of AI for KM in SMEs (Baabdullah et al., 2021).

Furthermore, Bettoni et al. (2021) identified five factors to consider for AI integration in SMEs, which include digital and smart factory, data strategy, human resources, organisational structures and organisational culture. The workforce should possess certain competencies to make use of the information collected through the data strategy. SMEs should help their employees acquire integrated, soft skills that will help them to understand the basic AI applications and processes used in different business functions (Bettoni et al., 2021). The adaptability of AI renders it particularly appealing for SMEs (Wei & Pardo, 2022). The adoption of AI by SMEs thus has the potential to enhance market share and generate increased revenues.

Scholars argue that computers perform tasks similar to human intelligence, but AI does not link itself to any biological procedures (Baabdullah et al., 2021; Rafique & Mujawinkindi, 2023). This implies that AI is programmatically developed in the form of human intelligence to solve human problems. Machine learning (ML) and natural language processing (NLP) are subsets of AI. While ML provides the learning capability for AI systems, NLP focuses on making human-language communication possible (Genty et al., 2025). Both can be used in SMEs' KM system operations as discussed below.

The Role of ML for KM in SMEs

ML refers to the 'method of designing or describing the sequence of actions to solve a problem, otherwise known as algorithms' (De la Hoz Domínguez et al., 2020, p. 3). It involves a deep structure of special hardware and software designs for writing and training (Burns et al., 2022). ML ensures that computer packages are smart, and this enables the users to identify problems, analyse them and make informed decisions. Intelligent ML applications like consumer and accounting systems, human asset and logistic systems, have been used by SMEs for operational efficiency (De la Hoz Domínguez et al., 2020). Due to SMEs' agility compared to larger enterprises, the adoption of ML applications in medium-sized firms has significantly increased (Bauer et al., 2020). Nevertheless, there are challenges at the process stage of the implementation of ML in SMEs. These include limited budgets to procure ML applications, insufficient know-how by SME employees, difficulties in identifying positive business cases and lack of management buy-in (Bauer et al., 2020).

NLP for KM in SMEs

NLP falls under the umbrella of AI. Just like ML, NLP is used to enhance operational efficiency. NLP applications are for enhancing operational performance, in areas such as maintenance, safety and continuous improvement. NLP plays a crucial role in digital transformation because it contributes to strengthening SMEs' resilience by boosting their preparedness for market disruptions (Mathieu et al., 2024). NLP can be used for tasks such as intelligent analysis, automating responses to customer queries and extracting innovative information from patent texts (Mathieu et al., 2024). Therefore, SMEs should embrace NLP usage for competitiveness. Some of the NLP tools that could be used to generate new knowledge for SMEs include ChatGPT, Google Cloud Vertex AI, Run Pod or Lambda.

AI-KM Implementation Frameworks for SMEs

SMEs' sustainability in the knowledge economy is dependent on effective KM systems. This implies that SMEs should thrive on knowledge-intensive operations. SMEs leveraging AI applications for KM are more creative and innovative (Gruneke et al., 2024). Hence, AI application in small businesses is a function of SMEs' readiness, support within the ecosystem and end users' satisfaction. Integrating AI in SMEs marks a pivotal shift, offering unprecedented opportunities for intelligent data capturing, retrieval and transmission of important business intelligence (Gruneke et al., 2024). However, SMEs are confronted with financial challenges for the effective implementation of AI-based KM systems. These are attributed to limited internal resources, capacities and most specifically the knowledge gap in that domain (Statistisches Bundesamt, 2023). Unlike large corporations that devote millions of dollars to technical AI development and adoption annually, SMEs are constrained by limited resources. Therefore, optimisation outcomes can only be sustained if the AI-KM system implementation framework is carried out in phases focused on the SMEs' readiness, strategic alignment, strategic goals and implementation.

SMEs' Readiness for AI Implementation in KM

SMEs must re-evaluate their adoption strategies and willingness to utilise AI technology for KM. The fundamentals needed for this to be achieved include readiness assessment, audit of the existing KM infrastructure by business owners or managers, mapping of current knowledge repositories among SMEs and establishing how knowledge dimensions are being created for a suitable AI adoption via tacit knowledge acquisition, and organisation, storage, retrieval and knowledge utilisation.

In contemporary businesses, AI has been automated into KM systems. This helps employees find useful information to make better decisions. Similarly, AI can be used to identify knowledge gaps by mapping knowledge repositories, as expressed earlier. This can help businesses ensure that their employees have the knowledge they need to do their jobs effectively. Once knowledge gaps have been identified, AI is instrumental in addressing those gaps by recommending or creating new knowledge resources.

SMEs often face a myriad of obstacles, such as insufficient funds for training, implementation and data-related issues, which can be frustrating (Ulrich & Frank, 2021). Thus, KM tools such as an intranet can be used not only to handle the complexity of AI adoption by SME owners but also to unlock potential business opportunities (Majumder & Dey, 2022). AI-powered KM

Table 4.1. Evaluating SMEs' Readiness for AI Adoption.

S/N	Factors to Consider	Activities
1.	Audit existing KM infrastructure	Map current knowledge repositories Identify gaps using AI analytics tools
2.	Evaluate SMEs readiness	Assess data quality/structure Secure leadership buy-in

Source: Authors' compilation, 2025

systems can analyse usage trends and predict knowledge needs. Therefore, SMEs should ensure that the existing knowledge base is well-organised and updated to optimise AI processing. SMEs need to select AI platforms that align with their business needs to ensure scalability and adaptation to future needs.

Table 4.1 indicates the first phase of SME assessment and readiness for AI integration into KM systems.

Strategic Alignment of AI for KM in SMEs

Strategic alignment is the second phase in the implementation of AI for KM in SMEs. After the assessment of SMEs' readiness through the evaluation of existing KM gaps, data quality and employee adaptability, the strategic alignment becomes imperative to enhance operational efficiency and innovative performance. The automation processes were identified as one of the strategic priorities of AI applications (Ghofrani, 2024). For example, AI can assist SMEs in synthesising information from various sources and creating comprehensive reports and manuals. The time spent on documentation is reduced, since the knowledge within the SME is up-to-date and easily accessible. Similarly, AI applications in KM are useful in analysing vast datasets and generating insights for strategic decision-making to predict market trends and customer expectations (Ghofrani, 2024).

Furthermore, Gruneke et al. (2024) argue that AI-powered search and retrieval tools like semantic search applications are often used by SMEs to streamline information retrieval, enabling employees to access contextually relevant knowledge. Similarly, KM serves as a strategic necessity in the contemporary business environment, facilitating data-driven decision-making and enhancing competitiveness in SMEs with the assistance of AI tools like Chatbots and blockchain technology (Muraleedharan & Velmurugan, 2025). These tools facilitate knowledge sharing and have the potential to bolster knowledge discovery and to empower decision-makers in SMEs.

Data-driven decision-making capability is an important strategic alignment of AI and KM in SMEs. Hence, predictive analytics, where AI analyses historical and real-time data to forecast market trends, customer behaviours and operational risks, empowering SMEs to allocate resources proactively (Ghofrani, 2024; Muraleedharan & Velmurugan, 2025). For example, the use of Chatbots enhances knowledge sharing as well as facilitates knowledge transfer and absorption in the SME. To mitigate knowledge loss, AI now captures institutional knowledge from departing employees, preserving expertise in centralised repositories and personalised training via Generative AI that tailors learning materials to suit individual employee needs. This helps to accelerate onboarding and upskilling (Ghofrani, 2024; Gruneke et al., 2024; Muraleedharan & Velmurugan, 2025).

Table 4.2 gives a synopsis of strategic alignment as a phase of implementing AI for KM in the SMEs.

Strategic Goals for AI-KM Implementation in SMEs

The implementation phase is the third stage in the AI-KM framework for SMEs. This should be executed in line with the strategic goals of SMEs. Incorporating AI applications for KM in SMEs involves several strategic steps. The integration of AI into SMEs is not merely about a technological upgrade but should also involve a strategic goal implementation that offers unparalleled opportunities and benefits. This phase centres on the implementation of AI action plans and KM strategic goals. According to Muminova et al. (2024), understanding the motivation behind AI implementation in SMEs requires a comprehensive analysis of the unique ecosystem in which the SMEs operate. Therefore, SME owners should endeavour to explore the multifaceted terrain of AI adoption by understanding the potential benefits and unravelling the broader socioeconomic impacts on these enterprises. The strategic KM of AI implementation in SMEs is essential to achieve the benefits highlighted earlier in the previous section. Hence, KM should be focused on setting a clear objective and developing an implementation roadmap for necessities such as assessing the current SMEs' infrastructure. Creating a timeline and milestones is also necessary to help achieve the strategic goals for AI-KM implementation in SMEs. The guidelines for AI-KM implementation in SMEs are presented in Table 4.3.

Sustainment and Optimisation of AI-KM in the SMEs

After the integration of AI in KM, optimisation is the final phase in the circle of AI-KM implementation. SMEs carry out AI-KM sustenance and optimisation through several strategies. By implementing these strategies, SMEs can optimise their AI-KM systems, leading to improved performance and competitiveness in the market (Bertilsson & Lindqvist, 2024). For instance, SMEs should ensure that employees are continuously trained on new AI technologies and KM practices. Leveraging external IT support and partnerships with technology providers is critical for overcoming resource constraints.

Table 4.2. Strategic Alignment of AI for KM in SMEs.

S/N	Elements	Implementation Strategy	AI Tools
1.	Knowledge accessibility and operational efficiency	Automated documentation and summarisation	Chatbots
		AI-powered search and retrieval	Semantic search applications
		Process optimisation	NLP-driven platform
2.	Data-driven decision making and innovation	Predictive analytics	Historical data
		Innovation acceleration	Enterprise resource planning (ERP) systems
3.	Scalable knowledge retention and talent development	Mitigating knowledge loss	Blockchain technology
		Personalised training	Generative AIs like Rasa
4.	Integration with SMEs' systems	AI synergy	ERP
		Collaboration tool	AI-powered chatbots
5.	Strategic implementation	Assess readiness	E.g. European digital innovation hubs (EDIHs)
		Adopt tailored AI tools	E.g. CRM
		Train a context-specific model	360 learning
		Monitor and iterate	H20 driverless

Source: Authors' compilation, 2025

Therefore, SMEs should rely on external expertise for implementation, maintenance and employee training, as internal IT teams often lack AI specialisation. Collaborative ecosystems, including government incentives and industry networks, help SMEs access cost-effective AI solutions and comply with data regulations. Similarly, a user-centric implementation strategy could also be adopted after AI-KM implementation by the SMEs. Here, user satisfaction would emerge as a central driver of sustained AI-KM adoption (Kovalskiy, 2024). Successful SMEs integrate feedback loops to refine AI tools based on employee needs. For instance, pilot projects allow iterative testing and minimise disruption, whereby training programmes empower employees to leverage AI for

Table 4.3. Strategic AI-KM Implementation Guidelines for SMEs.

S/N	Steps	AI Action Plans for Implementation	KM Strategic Goals Implementation
1.	Identify and prioritise needs and goals	Determine areas of SMEs that can benefit from AI	Align KM with the AI strategy to support SMEs' strategic objectives
2.	Pilot deployment	Begin with an AI pilot project focusing on a specific area	Determine areas where KM can add value
3.	Choose the right AI solutions	Select AI tools that are compatible with existing SMEs systems	SMEs leaders should define a clear direction for KM and foster a culture of knowledge sharing
4.	Invest in staff development	Provide training to ensure the SMEs team can effectively use AI tools	Invest in training Programmes to enhance employees' absorptive capacity for new ideas
5.	Track and optimise	Monitor AI performance regularly and adjust	Ensure information is accessible and easily transmitted across the SMEs
6.	Ensure compliance and security	Ensure AI systems comply with data privacy and security laws	Monitor and evaluate KM performance regularly to ensure it supports the SME's objectives
7.	Collaborate with professionals	Consider working with AI partners or consultants	Encourage a culture that rewards knowledge sharing and innovation

Source: Authors' compilation, 2025.

predictive analytics and customer segmentation. Fig. 4.1 illustrates how SMEs' AI-KM implementation can lead to sustainability and optimisation.

Benefits of AI Integration in SMEs

The benefits of AI cannot be underestimated because it has resulted in efficiency and productivity, enhanced decision-making, customer service experience, reduced wastages, enhanced innovation and creativity, as well as creating competitive advantages for the SMEs that embraced such applications. AI enables companies, including SMEs, to lower operational costs, accelerate production

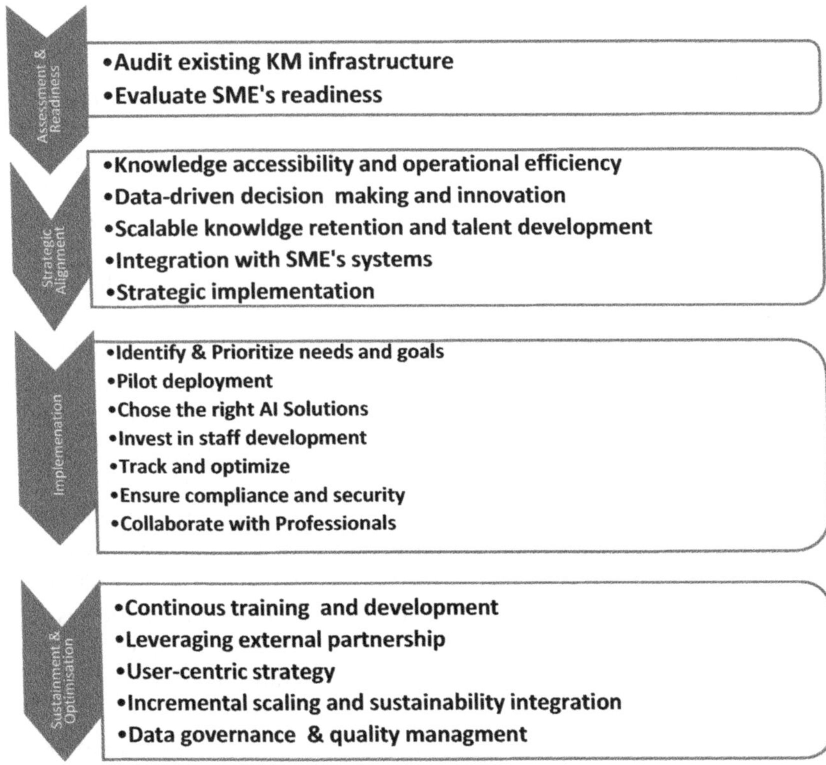

Fig. 4.1. AI-KM Implementation Frameworks for SMEs. *Source:* Authors' compilation, 2025

processes and develop innovative products or services that address the evolving needs of customers (Wei & Pardo, 2022).

In the agricultural sector, drones are used by farmers to plant and monitor crops, control weeds and ensure increased crop production. AI is also manifested in the education sector through tools such as gamified learning and project-based learning. Such tools are not only innovative and interesting, but they can also be fun for the learners. Karanth et al. (2021) posited that AI is used to foresee the impact of future climate change, which improves efforts aimed at improving food security. AI technologies in the construction industry can revolutionise project planning, execution and management, leading to improved productivity, reduced costs and enhanced safety (Abioye et al., 2021). Furthermore, AI has been credited with the deployment of autonomous vehicles, robotic surgeons, digital banks and other innovative uses in the transportation, health and financial sectors (Abioye et al., 2021; Hamza, 2024; Sabharwal, 2018).

Challenges of Implementing AIs in SMEs

Despite several benefits of AI applications, some barriers hinder the widespread adoption of AI in SMEs. These include a lack of technical expertise, limited financial resources to procure the AI tools and platforms, resistance to change on the part of SME owners and employees, as well as concerns about data security and privacy (Iyelolu et al., 2024).

Resource constraints: Resource constraints have been identified as a major challenge in the implementation of AI in SMEs. Resource constraints in this context include, but are not limited to, financial, human resources and infrastructure limitations. Despite the potential benefits of AI, the rate of adoption among SMEs has been relatively slow. This lag can be attributed to several challenges encountered during the implementation of AI in business processes. Key obstacles include concerns regarding the acceptability and transparency of AI, insufficient financial resources, a lack of a data-driven culture and the necessity for retraining both managers and employees, among others. The difficulties of integrating AI into business processes are also as challenging as getting access to financial resources for such investments (Bettoni et al., 2021; Wei & Pardo, 2022).

Data Quality and Management: Another major challenge in implementing AI in SMEs is the issue of data quality and management. That is, the availability of quality data in SMEs is crucial. Furthermore, the data need to be handled and operationalised in line with the business objectives of the SME.

Ethical Concerns: The ethical concerns pertain to issues of data mistrust, the consent of data providers and the necessity for transparency regarding the operations of AI. It is imperative that these aspects are explicitly articulated. Perceived risk and ethical concerns of AI in SMEs have become pervasive challenges in the implementation because of issues of data privacy and security risks (Colther & Doussoulin, 2024).

Socio-Cultural Issues: There are socio-cultural issues that pose challenges to AI integration into SMEs. These challenges can be linked to cultural changes whereby there is resistance due to a shift in organisational culture and processes, especially with the SMEs adopting AI for the first time. Decision-making in SMEs can easily be influenced using automated systems. There is a need for complementary adaptive skills to prepare people for a world where AI is prominent. This issue can be addressed through educational interventions, whereby incorporating collaborative learning and knowledge creation via networks leads to impactful knowledge formation (Colther & Doussoulin, 2024). Training and change management could also focus on the lack of technical expertise, whereby the issue of awareness and understanding of AI operations can be addressed.

Legal Challenges: The legal aspects are within various data management issues, such as transparency of the AI development process(es), allowing for independent audits as well as oversight functions to prevent biases and discrimination. The legal aspect should ensure that AI data users are fully informed about how the data are collected, used and stored, and they must have the option to opt out of data collection at any time. Respect for fundamental human rights will ultimately help the evolution of AI knowledge. This is because the ability to manage human knowledge will consolidate AI integration.

Strategies for Overcoming the Challenges of AI-KM in SMEs

Strategies to overcome the challenges hindering the proper implementation of AI for KM in SMEs include the provision of government incentives, public-private partnerships, affordable AI service models and platforms and specific training programmes to build AI competencies within SMEs (Iyelolu et al., 2024). Colther and Doussoulin (2024) suggest initiatives such as providing resources and training in the use of AI technologies to disadvantaged SME communities. That is, the SMEs should embrace a collaborative learning environment through mentorship programmes, and cross-functional teams can be developed to overcome the challenge of AI implementation in the SMEs.

A similar approach should be followed by SMEs with a digital divide among their employees, using effective KM strategies to enhance skills in areas such as digital literacy, project management and creative problem-solving (Iyelolu et al., 2024). This can be achieved through a series of investments in employees' training and upskilling by SME owners. The training of digitally disadvantaged employees could be in the form of workshops and online courses leading to certification. These should be seen as part of a continuous learning culture that provides hands-on practice and upskilling to employees. These types of initiatives can empower SMEs to navigate the complexities of innovation processes and leverage the new technologies for effective and efficient outcomes.

The integration of AI into SMEs requires effective KM systems through appropriate policies and regulations. AI has the potential to democratise access to knowledge in SMEs. Therefore, a comprehensive framework involving robust regulatory standards around KM, transparent AI development processes and active participation from a broad spectrum of stakeholders is essential (Colther & Doussoulin, 2024). Here, the SMEs could embrace strategic hiring practices such as targeted recruitment and emotional compensation to attract and retain AI professionals in SMEs. Similarly, leveraging external expertise could be encouraged, including consulting with AI vendors. This may prove to be a useful strategy for overcoming some of the challenges of AI-KM in SMEs.

Case Studies and Success Stories of Some Selected SMEs in Africa and Asia

This section probes the success stories of selected SMEs that have integrated AI into their operations in Asia and Africa. The SMEs were selected based on two criteria. First, the parameter of geographical location was used. Asia and Africa are continents in the Global South where many SMEs face a significant number of barriers (Yusuf et al., 2024). Therefore, examining the outcomes of AI implementation in any SME becomes pertinent. Second, the selection was based on the performance of SMEs in Asia and Africa, with a capital base of less than US$500. Thus, investigating how the AI implementation is conducted is germane, especially considering resource constraints as a major challenge.

Case studies from Emerald were used as secondary data, analysed and interpreted in this chapter to explain how the implementation of AI for KM in SMEs is carried out. AI platforms and tools such as Chatbots, Akiflow, Motion, Otter.ai, Levity, Hootsuite, Zoho CRM, Grammarly, Zia, and Jasper were adopted by SMEs across continents. These AI applications are efficient and effective based on the success stories of those SMEs. The adoption of AI is more pronounced among SME owners in other continents, particularly the more industrialised Europe and North America. The chosen cases are within Asia and Africa, with scant studies on AI integration in SME operations. In the United States and European countries, DocuSign, Dropbox, AIoD platform, ARISA Alliance and Fireflies.ai are integrated into SMEs' operations.

In Africa, AI tools such as Cloud and AIS have been adopted by SMEs for business process improvement. In South Africa, for instance, Queen Ndlovu, the CEO and founder of QP Drone Tech, a provider of drone business solutions as of April 2023, provided the following success story after facing a series of challenges in the year 2022.

> The CEO found practical support from The Innovation Hub, an incubator that was supporting her business, which enabled her to enhance the prototype of her drone. She then had to think about how she would manufacture drones locally by ensuring access to production infrastructure, funding, partners and customers.

In the above case study, the CEO viewed collaboration with professionals as a strategic implementation element, which is a strategy discussed earlier in this chapter under the section on the AI-KM implementation framework for SMEs. The SME first assesses its readiness before adopting a tailored AI tool within the trained context-specific model and monitors the progress of the AI adopted for sustainment and optimisation.

Another case of an SME AI-KM integration in Africa was Premier Wallet, an AI tool integrated into the banking sector in Somalia. This AI tool was developed as the go-to solution for bank consumers. The Head of Business Development of Premier Bank refers to the Premier Wallet as the first digital wallet in Somalia, which has transformed banking activities such that consumers can send and deposit money across the world through their smartphones. As reported by Hassan (2023):

> ...owing to the mobile wallet, consumers could, for the first time, engage in purchasing, withdrawing cash, shopping online and topping up without needing a bank account at Premier Bank. This allowed for the financial inclusion of the unbanked Somali population ...

The case scenario identifies and prioritises the needs and goals of bank consumers by knowledge accessibility and operational efficiency elements to automate documentation and summarisation with AI-powered search and retrieval elements. This helps to optimise bank operational processes. AI tools such as smartphones were embraced by the banks to provide the necessary applications for sustainment and optimisation.

Asian SMEs integrate AI solutions such as Velocity, DBS Ideal and digital platforms. In this chapter, the case of AI implementation among the SMEs in China was analysed using one of the digital platforms. Bai et al. (2022) documented the success of Meorient, a prominent exhibition SME in China. The outbreak of COVID-19 thrust the company into a state of emergency, compelling it to engage in efforts for survival. Due to this challenge, Meorient launched its digital exhibition platform in 2021. According to Bai et al. (2022):

> Over the past two decades, Meorient has amassed a substantial volume of data from both domestic and international exhibitors, as well as professional buyers, leading to the gradual establishment of a digital exhibition platform. The company is recognised as one of the pioneers in the digital transformation of China's exhibition industry. In the context of the post-pandemic era, China's national initiative known as "Digital China" has further accelerated the advancement of digital infrastructure.

The success of Meorient can be attributed to AI integration in various digital platforms. During this pivotal transitional phase, Meorient was compelled to make judicious decisions to ensure the sustainability of its profits and overall survival. The SME adopted data-driven decision-making and innovation elements as an implementation strategy whereby predictive analytics and innovation acceleration were used for sustainment and optimisation. Historical data and ERP were some of the adopted AI solutions.

Surplus Indonesia is a company founded with the belief in a harmonious balance between profitability and environmental stewardship. The founder's encounter with leftover food going to waste after buffets, therefore, Surplus Indonesia embarked on pioneering initiatives using application technology to address food wastage at the consumer level. An excerpt from Adhariani (2024) shows that:

> ...each meal saved through the Surplus app not only translated to reduced expenses for businesses but also contributed to reducing greenhouse gas emissions from landfills. Surplus' overarching mission was to cut food waste and loss in Indonesia by half by 2030, fostering an environment where food waste is virtually non-existent in the nation...

Scalable knowledge retention and talent development aspects can be argued as the elements adopted by the SME based on personalised training of the owner and investment in staff development for sustainment and optimisation. These cases show that AI-integrated KM systems in SMEs are a prerequisite for better outcomes. Therefore, SMEs that aspire for competitiveness should embrace AI adoption and integration into their business operations using the AI-KM implementation framework for SMEs.

Conclusion

With proper AI applications in developing KM strategies, SMEs can cultivate a continuous learning culture, adaptability and the achievement of innovative performance. Hence, responsible AI applications in SMEs can enhance business processes, leading to eco-efficiency and the launch of eco-friendly products and services. The human workforce should possess the soft skills to navigate AI-KM systems in SMEs. Therefore, AI should be integrated into the code of conduct in SMEs regarding knowledge sharing and storage of tacit knowledge. Moreover, SMEs should help their employees acquire soft skills to understand the basic AI applications and processes in SMEs' business operations.

References

Abioye, S. O., Oyedele, L. O., Akanbi, L., Ajayi, A., Delgado, J. M. D., Bilal, M., Akinade, O. O., & Ahmed, A. (2021). Artificial intelligence in the construction industry: A review of present status, opportunities and future challenges. *Journal of Building Engineering*, *44*, 103299. https://doi.org/10.1016/j.jobe.2021.103299

Abubakar, A. M., Elrehail, H., Alatailat, M. A., & Elçi, A. (2019). Knowledge management, decision-making style and organisational performance. *Journal of Innovation & Knowledge*, *4*(2), 104–114.

Adhariani, D. (2024). Surplus Indonesia: Tackling food waste through the app. *Emerald Emerging Markets Case Studies*, *14*(4). https://doi.org/10.1108/EEMCS-04-2024-0190

Ajibade, P. (2016). The role of knowledge management in improving small, micro and medium enterprises' productivity: A case of Nkonkobe municipality, South Africa. *Journal of Social Sciences*, *47*(3), 229–238.

Anane-Simon, R., & Atiku, S. O. (2024). Artificial intelligence and automation for the future of startups. In N. Baporikar (Ed.), *Ecosystem dynamics and strategies for startups' scalability* (pp. 133–153). IGI Global Scientific Publishing. https://doi.org/10.4018/979-8-3693-0527-0.ch007

Atiku, S. O. (2020). Knowledge management for the circular economy. In N. Baporikar (Ed.), *Handbook of research on entrepreneurship development and opportunities in circular economy* (pp. 520–537). IGI Global.

Atiku, S. O., Jeremiah, A., Semente, E., & Boateng, F. (Eds.). (2024). *Eco-innovation and sustainable development in Industry 5.0*. IGI Global. https://doi.org/10.4018/979-8-3693-2219-2

Baabdullah, A. M., Alalwan, A. A., Slade, E. L., Raman, R., & Khatatneh, K. F. (2021). SMEs and artificial intelligence (AI): Antecedents and consequences of AI-based B2B practices. *Industrial Marketing Management*, *98*, 255–270.

Bai, O., Yang, X., Hunter, K. O., & Wang, B. (2022). Meorient: A pioneer of the digital exhibition industry. *Emerald Emerging Markets Case Studies*, *12*(3). https://doi.org/10.1108/EEMCS-07-2021-0236

Bauer, M., van Dinther, C., & Kiefer, D. (2020). Machine learning in SME: An empirical study on enablers and success factors. In *AMCIS 2020 proceedings, Salt Lake City, Utah, USA* (Vol. 1–10). Americas Conference on Information Systems.

Bertilsson, W. A., & Lindqvist, M. (2024). *AI-Enabled automation for SMEs: Prerequisites and opportunities for implementation and operation*. https://www.diva-portal.org/smash/get/diva2:1862159/FULLTEXT01.pdf

Bettoni, A., Matteri, D., Montini, E., Gładysz, B., & Carpanzano, E. (2021). An AI adoption model for SMEs: A conceptual framework. *IFAC-PapersOnLine*, *54*(1), 702–708.

Burns, E., Laskowski, N., & Tucci, L. (2022). *What is artificial intelligence (AI)?* SearchEnterpriseAI (Blog). https://www.techtarget.com/searchenterpriseai/definition/AI-Artificial-Intelligence

Chiarini, A., Grando, A., Venturini, S., & Borgonovo, E. (2024). Do automation and AI impact on job reduction? A study on perceived risk of losing job among white-collars in Italian manufacturing companies. *Production Planning & Control*, *35*(16), 2198–2211.

Colther, C., & Doussoulin, J. P. (2024). Artificial intelligence: Driving force in the evolution of human knowledge. *Journal of Innovation & Knowledge*, *9*, 100625.

Dai, C. P., & Ke, F. (2022). Educational applications of artificial intelligence in simulation-based learning: A systematic mapping review. *Computers and Education: Artificial Intelligence*, *3*, 100087. https://doi.org/10.1016/j.caeai.2022.100087

De la Hoz Domínguez, E. J., Herrera, T. J. F., & Mendoza, A. A. M. (2020). Machine Learning and SMEs: Opportunities for an improved decision-making process. *Investigacióne Innovación en Ingenierías*, *8*(1), 21–36.

Genty, K., Elusope, M., & Semente, E. (2025). Human resource information system and operational efficiency among the professional ICT providers in Nigeria. In T. Ahram, A. L. Arquillos, J. Gandarias, & A. M. Casas (Eds.), *Human interaction and emerging technologies (IHIET-AI 2025) conference 3* (pp. 47–60). AHFE International. https://doi.org/10.54941/ahfe1005896

Ghofrani, J. (2024, February 29). *Application of generative AI for knowledge management in SMEs*. https://www.linkedin.com/pulse/application-generative-ai-knowledge-management-smes-javad-ghofrani-czsfe/

Gruneke, T., Guggenberger, T., Nusser, J., Oberlander, A. M., Stramm, J., & Varrentrap, A. (2024). Unlocking AI-based knowledge management potential for SMEs: Exploring semantic search adoption. In *19th international conference on Wirtschaftsinformatik September 2024*. Association of Information System. https://aisel.aisnet.org/wi2024/90

Hamza, U. M. (2024). *Developing an artificial intelligence maturity model (AIMM): Applicable to the UK construction industry* [Doctoral Dissertation]. University of the West of England.

Hassan, M. M. (2023). Premier wallet: Banking the unbanked population in Somalia. *Emerald Emerging Markets Case Studies*, *13*(4), 1–16. https://doi.org/10.1108/EEMCS-01-2023-0030

Intezari, A., & Gressel, S. (2017). Information and reformation in KM systems: Big data and strategic decision-making. *Journal of Knowledge Management*, *21*(1), 71–91. https://doi.org/10.1108/jkm-07-2015-0293

Iyelolu, T. V., Agu, E. E., Idemudia, C., & Ijomah, T. I. (2024). Driving SME innovation with AI solutions: Overcoming adoption barriers and future growth opportunities. *International Journal of Science and Technology Research Archive*, *7* (1). https://doi.org/10.53771/ijstra.2024.7.1.0055

Jarrahi, M. H., Askay, D., Eshraghi, A., & Smith, P. (2022). Artificial intelligence and knowledge management: A partnership between human and AI. *Business Horizons*, *66*(1), 87–99. https://doi.org/10.1016/j.bushor.2022.03.002

Karanth, S., Benefo, E. O., Patra, D., & Pradhan, A. K. (2022). Importance of artificial intelligence in evaluating climate change and food safety risk. *Journal of Agriculture and Food Research*, *11*, 100485. https://doi.org/10.1016/j.jafr.2022.100485

Khan, A. N., Mehmood, K., & Soomro, M. A. (2024). Knowledge management-based artificial intelligence (AI) adoption in construction SMEs: The moderating role of knowledge integration. *IEEE Transactions on Engineering Management*, *71*, 10874–10884. https://doi.org/10.1109/TEM.2024.3403981

Kovalskiy, V. (2024, February 8). *AI for SMEs: A practical guide to implementing AI for success*. https://www.bitrix24.com/articles/ai-for-smes-a-practical-guide-to-implementing-ai-for-success.php

Majumder, S., & Dey, N. (2022). *AI-empowered knowledge management*. Springer Nature.

Mathieu, B., Anas, N., Thomas, P., Robert, P., & Samir, L. (2024). Exploring the applications of natural language processing and language models for production, planning, and control activities of SMEs in Industry 4.0: A systematic literature review. *Journal of Intelligent Manufacturing*, 1–21. https://doi.org/10.1007/s10845-024-02509-w

Muminova, E., Ashurov, M., Akhunova, S., & Turgunov, M. (2024). AI in small and medium enterprises: Assessing the barriers, benefits, and socioeconomic impacts. In *International conference on knowledge engineering and communication systems (ICKECS)* (pp. 1–6). IEEE. https://doi.org/10.1109/ICKECS61492.2024.10616816

Muraleedharan, N. V., & Velmurugan, V. P. (2025). A review study on the influence and effect of knowledge management in small and medium enterprises. *Journal of Management World*, *2025*(1), 223–239. https://doi.org/10.53935/jomw.v2024i4.642

Rafique, S., & Mujawinkindi, F. (2023). *How can artificial intelligence (AI) help SMEs development in emerging economies: Qualitative from Pakistan* [Master Thesis]. Umea University.

Russ, M. (2021). Knowledge management for sustainable development in the era of continuously accelerating technological revolutions: A framework and models. *Sustainability*, *13*(6), 3353. https://doi.org/10.3390/su13063353

Sabharwal, C. L. (2018). The rise of machine learning and robo-advisors in banking. *IDRBT Journal of Banking Technology*, *2*(2), 28–43.

Sanzogni, L., Guzman, G., & Busch, P. (2017). Artificial intelligence and knowledge management: Questioning the tacit dimension. *Prometheus*, *35*(1), 37–56.

Statistisches Bundesamt. (2023). *Kleine und mittlere Unternehmen'.* https://www.destatis.de/DE/Themen/Branchen-Unternehmen/Unternehmen/Kleine-Unternehmen-Mittlere-Unternehmen/_inhalt.html

Ulrich, P. & Frank, V. (2021). Relevance and adoption of AI technologies in German SMEs - Results from survey-based research. *Procedia Computer Science 192*, 2152–2159.

Wei, R., & Pardo, C. (2022). Artificial intelligence and SMEs: How can B2B SMEs leverage AI platforms to integrate AI technologies? *Industrial Marketing Management*, *107*, 466–483.

Yusuf, S. O., Durodola, R. L., Ocran, G., Abubakar, J. E., Echere, A. Z., & Paul-Adeleye, A. H. (2024). Challenges and opportunities in AI and digital transformation for SMEs: A cross-continental perspective. *World Journal of Advanced Research and Reviews*, *23*(3), 668–678.

Chapter 5

Technology Using Artificial Intelligence (AI) to Enhance Productivity and Sustainability in Atlantic Salmon Production and Challenges From Knowledge Management

Per Harald Rødvei[a], *Knut Ingar Westeren*[a] *and Martin Munkeby*[b]

[a]Nord University, Norway
[b]CageEye AS, Norway

Abstract

Aquaculture fish proteins have considerably increased in volume and importance. High-tech artificial intelligence (AI)-based growth has enhanced the production productivity of Atlantic salmon; however, serious issues have arisen regarding sustainability, such as fish health and emissions. Surveillance of salmon in cages is crucial for conducting managerial tasks such as developing biomass and optimizing feed. In addition, fish health must be monitored, which is mainly achieved with underwater cameras as the main technological solution. Sonar equipment has recently been introduced at production sites, providing improved surveillance based on AI technologies. This led to the following research questions: (1) What characterizes the most recent solutions for analyzing the integration of sustainability and productivity needs using AI-based lasers for surveillance in salmon-based aquaculture? (2) How do these solutions challenge knowledge management? Our study is based on experience gained from installing sonar equipment on aquaculture sites through the high-tech company CageEye. Three key approaches play crucial roles in the development of AI-based sonars for use in aquaculture: (1) image processing, (2) machine learning, and (3) deep learning. Experience has demonstrated that operators and site managers must have a fundamental understanding of how AI is used.

AI-Driven Knowledge Management Assets, Volume 2, 81–104

doi:10.1108/978-1-83662-778-420261005

Therefore, companies must allocate resources to their employees to ensure the necessary knowledge level. Knowledge management challenges have changed as a result of modern management and human resource management (HRM) principles as well as substantial increases in education and knowledge levels.

Keywords: Salmon aquaculture; artificial intelligence; sustainability; knowledge transfers; sonars

Introduction

The numbers in a report from the Food and Agriculture Organization (FAO) (2024) on aquaculture showed considerable growth in produced volume in the last decennium, with aquaculture showing the potential to substantially contribute to meeting the increased global demand for seafood. The fundamental challenge is sustainability; the FAO report underlines this as well as clarifies that sustainability problems widely vary in scope and size. The main part of aquaculture production takes place in freshwater in Asia, with China being the main producer. Atlantic salmon accounts for approximately 6% of the total volume of world aquaculture production (FAO, 2024) but is important because of its status as a high value world market commodity.

Salmon-based aquaculture technology has radically changed, which has been accompanied by a formidable upscaling of the knowledge levels necessary to use new technologies. The other main driver of these developments is the need for sustainability and fish health. The natural habitat of salmon does not include up to 200,000 salmon living together in a cage with a 160 m circumference and a depth of 20–30 m; concerns regarding fish health and other sustainability issues thus arise. However, this production method has achieved cutting-edge results in transforming mainly plant-based feed into fish proteins, with the biological feed conversion rate (bFCR) approaching one or being even less than one (Westeren, 2025b). Companies providing Atlantic salmon-based aquaculture products have achieved profit margins above the general industrial level (Mowi, 2024), indicating the possibilities of using these fast high-tech developments with artificial intelligence (AI) to increase productivity.

The focus of this section is on discussing these important sustainability challenges and the fundamentals of AI as a basis for the technologies used in increasing productivity in the aquaculture production process while dealing with sustainability issues. We believe that, without understanding the fundamentals of AI, analyzing the knowledge management challenges of operating high-tech AI-based equipment is impossible. This led to the following two research questions:

- What characterizes the recent AI-based solutions when we analyze the integration of sustainability and productivity needs in salmon-based aquaculture?
- How do these AI-based solutions challenge knowledge management?

We examine the fundamentals of sustainability considerations related to aquaculture as well as describe recent and relevant AI developments. We then explain new AI-based equipment and how it can be used in salmon aquaculture production. Next, we outline the key issues in knowledge management and the importance of how knowledge can act as an enabler or a barrier to the use of high-tech AI-based equipment. Finally, we present our conclusions and discuss the need for further research.

Sustainability Considerations Related to Aquaculture

Aquaculture production involves an operational mode as well as sustainability considerations. These two factors are mutually dependent, but opinions on the importance and ranking of the different factors in the scientific literature vary, even within a production group like Atlantic salmon, which is our focus here.

Sustainability challenges in aquaculture have been discussed in many scientific contributions, and a historic perspective is provided by Westeren (2025a). The first widely used definition of sustainability was provided by the Brundtland Commission (United Nations, 1987), after which debate arose between ecologists/environmentalists, such as Daly (1992, 1997) and Georgescu-Roegen (1971), and market supporters, such as Solow (2014) and Stiglitz (2003). The sustainability and circular economy debates were, at least partly, integrated with the market economy in the 2010s, with contributions from the Ellen McArthur Ellen MacArthur Foundation (2013) and the European Union (EU; 2018). These contributions were based on a belief that sustainability/circularity can be achieved within the market economy paradigm. This market idea, coupled with sustainability principles, has been adopted by national policies in almost all countries that produce Atlantic salmon. This market is now highly competitive, with above-average profit margins.

Comprehending and delineating the concept of sustainability in terms of aquaculture involves a multifaceted discussion. Global-scale sustainability and aquaculture production discussions have been conducted by the FAO (2024). The FAO highlighted national responsibilities in its most recent report, including the following sustainability factors related to aquaculture production:

- Fish health and disease management;
- Resource (feed) use and efficiency;
- Feed sustainability;
- Carbon footprint of aquaculture and feed production;
- Discharge of sludge and pollutants;
- Genetic interactions;
- Land and sea area use;
- Societal/poverty aspects.

Many country-specific studies related to the sustainability of aquaculture have discussed the main or most important species the country is producing, including environmental and sustainability factors such as those mentioned above. However, how legal/governmental systems of the country can implement the necessary measures to increase sustainability is a problem that remains to be addressed (Bohnes et al., 2022; Bostock et al., 2016; Luthman et al., 2022; Naylor et al., 2023; Virapat, 2022; Wang et al., 2018).

Relevance and Use of AI for Technological Developments

Basic Aspects of AI

Production technologies have rapidly developed with the introduction of a variety of new technologies and equipment, and the important role of AI must be emphasized. In this section, we discuss the basic aspects of AI in relation to technologies for optimizing aquaculture production and sustainability surveillance.

The fundamental principle of AI is to create results from a computer-based machine that can reason similarly to a human. Although discussions on AI can be traced back more than a century, scientific developments place modern AI back to World War II and the work of Alan Turing (Hoffmann, 2022).

Many definitions of AI exist, most of which use formulations that depict AI as referring to all technologies aimed at conducting cognitive tasks traditionally performed by humans through computing. The aim of AI, where the main task in relation to technology, is to perform functions that require human capabilities, such as perception, learning, and reasoning. Haenlein and Kaplan (2019) provided the following (highly cited) definition of AI: "the ability of a system to correctly interpret external data, learn from that data, and use that learning to achieve specific goals and tasks through flexible adaptation" (p. 5). This definition is challenging and rigorous because the outcome of AI processes is classified as having to be usable and meet productivity expectations in organizations.

AI is essentially the use of a set of computer-based techniques founded on a combination of theories and algorithms that simulate human intelligence. Examples of AI use can be found in almost all production activities and aspects of social life.

AI has been a source of considerable technological progress, innovation, and productivity gains. Critical arguments have also been linked to AI on different levels, such as the societal, organizational, and personal levels; some of the limitations of AI are listed below. No general consensus has been reached on how seriously these arguments and opinions change as technology develops.

Limited emotional intelligence: AI systems are limited in their understanding and response to human emotions, which is called "emotional intelligence." AI can recognize some emotions but cannot fully understand human emotional complexity or respond appropriately to emotions owing to contextual factors that influence emotions.

Hardware limitations: AI operation is based on a network of semiconductors that interact quickly with each other. Although semiconductors development is ongoing, limitations exist, such as monopolization, restrictions on production, and increasing power consumption.

Limited creativity: AI systems have limited creative capacity. AI can generate new ideas and solutions from the data on which it has been trained; currently, AI only partly possesses creativity and innovation abilities up to the level of human beings.

AI Approaches in Aquaculture

Three key approaches play crucial roles in the development of technologies and equipment for use in aquaculture: (1) image processing, (2) machine learning, and (3) deep learning (DL). Image processing allows computers to see, analyze, and understand images similarly to those of human vision, whereas machine learning and DL are powerful tools for extracting information from data.

Image Processing

A digital image is represented as a matrix of numerical values corresponding to discrete, numerically defined intensities. The surface of a digital image is divided into elements (normally) called "pixels." Each pixel has a characteristic grayscale or color that is related to the corresponding location in the actual image or is calculated from a description of the image. This digital form allows exploitation using computer software tools.

Resolution is defined as the number of dots per unit area, expressed as dots per inch (dpi). A resolution of 300 dpi implies 300 columns and 300 rows of pixels in a square inch, resulting in a total of 90,000 pixels per square inch. The resolution of a digital image defines the degree of detail in the image, which is crucial for image recognition.

In the context of digital images, *noise* is generally a sudden change in the intensity of a pixel relative to its neighbors. Noise is caused by unwanted fluctuations in the illumination of the optical and electronic devices of the sensor used to capture the images. The *luminance* of an image is the brightness level of the points constituting an image. Luminance is defined as the ratio of the light intensity of a surface to its apparent area. A *histogram* is a statistical graphical tool that allows the visualization of the distribution of pixel intensities in an image. A histogram represents the number of pixels for each light-intensity value. Traditionally, raster *image formats* such as BMP, GIF, JPEG, and TIFF have been used; later developments involve the use of *vector images*, which represent data using mathematical formulas. This allows the image to be resized without limits. We show how these characteristics of image creation play a role in the usefulness and precision of systems in the empirical part of this section.

Image segmentation allows selecting and isolating objects of interest in an image, separating them from the rest of the image or background. Different segmentation techniques can be used, the simplest of which is thresholding. Segmentation can be performed manually, where a human operator delineates regions of interest, or automatically, whereby AI-based algorithms are used to perform this task through a program. Techniques such as this have been used for several years, for example, in the production of chicken meat. The traditional quality control method involved employing controllers (persons) to inspect the chickens along an assembly line. This method has changed to optical scanning using AI-based software (Westeren, 2014). This highlights the area of *image classification*, in which AI-based algorithms are used to predict the class to which a specific object in an image belongs. We can consider different levels of classification tasks using an image of a salmon that presents different challenges to determine the dominant content of an image:

Level 1: Identify whether the image contains salmon (e.g., not cod).
Level 2: Identify whether salmon contains traces of salmon lice.
Level 3: Identify when the salmon has lice wounds; that is, (i) the number of wounds and (ii) the size of the wounds are put into a classification system.

Other types of classifications include the following:

Continuous imaging 1: Evaluate the optimal start and end feeding times based on continuous sonar image sequences.
Continuous imaging 2: Calculate the increase in biomass using continuous sonar image sequences.

Machine Learning

Machine learning is an AI application in which systems (e.g., a surveillance system for feeding caged salmon) can improve the feeding process performance through AI-based data analysis, often using optimization criteria. Machine learning methods are diverse; however, they are commonly divided into supervised, unsupervised, and reinforced. No consensus has been reached on the definitions or delineation of these concepts (Kreuzberger et al., 2023).

Supervised learning is a machine learning method that uses a prelabeled set of data to predict outcomes. Supervised learning uses a representative database to construct a general model that works with data that was not previously included. Supervised AI can, for example, be based on linear or logistic regression algorithms. Using machine learning based on regression algorithms requires considering dependent and independent variables.

Unsupervised AI machine learning is based on unlabeled data with no target variable Y to predict, where supervised learning aims to build a model from labeled data $f(X) \rightarrow Y$. Unsupervised AI algorithms can be used to detect patterns in data. Clustering algorithms are categorized as unsupervised AI machine learning methods and allow data to be grouped into separate sets. One example is the use of surveillance sonar data to determine salmon positions in cages. In addition, data on feeding, temperature, salinity, and light can be collected. However, no or only fragmentary information can be obtained about causation and the possible choices of dependent/independent variables. Unsupervised AI machine learning can reveal potential patterns, which we discuss further in the empirical section.

Reinforced AI machine learning refers to an AI machine learning type of analysis that aims to find the best solution to a problem through iteratively interacting with the environment. Reinforcement learning requires the exploration of the environment to find the most suitable strategy, unlike supervised and unsupervised methods. The algorithm attempts several solutions, observes the response of the environment, and accordingly adapts its behavior to determine the optimal strategy. The exploration and exploitation phases must be balanced in these types of problems, which are particularly suited to situations requiring tradeoffs between possible outcomes. Reinforcement learning is used for tasks such as operating a robot in a new environment or managing a self-driving car.

DL is an AI method that stems from machine learning. The main goal of DL is to create algorithms that can autonomously learn and improve, unlike traditional programming, in which machines follow predetermined rules. DL uses successive layers of nonlinear processing units to extract and transform data features. The output of one layer is the input of the next layer. DL algorithms can be supervised (allowing data to be classified) or unsupervised. They can process large amounts of data compared to other current machine-learning methods, allowing them to achieve superior performance.

DL is based on artificial neural networks. These networks are inspired by the function of neurons in the human brain. Artificial neural networks have contributed to the development of technologies such as image recognition and robotic vision. A large amount of scientific literature exists in the field of DL, which has led to rapid DL developments.

Sustainability Considerations, Developments, and Experiences with Sonar Technologies Based on AI in Aquaculture

Sustainability Aspects

Many researchers have studied new AI-based technologies in aquaculture, and relevant review articles have been published (Gladju et al., 2022; Hu et al., 2020; Li et al., 2020; Mandal & Ghosh, 2023, 2024; Zhou et al., 2018). Views have changed considerably regarding the importance and applicability of new technologies in the six years from the first to the last of these reviews. One reason for this shift is the rapid change in AI. In addition, technological assessments widely differ from production methods and geographical standpoints. Jiang et al. (2023) analyzed how technological progress contributes to aquaculture production in China, whereas McIntosh et al. (2022) analyzed global changes in the farm technology used for salmon production. China hosts a large proportion of the global freshwater aquaculture, in which surveillance and feeding technologies substantially differ from those used in open-cage salmon saltwater aquaculture production.

The focus of this section is on analyzing how technologies using AI can enhance the productivity and sustainability of Atlantic salmon production. The following factors are central to these aspects:

(1) Monitoring and optimizing feeding;
(2) Control of water quality and other environmental factors, such as oxygen content, temperature, current, and light;
(3) Assessing the status of salmon biomass and growth rate, including counting and weight class sorting;
(4) Fish health surveillance, especially the salmon lice situation;
(5) Observation and interpretation of fish behavior;
(6) Escape from cages and genetic interactions.

Factors 1–6 are aspects of sustainability, and we discuss some of them here. Salmon feed optimization to increase sustainability has received considerable attention from companies, and research has led to the development of innovative and cost-effective solutions. The two main sustainability challenges are increasing feed quality and reducing the feed waste in the cages during salmon growth. Salmon feed has considerably changed, and Hansen (2019) reported that plant oil and plant protein contents increased from 22% in 2000 to 61% in 2016 in the feed used in Norwegian aquaculture, while the marine oil and protein contents reduced from 65% to 25%. One important factor of this change is “The Brazilian Green Revolution” (Nehring, 2022), in which the production of soybeans doubled from 2012–2013 to 2022–2023. Brazil now produces 162 million metric tons of soybeans annually, which is approximately 35% of the world’s production. The environmental effects of this development have been discussed (D’Abramo, 2021; Hansen, 2019; Sarker, 2023), and producers now state whether the Brazilian soy used has a sustainability certification. Most scientists think that the substitution of plant proteins for animal proteins in salmon feed is a good idea (see the above citations); however (Sarker, 2023), argues for the introduction of a larger proportion of ingredients based on microalgae and insects (Sarker, 2023).

The utilization of feed by the salmon is a key aspect in aquaculture production, which faces a number of challenges (Ytrestøyl et al., 2015). Here, we focus on the feed conversion rate, which includes two components: the biological feed conversion rate (bFCR) and the economic feed conversion rate (eFCR). bFCR is the amount of feed required to produce one unit of salmon. The eFCR also considers production losses such as mortality. The bFCR for one of the main salmon producers in Norway was 1.15 (Lerøy Sea Food, 2024) and the eFCR was 1.3 (Mowi, 2024) in 2023. These numbers depend on several factors, such as feed quality and composition, but are representative of Norwegian salmon aquaculture production. The bFCR is expected to reach values of approximately 1.0 (or even lower) in the near future, with these results already being obtained in some areas (Hevrøy, 2021; Westeren, 2025b).

Fish health is a major factor affecting salmon aquaculture in Norway and other countries. Salmon lice (*Lepeophtheirus salmonis*) are the main challenge affecting salmon. Salmon lice float with the current under normal conditions and cannot live deeper than approximately 10 m. Delicing has been the major form of treatment for more than 20 years, and producers have now shifted from medical treatment to the use of heated water, fresh water, and/or other flushing techniques. These treatments increase fish mortality and reduce fish welfare (Aldrin et al., 2023; Overton et al., 2019; Stige et al., 2024). Another method of coping with salmon lice is preventing the lice from entering the cage using skirts extending to a water depth of 30 m (Westeren, 2023) or closed cages (Westeren, 2025b). These solutions have produced promising results in creating lice-free environments; however, these methods are expensive. An Aquatraz cage with a 30 m lice skirt costs NOK 30–50 million; a traditional open cage costs up to NOK 2 million (Westeren, 2023). Two-thirds of all Norwegian salmon production units in 2017 used cleaner fish to reduce the salmon lice problem; however, this method may not be sustainable (Overton et al., 2019). A new method being tested is the salmon lice laser, which is mentioned in the empirical section.

The future of aquatic salmon in Norway depends on finding a solution to the salmon lice problem. Norwegian authorities have introduced the "traffic light system" to "deal" with lice. Whether this system is fair to the producer, optimal for finding solutions to salmon lice, and sustainable in general is the subject of debate (Bailey & Eggereide, 2020; Hersoug, 2022; van Nes et al., 2025).

Salmon in Cages Analyzed Using Imaging Sonars

Underwater cameras are currently the standard equipment used in industrial salmon aquaculture cages. Camera quality has considerably increased in terms of their resolution, movability, and handling of low-light situations. Learning how to use underwater cameras is part of the education of aquaculture operators. However, not all vital information about salmon in cages can be acquired from cameras; until recently, no satisfactory methods were available for obtaining reliable information about the following:

- The number and size of the salmon for estimating growth and biomass;
- The fish health and disease situation, especially regarding the salmon lice status;
- Fish behavior in general;
- The relationships between fish behavior in general, (1) feeding data, and (2) environmental data, such as temperature, oxygen, salinity, light, and current.

Early attempts to use sonar to address these problems started in 2017 (Folkedal et al., 2022); Wei et al. (2022) stated that sonar technology had emerged in the prior decade and had been closely linked to AI development in a review on monitoring fish using sonar. In principle, sonar technology can provide solutions to all the abovementioned problems; however, the research on and knowledge of the factors affecting salmon growth, the ability to resist health challenges, and managing environmental factors must be advanced to industrially use sonar data.

Sonar technology has rapidly developed with advances in AI to improve image construction and further software development. Different hardware configurations are discussed in the empirical section. The sonar sends out beams that are interpreted and transferred into images, which are then processed into customized formats for selected analyses. AI is necessary for this process. The focus can be on different aspects, such as fish health surveillance, behavioral characteristics, counting, sizing, and biomass estimation. Sonar has been used for sizing and counting different types of fish (Feng et al., 2023; Gutiérrez-Estrada et al., 2022; Helminen et al., 2020; Li et al., 2020; Wei et al., 2022), and sonar produced more accurate results than prior methods.

Two methods are available for detecting fish behavior: underwater cameras or sonar equipment combined with matching software. Banno et al. (2024) compared these technologies and concluded that sonar is preferable because it can collect and handle much larger quantities of data. However, underwater cameras will continue to be used because they provide easy access to vital information during daily site operations. Fish behavior is often analyzed in combination with meal behavior. Folkedal et al. (2022) and Westeren et al. (2022) found interesting correlations between environmental characteristics and fish meal behavior. Folkedal et al. (2022, p. 10) concluded with "In this study, a hydroacoustic system was successfully used to autonomously control the meal duration of sea-caged Atlantic salmon by monitoring fish biomass within a defined observation volume." Westeren et al. (2022) reported salmon behavior over a 24-hour period for most of the total production time of approximately 420 days. Distinct behavioral patterns were observed when the feeding periods were included in the analysis. Westeren et al. (2022) analyzed the relationships between fish behavior and (1) feeding data and (2) environmental data, such as temperature, oxygen, salinity, light, and current.

Empirical Results

This section is based on data from the CageEye company, and the information presented here can be found in CageEye (2025). Salmon aquaculture in Norway normally involves the use of cages with a circumference of 160 m, each holding 50,000–200,000 fish. The sonar equipment from CageEye is called the Echosounder, and Fig. 5.1 illustrates how the system works using two transponders: one at the top and one at the bottom of the cage.

Each fish was recorded with datasets for each observation, such as position and movement speed. The data streams were captured in real time, as documented by Westeren et al. (2022), and the system was structured to create a new dataset every 12 s. The fish distribution in the cage was recorded in 1 m depth intervals over 25 m. This resulted in 180,000 observations per hour. Data were

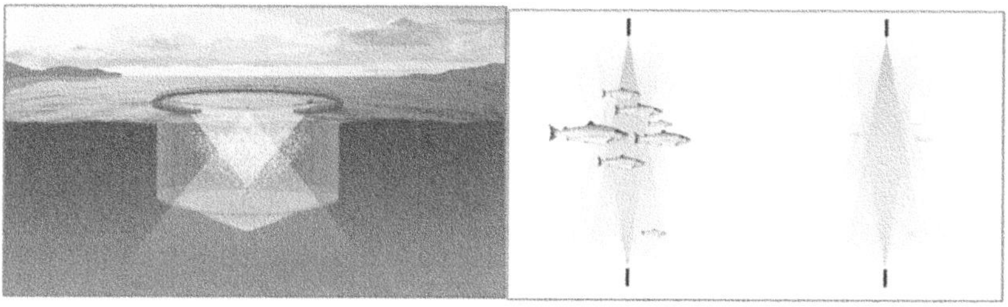

Fig. 5.1. Outline of a Two-Transponder Echosounder System. *Source:* CageEye (2025).

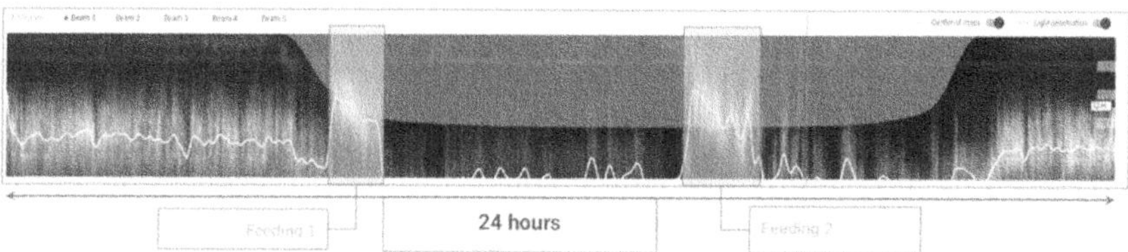

Fig. 5.2. Scan of a 24-hour Cycle of Average Depth (White Line) and Distribution Density (Feeding Periods in Green). *Source:* CageEye (2025).

used to produce a scan, as shown in Fig. 5.2. The positioning data were combined with the feeding data, and the feeding periods are marked in green in Fig. 5.2.

Fig. 5.3 shows how the changes in the environmental conditions using underwater light affected the salmon. Salmon normally avoid light and change their behavioral pattern when a light is turned on at the bottom of the cage. We can analyze how new light positioning influences salmon growth patterns.

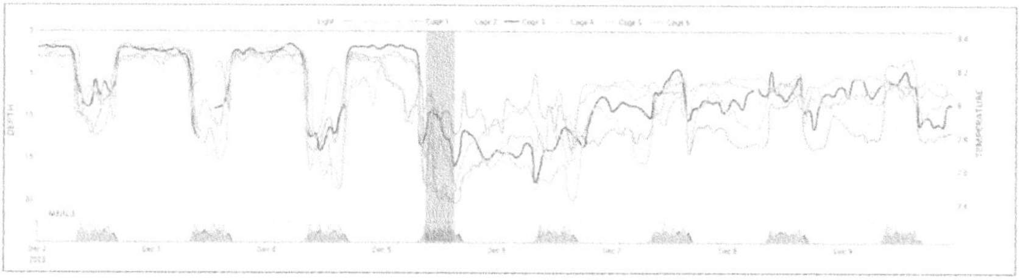

Fig. 5.3. Scan of Positioning Data for a Seven-Day Period (December 2–9); Artificial Underwater Light was Introduced on December 5–6. *Source:* CageEye (2025).

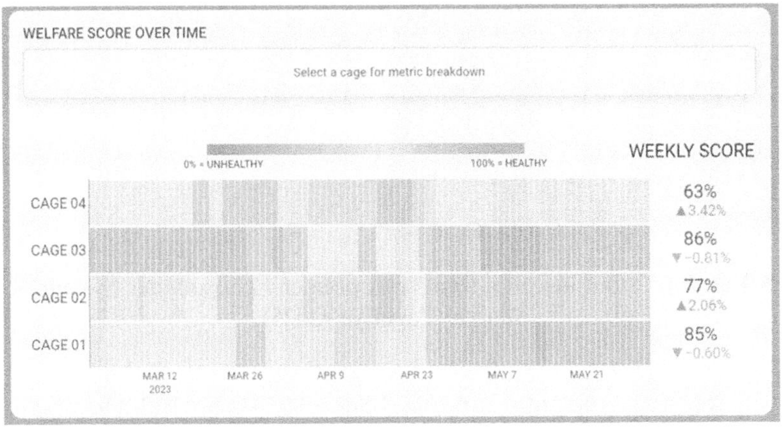

Fig. 5.4. Welfare Scores Over Time. *Source:* CageEye (2025).

Variations in temperature also affect salmon, where Westeren et al. (2022) showed that growth rates differed between a low-temperature winter month and a high-temperature spring month. Similar analyses can be conducted for changes in environmental factors such as salinity and current.

Fig. 5.4 shows the welfare scores calculated during actual salmon production in four cages from March to May 2023. The scores originate from AI models that analyze cage behavior indicators and environmental factors. Key elements include:

Behavior Metrics: (i) Activity: Assesses daily movement patterns in the water column, referencing normal circadian rhythms (dawn, dusk, day, and night). (ii) Stability: Evaluates consistency in swimming depth and movement. Rapid or erratic changes lower stability. (iii) Rhythm: Looks for alignment with typical diel movement (e.g., avoiding sunlight by descending in the water column), a hallmark of healthy salmon behavior.

Environmental Indicators: (i) Temperature and Oxygen: A 100% score means the measured conditions are optimal according to the AI model. (ii) Current: Assesses whether water movement remains within tolerance levels that do not stress fish. (iii) Sunlight Penetration: Excessive penetration and brightness at depth can trigger stress responses.

Feeding Response: (i) Feeding Variation/Appetite: A well-functioning cage will show consistent, robust feeding unless environmental conditions disrupt normal patterns. (ii) Mortality: A spike here signals potential welfare problems that may not be visible solely through behavior metrics.

These factors are automatically aggregated into a single "overall welfare metric" by assigning a weight to each component. For instance, repeated fluctuations in fish depth (low stability) combined with suboptimal temperatures will reduce the welfare score. If a cage has minimal movement, strong feeding response, optimal temperature, and stable daily rhythms, the cage attains a higher overall welfare rating.

Fig. 5.5. Illustration of the Use of a Lice Laser. *Source:* CageEye (2025).

The Lice Laser, see Fig. 5.5, is a new type of equipment that incorporates several aspects of AI (Gurugain et al., 2021). Cage operators must position their lice lasers as effectively as possible, and the Echosounder can estimate the optimal positioning based on the calculation of the highest biomass density.

Knowledge Management (KM) Challenges

Some KM Fundamentals Relevant for the AI Discussion

Knowledge as a foundation for the success of an organization has long been acknowledged, but KM as a discipline emerged during the 1990s, with early contributions from Wiig (1997) and Davenport and Prusak (1998). This coincided with two fundamental shifts in policy: the Lisbon Declaration from the European Union, where the primary goal shifted to enhancing knowledge competitiveness, and the change in the World Bank strategy to focus on knowledge development, as discussed in Westeren (2018). Another important driver of KM development was the possibility of introducing immaterial (knowledge-based) assets into the balance accounts of firms in Europe and North America.

The discussion of KM as a scientific genre began in the 1990s with a book by Nonaka and Takeuchi (1995) about knowledge-creating companies. The analysis provided by Nonaka and Takeuchi (which is the foundation of the SEKI model) builds on the assumption that we can separate the concepts of explicit and tacit knowledge and that we have an operational understanding of tacit knowledge and how the processes of change occur between explicit and tacit knowledge. Thirty years after the book by Nonaka and Takeuchi (1995), no common scientific agreement has been reached about explicit and tacit knowledge, but most scientists relate the tacit knowledge concept to Polanyi (1961). The article by Tsoukas (2005) is often used.

The definitions of KM have focused on the process of creating value and improving the situation of an organization; this normally refers to enhancing competitiveness for companies. This definition scientifically indicates that testing whether this phenomenon occurs is possible. Hislop (2010) discussed whether KM is a transient management approach, concluding that a reasonable number of scientific contributions support this notion. Westeren (2018) discussed several criteria from the philosophy of science that should be considered when establishing KM as a scientific genre. An important delineation is between the cognitivist and connectionist approaches. The cognitivist approach assumes that the study objects are measurable in the sense of Popper (2005), which most KM studies do not claim. The connectionist approach relates to hermeneutic and phenomenological traditions, which have been applied in many scientific studies related to KM. North and Kumta (2018) and Natek and Lesjak (2021) argued that ambiguities about concepts, such as tacit knowledge, may exist that do not preclude the scientific level of these studies being satisfactory as long as fundamental rules from the philosophy of science and methodological analysis are followed.

KM and AI

KM is process-oriented in its formulation for use by organizations; KM is often formulated as creating, storing, sharing, and exploiting knowledge, as described by Hislop et al. (2018). KM allows for technological inputs in all these areas, and the central argument now is that we must also allow for AI contributions in all these areas, as exemplified by Vadari and Desik (2021) and Yang (2024) (Fig. 5.6). AI has enabled the creation of new knowledge-based technological solutions that challenge firms in areas such as:

- Managerial set up;
- Organizational structure;
- Internal and external knowledge exchange procedures.

The reasons for introducing AI as a new technology do not, in principle, change the fundamental goals of a firm, such as the optimal combination of profit maximization and competitiveness.

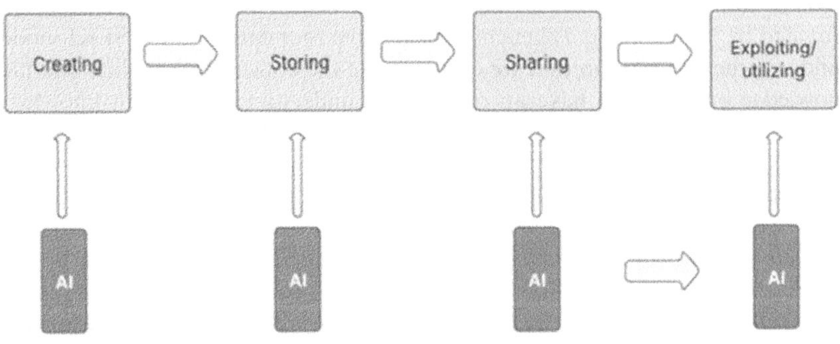

Fig. 5.6. The KM Process and AI. *Source:* Own elaboration.

Hansen et al. (1999) analyzed KM strategies by dividing them into codification and personalization. This model has been used, amended, and criticized by, e.g., Scheepers et al. (2004), Haesli and Boxall (2005), and Ajith Kumar and Ganesh (2011). The model is still relevant (Haug, 2024; Yang, 2024). This model is related to explicit and tacit knowledge. The codification strategy involves the use of explicit knowledge that can be codified, stored, and retrieved. The personalization strategy is founded on the communication of knowledge between persons, where fulfilling both criteria for trust is crucial—the cognitive (the information you give me is correct) and the affective (I can trust that you will not betray me). Hansen et al. (1999) opined that organizations must choose which strategy to prioritize, but later changed their view that organizations must seek the optimal combination of strategies. Transfers of tacit knowledge, as defined by Polanyi (1962), play an important role in the personalization of KM strategies but have a wider definition than the concept of tacit knowledge.

We use two empirical examples of the different steps of the KM process and their relationship to AI: one from image processing and the other from machine learning. The knowledge creation step represents the largest change in new knowledge obtained from AI. Image recognition of health problems in salmon is not yet systematically and verifiably possible. An example of the application of machine learning is AI enabling the modeling of salmon behavior so that less waste is produced during feeding. Storing knowledge requires a high-capacity IT system; however, this does not represent a new challenge because this is codified knowledge. A new situation arises in the knowledge sharing. Here, the personalization concept applies, as described by Hansen (1999). Image recognition requires knowledge sharing among employees about which salmon health problems, as determined with AI, are dependent on interpretation. The images from the AI system indicate health problem similarities among the salmon, as described by the statistical criteria. The site staff must find a common interpretation based on the criteria and determine what and when action is required. AI reduces uncertainty in the decision-making process and provides knowledge based on statistical criteria, but AI cannot interpret the health situation of a salmon, as shown in this empirical case.

The case of feeding salmon is different from that above because this task is based on unsupervised AI machine learning, starting from unlabeled data with no target variables. Site staff must first share knowledge and agree on how to model salmon behavior. After a model is established, the staff must agree on how to establish intervention criteria, which refer to the time period and intensity of the feeding process in practice. In addition, the goal is the same: optimization of the feeding process, and thereby optimization of salmon growth, which again leads to the maximization of profit and competitiveness.

Context dependency is a central aspect to consider when KM strategies are implemented, especially when AI is used. "The incorporation of AI into KM equips organizations with advanced tools for data management, offers insightful analytics, improves user interactions, drives innovation, and efficiently manages an abundance of information" (Yang, 2024, p. 38), a statement reflected in many scientific studies on KM and AI. However, AI offers possibilities as well as creates challenges for the organization in terms of increased resource use, necessitating investing in the accrual of codified and personalized knowledge, as well as for KM specifically tailored to the context.

Barriers to Knowledge Transfer

Riege (2005) discussed barriers to knowledge transfer, and provided criteria for evaluating relevant knowledge barriers that still remain relevant. Ferrer-Serano et al. (2022, pp. 1369–1372) presented several of the same key points as Riege (2005) in an update on the development of knowledge strategies over the prior two decades. Table 5.1 presents the original 17 barriers, which we subdivided into relevant and irrelevant barriers to knowledge transfer related to AI-based high-tech technologies in salmon aquaculture. The comments in the Table 5.1 are based on the cited literature and the experiences with CageEye.

Riege's argument (2005) shown in Table 5.1 shows that resources being a problem for communication and knowledge management is valid in our AI case and is based on international experience (Chiu et al., 2022). Norwegian aquaculture sites generally have a flat organizational structure with the strong involvement of the entire team (Stiklestad et al., 2019). This requires all operators and site managers to have a fundamental understanding of how AI data is input to feeding programs and how the programs work by using AI data. This requires companies to allocate resources to employees to teach the necessary knowledge, and that the information to date points that these resources have been devoted to this task.

The KM discussion can be divided into that on tacit and explicit knowledge. Underwater cameras considerably affect operator reliability regarding tacit knowledge, as defined and discussed by Polanyi (1962) and Tsoukas (2005), because of their limited visibility. AI-based equipment collects data, including (nearly) all fish in the cage, which requires an understanding of how the information output is produced but partly removes the importance of the tacit knowledge component. The knowledge transfer challenge changed to combining explicit and tacit knowledge to correctly interpret the situation in a cage after the introduction of AI.

The arguments about differences in experience levels are placed on the relevant side of barriers to knowledge transfer in Table 5.1. Individual differences arise because of differences in backgrounds, education, and job requirements. Stiklestad et al. (2019) stated that Norwegian salmon production sites aim to improve job performance more than those in Chile, which reduces the scope of the problem of knowledge transfer.

The concept of trust has been debated and has been delineated into three groups: personal, generalized/scientific, and political/societal trust (Newton & Zmerli, 2011). Riege (2005) assumed that personal and scientific perspectives are of interest, but, based on our findings, the lack of trust in people as a barrier to knowledge transfers is negligible (Table 5.1). Generalized or scientific trust is important in AI relationships. We did not find a lack of trust of the operators in

Table 5.1. The 17 Barriers for Knowledge Transfers from Riege (2005) are Divided into Relevant and Non-relevant Transfers Based on an Evaluation of Utilizing High-tech AI-based Equipment in Salmon Aquaculture.

Relevant barriers to knowledge transfers	Nonrelevant barriers to knowledge transfers
(1) Lack of time and resources	(1) Apprehension of fear
(2) The explicit–tacit knowledge split	(2) Low awareness and realization of value and benefit of possessed knowledge
(3) Differences in experience levels	(3) Hierarchy, status, and formal power-based arguments
(4) Lack of contact time and interaction between knowledge sources and recipients	(4) Insufficient tolerance of past mistakes
(5) Age differences	(5) Poor verbal/written communication and interpersonal skills
(6) Lack of trust in the accuracy and credibility of knowledge from external sources	(6) Age differences
	(7) Gender differences
	(8) Lack of social network
	(9) Differences in education levels
	(10) Fear of not receiving recognition and accreditation from managers and colleagues
	(11) Lack of trust in people
	(12) Lack of trust in the accuracy and credibility of knowledge from external sources
	(13) Differences in culture or ethnic background.

the actual developers of systems and equipment but of more AI in general being a "black box." This is why we also placed age differences on both sides of Table 5.1. The conclusion is that the effects of Items 10 (age differences) and 16 (lack of trust in the accuracy and credibility of knowledge from external sources) are less clear than those of the other items.

Many items classified as irrelevant barriers to knowledge transfer (Items 2, 3, 5, 6, 9, 11, 12, 13, and 14) are not discussed further, other than to say that crews at Norwegian salmon-producing sites have implemented modern human resource management (HRM) practices. One company normally has several sites in operation and is managed with a flat structure, open information channels, and responsibility sharing, which are combined with a commitment to increasing educational levels; each site is independent in making its own managerial decisions. This ideal situation is also in the company's interest in maximizing profit (Stiklestad et al., 2019).

Final Discussion, Conclusions, and Future Research

Discussing the AI technologies employed in salmon production to increase productivity and sustainability requires an understanding of the principles of AI development, such as image processing and machine learning. Underwater cameras have long been in use and are expected to be widely used in the future. These cameras produce images of the salmon in a cage so that operators can see how individual salmon behave when they feed. Underwater cameras can also be used to study the health of the salmon; for example, the number of lice attached to a few individual salmon at a time. The skills of operators were largely based on intuition prior to the introduction of sonar because underwater cameras could not provide complete observations or calculations of the situation of the salmon in the cage. The introduction of sonar enables the use of single- and multibeam equipment. CageEye is based on a multibeam (two sonar heads) system (Fig. 5.1), which covers approximately 75% of the fish in the cage. This created two AI-related challenges: The first is also experienced with single-beam systems, namely, identifying and producing digital images of all the salmon within the range of the sonar through obtaining identifying information such as depth and size. A single beam only covers 30–40% of the fish, so the uncertainty margins of the results are high. The two-sonar-head multibeam system largely reduces the uncertainty in the results but requires the integration of two data sources. Finding solutions to this problem requires substantial data capacity and advanced programming; however, multibeam systems are based on supervised AI machine learning, based on a target variable, which is the individual salmon.

Image classification is a central AI task that must be performed to obtain the information needed. Salmon weight is calculated by comparing the size of the salmon to predefined standards. The statistical error margins are small with up to 200,000 salmon in a cage. Determining fish health, in particular the lice situation, is a more challenging task. Standard images of lice adhered to a salmon can easily be produced so lice can be counted, but understanding the severity of the health problem is challenging. Other health problems, such as wounds, are more difficult to analyze because of the uncertainty related to classifying the object.

The use of sonar to monitor and analyze fish behavior creates another AI-related challenge. Fish behavior involves the time dimension, which can be addressed by linking snapshots together or with continuous surveillance. The latter method is more complicated, requiring two vectors: identification and movement data. Continuous methods have not yet been scientifically documented and are still in the testing stage. Different methods can be used to link observations (CageEye, 2025; Westeren et al., 2022) and analyze the behavior of salmon over a 24-hour period or in experimental situations where lights are introduced at the bottom of the cage (Figs. 5.2 and 5.3). Obtaining these scans is straightforward, but analyzing this data is another AI challenge. The problem is that we have no complete knowledge of fish/salmon behavior, which raises questions such as:

- Do we have a behavioral pattern that can be modeled and entered into an analytical system?
- What period is appropriate when searching for behavior patterns that produce significant results (e.g., 20-s or 2-minute intervals)?
- Should we assume linear or circular relationships?

Such questions favor reasoning based on unsupervised and reinforced AI machine learning as well as emphasize the importance and need for the human brain, which plays a decisive role in determining the model structures.

The analysis of KM challenges reveals that the evaluation criteria from Riege (2007) are still relevant; however, the production mode and sustainability challenges have considerably changed:

(1) Modern management and HRM principles.
(2) A large increase in education and knowledge levels.
(3) The introduction of AI-based high-tech equipment.

Factors 1–3 contribute to Items 2, 3, 5, 6, and 14 in Table 5.1, not acting as barriers to knowledge transfer. Trust remains an important issue, the influence of which on the system has changed. The lack of personal trust as a KM problem is now of little relevance, whereas developments in using black-box-like AI technologies have remained in discussions on explicit and tacit knowledge. Resource questions regarding knowledge acquisition and transfer remain. Founders of KM science, such as Davenport (2005), stated that from a productivity viewpoint, all employees having all the knowledge about all business operations would never be optimal. The experiences described in this section indicate that this remains true but the perspective has changed. Aquaculture sites now function as integrated groups that provide resources for knowledge sharing. The speed of AI developments requires more resources, but the resources are more collective than individual learning.

Research into the use of AI-based technologies in aquaculture has expanded from this perspective. Developments in image creation and machine learning will continue. The debate is ongoing whether people should accept that AI is a black box or whether people should understand the main AI processes. We recommend that users have a fundamental understanding of AI for applications in aquaculture, based on our discussions, as we assume causality or use models based on unsupervised and/or reinforced AI machine learning developments.

References

Ajith Kumar, J., & Ganesh, L. (2011). Balancing knowledge strategy: Codification and personalization during product development. *Journal of Knowledge Management*, *15*(1), 118–135.

Aldrin, M., Huseby, R. B., Stige, L. C., & Helgesen, K. (2023). Estimated effectiveness of treatments against salmon lice in marine salmonid farming. *Aquaculture*, *575*, 739749. https://doi.org/10.1016/j.aquaculture.2023.739749

Bailey, J. L., & Eggereide, S. S. (2020). Indicating sustainable salmon farming: The case of the new Norwegian aquaculture management scheme. *Marine Policy*, *117*, 103925. https://doi.org/10.1016/j.marpol.2020.103925

Banno, K., Gao, S., Anichini, M., Stolz, C., Tuene, S. A., & Gansel, L. C. (2024). Expanded vision for the spatial distribution of Atlantic salmon in sea cages. *Aquaculture*, *588*, 740879. https://doi.org/10.1016/j.aquaculture.2024.740879

Bohnes, F. A., Hauschild, M. Z., Schlundt, J., Nielsen, M., & Laurent, A. (2022). Environmental sustainability of future aquaculture production: Analysis of Singaporean and Norwegian policies. *Aquaculture*, *549*, 737717. https://doi.org/10.1016/j.aquaculture.2021.737717

Bostock, J., Lane, A., Hough, C., & Yamamoto, K. (2016). An assessment of the economic contribution of EU aquaculture production and the influence of policies for its sustainable development. *Aquaculture International*, *24*, 699–733. https://doi.org/10.1007/s10499-016-9992-1

CageEye. (2025). *Using fish location data from echosounders to position equipment in aquaculture cages*. Retrieved 16.01 from https://www.cageeye.com/2024/02/20/using-echosounder-data-to-position-equipment-in-aquaculture-cages/

Chiu, M.-C., Yan, W.-M., Bhat, S. A., & Huang, N.-F. (2022). Development of smart aquaculture farm management system using IoT and AI-based surrogate models. *Journal of Agriculture and Food Research*, *9*, 100357. https://doi.org/10.1016/j.jafr.2022.100357

D'Abramo, L. R. (2021). Sustainable aquafeed and aquaculture production systems as impacted by challenges of global food security and climate change. *Journal of the World Aquaculture Society*, *52*(6), 1162–1167. https://doi.org/10.1111/jwas.12867

Daly, H. E. (1992). Allocation, distribution, and scale: Towards an economics that is efficient, just, and sustainable. *Ecological Economics*, *6*(3), 185–193.

Daly, H. E. (1997). Georgescu-roegen versus Solow/Stiglitz. *Ecological Economics*, *22*(3), 261–266.

Davenport, T. H. (2005). *Thinking for a living: How to get better performances and results from knowledge workers*. Harvard Business Press.

Ellen MacArthur Foundation. (2013). *Towards the circular economy, economic and business rationale for an accelerated transition* (Vol. 1). Ellen MacArthur Foundation.

EU. (2018). *A sustainable bioeconomy for Europe: Strengthening the connection between economy*. Society and The Environment.

FAO. (2024). *The state of world fisheries and aquaculture 2024 – blue transformation in action*. https://doi.org/10.4060/cd0683en

Feng, Y., Wei, Y., Sun, S., Liu, J., An, D., & Wang, J. (2023). Fish abundance estimation from multi-beam sonar by improved MCNN. *Aquatic Ecology*, *57*(4), 895–911. https://doi.org/10.1007/s10452-023-10007-z

Ferrer-Serrano, M., Fuentelsaz, L., & Latorre-Martinez, M. P. (2022). Examining knowledge transfer and networks: An overview of the last twenty years. *Journal of Knowledge Management*, *26*(8), 2007–2037. https://doi.org/10.1108/JKM-04-2021-0265

Folkedal, O., Macaulay, G., Fosseidengen, J., Mikkelsen, G., Myrland, J., Søvegjarto, B., Klepaker, T., Fernö, A., Dempster, T., & Oppedal, F. (2022). Deployment of hydroacoustic feeding control in salmon sea-cages: Biological and technical considerations. *Aquaculture*, *561*, 738700. https://doi.org/10.1016/j.aquaculture.2022.738700

Georgescu-Roegen, N. (1971). *The entropy law and the economic process*. Harvard University Press.

Gladju, J., Kamalam, B. S., & Kanagaraj, A. (2022). Applications of data mining and machine learning framework in aquaculture and fisheries: A review. *Smart Agricultural Technology*, *2*, 100061. https://doi.org/10.1016/j.atech.2022.100061

Guragain, P., Tkachov, M., Båtnes, A. S., Olsen, Y., Winge, P., & Bones, A. M. (2021). Principles and methods of counteracting harmful salmon–arthropod interactions in salmon farming: Addressing possibilities, limitations, and future options. *Frontiers in Marine Science*, *8*, 701793. https://doi.org/10.3389/fmars.2021.701793

Gutiérrez-Estrada, J. C., Pulido-Calvo, I., Castro-Gutiérrez, J., Peregrín, A., López-Domínguez, S., Gómez-Bravo, F., Garrocho-Cruz, A., & De la Rosa-Lucas, I. (2022). Fish abundance estimation with imaging sonar in semi-intensive aquaculture ponds. *Aquacultural Engineering*, *97*, 102235. https://doi.org/10.1016/j.aquaeng.2022.102235

Haenlein, M., & Kaplan, A. (2019). A brief history of artificial intelligence: On the past, present, and future of artificial intelligence. *California Management Review*, *61*(4), 5–14.

Haesli, A., & Boxall, P. (2005). When knowledge management meets HR strategy: An exploration of personalization-retention and codification-recruitment configurations. *The International Journal of Human Resource Management*, *16*(11), 1955–1975.

Hansen, L. (2019). The weak sustainability of the salmon feed transition in Norway–a bioeconomic case study. *Frontiers in Marine Science*, *6*, 764. https://doi.org/10.3389/fmars.2019.00764

Hansen, M. T., Nohria, N., & Tierney, T. (1999). What's your strategy for managing knowledge?. In *The knowledge management yearbook 2000-2001* (pp. 55–69). Routledge.

Haug, A. (2024). Critical success factors for knowledge management systems in new product development. *Knowledge Management Research and Practice*, 1–13. https://doi.org/10.1080/14778238.2024.2424290

Helminen, J., Dauphin, G. J., & Linnansaari, T. (2020). Length measurement accuracy of adaptive resolution imaging sonar and a predictive model to assess adult Atlantic salmon (Salmo salar) into two size categories with long range data in a river. *Journal of Fish Biology*, *97*(4), 1009–1026. https://doi.org/10.1111/jfb.14456

Hersoug, B. (2022). "One country, ten systems"–The use of different licensing systems in Norwegian aquaculture. *Marine Policy*, *137*, 104902. https://doi.org/10.1016/j.marpol.2021.104902

Hevrøy, E. M. (2021). *Impact of different lots of the same feed product on short-term feed intake and growth in farmed Atlantic Salmon*. Mowi.

Hislop, D. (2010). Knowledge management as an ephemeral management fashion?. *Journal of Knowledge Management*, *14*(6), 779–790.

Hislop, D., Bosua, R., & Helms, R. (2018). *Knowledge management in organizations: A critical introduction*. Oxford University Press.

Hoffmann, C. H. (2022). Is AI intelligent? An assessment of artificial intelligence, 70 years after turing. *Technology in Society*, *68*, 101893.

Hu, Z., Li, R., Xia, X., Yu, C., Fan, X., & Zhao, Y. (2020). A method overview in smart aquaculture. *Environmental Monitoring and Assessment*, *192*, 1–25. https://doi.org/10.1007/s10661-020-08409-9

Jiang, Q., Wu, M., & Zhang, D. (2023). Evidence of the contribution of the technological progress on aquaculture production for economic development in China—research based on the transcendental logarithmic production function method. *Agriculture*, *13*(3), 544. https://doi.org/10.3390/agriculture13030544

Kayworth, T., & Leidner, D. (2004). Organizational culture as a knowledge resource. In *Handbook on knowledge management 1: Knowledge matters* (pp. 235–252).

Kreuzberger, D., Kühl, N., & Hirschl, S. (2023). Machine learning operations (mlops): Overview, definition, and architecture. *IEEE Access*, *11*, 31866–31879.

Leroyseafood. (2023). *Sustainability-library-2023*. Leroyseafood. Retrieved 14.01 from www.leroyseafood.com/en/sustainability/sustainability-library-2023/

Li, D., Wang, Z., Wu, S., Miao, Z., Du, L., & Duan, Y. (2020). Automatic recognition methods of fish feeding behavior in aquaculture: A review. *Aquaculture*, *528*, 735508. https://doi.org/10.1016/j.aquaculture.2020.735508

Luthman, O., Jonell, M., Rönnbäck, P., & Troell, M. (2022). Strong and weak sustainability in Nordic aquaculture policies. *Aquaculture*, *550*, 737841. https://doi.org/10.1016/j.aquaculture.2021.737841

Macaulay, G., Bui, S., Oppedal, F., & Dempster, T. (2021). Challenges and benefits of applying fish behaviour to improve production and welfare in industrial aquaculture. *Reviews in Aquaculture*, *13*(2), 934–948. https://doi.org/10.1111/raq.12505

Måløy, H. (2020). Echobert: A transformer-based approach for behavior detection in echograms. *IEEE Access*, *8*, 218372–218385.

Mandal, A., & Ghosh, A. R. (2023). AI - Driven surveillance of the health and disease status of ocean organisms: A review. *Aquaculture International*, *192*. https://doi.org/10.1007/s10499-023-01192-7

Mandal, A., & Ghosh, A. R. (2024). Role of artificial intelligence (AI) in fish growth and health status monitoring: A review on sustainable aquaculture. *Aquaculture International*, *32*(3), 2791–2820. https://doi.org/10.1007/s10499-023-01297-z

McIntosh, P., Barrett, L., Warren-Myers, F., Coates, A., Macaulay, G., Szetey, A., Robinson, N., White, C., Samsing, F., & Oppedal, F. (2022). Supersizing salmon farms in the coastal zone: A global analysis of changes in farm technology and location from 2005 to 2020. *Aquaculture*, *553*, 738046. https://doi.org/10.1016/j.aquaculture.2022.738046

Mowi. (2024). *Salmon farming industry handbook 2024*. Mowi.

Mustapha, U. F., Alhassan, A. W., Jiang, D. N., & Li, G. L. (2021). Sustainable aquaculture development: A review on the roles of cloud computing, internet of things and artificial intelligence (CIA). *Reviews in Aquaculture*, *13*(4), 2076–2091. https://doi.org/10.1111/raq.12559

Natek, S., & Lesjak, D. (2021). Knowledge management systems and tacit knowledge. *International Journal of Innovation and Learning*, *29*(2), 166–180.

Naylor, R., Fang, S., & Fanzo, J. (2023). A global view of aquaculture policy. *Food Policy*, *116*, 102422. https://doi.org/10.1016/j.foodpol.2023.102422

Nehring, R. (2022). The Brazilian green revolution. *Political Geography*, *95*, 102574. https://doi.org/10.1016/j.polgeo.2021.102574

Nesbø, O., & Westeren, K. I. (2018). Innovations and knowledge transfers in aquaculture production in Norway and Chile. In *European conference on knowledge management, ECIE.*

Newton, K., & Zmerli, S. (2011). Three forms of trust and their association. *European Political Science Review*, *3*(2), 169–200.

Nonaka, I., & Takeuchi, H. (1995). *The knowledge creating company: How Japanese companies create the dynamics of innovation*. Oxford University Press.

Nonås, S. V., & Bratseth, K. O. (2023). *Open Innovation and Knowledge Sharing-Towards a sustainable offshore aquaculture* [Master's thesis. University of Stavanger.

North, K., & Kumta, G. (2018). *Knowledge management: Value creation through organizational learning*. Springer.

Overton, K., Dempster, T., Oppedal, F., Kristiansen, T. S., Gismervik, K., & Stien, L. H. (2019). Salmon lice treatments and salmon mortality in Norwegian aquaculture: A review. *Reviews in Aquaculture*, *11*(4), 1398–1417. https://doi.org/10.1111/raq.12299

Polanyi, M. (1962). *Personal knowledge: Towards a post-critical philosophy*. Chicago University Press.

Popper, K. (2005). *The logic of scientific discovery*. Routledge.

Riege, A. (2005). Three dozen knowledge sharing barriers managers must consider. *Journal of Knowledge Management*, *9*(3), 18–35.

Sarker, P. K. (2023). Microorganisms in fish feeds, technological innovations, and key strategies for sustainable aquaculture. *Microorganisms*, *11*(2). https://doi.org/10.3390/microorganisms11020439

Scheepers, R., Venkitachalam, K., & Gibbs, M. R. (2004). Knowledge strategy in organizations: Refining the model of Hansen, Nohria and Tierney. *The Journal of Strategic Information Systems*, *13*(3), 201–222.

Solow, R. (1993). An almost practical step toward sustainability. *Resources Policy*, *19* (3), 162–172.

Stige, L. C., Qviller, L., Viljugrein, H., & Tavornpanich, S. (2024). A salmon lice prediction model. *Preventive Veterinary Medicine*, 106405. https://doi.org/10.1016/j.prevetmed.2024.106405

Stiglitz, J. (2003). Towards a new paradigm of development. In *Making globalization good: The moral challenges of global capitalism* (pp. 76–107). Oxford University Press.

Stiklestad, T., Westeren, K. I., & Yeong, M. (2019). Knowledge utilization, communication and innovations in aquaculture in an international perspective. In *International conference on intellectual capital and knowledge management and organisational learning*. ECIE.

Tsoukas, H. (2005). Do we really understand tacit knowledge. In M. E.-S. a. M. A. Lyles (Ed.), *Handbook of organizational learning and knowledge* (pp. 1–18). Blackwell.

United Nations. (1987). *Report of the world commission on environment and development: Our common future.*

Vadari, S., & Desik, P. A. (2021). The role of AI/ML in enhancing knowledge management systems. *IUP Journal of Knowledge Management*, *19*(2), 7–31.

van Nes, S., Imsland, A. K. D., & Jones, S. R. (2025). Salmon lice biology, environmental factors, and smolt behaviour with implications for the Norwegian salmon farming management system: A critical review. *Reviews in Aquaculture*, *17* (1), e12953. https://doi.org/10.1111/raq.12953

Virapat, C. (2022). The current challenges of sustainable aquaculture in the Asia-pacific region and the measures recommended. *Asia-Pacific Journal of Rural Development*, *32*(2), 207–216.

Wang, Q., Li, Z., Gui, J.-F., Liu, J., Ye, S., Yuan, J., & De Silva, S. S. (2018). Paradigm changes in freshwater aquaculture practices in China: Moving towards achieving environmental integrity and sustainability. *Ambio*, *47*, 410–426.

Wei, Y., Duan, Y., & An, D. (2022). Monitoring fish using imaging sonar: Capacity, challenges and future perspective. *Fish and Fisheries*, *23*(6), 1347–1370. https://doi.org/10.1111/faf.12693

Westeren, K. I. (2017). Epistemological perspectives in the analysis of human capital and human assets and the development of the knowledge-based economy. In *Human capital and assets in the networked world* (pp. 3–18). Emerald Publishing Limited.

Westeren, K. I. (2023). Hvordan kan innovative merdteknologier bidra til mer bærekraftig produksjon innen akvakultur?. In *Samskapt bærekraft i norsk arbeidsliv* (pp. 126–149). Universitetsforlaget.

Westeren, K. I. (2025a). Perspectives on the concepts of the circular economy and circular bioeconomy. In *Research handbook on innovation for a circular bioeconomy*. Edward Elgar Publishing. https://doi.org/10.4337/9781035307968.00010

Westeren, K. I. (2025b). New innovative solutions for waste management as part of a circular production setup in salmon-based aquaculture. In *Research handbook on innovation for a circular bioeconomy*. Edward Elgar Publishing. https://doi.org/10.4337/9781035307968.00022

Westeren, K. I., Cader, H., de Fátima Sales, M., Similä, J. O., & Staduto, J. (2018). *Competitiveness and knowledge: An international comparison of traditional firms*. Routledge. https://doi.org/10.4324/9781315625331

Westeren, K. I., Helbæk, M., & Korsøen, Ø. (2022). The use of algorithm-assisted feeding for innovation and increased productivity in aquaculture. In *European conference on innovation and entrepreneurship, ECIE*.

Wiig, K. M. (1997). Knowledge management: An introduction and perspective. *Journal of Knowledge Management*, *1*(1), 6–14. https://doi.org/10.1108/13673279710800682

Yang, S. S. (2024). *The impact of artificial intelligence on knowledge management practices* Lappeenranta–Lahti University of Technology LUT].

Ytrestøyl, T., Aas, T. S., & Åsgård, T. (2015). Utilisation of feed resources in production of Atlantic salmon (Salmo salar) in Norway. *Aquaculture*, *448*, 365–374. https://doi.org/10.1016/j.aquaculture.2015.06.023

Zhou, C., Xu, D., Lin, K., Sun, C., & Yang, X. (2018). Intelligent feeding control methods in aquaculture with an emphasis on fish: A review. *Reviews in Aquaculture*, *10*(4), 975–993. https://doi.org/10.1111/raq.12218

Chapter 6

Transforming Knowledge Management Through Synergistic Artificial Intelligence–Human Collaboration

Viraj Dawarka[a] *and Geshwaree Huzooree*[b]

[a]University of Staffordshire, UK
[b]Edinburgh Napier University, UK

ABSTRACT

As organizations increasingly navigate the complexities of the digital age, the incorporation of artificial intelligence (AI) into knowledge management (KM) frameworks is becoming indispensable for the attainment of sustained competitive advantage. This chapter explores the transformative capabilities of AI within KM, underscoring the pivotal significance of human–AI collaboration. We will investigate how emerging technologies, including AI, machine learning (ML) and natural language processing (NLP), can enhance key KM dimensions: the creation, storage, retrieval, sharing and application of knowledge. Furthermore, the chapter considers the essential contributions of human expertise, contextual understanding and decision-making in KM practices. By elucidating the synergy between the advantages of AI, like scalability, data analysis, human competencies, creativity and empathy, the chapter further explores specific implementations of AI–human collaboration, encompassing automated knowledge repositories for knowledge generation, NLP for knowledge retrieval and tailored recommendations for knowledge application. We will also address the ethical challenges and implications that accompany AI integration, focusing on issues such as bias, the need for transparency, trust in AI systems, data privacy and the balance between human oversight and AI control. Finally, we outline practical implications for organizations aiming to empower talent, create AI-friendly infrastructures and streamline knowledge processes to foster successful human–AI partnerships. We conclude by discussing the future of AI–human collaboration in KM, identifying

AI-Driven Knowledge Management Assets, Volume 2, 105–131

Published under exclusive licence by Emerald Publishing Limited
doi:10.1108/978-1-83662-778-420261006

emerging trends and the long-term benefits of integrating AI into organizational learning and innovation.

Keywords: Knowledge management (KM); AI–human collaboration; artificial intelligence (AI); AI ethics in knowledge management; cross-functional knowledge exchange

Introduction

The value of knowledge management (KM) in the contemporary sphere of artificial intelligence (AI) is gradually acknowledged as organizations work to effectively capitalize on AI technologies. KM functions as a crucial foundational structure that bolsters the assimilation of AI into organizational processes, thereby promoting knowledge dissemination and fostering innovation. This interconnection is vital for optimizing the advantages of AI while simultaneously addressing its inherent constraints. KM operates as a strategic framework for AI integration, wherein it facilitates the adoption of AI by offering guidelines for its implementation within business communications, thereby underscoring the necessity for skills enhancement and knowledge exchange (Iaia et al., 2023). Sophisticated KM systems that integrate semantic reasoning possess the potential to augment data accessibility and analytical capabilities, consequently enhancing decision-making processes across sectors such as life sciences (Taherdoost & Madanchian, 2023). The integration of AI into KM creates a self-reinforcing cycle of knowledge activities, thereby enhancing the effectiveness of knowledge flows and the potential for innovation within organizations (Fowler, 2000). To fully harness the capabilities inherent in digital knowledge engineering, organizations are compelled to confront challenges in data management and the integration of technology. Although AI possesses the capacity to replicate human judgement, it is incapable of supplanting emotional intelligence, which underscores the imperative for a judicious approach in the practices of KM (Iaia et al., 2023). In contrast, there exists a perspective suggesting that the swift advancement of AI may surpass the evolution of KM practices, potentially resulting in discrepancies in the sharing and application of knowledge. This emphasizes the critical need for the ongoing modification of KM strategies to align with the rapid progression of technological innovations.

The rise of digital technologies has greatly influenced KM approaches in a wide range of sectors, especially in the contexts of education and engineering. These technologies enhance access to knowledge, promote collaborative efforts and optimize KM processes, ultimately resulting in heightened innovation and a competitive edge. The subsequent sections delineate the principal effects of these technologies on KM. A significant effect of these technologies on KM pertains to augmented access and adaptability, wherein digital technologies afford learners the ability to engage with extensive open-source knowledge repositories, thereby enabling flexible and individualized learning experiences (Gurukkal, 2023). This level of accessibility fosters the establishment of global learning communities, thereby encouraging interactive and reciprocal learning (Gurukkal, 2023). Furthermore, there exists an enhancement in KM processes, as in the field of engineering, digital technologies facilitate four essential KM processes: creation, storage and retrieval, sharing and application (Yao et al., 2023). Technologies function as repositories, communication environments and boundary objects, thereby augmenting the overall efficacy of KM practices. Moreover, it facilitates innovation and competitive advantage, wherein knowledge digitization is associated with enhanced innovation performance within organizations, with attributes such as codability and generativity serving pivotal roles (Cheng et al., 2023). A comprehensive strategy towards KM, which incorporates digital technologies, can generate substantial organizational value and competitive benefits (Yao et al., 2023). Conversely, although digital technologies bolster KM, challenges including cultural impediments and the necessity for a unified strategy continue to be widespread. Organizations are required to navigate these challenges to fully capitalize on the advantages presented by emerging technologies in KM practices.

Human–AI collaboration is increasingly acknowledged as a fundamental component in the field of KM, especially for addressing multifaceted and exploratory tasks that necessitate both human cognitive insights and AI capabilities. This collaborative effort enhances the processes of problem-solving, elevates decision-making efficacy and optimizes performance across a multitude of domains. Such collaboration is instrumental in hybrid problem-solving methodologies, particularly in exploratory tasks where the interplay between humans and AI enables organizations to confront complex challenges through hybrid strategies, including autonomous, sequential and interactive searches, which generate a spectrum of solutions (Raisch & Fomina, 2023). In the field of medical imaging, the amalgamation of expert knowledge with AI markedly enhances the detection of rare conditions, thereby illustrating the efficacy of collaborative frameworks within specialized domains (Kamboj et al., 2024). Furthermore, it contributes to the enhancement of task performance through AI delegation; permitting AI systems to assign tasks to human collaborators can improve performance and satisfaction, as it cultivates a sense of self-efficacy among human participants (Hemmer et al., 2023). Variables such as motivation and the provision of accurate information can significantly augment the effectiveness of human–AI collaborations, resulting in superior decision-making outcomes (Eisbach et al., 2023). Although human–AI collaboration presents a plethora of advantages, it is imperative to address potential disparities in trust and to ensure that AI systems operate with transparency and reliability to maximize their efficacy in KM.

Human–AI Collaboration in KM

The Role of AI in KM: Overview of Tools and Technologies

The role of AI in KM has evolved significantly in recent years, transforming the methods by which organizations capture, organize, store, share and apply knowledge. In the past, KM has emphasized manual methods concerning the governance of documents, expertise and information. In contemporary contexts, AI technologies facilitate the automation and enhancement of these processes, thereby augmenting the efficiency, precision and accessibility of knowledge within organizational frameworks. AI is not replacing human knowledge, but it fosters more effective collaboration between humans and machines, thereby unlocking insights, refining decision-making and optimizing workflows. AI is causing a revolution in KM by introducing a wide range of tools and technologies that improve knowledge capture, organization, sharing and application. These AI-driven technologies enable organizations to manage large amounts of information more efficiently, allow data-driven decision-making and encourage employee collaboration. The following section presents an overview of the key AI tools and technologies that are bringing change to the realm of KM.

Natural Language Processing

A branch of AI, namely natural language processing (NLP), examines how computers and human language interact, allowing machines to understand, interpret and produce human language (Rane et al., 2024a). NLP is used in KM to process and extract important data from unstructured content including emails, reports, documents and articles. The applications of NLP in KM encompass text extraction, where AI algorithms retrieve salient information from documents, identifying crucial phrases, terms or concepts. Document summarization represents another application of NLP in KM, wherein concise summaries are autonomously generated from extensive textual materials (Sawalha & Akinci, 2024). Furthermore, sentiment analysis serves as a viral application, where the emotional tone or sentiment of customer feedback, internal communications or social media interactions is conscientiously examined. Some examples of tools that may be used within this context include OpenAI GPT for content generation, IBM Watson NLP for natural language understanding and spaCy as an open-source NLP library (Raiaan et al., 2024).

Machine Learning

Machine learning (ML) allows systems to automatically learn from experience and improve without explicit programming. ML significantly improves the efficiency and accuracy of KM systems by automating tasks and providing predictive insights, which lead to better organizational performance and innovation (Smith, 2024). In KM, ML algorithms are very helpful for automating suggestions, forecasts and classification. The integration of ML into KM enables the analysis of big data, allowing organizations to manage knowledge as an asset effectively (Anshari et al., 2023). Predictive analytics, which uses historical data to forecast future knowledge gaps, recommendation systems, which suggest pertinent documents, experts or knowledge resources to users based on their needs, and content categorization, which automatically groups documents or content into predefined categories, are examples of applications in KM. Furthermore, ML enhances knowledge-sharing platforms by customizing content and anticipating user needs, thus enhancing user experience and collaboration (Akanbiemu, 2024). Examples of tools include Azure Machine Learning for predictive modelling, Amazon SageMaker for creating and deploying ML models and Google AutoML for creating and training bespoke models.

Semantic Search

In KM, semantic search refers to a system's capacity to comprehend and interpret user queries to improve the retrieval of pertinent data (Huang & Yuan, 2024). This method makes use of ontologies and structured data to better match user requests with existing knowledge, which eventually leads to more efficient decision-making and problem-solving across a range of fields. In contrast to conventional keyword-based search, semantic search uses AI to comprehend the context, intent and meaning of a query. This makes search results more accurate and relevant, particularly when users use alternative wording. Semantic search has several uses in KM, such as providing more precise search results by comprehending the user's purpose rather than simply matching keywords (Taherdoost & Madanchian, 2023) and knowledge discovery, which assists users in finding relevant information based on semantic links within documents (Huang & Yuan, 2024). Elasticsearch with AI integration for semantic search (Konda, 2024), Lucidworks Fusion for AI-powered search platform and Coveo for AI-powered enterprise search solution (Feng et al., 2024) are a few examples of technologies.

Chatbots and Virtual Assistants

Chatbots and virtual assistants driven by AI are transforming how workers access and engage with knowledge through the simplification of communication, the facilitation of information access and the encouragement of a culture of continuous learning. These tools offer conversational, real-time interfaces for information retrieval, question answering and repetitive job automation. Chatbots in KM assist staff members in rapidly locating resources, and answers in repositories, improving productivity and decision-making processes (Jo & Park, 2024; Sumbal & Amber, 2024). Routine chores like scheduling, reminders and basic data retrieval can be automated by virtual assistants. According to their areas of expertise, AI assistants can also aid staff members in locating specialists within the company through Expert Discovery. Among the often-used tools are IBM Watson Assistant for internal KM and customer service, Google Dialogflow for creating conversational AI systems, Microsoft Power Virtual Agents for creating chatbots and Intercom for knowledge automation and AI-based assistance (Sumbal & Amber, 2024).

Knowledge Graphs and Predictive Analytics

Semantic networks that depict the connections between objects, ideas or pieces of data are called knowledge graphs. Organizations can visualize, connect and explore intricate networks of knowledge across systems with the use of AI-driven knowledge graphs (Zheng et al., 2022). One use of knowledge graphs in KM is knowledge mapping, which aids in creating a visual depiction of the connections between various knowledge items, including documents and projects. It facilitates the identification and visualization of the connections among information, expertise and skills inside an organization (Guy, 2013). Moreover, it enables users to uncover related knowledge based on interconnected data points. Tools like Microsoft Azure Knowledge Graph for enterprise knowledge mapping, AWS Neptune for Amazon's managed graph database service and Neo4j for creating knowledge graphs can be utilized to do these tasks.

Predictive analytics technologies driven by AI assist businesses in understanding possible future events by analysing past data, user patterns and trends (Rane et al., 2024b). This is especially helpful for spotting new opportunities, user behaviours or knowledge gaps. Trend analysis is used in some KM use cases to forecast changes in industry trends, knowledge gaps or knowledge usage. Additionally, it aids in the identification of knowledge gaps by forecasting areas where there might be a lack of training or expertise. Tools such as Google AI for creating predictive models in KM systems, SAP Predictive Analytics for knowledge forecasting and IBM SPSS for predictive analytics in trend and pattern analysis are used in this context (Delen, 2020).

By enhancing knowledge-sharing quality, automating repetitive operations and providing insightful data, AI tools and technology are transforming KM. Organizations can better capture, organize and apply knowledge by utilizing AI-driven tools such as NLP, ML, Semantic Search, Chatbots, Knowledge Graphs and others. The role of AI in KM extends beyond task automation; it also involves embracing human decision-making and fostering better teamwork. The influence of AI on KM will only increase as it develops further, enabling additional intelligent and effective knowledge ecosystems that motivate innovation and business success.

The Role of Human Intelligence: Expertise and Decision-Making

The collaboration between human intelligence and AI is becoming more and more important as businesses include AI in their KM procedures. Human intelligence provides context, judgement and knowledge that AI cannot match, even while AI is strong at processing huge amounts of data, seeing patterns and automating repetitive jobs (Korteling et al., 2021). Knowledge production, sharing and decision-making become more dynamic and effective when human and AI strengths are combined. Human intelligence, particularly expertise and decision-making, continues to play a crucial role in KM. AI technologies are not meant to replace human abilities; rather, they are meant to enhance them. Collaboration between humans and AI allows organizations to take advantage of both the computing power of AI and the rich, varied knowledge that human experts bring to complicated issues (Dwivedi et al., 2021).

Human expertise is important in KM as they offer crucial insights that AI systems might overlook particularly in situations that are unclear or complicated. KM still heavily depends on human skill, especially when it comes to understanding, implementing and contextualizing knowledge in challenging real-world scenarios (Holtshouse, 2013). While AI can analyze data and identify trends, it frequently lacks the context required to completely comprehend the subtle aspects of a given business, circumstance or person. AI can gather and process large amounts of data, but people are better at combining these data with established knowledge and using experience and an awareness of organizational objectives to make decisions (Rajagopal et al., 2022). Humans are usually superior at handling ambiguous problems that call for judgement and creative thinking, even though AI may make suggestions or come up with answers. While AI tools can help organizations identify their areas of expertise, information transmission to others is still done by humans (Duan et al., 2019). An essential component of KM is the natural human exchange of knowledge through teamwork, mentoring or casual conversations. AI may compile data from scientific publications in a research setting, but scientists use their subject-matter knowledge to plan experiments and analyze findings.

As for decision-making, AI systems are good at processing data and producing insights, but they cannot completely replace a human's capacity for morally sound, context-sensitive and well-informed decision-making (Van Berkel et al., 2022). Human judgement is essential to the decision-making process, especially when ethics, values and ambiguity are involved. Human judgement plays a part in KM by enabling ethical decision-making about the sharing of information, the protection of knowledge and the management of privacy. Additionally, human judgement is needed to evaluate the dangers involved in putting AI-generated recommendations into practice. Furthermore, in KM, decision-making involves more than just operational effectiveness; it also involves matching knowledge strategies with long-term organizational objectives (Ramos Cordeiro et al., 2024). AI can recommend individuals in the hiring process based on their background and expertise, but human recruiters use their judgement to evaluate team dynamics, long-term potential and cultural fit.

In KM, human–AI collaboration aims to improve human intellect rather than replace it. Human intelligence gives judgement, context, creativity and moral decision-making, whereas AI offers speed, automation and data-driven insights. AI and humans work in harmony when they complement one another's abilities, which improves KM, creativity and decision-making.

The Synergy Between AI and Human Skills

Human–AI collaboration in KM improves decision-making and problem-solving techniques by utilizing the complementary qualities of artificial and human intelligence. One of the main forces behind creativity, productivity and decision-making in the contemporary workplace is the combination of AI and human abilities. In a variety of situations, especially educational and organizational ones, where AI can enhance rather than replace human capabilities, this synergy is essential. The following sections outline key aspects of this collaboration.

Enhancing Learning and Communication

Collaboration between humans and AI in KM has the potential to greatly improve communication and learning inside businesses. Organizations can create more productive learning environments and communication channels by fusing human skills like creativity, emotional intelligence and contextual awareness with AI's advantages, such as its capacity to process vast amounts of data and spot patterns. AI can help find and extract pertinent information from massive volumes of unstructured data. By promoting metacognitive abilities, AI technologies can help students learn, enabling teachers to cooperate with AI to teach vital workforce skills (Atchley et al., 2024). A more dynamic learning environment can be created by integrating AI into educational settings, which can enhance student–teacher collaboration and communication (Atchley et al., 2024). However, by providing contextual information, evaluating the material's applicability and using expertise that AI would find difficult to capture or encode, humans can improve the search process.

Collective Intelligence in Organizations

The combined problem-solving, decision-making and creative skills that arise when people work together and integrate their knowledge, skills and insights are referred to as collective intelligence in organizations. In the field of KM, collective intelligence assists companies in utilizing their human resources in conjunction with technical innovations such as AI to enhance learning, creativity and organizational success. By finding pertinent expertise, initiatives or subjects and encouraging relationships between individuals, AI may assist in dismantling organizational barriers and enabling more effective information exchange. When human insights and AI skills are combined, collective intelligence can be improved and better decisions can be made (Gupta et al., 2023). Compared to traditional approaches, organizations that use a hybrid approach to problem-solving and integrating human and AI efforts can provide more creative solutions (Raisch & Fomina, 2023). Platforms for collaboration powered by AI can suggest content, lead conversations or even build online communities around common interests or objectives. However, AI may not yet be able to entirely replace the social and emotional intelligence that humans offer to foster trust, promote information exchange and have meaningful interactions.

Task Performance and Satisfaction

AI is exceptionally effective at automating time-consuming, repetitive jobs. This could involve organizing knowledge repositories, identifying content or arranging documents in a KM setting. AI-powered solutions can also help with resource recommendations, predictive analytics and even report generation using historical data. Employees can concentrate their mental energies on higher-value jobs that call for human judgement by assigning certain chores to AI. It has been demonstrated that AI delegation in task management increases team members' self-efficacy, which in turn improves human work performance and satisfaction (Hemmer et al., 2023). To fully utilize AI's potential, organizations must adhere to the human–AI collaboration principles of relevance and diversity (Kolbjørnsrud, 2023). Humans contribute the vital abilities of decision-making, problem-solving and context-specific judgement, even though AI can automate many repetitive jobs. Human involvement is still vital for tasks requiring strategic thinking, ethics and sophisticated understanding. Workers evaluate, decipher and act upon AI-generated insights using their domain expertise. AI enables workers to perform more valuable, meaningful work by lessening the cognitive load of repetitive tasks. Employees may be more satisfied with their jobs because of this change since they will have more chances to solve problems creatively and be less frustrated by administrative or repetitive tasks. Although working together with AI has many advantages, there are concerns about relying too much on AI, which could eventually result in a decline in human abilities.

Applications of AI–Human Collaboration in KM

Knowledge Creation: Automated Repositories and Data Categorization

KM collaboration between AI and humans is transforming how businesses produce, classify and share knowledge. AI applications in knowledge creation like data categorization and automated repositories are significantly improving KM procedures (Tsui et al., 2000). In addition to automating procedures, these technologies are actively fostering innovation and knowledge advancement within organizations.

Knowledge repository management and organization can be significantly simplified with AI. Manual input and updates are frequently used in traditional KM systems, which can be tedious and prone to mistakes. Large volumes of data from many sources can be automatically categorized, tagged and indexed by AI-powered systems, especially those that use ML and NLP (Meesad & Mingkhwan, 2024). This guarantees that employees have easy access to pertinent knowledge, irrespective of its creation date or storage location. By examining fresh data, spotting patterns and drawing forth significant insights, AI systems can also update these repositories regularly, contributing to the development of a constantly evolving knowledge base.

The capacity of AI to classify data has revolutionary effects on KM. AI can identify themes, correlations and patterns in a wide range of content forms, such as emails, research papers and documents, by examining huge datasets. AI can categorize data into distinct groups using algorithms, which improves organization and searchability. In addition to being automated, this procedure can be tailored to the requirements of the company, enhancing the relevancy of search results and guaranteeing that knowledge is arranged logically for users in the future (Baviskar et al., 2021). Additionally, by recommending similar pieces of knowledge, AI systems can facilitate teamwork and promote a more integrated approach to knowledge development.

Knowledge Storage and Retrieval: Facilitating Knowledge Sharing through NLP

The collaboration between AI and humans in KM greatly improves the methods of knowledge storage and retrieval, especially with the application of NLP. This integration of AI and human skills promotes more effective and contextually appropriate knowledge sharing within organizations.

Traditional knowledge storage systems frequently depend on manual data entry, which can be labour-intensive and susceptible to mistakes. AI-powered solutions, particularly those utilizing NLP, enhance this procedure by automatically sorting, categorizing and tagging information according to its content and context (Sarker, 2022). NLP equips AI systems with the capability to comprehend human language on a more profound level, recognizing essential themes, entities and connections within documents (Wu et al., 2022). This allows the system to categorize and organize knowledge more intuitively and systematically, facilitating easier access to pertinent information for users when necessary. Over time, these systems can also evolve and learn from new information, ensuring that the knowledge repository adapts to the organization's evolving requirements.

NLP significantly improves the extraction of knowledge from extensive and intricate databases. Rather than depending exclusively on keyword-based searches, NLP-driven systems comprehend the intent behind inquiries, facilitating more precise and context-sensitive search outcomes (Nuccio & Mogno, 2023). By interpreting queries in natural language, users can engage with the system more seamlessly, without the requirement to structure their requests in a particular format (Chen et al., 2024). AI algorithms are also capable of evaluating user behaviour and past interactions, discerning which information holds the greatest relevance and customizing the search results accordingly. This approach reduces the time spent searching for information while enhancing the relevance of the retrieved knowledge.

By facilitating more effective storage and retrieval, NLP-driven AI systems enhance knowledge sharing among employees. These systems assist users in swiftly finding information, exchanging insights and working together on projects, thereby fostering a culture of perpetual learning and innovation within the organization. In conclusion, the collaboration between AI and humans, especially through NLP, is revolutionizing the ways organizations manage the storage, retrieval and sharing of knowledge, thereby improving both efficiency and effectiveness in KM practices.

Knowledge Sharing: Visualization Tools and Semantic Enrichment

Knowledge sharing has been profoundly changed by AI–human collaboration in KM, especially with the use of visualization tools and semantic enrichment. Organizations can better share insights thanks to these tools, which enhance team learning, decision-making and cooperation.

In KM systems, AI-driven visualization tools are quite useful, particularly when it comes to making complex data and knowledge easier to comprehend and use. These tools can analyze big datasets and display the findings in dynamic visual representations like graphs, heat maps and interactive dashboards by utilizing AI techniques like ML and data mining (Deekshith, 2020). Users may make better decisions by using these graphics to swiftly spot patterns, correlations and anomalies. AI, for instance, can recognize important findings from several studies and present them in a way that emphasizes their relevance and connections, facilitating knowledge sharing and helping staff members understand difficult ideas in a research-driven company (Acworth, 2008). Furthermore, interactive visualizations facilitate deeper insights and cooperative problem-solving by enabling users to examine data from many perspectives. This method facilitates communication, particularly in interdisciplinary teams.

Semantic enrichment enhances the context and relevance of data by adding meaning through AI, specifically NLP. Key concepts in knowledge repositories can be automatically identified and categorized by AI systems using entity recognition and semantic tagging. By offering deeper insights into the links between different data points, this semantic layer enhances the information and enables people to comprehend not only the content but also the implications and connections that drive it (Lan et al., 2021). AI can highlight ideas that users might not have first thought of, link similar documents and recommend pertinent resources, facilitating more efficient knowledge sharing. By ensuring that workers are not only obtaining information but also comprehending its significance in a larger organizational context, this contextualization enhances how they access and engage with shared knowledge. When used in parallel, visualization tools and AI-powered semantic enrichment make information more accessible, perceptive and connected, which promotes increased cooperation and creativity inside businesses.

Knowledge Application: Personalized Recommendations and Problem-Solving

Knowledge application has evolved because of AI–human collaboration in KM, especially through personalized recommendations and problem-solving skills. These technologies enable employees to resolve complex issues, obtain pertinent information quickly and make better decisions.

Personalized recommendations are one of the main ways AI improves knowledge application. To recommend specialized information, AI systems employ ML algorithms to examine a person's prior interactions, preferences and work habits. For instance, depending on a user's function, ongoing tasks or knowledge gaps, AI can suggest pertinent articles, case studies or training materials. By ensuring that workers can swiftly locate the most relevant information for their activities, these tailored recommendations save time and improve learning and productivity (Paleyes et al., 2022). Furthermore, AI systems are always learning and changing, improving their suggestions in response to user input and changing requirements. This results in a dynamic, adaptable environment for exchanging knowledge that suits each person's particular requirements.

AI is also important to KM systems' problem-solving capabilities. AI can process vast amounts of data to find patterns and insights that people would miss by utilizing NLP and advanced data analytics (Rane et al., 2024c). When an issue arises, staff members can ask AI systems for recommendations based on previous fixes, industry best practices or comparable issues that have arisen within the company. For instance, by examining similar cases or documents that deal with related concerns, AI-powered systems can find and suggest the best solutions, giving staff members a head start on solving challenging challenges. Additionally, AI can support creative problem-solving during brainstorming sessions by putting forward novel ideas or tying disparate pieces of information together (Boussioux et al., 2024). By providing tailored recommendations and assisting with problem-solving, AI–human collaboration improves knowledge application. By providing employees with timely access to relevant details, these technologies enhance both individual and organizational performance.

Challenges in Developing and Implementing AI-Based Knowledge Management Systems

As AI technology progresses, organizations are increasingly integrating AI-driven KM systems. However, this integration presents challenges such as technological adaptation, cost considerations, system compatibility and the need to update traditional KM practices. Successfully blending AI and KM requires a deep understanding of both fields and a strategic approach to align them effectively, ensuring that AI enhances existing KM workflows (Chowdhury et al., 2022).

Technical Challenges and Limitations

Integrating AI with KM presents several challenges, particularly AI's inability to capture tacit knowledge, which is implicit and experiential (Sanzogni et al., 2017). While AI and ML enhance KM by processing large datasets, they cannot autonomously generate or innovate knowledge (Vadari & Desik, 2021). A survey by Moradi & Dass (2022) found that only 37% of companies in business marketing have adopted AI, with barriers including low-quality data, privacy concerns and high integration costs.

A key challenge is handling unstructured data such as images and social media content, which lack standardized formats. Developing sophisticated algorithms to process such data requires significant expertise and resources (Chowdhury et al., 2022). Moreover, data quality directly impacts AI's reliability; poor data lead to biased or inaccurate results, necessitating rigorous cleaning and organization for effective decision-making (Bhbosale et al., 2020).

AI systems also lack creative problem-solving abilities and adaptability, making them unsuitable for tasks requiring innovation. Their reliance on pre-programmed algorithms limits flexibility, underscoring the need for precise objective-setting in KM applications (West & Allen, 2018).

Traditional KM systems often struggle to keep pace with AI advancements, leading to inefficiencies (Fteimi & Hopf, 2021). Integrating AI into KM requires substantial transformation, including updating knowledge storage and sharing processes, demanding significant investment (Bhbosale et al., 2020). Compatibility with existing systems and adaptability for future growth is critical, requiring technical expertise for successful implementation (Bharadiya, 2023; Taherdoost & Madanchian, 2023).

Ethical, Legal and Socio-Technical Considerations

Integrating AI into KM systems presents significant technical, ethical, legal and socio-technical complexities. Organizations must navigate challenges such as bias, data privacy, transparency and the socioeconomic impacts of automation while aligning these concerns with broader strategic goals (Carter et al., 2020; Munoko et al., 2020). A multi-faceted approach is crucial to mitigate risks and maximize AI's benefits.

A primary ethical concern in AI integration is data bias. AI systems rely on the datasets used during training, and any biases in these datasets can result in unfair or skewed outcomes. For example, incomplete or non-representative data can produce algorithms that fail to account for diverse contexts, populations or use cases, thereby perpetuating or exacerbating inequalities (Akter et al., 2021; Aquino, 2023; Ntoutsi et al., 2020). Mitigating bias requires continuous monitoring, robust dataset curation and algorithmic transparency. Regular audits can help identify and address biases, ensuring that AI models operate equitably and inclusively (Ferrara, 2023).

Data privacy and security are also critical concerns, as KM systems often manage vast amounts of sensitive information such as proprietary knowledge and employee records. AI's reliance on large datasets increases the risk of data breaches or misuse. Organizations must adopt rigorous data protection measures to comply with privacy regulations like the General Data Protection Regulation (GDPR) while maintaining user trust. Transparency about data collection, use and security is essential to ethical AI deployment (Bharadiya, 2023). Balancing data innovation with privacy laws requires nuanced policies and strong governance frameworks (Chowdhury et al., 2022).

Transparency extends beyond data practices to the AI decision-making process. Many AI systems, particularly those based on ML, operate as 'black boxes,' making it difficult for users to understand how decisions are made. Ensuring transparency is crucial for fostering user trust and accountability. Explainable AI methods aim to make decision-making more interpretable, allowing organizations to align AI outputs with ethical standards and organizational goals (Dwivedi et al., 2023; Kaplan & Haenlein, 2019). Incorporating user feedback and ensuring human oversight further enhance the accountability of AI-driven decisions (Tatineni & Allam, 2024).

The socio-economic implications of AI integration are also significant. Automation driven by AI can displace jobs, particularly in roles involving repetitive tasks. While automation frees workers to engage in more strategic or creative roles, it also risks workforce disruption. To address this, organizations must invest in upskilling and reskilling programs to help employees transition into roles that leverage human creativity alongside AI tools (Bhbosale et al., 2020). This approach helps ensure that AI adoption does not exacerbate social inequities but promotes a balanced partnership between humans and machines.

The rise of generative AI technologies like ChatGPT has sparked debates about authorship, originality and intellectual property. As AI contributes more to content creation and decision-making, distinguishing between human and AI outputs becomes challenging. This raises legal and ethical questions regarding accountability and intellectual property rights (Aydın & Karaarslan, 2023; Nah et al., 2023). Organizations need to establish clear guidelines to ensure that AI is used responsibly and respects human creativity.

AI integration must also align with organizational values and goals. Ethical AI deployment is not a one-size-fits-all approach; it must reflect the unique needs, values and cultural contexts of each organization. Cross-disciplinary collaboration between AI developers, ethicists, legal experts and business leaders is essential to ensure AI systems are designed and implemented in ways that uphold integrity and address ethical concerns (Olan et al., 2022).

Finally, AI's integration into KM systems requires rethinking traditional KM practices. Traditional approaches may lack the flexibility needed to keep pace with AI advancements, potentially leading to inefficiencies or underutilization of AI capabilities (Barrantes-Briceño et al., 2024; Fteimi & Hopf, 2021). Organizations must rethink how knowledge is created, stored and shared, embedding ethical principles into KM processes.

As AI systems continue to evolve, organizations face challenges related to intellectual property, liability and regulatory compliance. Defining accountability for AI decisions, especially when outcomes deviate from expectations, remains a grey area. Clear governance guidelines and regulatory frameworks are needed to mitigate risks and ensure compliance, ensuring organizations can responsibly harness AI's potential in KM systems (Piraianu et al., 2023; West & Allen, 2018).

Practical Implications

Empowering Talent for AI

As AI continues to evolve, organizations must adapt their workforce strategies to effectively integrate these technologies. This shift requires a rethinking of roles, skillsets and organizational structures to ensure that human workers are equipped to collaborate with AI systems in ways that maximize their potential.

Redefining Workforce Roles in the AI Field

The integration of AI into the workplace calls for a new understanding of workforce roles, moving beyond concepts like 'human-in-the-loop' AI, which often limits human involvement in supporting or correcting AI systems. Instead, human–AI partnerships should be seen as symbiotic, with humans actively shaping AI applications to meet real-world needs. Frontline workers play a crucial role in operationalizing AI, adapting its capabilities to the complex demands of their work. Rather than replacing human expertise, AI enhances decision-making, creativity and focus on high-value tasks. In customer service, for instance, AI handles routine queries, freeing agents to address complex cases requiring emotional intelligence. This shift transforms these roles into 'experience curators,' blending AI insights with strategic customer engagement. Similarly, in healthcare, AI diagnostic tools allow doctors to focus on nuanced care and empathetic interactions which emphasize human strengths. This evolving dynamic fosters a feedback loop where human expertise not only complements AI but also refines its outputs and integration into workflows. Workers train and improve AI models while ensuring alignment with organizational goals and ethics. Such partnerships create adaptive roles, evolving alongside advancements in AI and workplace demands.

Developing Skills for Knowledge-Centric AI Applications

To thrive in an AI-integrated workplace, knowledge workers must acquire skills that enable them to effectively collaborate with AI systems. AI is increasingly being used to automate routine tasks and provide insights into complex decision-making processes (Mishra, 2024). Consequently, workers must develop competencies that blend technical expertise with contextual knowledge. This dual competency involves not only understanding AI tools but also knowing how to interpret and apply their outputs meaningfully. The development of these skills requires an emphasis on interdisciplinary collaboration, critical thinking and workflow adaptation. For example, healthcare professionals and legal experts increasingly rely on AI for diagnostics and contract analysis. In these fields, the ability to combine AI insights with human judgement is crucial. Platforms like EdCast exemplify how AI can identify skill gaps and create tailored learning pathways, ensuring workers' capabilities align with the evolving demands of their respective sectors (Gryncewicz et al., 2023). Furthermore, the emergence of new roles such as 'knowledge scientists,' who curate data for strategic decisions, and 'AI champions,' who advocate for effective AI use, highlights the need for specialized skill sets. These roles integrate technical proficiency with leadership, business analysis and ethical considerations.

Cultivating AI Specialists

The rapid development of AI technologies has significantly increased the demand for specialized roles such as knowledge scientists and data scientists. These professionals are critical in bridging the gap between symbolic AI, which relies on rules and logic, and statistical AI approaches that leverage neural networks and ML (Doran et al., 2017). Knowledge scientists play a vital role in constructing knowledge graphs in structured representations of domain knowledge that improve the explainability and transparency of AI systems. These graphs complement training data by embedding contextual knowledge, making AI systems more interpretable and enhancing trust in AI decisions (Arrieta et al., 2020). Moreover, knowledge scientists are central to the adoption of AI within organizations. Their expertise in KM allows them to communicate the 'know-why' behind AI outputs, addressing any concerns and persuading stakeholders of the value of AI implementations (Von Krogh, 2018; Gkeredakis & Constantinides, 2019). This communication is essential for fostering organizational trust in AI systems, which is crucial for their successful deployment and continuous improvement. As AI technologies evolve, the role of knowledge scientists becomes even more critical in ensuring that AI solutions are aligned with organizational goals and ethical standards.

Cultivating AI Champions

AI champions are key agents of change within organizations, serving as advocates for AI's potential to augment human capabilities rather than replace them. These individuals are not just enthusiastic about AI but possess a deep understanding of both AI technologies and organizational processes. They are strategic thinkers who align AI capabilities with specific KM functions, demonstrating how AI can enhance decision-making and task quality across the organization. AI champions are essential for bridging the gap between technical advancements and business needs. They identify opportunities to leverage AI to streamline processes, improve knowledge sharing and enhance productivity. Effective AI champions also excel in business analysis and problem-solving, ensuring that AI initiatives address organizational challenges and deliver meaningful results (Davenport & Mahidhar, 2018; Sætra, 2022). Their ability to communicate the value of AI to diverse stakeholders, including those with varying levels of technical expertise, makes them indispensable in fostering organizational support for AI adoption. To cultivate AI champions, organizations often need to invest in training programmes that develop both technical and leadership skills. These individuals must be able to lead AI initiatives, facilitate cross-functional collaboration and drive cultural change within the organization.

Raising AI and Data Literacy in Organizations

As AI automates routine tasks, organizations must prioritize AI literacy to ensure employees can effectively leverage these systems. AI literacy extends beyond technical skills, requiring workers, including managers, to understand how AI systems function, the algorithms behind them and their decision-making processes. This knowledge enables employees to interpret AI-generated insights in context, ensuring AI complements rather than replaces human decision-making.

A deeper 'know-why' understanding, as described by Jarrahi et al. (2021, 2023), is essential for critically evaluating AI outputs and challenging them when necessary. Professionals must actively engage with AI results, as argued by Bersin and Zao-Sanders (2020) and Schmarzo (2023), rather than passively accepting them. Organizations can foster this critical engagement by promoting a culture of inquiry and continuous learning.

However, AI adoption often encounters resistance due to concerns about job displacement, lack of trust in algorithmic decision-making and uncertainty regarding AI's role in existing workflows. Overcoming these challenges requires a structured approach. One effective model is the technology acceptance model (Davis, 1989), which emphasizes perceived usefulness and ease of use as key factors influencing AI adoption. Organizations can enhance AI acceptance by demonstrating its tangible benefits and ensuring user-friendly interfaces that integrate seamlessly with established practices.

Additionally, Kotter's 8-Step Change Model (Kotter, 1995) provides a roadmap for navigating AI-driven transformation. Key steps include creating a sense of urgency around AI's value, building coalitions of AI champions and embedding AI literacy into organizational culture through continuous training and iterative feedback loops. By integrating AI education into professional development programs, organizations can mitigate resistance and foster a workforce that actively engages with AI tools.

By equipping employees with the skills to question and refine AI-driven decisions, organizations enable workers to play an active role in improving AI systems. This approach ensures AI evolves in alignment with ethical standards, organizational goals and workplace demands. Ultimately, AI literacy, coupled with strategic change management frameworks, strengthens organizational resilience, allowing businesses to adapt to AI advancements while maintaining trust, efficiency and human oversight.

Creating AI-Friendly Infrastructure

Optimizing Data Quality

The effectiveness of AI systems relies on high-quality data, which is crucial for training and operation (Paschen et al., 2020). While deep learning applications benefit from large datasets, data quality is equally important. Organizations must prioritize building accurate, consistent and comprehensive datasets to support AI effectively. Achieving this requires cross-functional collaboration to eliminate data silos and ensure seamless integration.

Data quality optimization involves multiple stages, including data collection, cleaning, storage, governance and security (Palakurti, 2024). Each step ensures reliable, unbiased data for training AI models. Additionally, organizations should integrate both internal data and external insights, such as market trends, to create richer datasets. This enhances AI's ability to make robust, accurate decisions.

Continuous improvement of data quality is vital. AI models are only as effective as the data they are trained on, necessitating iterative refinement and validation. As AI technologies advance, data sources must adapt to include real-time, contextually relevant information. This ensures AI systems can respond to changing environments and provide precise, actionable insights. By focusing on high-quality, dynamic data, organizations can maximize the potential of their AI initiatives while maintaining accuracy and reliability.

Enforcing Transparency and Ethics

As AI becomes integral to organizational operations, ensuring transparency and ethical deployment is critical. Many AI models, particularly in business, function as 'black boxes,' making it difficult for stakeholders to understand decision-making processes. This lack of interpretability can lead to distrust and hinder adoption. Prioritizing transparency ensures AI decisions are explainable, fostering trust and accountability (Ahlawat et al., 2024; Gaske, 2023).

Organizations must implement mechanisms that clarify AI outputs, especially in high-stakes areas like healthcare, finance and customer service. Supervised learning models, which rely on labelled data, offer greater transparency by providing traceable decision pathways. However, these models require precise data preparation and cross-functional collaboration to achieve interpretability (Ahlawat et al., 2024).

Alongside transparency, embedding ethical standards is essential. AI systems must prioritize fairness, avoid bias and protect privacy throughout development and deployment. Organizations should establish guidelines ensuring AI aligns with legal and societal values, addressing risks like discrimination or privacy violations. By emphasizing transparency and ethics, organizations can build trust, enhance accountability and ensure AI systems contribute positively to both business goals and societal expectations.

Using Knowledge Graphs for Knowledge Forecasting

Modern KM faces the challenge of harnessing vast, dynamically generated, and often unstructured data. While rich in potential insights, these data require a structured approach for effective analysis. Knowledge graphs offer a solution by organizing complex relationships between data points, terms and entities, enabling advanced AI-driven analysis (Ji et al., 2021). These graphs capture data and their interconnections, creating a comprehensive view of an organization's information landscape.

For instance, knowledge graphs can model relationships between supply chain logistics, cost fluctuations and external factors like weather conditions. This enables businesses to predict how variables influence each other, helping forecast disruptions or opportunities. AstraZeneca uses knowledge graphs to enhance drug discovery by mapping relationships between compounds, diseases and biological pathways, driving informed research decisions (Fang et al., 2024).

AI plays a critical role in creating and evolving knowledge graphs, dynamically interpreting and assigning meaning to data relationships. This synergy allows organizations to extract actionable insights from diverse, unstructured data sources, enhancing decision-making and operational efficiency. By integrating knowledge graphs, businesses can unlock the full potential of their data in real time.

Streamlining Knowledge Processes for Human–AI Collaboration

Fostering Collaborative Learning Between Humans and AI

Effective collaboration between humans and AI in KM requires a continuous exchange of insights and corrective feedback. While AI excels at processing large datasets and identifying patterns, it lacks the nuanced, contextual understanding essential for managing knowledge effectively. Human oversight is crucial to guide AI applications and address their limitations.

AI's capabilities depend on the quality and scope of the data it is trained on, making it susceptible to perpetuating or amplifying biases within organizational structures.

For instance, in recruitment processes, AI systems trained on historical hiring data may inadvertently reflect past biases, leading to unfair candidate evaluations. Human intervention is essential to identify and mitigate these risks. Organizations like IBM have implemented bias detection frameworks that analyze AI-driven hiring decisions, ensuring equitable treatment across diverse candidate pools. Furthermore, in the financial sector, AI algorithms are commonly used for credit scoring and fraud detection. Companies like Mastercard have integrated human review panels to evaluate flagged transactions, balancing AI's efficiency with human judgement. These biases can distort AI-generated knowledge, presenting it as objective when it may carry inherent flaws from human decision-making processes. Human intervention is essential to identify and mitigate these risks.

Establishing a feedback loop where human experts regularly review AI outputs is vital. Such audits ensure the accuracy and fairness of AI-driven insights while allowing algorithms to be adjusted to align with evolving organizational goals and values. This approach positions AI as a complementary tool, enhancing human expertise while maintaining objectivity and transparency. By combining AI's analytical power with human oversight, organizations can ensure the knowledge generated is accurate, relevant and ethically sound (Metaxa et al., 2021).

Promoting Cross-Disciplinary Collaboration

Cross-disciplinary collaboration is pivotal in effectively implementing AI-driven KM systems, as it facilitates the integration of domain-specific expertise with algorithmic proficiency. The effective deployment of AI within organizations demands not only technological capabilities but also a deep understanding of the business context in which AI operates. This integration requires collaboration between AI specialists, data scientists, domain experts and frontline workers who can bridge the gap between the technical and operational aspects of AI systems (Mohapatra, 2020). By leveraging the strengths of various disciplines, organizations can ensure that AI tools are not only technically robust but also aligned with the unique needs and nuances of specific business processes.

Moreover, interdisciplinary teams play a crucial role in continuously refining and adapting workflows to accommodate AI's capabilities. This requires ongoing dialogue between technology and domain experts to ensure that AI systems augment rather than replace existing knowledge activities. Such collaboration empowers knowledge workers to make informed decisions about how to integrate AI solutions into their workflows, fostering trust and ownership of the technology. It also promotes a culture where AI is seen as a partner in enhancing human decision-making, rather than as a tool that imposes top-down directives. Ultimately, cross-functional collaboration ensures that AI adoption is both effective and sustainable, driving organizational growth and innovation (Paschen et al., 2020).

Redesign and Revamp Processes

The process redesign in organizations must balance automation with human augmentation to maximize the effectiveness of AI technologies. Rather than viewing automation as a replacement for human expertise, it should be seen as an enabler that liberates knowledge workers from repetitive and time-consuming tasks. By automating mundane activities, such as scheduling meetings or sorting invoices, AI systems can free up valuable human resources to focus on more strategic, complex and creative tasks (El-Farr & Kertechian, 2024). For example, AI can identify discrepancies in financial data, such as missing order numbers or inconsistencies in invoices, enabling staff to address these issues more efficiently and redirect their efforts towards higher-value decision-making.

When redesigning organizational processes, it is essential to integrate both AI and human capabilities in ways that enhance decision-making and knowledge-sharing. Organizations should consider processes where AI and humans collaborate in parallel, allowing both parties to contribute their strengths. For instance, AI can propose solutions, while humans validate and refine them based on contextual knowledge. Alternatively, in a sequential approach, humans can verify and improve AI-generated decisions, fostering an ongoing feedback loop that promotes mutual learning. Such a dual approach not only strengthens decision-making but also enhances transparency and trust, as AI's logic is made explainable, allowing human workers to better understand and engage with the AI's reasoning (Marr, 2019).

Conclusion

This chapter explores how AI–human collaboration is reshaping KM, offering opportunities and challenges for organizations in a data-driven world. AI enhances KM by automating processes, generating insights and driving innovation. However, it cannot fully manage tacit knowledge, which depends on human intuition, experience and context. This limitation underscores the need for systems where AI complements human decision-making rather than replacing it.

AI's reliance on high-quality, unbiased and comprehensive data is a significant challenge. Poor data quality can distort AI-driven insights, while ethical concerns such as transparency, accountability and data privacy further complicate integration. Organizations must address these issues through robust governance frameworks to ensure fairness, inclusivity and trust in AI systems. Establishing a collaborative culture is equally critical, encouraging employees to see AI as an augmentative tool rather than a threat to their roles.

Future research should focus on practical implementations of AI–human collaboration in KM. Case studies across industries could highlight best practices, challenges and comparative insights between AI-driven and traditional KM models. Advancing AI systems to better handle tacit knowledge, using tools like NLP and interactive AI, could bridge gaps between explicit and tacit domains, preserving the creativity and innovation inherent in human expertise.

Ethical and socio-technical considerations also require sustained attention. Organizations must address concerns about data privacy, intellectual property and the equitable distribution of AI benefits. Interdisciplinary research can provide holistic solutions to these challenges, combining expertise from AI, KM, ethics and organizational behaviour.

Generative AI tools like ChatGPT hold particular promise in KM. These tools can create knowledge artefacts, assist in brainstorming and enhance decision-making. Research should explore their integration into collaborative environments while addressing ethical questions, such as transparency and authorship dilemmas, to build trust.

Cultural and organizational factors play a crucial role in successful AI adoption. Resistance to change, lack of trust in AI and inadequate training are common barriers. Future studies should examine strategies to foster adaptability, trust and continuous learning in organizations. Longitudinal research tracking AI's long-term impact on KM practices, performance and innovation could offer deeper insights.

In summary, AI–human collaboration has immense potential to revolutionize KM. By addressing challenges and pursuing targeted research, organizations can create systems that leverage AI and human strengths, driving adaptive, ethical and innovative knowledge practices.

References

Acworth, E. B. (2008). University–industry engagement: The formation of the knowledge integration community (KIC) model at the Cambridge-MIT Institute. *Research Policy*, *37*(8), 1241–1254.

Ahlawat, A., Winecoff, A., & Mayer, J. (2024). Minimum viable ethics: From institutionalizing industry AI governance to product impact. *arXiv preprint arXiv: 2409.06926*.

Akanbiemu, A. A. (2024). Enhancing knowledge sharing platforms with Machine Learning. *Journal of Applied Sciences, Information and Computing*, *5*(1), 40–46.

Akter, S., Grace, M., Shahriar, S., Katina, M., Yogesh, K. ., D., John, D., & Shen, K. N. (2021). Algorithmic bias in data-driven innovation in the age of AI. *International Journal of Information Management*, *60*, 102387.

Anshari, M., Syafrudin, M., Tan, A., Fitriyani, N. L., & Alas, Y. (2023). Optimisation of knowledge management (KM) with machine learning (ML) enabled. *Information*, *14*(1), 35. https://doi.org/10.3390/info14010035

Aquino, Y. S. (2023). Making decisions: Bias in artificial intelligence and data-driven diagnostic tools. *Australian Journal of General Practice*, *52*(7), 439–442.

Arrieta, A. B., Natalia, D.-R., Javier, D. S., Adrien, B., Siham, T., Alberto, B., & Chatila, R. (2020). Explainable Artificial Intelligence (XAI): Concepts, taxonomies, opportunities and challenges toward responsible AI. *Information Fusion*, *58*, 82–115.

Atchley, P., Pannell, H., Wofford, K., Hopkins, M., & Atchley, R. A. (2024). Human and AI collaboration in the higher education environment: Opportunities and concerns. *Cognitive Research: Principles and Implications*, *9*(1), 20.

Aydın, Ö., & Karaarslan, E. (2023). Is ChatGPT leading generative AI? What is beyond expectations? *Academic Platform Journal of Engineering and Smart Systems*, *11*(3), 118–134.

Barrantes-, B., Christian, E., Fernando César Almada, S., & Marcelo, S. N. (2024). Bridging excellence, knowledge management and sustainability: Introducing the 'Knowledge Management Excellence Model 21', a model for sustainable development goals alignment. *Journal of Cleaner Production*, *455*, 142326.

Baviskar, D., Ahirrao, S., Potdar, V., & Kotecha, K. (2021). Efficient automated processing of the unstructured documents using artificial intelligence: A systematic literature review and future directions. *IEEE Access*, *9*, 72894–72936.

Bersin, J., & Zao-Sanders, M. (2020, 02 12). *Analytics and Data Science - boost your team's data literacy*. Retrieved 04 12, 2025, from Harvard Business Review: https://hbr.org/2020/02/boost-your-teams-data-literacy

Bharadiya, J. P. (2023). Artificial intelligence and the future of Web 3.0: Opportunities and challenges ahead. *American Journal of Computer Science and Technology*, *6*(2), 91–96.

Bhbosale, S., Vinayak, P., & Zameer, M. (2020). Advantages and disadvantages of artificial intelligence. *Aayushi International Interdisciplinary Research Journal, 77*, 227–230.

Boussioux, L., Lane, J. N., Zhang, M., Jacimovic, V., & Lakhani, K. R. (2024). The crowdless future? Generative AI and creative problem-solving. *Organization Science, 35*(5), 1589–1607.

Carter, S. M., Wendy, R., Khin, T. W., Helen, F., Bernadette, R., & Nehmat, H. (2020). The ethical, legal and social implications of using artificial intelligence systems in breast cancer care. *The Breast, 49*, 25–32.

Chen, J., Liu, Z., Huang, X., Wu, C., Liu, Q., Jiang, G., & Zheng, K. (2024). *When large language models meet personalization: Perspectives of challenges and opportunities* (Vol. 27, 4, p. 42). World Wide Web.

Cheng, Q., Liu, Y., Peng, C., He, X., Qu, Z., & Dong, Q. (2023). Knowledge digitization: Characteristics, knowledge advantage and innovation performance. *Journal of Business Research, 163*, 113915.

Chowdhury, S., Pawan, B., Prasanta, K. D., Sian, J.-E., & Amelie, A. (2022). AI-employee collaboration and business performance: Integrating knowledge-based view, socio-technical systems and organisational socialisation framework. *Journal of Business Research, 144*, 31–49.

Davenport, T. H., & Mahidhar, V. (2018, 05 10). *What's your cognitive strategy*? Retrieved 04 12, 2025, from MIT Sloan Management Review https://sloanreview.mit.edu/article/whats-your-cognitive-strategy/

Davis, F. D. (1989). Technology acceptance model: TAM. In M. N. Al-Suqri & A. S. Al-Aufi (eds), Information seeking behavior and technology adoption. *IGI global* (pp. 205–219).

Deekshith, A. (2020). AI-enhanced data science: Techniques for improved data visualization and interpretation. *International Journal of Creative Research In Computer Technology and Design, 2*(2).

Delen, D. (2020). Predictive analytics uCertify labs access code card: Data mining. In *Machine learning and data science for practitioners*. FT Press.

Doran, D., Sarah, S., & Besold, T. R. (2017). What does explainable AI really mean? A new conceptualization of perspectives. *arXiv preprint arXiv:1710.00794*.

Duan, Y., Edwards, J. S., & Dwivedi, Y. K. (2019). Artificial intelligence for decision making in the era of Big Data–evolution, challenges and research agenda. *International Journal of Information Management, 48*, 63–71.

Dwivedi, R., Devam, D., Het, N., Smiti, S., Rana, O., Pankesh, P., & Bin, Q. (2023). Explainable AI (XAI): Core ideas, techniques, and solutions. *ACM Computing Surveys, 55*(9), 1–33.

Dwivedi, Y. K., Hughes, L., Ismagilova, E., Aarts, G., Coombs, C., Crick, T. ., & Williams, M. D. (2021). Artificial Intelligence (AI): Multidisciplinary perspectives on emerging challenges, opportunities, and agenda for research, practice and policy. *International Journal of Information Management, 57*, 101994.

Eisbach, S., Langer, M., & Hertel, G. (2023). Optimizing human-AI collaboration: Effects of motivation and accuracy information in AI-supported decision-making. *Computers in Human Behavior: Artificial Humans, 1*(2), 100015. https://doi.org/10.1016/j.chbah.2023.100015

El-Farr, H., & Kertechian, K. S. (2024). Knowledge management and knowledge leadership in the fourth industrial revolution: Resolving the automation-augmentation paradox. In *In the changing landscape of workplace and workforce.*

Fang, C., Gustavo, A. A., Ioannis, K., Mohammad, H. K., Etai Jacob, K. C., & Natasha, M. (2024). Integrating knowledge graphs into machine learning models for survival prediction and biomarker discovery in patients with non–small-cell lung cancer. *Journal of Translational Medicine*, *22*(1), 726.

Feng, C. M., Botha, E., & Pitt, L. (2024). From HAL to GenAI: Optimizing chatbot impacts with CARE. *Business Horizons*, *67*(5), 537–548.

Ferrara, E. (2023). Fairness and bias in artificial intelligence: A brief survey of sources, impacts, and mitigation strategies. *Science*, *6*(1).

Fowler, A. (2000). The role of AI-based technology in support of the knowledge management value activity cycle. *The Journal of Strategic Information Systems*, *9* (2–3), 107–128.

Fteimi, N., & Konstantin, H. (2021). Knowledge management in the era of artificial intelligence: Developing an integrative framework. In *29th European Conference on information systems 2021.* Marrakech, Morocco: ECIS 2021 Proceedings.

Gaske, M. R. (2023). *Artificial intelligence regulation, minimum viable products, and partitive innovation* (Vol. 73, p. 17). Emory LJ Online.

Gkeredakis, M., & Constantinides, P. (2019). Phenomenon-based problematization: Coordinating in the digital era. *Information and Organization*, *29*(3), 100254.

Gryncewicz, W., Pilch, A., & Ryszard, Z. (2023). Organizational, technological and economic facets of AI implementation in HRM trainings. In *CEUR Workshop proceedings* (Vol. 3624).

Gupta, P., Nguyen, T. N., Gonzalez, C., & Woolley, A. W. (2023). Fostering collective intelligence in human–AI collaboration: Laying the groundwork for COHUMAIN. *Topics in Cognitive Science*. https://doi.org/10.1111/tops.12679

Gurukkal, R. (2023). Digital influx in knowledge fields. *Higher Education for the Future*, *10*(1), 7–10.

Guy, I. (2013). Mining and analyzing the enterprise knowledge graph. In *Proceedings of the 22nd International Conference on world wide Web* (pp. 497–498).

Hemmer, P., Westphal, M., Schemmer, M., Vetter, S., Vössing, M., & Satzger, G. (2023). Human-AI collaboration: The effect of AI delegation on human task performance and task satisfaction. In *In Proceedings of the 28th International Conference on intelligent user interfaces* (pp. 453–463). https://doi.org/10.1145/3581641.3584052

Holtshouse, D. K. (2013). *Information technology for knowledge management.* Springer Science & Business Media.

Huang, Z., & Yuan, L. (2024). Enhancing learning and exploratory search with concept semantics in online healthcare knowledge management. *Expert Systems with Applications*, *237*, 121558.

Iaia, L., Nespoli, C., Vicentini, F., Pironti, M., Genovino, C. (2024, January 5). Supporting the implementation of AI in business communication: The role of knowledge management. *Journal of Knowledge Management*, *28*(1), 85–95. https://doi.org/10.1108/JKM-12-2022-0944

Jarrahi, M. H., Askay, D., Eshraghi, A., & Smith, P. (2023). Artificial intelligence and knowledge management: A partnership between human and AI. *Business Horizons*, *66*(1), 87–99.

Jarrahi, M. H., Gemma, N., Min Kyung, L., Christine, T. W., Eliscia, K., & Will, S. (2021). Algorithmic management in a work context. *Big Data & Society*, *8*(2), 20539517211020332.

Ji, S., Shirui, P., Erik, C., Pekka, M., & Philip S, Y. (2021). A survey on knowledge graphs: Representation, acquisition, and applications. *IEEE Transactions on Neural Networks and Learning Systems*, *33*(2), 494–515.

Jo, H., & Park, D. H. (2024). AI in the workplace: Examining the effects of ChatGPT on information support and knowledge acquisition. *International Journal of Human-Computer Interaction*, *40*(23), 8091–8106.

Kamboj, P., Banerjee, A., & Gupta, S. K. (2024). Expert knowledge driven human-AI collaboration for medical imaging: A study on epileptic seizure onset zone identification. *IEEE Transactions on Artificial Intelligence*. https://doi.org/10.1109/tai.2024.3396421

Kaplan, A., & Haenlein, M. (2020). Rulers of the world, unite! The challenges and opportunities of artificial intelligence. *Business Horizons*, *63*(1), 37–50.

Kolbjørnsrud, V. (2024). Designing the intelligent organization: Six principles for human-AI collaboration. *California Management Review*, *66*(2), 44–64.

Konda, M. (2024). *Elasticsearch in action*. October 31, 2023.

Korteling, J. H., van de Boer-Visschedijk, G. C., Blankendaal, R. A., Boonekamp, R. C., & Eikelboom, A. R. (2021). Human versus artificial intelligence. *Frontiers in Artificial Intelligence*, *4*, 622364.

Kotter, J. P. (1995). *Leading change: Why transformation efforts fail*. Harvard Business Review. Retrieved 04 12, 2025, from https://web.mit.edu/curhan/www/docs/Articles/15341_Readings/Organizational_Learning_and_Change/Kotter_1995_Leading_change.pdf

Lan, Q., Wen, D., Zhang, Z., Zeng, Q., Chen, X., Popovski, P., & Huang, K. (2021). What is semantic communication? A view on conveying meaning in the era of machine intelligence. *Journal of Communications and Information Networks*, *6*(4), 336–371.

Marr, B. (2019). *Artificial intelligence in practice: How 50 successful companies used AI and machine learning to solve problems*. John Wiley & Sons.

Meesad, P., & Mingkhwan, A. (2024). AI-powered smart digital libraries. In *Libraries in transformation: Navigating to AI-powered libraries* (pp. 391–428). Springer Nature.

Metaxa, D., Joon, S. P., Robertson, R. E., Karrie, K., Christo, W., & Jeff, H. C. (2021). Auditing algorithms: Understanding algorithmic systems from the outside in. *Foundations and Trends® in Human–Computer Interaction*, *14*(4), 272–344.

Mishra, A. (2024). *Empowering AI-powered product companies: Enhancing design with knowledge management*. OCAD University.

Mohapatra, A. (2020). *Designing for AI: A collaborative framework to bridge the gap between designers and data scientists, and enabling designers to create human-centered AI products and services*. KTH Royal Institute of Technology, School of Industrial Engineering and Management (ITM), Machine Design (Dept.), Integrated Product Development. https://kth.diva-portal.org/smash/get/diva2:1501764/FULLTEXT01.pdf

Moradi, M., & Mayukh, D. (2022). Applications of artificial intelligence in B2B marketing: Challenges and future directions. *Industrial Marketing Management*, *107*, 300–314.

Munoko, I., Helen, L., Brown, L., & Miklos, V. (2020). The ethical implications of using artificial intelligence in auditing. *Journal of Business Ethics*, *167*(2), 209–234.

Nah, F., Ruilin, Z., Jingyuan, C., Keng, S., & Langtao, C. (2023). Generative AI and ChatGPT: Applications, challenges, and AI-human collaboration. *Journal of Information Technology Case and Application Research*, *25*(3), 277–304.

Ntoutsi, E., Fafalios, P., Gadiraju, U., Iosifidis, V. N. W., Vidal, M., & Kompatsiaris, I. (2020). Bias in data-driven artificial intelligence systems—an introductory survey. *Wiley Interdisciplinary Reviews: Data Mining and Knowledge Discovery*, *10*(3), e1356.

Nuccio, M., & Mogno, S. (2023). *Mapping digital skills in cultural and creative industries in Italy*. Springer Nature. https://doi.org/10.1007/978-3-031-26867-0

Olan, F., Emmanuel, O. A., Jana, S., Franklin, N., & Nadja, D. U. (2022). Artificial intelligence and knowledge sharing: Contributing factors to organizational performance. *Journal of Business Research*, *145*, 605–615.

Palakurti, N. R. (2024). Building blocks of artificial intelligence and machine learning: A framework for sustainable development. In *In artificial intelligence and machine learning for sustainable development* (pp. 86–99).

Paleyes, A., Urma, R.-G., & Lawrence, N. D. (2022). Challenges in deploying machine learning: A survey of case studies. *ACM Computing Surveys*, *55*(6), 1–29.

Paschen, U., Pitt, C., & Kietzmann, J. (2020). Artificial intelligence: Building blocks and an innovation typology. *Business Horizons*, *63*(2), 147–155.

Piraianu, A.-I., Ana, F., Carmina, L. M., Oana-Roxana, C., Diana, G. P., Elena, S., & Octavian, C. I. (2023). Enhancing the evidence with algorithms: How artificial intelligence is transforming forensic medicine. *Diagnostics*, *13*(18), 2992.

Raiaan, M. A., Mukta, M. S., Fatema, K., Fahad, N. M., Sakib, S., Mim, M. M., & Azam, S. (2024). A review on large language models: Architectures, applications, taxonomies, open issues and challenges. *IEEE Access*, *12*, 26839–26874.

Raisch, S., & Fomina, K. (2023). Combining human and artificial intelligence: Hybrid problem-solving in organizations. *Academy of Management Review*, amr-2021.

Rajagopal, N. K., Qureshi, N. I., Durga, S., Ramirez Asis, E. H., Huerta Soto, R. M., Gupta, S. K., & Deepak, S. (2022). Future of business culture: An artificial intelligence-driven digital framework for organization decision making process. *Complexity*, *1*, 7796507.

Ramos Cordeiro, E., Lermen, F. H., Mello, C. M., Ferraris, A., & Valaskova, K. (2024). Knowledge management in small and medium enterprises: A systematic literature review, bibliometric analysis, and research agenda. *Journal of Knowledge Management*, *28*(2), 590–612.

Rane, N. L., Mallick, S. K., Kaya, Ö., & Rane, J. (2024a). *Applied machine learning and deep learning: Architectures and techniques*. Deep Science Publishing.

Rane, N. L., Paramesha, M., Choudhary, S. P., & Rane, J. (2024b). Artificial intelligence, machine learning, and deep learning for advanced business strategies: A review. *Partners Universal International Innovation Journal*, *2*(3), 147–171.

Rane, N. L., Paramesha, M., Rane, J., & Kaya, O. (2024c). Emerging trends and future research opportunities in artificial intelligence, machine learning, and deep learning. *Artificial Intelligence and Industry in Society*, *5*, 2–96.

Sanzogni, L., Gustavo, G., & Busch, P. (2017). Artificial intelligence and knowledge management: Questioning the tacit dimension. *Prometheus*, *35*(1), 37–56.

Sarker, I. H. (2022). AI-based modeling: Techniques, applications and research issues towards automation, intelligent and smart systems. *SN Computer Science*, *3*(2), 158.

Sætra, H. S. (2025). Scaffolding human champions: AI as a more competent other. *Human Arenas*, *8*(1), 56–78.

Sawalha, L., & Akinci, T. C. (2024). Shallow learning versus deep learning in natural language processing applications. In *Shallow learning vs. Deep learning: A practical guide for machine learning solutions* (pp. 179–206).

Schmarzo, B. (2023). *AI & data literacy: Empowering citizens of data science*. Packt Publishing Ltd.

Smith, P. (2024). Machine learning applications in knowledge management. *European Journal of Information and Knowledge Management*, *3*(2). https://doi.org/10.47941/ejikm.2060

Sumbal, M. S., & Amber, Q. (2024). *ChatGPT: A game changer for knowledge management in organizations*. Kybernetes. https://doi.org/10.1108/K-06-2023-1126

Taherdoost, H., & Madanchian, M. (2023). Artificial intelligence and knowledge management: Impacts, benefits, and implementation. *Computers*, *12*(4), 72.

Tatineni, S., & Allam, K. (2024). AI-driven continuous feedback mechanisms in DevOps for proactive performance optimization and user experience enhancement in software development. *Journal of AI in Healthcare and Medicine*, *4*(1), 114–151.

Tsui, E., Garner, B. J., & Staab, S. (2000). The role of artificial intelligence in knowledge management. *Knowledge-Based Systems*, *13*(5), 235–239.

Vadari, S., & Desik, P. A. (2021). The role of AI/ML in enhancing knowledge management systems. *Journal of Knowledge Management*, *19*(2), 7–31.

Van Berkel, N., Tag, B., Goncalves, J., & Hosio, S. (2022). Human-centred artificial intelligence: A contextual morality perspective. *Behaviour & Information Technology*, *41*(3), 502–518.

Von Krogh, G. (2018). Artificial intelligence in organizations: New opportunities for phenomenon-based theorizing. *Academy of Management Discoveries*, *4*(4), 404–409.

West, D. M., & Allen, J. R. (2018). *How artificial intelligence is transforming the world*. Brookings. Retrieved 03 2025, from https://www.brookings.edu/articles/how-artificial-intelligence-is-transforming-the-world/

Wu, C., Li, X., Guo, Y., Wang, J., Ren, Z., Wang, M., & Yang, Z. (2022). Natural language processing for smart construction: Current status and future directions. *Automation in Construction*, *134*, 104059.

Yao, Y., Patterson, E. A., & Taylor, R. J. (2023). The influence of digital technologies on knowledge management in engineering: A systematic literature review. *IEEE Transactions on Knowledge and Data Engineering*, *36*(2), 854–867.

Zheng, L., Niu, J., Long, M., & Fan, Y. (2023). An automatic knowledge graph construction approach to promoting collaborative knowledge building, group performance, social interaction and socially shared regulation in CSCL. *British Journal of Educational Technology*, *54*(3), 686–711.

Chapter 7

Architectural Artificial Intelligence Design Patterns for Knowledge Management Processes

Giovanna Di Marzo Serugendo and Lamia Friha

University of Geneva, Switzerland

ABSTRACT

This paper explores the emerging architectural artificial intelligence (AI) design patterns that support today's knowledge management processes. It summarises first various AI disciplines, then reviews related works aiming at providing design patterns. It then presents innovative solutions based on real-world use cases developed with our students and discusses the AI-based systems lifecycle as well as common underlying patterns such as agents, RAG or GraphRAG. For each pattern, we describe the problem it addresses, the solution it proposes, as well as its main benefits and illustrate with business use cases. Design patterns are a well-known technique for improving software engineering and the quality of software. As AI-based systems evolve, it becomes increasingly important to document emerging AI design patterns.

Keywords: Knowledge graphs; large language models; agentic; retrieval augmented generation techniques; embeddings; AI-based design patterns

Introduction

The inherent distributed and heterogeneous nature of knowledge management in business makes it a relevant candidate for several disciplines of artificial intelligence (AI). Indeed, AI offers a great potential for knowledge management in businesses, such as analysing customers behaviour and preferences; processing customers reviews and social media mentions; identifying markets trends,

AI-Driven Knowledge Management Assets, Volume 2, 133–151

doi:10.1108/978-1-83662-778-420261007

investments risks; inventory management, demand forecasting, logistics; recruitment and productivity analysis; tracking environmental impact; business insights; regulations and compliance checking; or legal documents analysis.

If we look individually at the different AI disciplines, we can identify: distributed artificial intelligence (DAI), semantic knowledge representation, machine learning (ML), natural language processing (NLP) (Russel & Norvig, 2020), as well as large language models (LLMs) (Wang et al., 2024) and Generative AI (Sengar et al., 2024).

DAI is a form of advanced multi-agent architecture, where complex tasks can efficiently be managed by several specialised autonomous agents and contribute to an overall solution (Russel & Norvig, 2020; Wooldridge, 2009).

Semantic knowledge representation enables to capture domain-specific knowledge and provides a meaningful interaction with data facilitating reasoning, knowledge accessibility and discovery (Ryś et al., 2024).

ML is a class of techniques that allow a system to learn and predict outcomes and to identify patterns from large amounts of data without explicit programming (Russel & Norvig, 2020).

NLP uses various techniques to process human language, among others tokenisation, part of speech, named entity recognition or sentiment analysis (Egger & Gokce, 2022).

Generative AI is a class of advanced ML algorithms capable of generating new content in the form of text, media or music by learning from a major corpus of data (Sengar et al., 2024).

LLMss are deep learning techniques, trained on a vast amount of text data, able to process (understand and generate) human-like text (Wang et al., 2024).

Hybrid approaches: Future AI systems will likely integrate multiple AI techniques above to enhance their functionality. Agents can incorporate any of the other mentioned techniques, enabling them to specialise in distinct tasks while coordinating efforts to achieve a shared objective. The combination of multi-agent systems (MASs) and LLM-based agents facilitates a structured approach where specialised agents handle specific functions while interacting efficiently. Other emerging trends are RAG (Gao et al., 2023) approaches, which retrieve contextual data before feeding it to an LLM, and GraphRAG (Graph Retrieval-Augmented Generation) (Khorashadizadeh et al., 2024; Peng et al., 2024) approaches, which merge semantic knowledge representation with RAG and LLM-based solutions. This integration enhances AI's ability to process structured knowledge while leveraging the generative capabilities of LLMs. Following similar ideas, TAG (Table-Advanced-Generation) (Biswal et al., 2024) supports interactions through natural language queries with tables or structured (quantitative) data.

The above AI disciplines have broadened the innovation solutions to very complex problems and created new opportunities for knowledge management for business processes.

All these new digital systems share common patterns and need to be formalised, defined and made accessible for all digital systems and services designers.

In this paper, we dive into selected use cases developed under the innovative process we set up at the University of Geneva. Based on this experience, we document the AI-based system lifecycle we experienced during these developments. We also derive and document preliminary architectural AI design patterns offering recurrent solutions relevant to business knowledge management. We describe these patterns and their relationships, exemplifying them with business use cases.

Related Works

Design Patterns

Software engineering requires care to develop correct software. Design patterns emerged in the 90s in the wake of object-oriented languages as a technique to improve the quality of software. The notable reference in the field is the work of Gamma et al. (1994) defining a series of design patterns, which represent standardised, reusable solutions to recurring challenges in software development. Since then, different types of patterns have emerged from patterns addressing software design (e.g., creational, structural or behavioural patterns) to concurrency, security or testing patterns, as well as to architectural considerations (e.g., client-server, micro-services patterns).

AI-based systems come with new paradigms that equally need to be formalised and standardised to be easily reusable for solving common issues to implement new AI-based services.

Design Patterns for AI-Based Systems

For AI-based systems, design patterns address central aspects such as data processing, model deployment, human–AI interaction and continuous learning and integration. By adopting proven design patterns, organisations ensure scalability, maintainability, dependability and adaptability in deploying AI-driven business solutions.

Research on such design patterns is emerging. For instance, Fowler & Subramaniam (2025) provide a formal definition of three emerging patterns in AI-based systems: '*Direct Prompting*: A direct interaction between the user and the LLM; *Evals*: Evaluating the responses of an LLM in the context of a specific task; *Embeddings*: Transforming large data blocks into numeric vectors so that embeddings near each other represent related concepts.'

Bauer & Smith (2023) have identified design patterns for AI-based systems of which 34 are new patterns and 36 are adapted from traditional software engineering.

According to Bhat (2025), there is a need to understand AI design patterns. The *Retrieval-Augmented Generation* (RAG) described in this paper is currently one of the most important patterns. It is used to enhance response generation by providing relevant context from proprietary and external data sources. The article also describes the system AI lifecycle steps, including data collection and preparation, model training, deployment and continuous learning.

Design Patterns for Agentic-Based Systems

The notion of autonomous agents and MASs emerged in the 1990s. Several researchers have provided various types of agent-based design patterns: from agent-oriented design patterns, aiming at developing applications from agents (Oluyomi et al., 2007), to agent-modelling design patterns (North & Macal, 2011), to specific patterns for their coordination. Among this last category, Fernandez-Marquez et al. (2013) define a catalogue of bio-inspired mechanisms for self-organising MASs with emergent behaviour. These mechanisms are expressed in terms of modular and reusable design patterns, together with their relationships. Among other patterns, we can also mention the agentic collaboration pattern and the agentic planning pattern to solve efficiently a complex problem.

LLM-based agents' patterns combine traditional agents' patterns with *direct prompting*, *evaluation*, *RAG* and *embedding patterns* to provide agents based on foundation models to ease their design and specifications as identified by Liu et al. (2024).

In DeepLearning.AI, 2023, a very promising set of agentic design patterns is presented: '*Reflection*', in which the agent improves its answer continuously and builds step by step higher-quality answers; '*Tool of Use*', which takes advantage of gathering information from external and several sources to enhance output; and '*Planning and Multi-agent collaboration*', whose aim is to divide a problem into tasks and set goals to reach an overall objective and solve the problem.

To conclude, we observe that there are a lot of emerging patterns for AI-based systems at different levels and granularity: architectural, internal behaviour of LLM-based agents, agents' coordination and interaction, or a combination of patterns.

The goal of design patterns is to help develop reliable and sound software, providing well-proven solutions. The current rapid evolution of AI-based systems brings a series of proposals for corresponding design patterns, which still require validation and proper cataloguing and formalisation. This paper focuses on clarifying the links among architectural AI design patterns.

Digital Innovation Process at the University of Geneva

We set up an innovation process at the University of Geneva (Unige), an innovation process aiming at developing innovative digital services for the University. This unique process follows a service science approach (Di Marzo Serugendo & Friha, 2021), where researchers, students, information systems experts and stakeholders team up to ideate services, develop ideas into functional prototypes and industrialise and deploy them for the whole University community. This innovation process is a funnel, where some of the produced ideas are transformed into prototypes and the most promising prototypes are turned into an industrial service.

As part of this digital innovation process, we regularly coach students and manage innovation projects. With the recent development in Generative AI, in particular text analysis, we are brought to investigating all the knowledge gathered in an organisation. The University of Geneva as well as external organisations have their own various and heterogeneous knowledge sources and data to be processed. Stakeholders are now interested in leveraging all the accumulated knowledge for various purposes, such as to better present information to users and facilitate access and information search, to visualise structured data and facilitate decision-making.

On the students' side, during the past three years, there has been a great enthusiasm for generative AI and the new possibilities it offers. Students are keen on new technologies and at the same time expanding their project portfolios, especially with real-world projects. In this context, various projects have emerged. Some of these projects have highlighted the need to create skills and internal hardware infrastructure for new AI-based services, while others have shown the potential of providing extracted and federated knowledge from various sources, accessible to everyone in natural language.

In this context, we have also implemented continuous training to accompany the transition to adopt AI and enable the use of the most widespread tools.

Consequently, we have focused on the following main axes for business process innovation:

(1) Continuous training for all employees
(2) Defining and specifying the prerequisites to establish the necessary hardware infrastructure and resources to sustain innovative services
(3) Demonstrating, through prototypes or pilots, the potential of leveraging heterogeneous data in various formats available within the organisation
(4) Establish governance and policies on data lifecycle management, data protection and ethical use of AI to ensure a responsible implementation
(5) Define guidelines to support SMEs in their AI transformation with expert knowledge and training (Friha et al., 2025).

AI-Based Systems Lifecycle

Since 2016, we have experimented and built conversational agents for several use cases. Most of them were for the university community. The agents are designed either to assist students, to onboard and facilitate enrolment, help students to organise their work or to help discover cultural and sports activities on the campus. These chatbots have different levels of maturity and rely on different sources of information. With the advent of ChatGPT and the new possibilities of LLMs and the first open-source models, we focused on defining the appropriate personas for the chatbots, assessing their maturity level, choosing the appropriate data sources and building information bases, evaluating the system performances (results and computing time) and experiencing the development lifecycle of systems based on LLM. Globally, we observe that the overall development lifecycle of such AI-based systems is different from more traditional software development, since there is a need for regular maintenance, fine-tuning and control.

A usual lifecycle for AI-based projects is as follows:

- Collecting and curating data, constituting a sound and pertinent information base
- Selecting the appropriate technique:

    a. Non-AI-based solution
    b. AI-based solution

        - With/without generative AI
        - With/without MAS
        - With/without knowledge engineering technology
        - With/without a combination of the above

- If it is an AI-based solution, select the appropriate model (e.g., LLM, ML algorithm) and determine which higher-level technique(s) to use (RAG, GraphRAG, MASs, etc.).
- Designing the workflow, which involves tasks such as:

    a. Identification of agents' responsibilities and tasks
    b. Coordination of agents' tasks
    c. Retrieving information from unstructured, semi-structured and structured data (own data and/or from the Web)
    d. Generating an answer from the information base
    e. Providing a user interface through fluid interaction in natural language

- Evaluating the overall system
- Testing, adjusting, fine-tuning
- Continuous improvement

From our experience and the use case below, we highlight the following design patterns for AI-based systems.

AI Design Patterns Catalogue

As said above, software design patterns represent well-known and assessed solutions to recurrent problems. Patterns can be used alone or in conjunction with other patterns to provide solutions to more complex problems. Some patterns require other patterns in their design. Fig. 7.1 shows relationships between a set of architectural AI-based systems design patterns. This figure is by no means exhaustive but highlights the patterns used in the use cases we describe in the next section. In Fig. 7.1, patterns are organised into three layers: *basic patterns* are those that are not further decomposed or combined with other patterns to

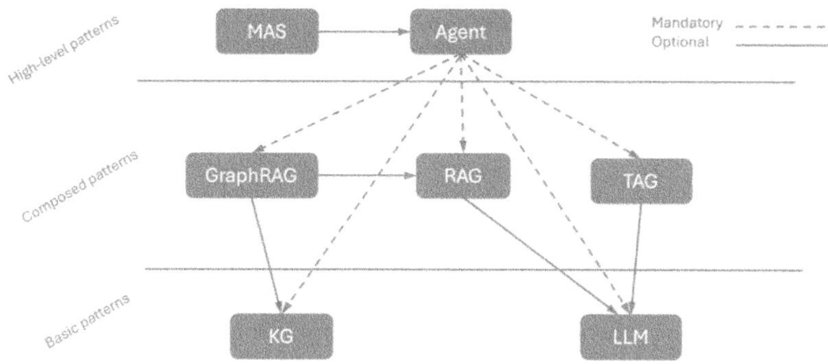

Fig. 7.1. AI Design Patterns and Their Relationships.

provide their solution, *composed patterns* are those that require other patterns to fully propose a solution, and *high-level patterns* are those that act at the level of an application and require lower-level patterns. Arrows indicate relationships among patterns either mandatory or optional. An arrow from pattern A to pattern B means pattern A requires pattern B in its design.

Design patterns are usually described according to a very specific format (Gamma et al., 1994). As we are at a preliminary stage of identification and explanation, we will limit the description to the problem they address and the solution they provide.

Agent Pattern

Problem: Some artificial systems suffer from limited autonomy and need human oversight or intervention. Systems lack adaptability to unanticipated or dynamically changing situations, thus also preventing scalability.

Solution: Employing software agents capable of operating independently, making decisions, perceiving their environment and acting on it. Agents come in many flavours (mobile, reactive, cognitive, learning, bio-inspired, etc.). Their capabilities may vary. They usually are autonomous – taking actions based on their objectives without human supervision; they adapt through specific mechanisms; are goal-oriented and able to perceive their environment and act on it; and perceive other agents and interact with them.

Other patterns: Agents may be equipped with any capability and so with any other pattern.

Benefits: Agents improve adaptability to dynamically changing situations, support scalability through their autonomy as human intervention is strongly reduced.

Business use cases: Single agents are typically bots or robots performing specific tasks. Examples include trading agents, bots buying or selling energy, manufacturing robots or autonomous vehicles. Specialised LLM-based agents are configured to interact with users on a specific topic. For instance, specialised in writing newsletters of the company, or checking information against regulations.

MAS (Multi-Agent-Systems) Pattern

Problem: Single-agent systems provide limited specialisation and scalability. A single agent handling a complex task is more difficult to programme. Single-agent systems may suffer a single point of failure.

Solution: Employing multiple autonomous agents that work collaboratively to achieve a common goal. Agents in the system may specialise in different tasks and roles, communicate with other agents and coordinate their actions. They also provide redundancy when several agents perform the same tasks and thus enhance resilience and fault tolerance. Finally, MAS also supports distributed problem solving as agents work on different parts of the problem simultaneously, leveraging their specialised skills.

Other patterns: Agent pattern.

Benefits: MAS enhances scalability as it can handle complex tasks and large volumes of data by distributing work among multiple agents. MASs are more robust, since agents adapt to changing conditions, and resilient to failures, as tasks are distributed among several agents and many agents provide redundancy in the system. Agents can be designed with specific expertise, improving the overall efficiency and effectiveness of the system.

Business use cases: MASs are used for: optimisation (e.g., complex constraint solving problems); modelling (e.g., providing micro-modelling of urban settings) or engineering and distributed computing (e.g., managing fleets of autonomous vehicles, managing energy distribution and consumption in smart grids through collaborative agent-based systems).

RAG (Retrieval-Augmented-Generation) Pattern

Problem: AI-based systems rely on pre-trained data or data freely found on the Web and do not cover specific or proprietary information needed for certain applications.

Solution in three steps:

(1) *Retrieval*: The system first retrieves relevant documents or data from the provided knowledge base (proprietary data or specific information or specific websites). Retrieval uses lower-level patterns such as data access, vectorisation or embedding.
(2) *Augmentation*: The retrieved information is then used to augment the input provided to the AI-based component that will generate the answer.
(3) *Generation*: The language model processes the augmented input to generate a more accurate and contextually relevant response.

Other patterns: Retrieval requires lower-level patterns (data access, vectorisation or embedding). Generation requires the choice of an LLM to generate the answer.

Benefits: This pattern generally reduces hallucinations as it enhances the quality of response by providing proprietary context to the AI-based system.

Business use cases: Any business domain such as finance, HR or customer relations benefits from an AI-based system that retrieves and generates information based on well-identified proprietary data, thus improving the accuracy of answers for financial forecasts, HR information or customer answers.

GraphRAG (Graph Retrieval-Augmentation Generation) Pattern

Problem: AI-based systems do not capture the relationships between pieces of data or do not possess domain-specific knowledge.

Solution: It consists of a RAG method based on knowledge graphs (KGs). It provides domain-specific knowledge to the AI-based system and retrieves information from a KG, not only from general unstructured data. It involves the following steps:

(1) *KG construction*: Capturing the data and domain of interest as a graph of entities and relationships (see KG pattern);
(2) *Enhanced retrieval*: Retrieve information from the KG, exploiting relationships and context within the graph;
(3) *Augmentation*: The retrieved information from the KG provides richer and more domain-specific information, which is then used to augment the input provided to the AI-based component that will generate the answer;
(4) *Generation*: The language model processes the augmented input to generate a more accurate and contextually relevant response. Generation requires the choice of an LLM to generate the answer.

Other patterns: Requires both the RAG pattern and the KG pattern in its design.

Benefits: This pattern improves understanding, accuracy and interaction among data as it is based on well-defined domain-specific knowledge and/or proprietary data and their well-established relationships.

Business use cases: Combines the benefit of RAG and KG, thus improving accuracy with domain-specific knowledge and exploiting proprietary data. Business intelligence is one of the application domains that benefits from the GraphRAG approach. It can be used mainly for generating reports by gathering data from multiple sources. It enhances customer support by retrieving accurate answers.

KG (Knowledge-Graph) Pattern

Problem: Information is scattered in data silos across various systems, making it difficult to integrate and access. Traditional databases do not capture the relationships and semantics between different pieces of data. Complex queries require an understanding of intricate relationships between entities.

Solution: Structuring data in a graph format, where nodes represent entities and edges represent relationships. This approach is highly relevant to query and manage data. It requires:

(1) *Graph construction*: Build a KG that represents the application domain, defining entities (nodes) and their relationships (edges);
(2) *Data integration*: Integrate data from multiple sources into the KG, ensuring that all relevant information is represented and accessible;
(3) *Contextual understanding*: Use the graph structure to capture the knowledge behind the represented data;
(4) *Advanced querying*: Leverage the graph's structure to perform complex queries, utilising graph traversal and pattern matching techniques. For an advanced and superior version, the use of ontologies further defines the concepts and their relationships, de facto defining the knowledge about a domain. KGs then follow the ontologies' structure. We speak about linked data when KGs have no underlying ontologies.

Other patterns: No other pattern.

Benefits: Improved data integration, enhancing results through links among data. Federating queries across different databases and domains. Enhanced understanding due to the integration of domain-specific knowledge and its semantics (when using ontologies).

Business use cases: KG supports compliance checking or compliance by design by mapping out the relationships between regulations, policies and business processes. KG enhances search capabilities thanks to contextual understanding. In healthcare and pharma, KG helps uncover relationships (e.g., incompatibility) among drugs, or between drugs and diseases (e.g., contraindication).

TAG (Table-Advanced-Generation) Pattern

Problem: Interacting through natural language queries with traditional (e.g., relational) databases or structured (quantitative) data.

Solution in three steps:

(1) *Query synthesis*: Translates the user's natural language query into an executable database query.
(2) *Query execution*: Runs the query to retrieve relevant data from the database.
(3) *Answer generation*: Uses the retrieved data along with the original query to generate a natural language answer.

Other patterns: Requires LLM pattern.

Benefits: This pattern improves the interaction with databases and enhances accuracy compared to regular LLMs.

Business use cases: TAG helps generate financial reports by extracting (quantitative) data from financial tables.

LLM (Large-Language-Model) Pattern

Problem: Traditional software systems often struggle with tasks that require understanding and generating human-like text, handling unstructured data or adapting to new contexts without extensive reprogramming.

Solution: LLM-based systems are trained on a vast number of texts in natural language and equipped with specific NLP capabilities. They can perform tasks like text generation, summarisation and translation. To some extent, they capture context across large portions of text. LLMs can perform multiple tasks without task-specific training, offering flexibility and reducing the need for extensive reprogramming. Finally, they provide generative capabilities for creating new content or code.

Other patterns: No other pattern.

Benefits: LLMs serve as de facto user interfaces providing fluid interactions in natural language. They simplify tasks related to text processing such as translations, summaries, extraction of information or text generation.

Business use cases: Personalised and natural interaction with customers through smart agents that benefit from LLMs' ability to understand and generate human-like text. Improving efficiency when summarising or generating reports. Generating emails. Writing programming code.

Use Cases

Compliance with Regulations

Compliance by design and compliance checking are two important approaches that ensure that systems or processes satisfy regulations. *Compliance by design* aims to ensure compliance *during the design phase* by embedding regulatory requirements from the outset. *Compliance checking* focuses on *assessing compliance after development* or implementation to ensure the system or process meets legal and regulatory standards.

As part of various research projects undertaken with industry, we worked on the notion of compliance by design and automated compliance checking. In all cases, we exploited semantic knowledge representation in particular ontologies and data stored in KGs. We additionally used ML or LLMs to complement some parts of the system.

Services Exploiting Underground Data

When planning and constructing new buildings, it is of the utmost importance to know precisely the location of underground objects: electricity, water or gas pipes, as well as root trees, or other objects linked to nearby buildings. Underground data may be uncertain or incomplete (2D information available but not precise, and no information on depth), and thus not always reliable. The first project aimed at: (1) complementing 2D underground data with a 3D dimension; (2) compensating for the uncertainty of the data; (3) calculating any underground conflict (a gas pipe is too close to an electricity network or water pipe). We based our system on urbanistic and underground objects regulations. We then inferred further information: a gas pipe installed in the 80s should be at a well-specified metre depths, because the regulation was as such at that time; uncertainty should be accounted for and we set up a zone across each object where the probability of finding it is high; conflicts among objects arise from a discrepancy between their current location and the regulations (e.g., the distance between two pipes is too small). We developed an ontology of the underground objects and defined the regulations with SHACL to complement (with 3D and uncertainty information) an existing database of underground objects. We also further identified specific conflicts among objects of a given zone (Métral et al., 2020). This work was done in collaboration with an SME and data from the Geneva utility company (SIG).

Patterns used: KG pattern.

Our second example relating to underground data concerns the automatic update of the database storing the underground pipes (gas, water, thermic) after roadworks have modified those pipes. We used here two AI techniques: machine learning for automatically classifying images of underground pipe segments (e.g., elbow and tap) and semantic knowledge representation for verifying that the classified segments matched together and for automatically updating the original database of the utility company. Similarly to above, we based our work on underground regulations, we defined an ontology of the pipes segment, defined rules for their combination and for detecting changes. This work was done in collaboration with the Geneva utility company (SIG) (Di Marzo Serugendo, Cappelli, Falquet, et al., 2024).

Patterns used: KG pattern.

Administrative Service for Tax Return

Processing administrative documents for tax returns is a time-consuming task for fiduciaries. This projects aimed at automating this task, in particular at: (1) identifying the type of document (health insurance policy, doctor's bill or salary certificate); (2) tagging those documents by category (health, taxes, etc.) and by household (taxpayer, any spouse, children); (3) defining household profiles (widower, employee, or self-employer, retired, family with children, etc.); (4) and finally verifying that every household correctly provided the necessary documents or updating the household profile in case of a change (e.g., a new child requires to add a new health insurance policy in Switzerland; an employee is now retired). We developed an ontology for the Geneva Canton tax return and defined the rules for household documents linked to household profiles (Di Marzo Serugendo, Cappelli, Falquet, et al., 2024).

This work was done before 2023 with an SME active in the management of administrative documents. This is the reason why we did not use LLMs but only ML.

Patterns used: KG pattern.

University Programmes Regulations

Tracking university students' academic progress in an interactive, synchronised and well-coordinated manner across an entire study programme presents a significant challenge. University stakeholders—including students, study advisors, faculty members, scientific committees and the admissions office—require a system that provides personalised access and actions based on their specific roles. This system must also be integrated with a unified information framework while ensuring compliance with study regulations. We developed a method to automatically generate a regulation-compliant service (i.e., compliant by design) that delivers tailored views to different stakeholders. This automated implementation is built on a set of generic rules that define the regulatory requirements applicable across all curricula and programmes. Our case study concerns PhD student programmes regulations. Our proof-of-concept demonstrates how the system dynamically instantiates the service from predefined rules, generates role-specific interface views and operates through a semantic reasoning engine. We developed an ontology for the University of Geneva's programme regulations and defined the rules for the specific PhD student programme. The proposed solution has the potential to enhance and streamline student progress monitoring, extending beyond PhD programmes to any academic level. By automating the implementation of study programmes, this approach offers a scalable solution adaptable to universities worldwide. (Di Marzo Serugendo & Friha, 2021, 2022). We are currently working on automatically extracting rules from regulations (from PDF files) using existing LLM-based systems and transforming them into semantic rules our system can use.

In contrast to the previous examples focusing on compliance checking, this case aims at developing a system that is, by design, compliant with the regulations.

Patterns used: KG pattern, LLM pattern.

Application to businesses and organisations: Organisations must ensure compliance with regulations, understand the regulatory landscape and conduct regular audits to reduce risks and enhance competitiveness.

Medical/Pharmaceutical Knowledge Exploration

Several application areas benefit from the integration of semantic knowledge representation and advanced User eXperience allowing effortless interaction with large datasets and finding relevant information, recommendations and discoveries.

One of the promising and challenging works done, as two joint master's theses, by our students (Guetarni, 2023; Sedoh, 2023), addresses the crucial issue of drug interaction. The idea was to describe interactions with drug and medical knowledge ontologies exploited by an intelligent agent to answer questions on: (1) drug–drug interactions, (2) drug–food/beverage interactions and (3) drug–patient's condition interactions. Unintended drug interactions can have unexpected side effects (e.g., be harmful to the patient); it is then important for the patient to be able to check those interactions, possibly on her own, at any time.

Patterns used: KG pattern, LLM pattern.

Application to businesses and organisations: Using KG, organisations structure and organise effectively their data and hence enhance decision-making, or provide personalised recommendations tailored to customer-specific needs.

ERP, Multi-Agent Systems and Generative AI

Enterprise resource planning (ERP) is a software system that is used to manage human resources, finance, inventory, planning and risk management in an organisation. These are called functions, structured in a modular manner and shared in a centralised database. Software agents can be designed to collaborate and manage information from different sources and help in decision-making.

Patterns used: KG pattern, LLM pattern, MAS pattern.

Interacting with Structured and Unstructured Data

The University of Geneva (Unige) Memento Use Case

The Unige Memento is a website that gathers various information and important documents such as regulations, academic calendars, HR directives, etc. This website is equipped with a search engine that is limited in obtaining relevant results. We have built an intelligent search in the form of a smart chatbot that understands the context and the user's intent to provide accurate and relevant results. Moreover, it enhances user experience through a natural language interaction. For this project, we first gathered all web pages of the memento, then considered a RAG approach to first retrieve the most relevant pages corresponding to the user query, before feeding these pages to an LLM for further generation of the response. Another variant using the GraphRAG approach is also being evaluated.

A similar approach was used for another project for the Geneva state, where a large amount of data was curated and processed to feed a RAG system.

Pattern used: RAG pattern, GraphRAG pattern, LLM pattern.

Application to businesses and organisations: A GraphRAG-based system provides appropriate proprietary context to a conversational agent to retrieve and deliver accurate information.

Patent Management Project

An exploratory work has recently started in collaboration with the technology transfer service of the University of Geneva (UNITEC), which manages university patents. The project aims to build an AI agent that helps employees along the different steps of the Unitec technology transfer process. The AI agent's mission is to understand the innovation described by a document and find a similar existing patent and provide the user with the appropriate documentation.

Pattern used: RAG pattern, GraphRAG pattern, Agent pattern.

Application to businesses and organisations: Efficient patent management systems empower organisations with the appropriate rights to their invention and prevent competitors from using them.

Extracting Tabular Information

Moving from natural language and texts, companies are also interested in automatically processing tables containing numbers, be they stored in digital structured format (e.g., .csv files) or appearing in PDFs as a piece of text. We coached various projects aiming at processing tables, notably: (1) automatically creating graphic visualisation (e.g., pie charts) out of a digital structured file; (2) automation of data extraction from tabular formats within ISO standard documents and comparison of various techniques (NLP vs LLMs). Challenges faced by these systems encompass the quality of the tabular data (not complete, mix of text and numbers, special characters).

Patterns used: TAG pattern.

Application to businesses and organisations: Using TAG-based systems, organisations are equipped with dynamically generated and updated dashboards, thus improving monitoring and decision-making.

Business Context

We summarise here in Table 7.1, the AI design patterns discussed above, highlighting their main characteristics and providing examples of each in the business context.

Conclusion

This paper presents a preliminary definition of a series of architectural AI design patterns, derived from our extensive experience in software engineering, AI and innovation. Our work, initiated in 2016, focuses on developing innovative AI-based digital services, including conversational agents, regulatory compliance services, knowledge exploration and interactions with structured and unstructured data through natural language queries. These services were developed through our innovation process with students at the University of Geneva. Additionally, this paper outlines the AI-based system lifecycle we encountered during development.

Table 7.1. AI Design Patterns, Characteristics and Business Examples.

Design Patterns	**Main Characteristics**	**Business Context Examples**
LLM	Dynamically processing natural language (understanding and generating)	Fluid user interface using natural language (understanding requests and providing answers) Unstructured data (text) processing: summaries, information extraction, code and text generation (email, marketing, reports)
TAG	Interacting through natural language queries with structured (quantitative) data	Dynamically creating and updating dashboards Explaining the content of a database Financial analysis/business intelligence: generating reports from complex queries expressed in natural language
KG	Capturing domain-specific knowledge and structuring data in a graph format	Discovering links and relationships among data Federating queries across databases and domains Providing semantics to information Integrating data from different sources and domains Improving search results based on semantics Supporting compliance checking or compliance by design
GraphRAG	Capturing domain-specific knowledge and exploiting proprietary data	Providing context and improving accuracy Recommendation systems for customers Enhancing internal document management systems
RAG	Exploiting proprietary data	Improved customer support providing pertinent

Table 7.1. *(Continued)*

Design Patterns	Main Characteristics	Business Context Examples
		information based on proprietary data Managing internal knowledge bases and retrieving relevant documents and data, helping employees find the information they need quickly
MAS	Multiple autonomous agents work collaboratively to achieve a common goal	Swarm robotics, warehouse automation Financial market and trading Smart grid monitoring and management
Agent	Autonomous software, perceiving its environment and acting on it	Specialised agents for negotiations (buying/selling real estate, planning and booking travel, etc.) or managing investments (e.g., stockbrokers)

Our exploration of the state-of-the-art reveals various approaches to classifying emerging design patterns. The demand for new AI-based services is high, and the problems to be solved are complex. Therefore, properly documenting and defining AI design patterns is crucial, as AI-based systems, like any other software, need to be accurate, robust, ethical and scalable.

In this paper, we identify several architectural AI design patterns and explain their interrelationships. We provide examples through case studies developed with our students and illustrate each pattern with business use cases.

We plan to expand the current AI design pattern catalogue with additional patterns and provide comprehensive documentation for all of them, adhering to the formal definition of design patterns established by Gamma et al. (1994).

Acknowledgements

The authors wish to thank all students who developed the various projects mentioned in this paper, as well as the Unige or external organisation stakeholders who supported the projects. We also wish to thank the two Innosuisse-funded projects RAR 100.851 IP-ICT and SUBSURFACE 35265.1 IP-ICT. We would like to acknowledge the use of Microsoft Copilot (GPT-4) for the reformulation of some sentences of this paper.

References

Bauer, A., & Smith, J. (2023). Design patterns for AI-based systems: A multivocal literature review and pattern repository. *arXiv*. https://arxiv.org/abs/2303.13173

Bhat, A. K. (2025, March 18). *AI design patterns: Understanding RAG pattern*. IEEE Computer Society. Retrieved April 15, 2025 from https://www.computer.org/publications/tech-news/trends/ai-design-patterns

Biswal, A., Patel, L., Jha, S., Kamsetty, A., Liu, S., Gonzalez, J. E., Guestrin, C., & Zaharia, M. (2024). Text2SQL is not enough: Unifying AI and databases with TAG. *arXiv*. https://arxiv.org/abs/2408.14717

DeepLearning.AI. (2023, October 5). *Agentic design patterns part 2: Reflection*. Retrieved April 15, 2025 from https://www.deeplearning.ai/the-batch/agentic-design-patterns-part-2-reflection/

Di Marzo Serugendo, G., Cappelli, M. A., Falquet, G., Métral, C., Wade, A., Ghadfi, S., Cutting-Decelle, A.-F., Caselli, A., & Cutting, G. (2024). Streamlining tax and administrative document management with AI-powered intelligent document management system. *Information*, *15*(8), 461. https://doi.org/10.3390/info15080461

Di Marzo Serugendo, G., Cappelli, M. A., Glass, P., & Caselli, A. (2024). *The semantic approach to recognise the components of the underground cadastre - Relevé Automatique des réseaux (RAR) Project*. Computer Science Center, University of Geneva. Technical report. https://access.archive-ouverte.unige.ch/access/metadata/6c7c5b19-fed1-42f0-8962-75e9cd153620/download

Di Marzo Serugendo, G., Caselli, A., Cappelli, M. A., Friha, L., Hugentobler, A., Cissé, K., Mulard, P., Missiri, N., Martelli, A., Huyhn, B., Turhan, I. C., Sadeghi, O., Bauch, S., & Buzgheiba, A. (2023). *A semantic-based approach for automating compliance by the design of digital services - a case study in the academic sector*. In *International Conference on Exploring Service Science (IESS 2.3)* (Vol. 51, p. 05004) ITM Web Conf. https://doi.org/10.1051/itmconf/20235105004

Di Marzo Serugendo, G., & Friha, L. (2021). Digital innovation process in the academic sector - the case of the University of Geneva. *International Conference on Exploring Service Science (IESS 2.1)*, *38*, 03004. ITM Web Conf. https://doi.org/10.1051/itmconf/20213803004

Di Marzo Serugendo, G., Friha, L., Burgi, P. Y., Döbeli, J., Wade, A., Cappelli, M. A., Cutting-Decelle, A. F., Vonlanthen, M., Durand, N., & Hugentobler, A. (2022). *Towards a digital service to help the elaboration, implementation and follow-up of study regulations at the University of Geneva - a hands-on experiment*. *International Conference on Exploring Service Science (IESS 2.2)* (Vol. 41, p. 03004). ITM Web Conf. https://doi.org/10.1051/itmconf/20224103004

Egger, R., & Gokce, E. (2022). Natural Language processing (NLP): An introduction. In R. Egger (Ed.), *Applied data science in tourism. Tourism on the verge* (pp. 307–334). Springer. https://doi.org/10.1007/978-3-030-88389-8_15

Fernandez-Marquez, J. L., Di Marzo Serugendo, G., Montagna, S., Viroli, M., & Arcos, J. L. (2013). Description and composition of bio-inspired design patterns: A complete overview. *Natural Computing*, *12*(1), 43–67. https://doi.org/10.1007/s11047-012-9324-y

Fowler, M., & Subramaniam, B. (2025). *Emerging patterns in building GenAI products*. Retrieved April 15, 2025 from https://martinfowler.com/articles/gen-ai-patterns/

Friha, L., Hugentobler, A., Kastanis, I., Koehler, J., Kugler, M., Kurpicz-Briki, M., Moi, G., Rizzoli, A., Sawicki, B., & Schwarz, G. (2025). *Orientation IA : Défis et opportunités pour les PME suisses*. Zenodo. https://doi.org/10.5281/zenodo.14755699

Gamma, E., Helm, R., Johnson, R., & Vlissides, J. (1994). *Design patterns: Elements of reusable object-oriented software*. Addison-Wesley.

Gao, Y., Xiong, Y., Gao, X., Jia, K., Pan, J., Bi, Y., Dai, Y., Sun, J., Wang, M., & Wang, H. (2023). Retrieval-augmented generation for Large Language models: A survey. *arXiv*. https://arxiv.org/abs/2312.10997

Guetarni, A. (2023). Analysis, design and development of an ontology-based chatbot for drug interactions. *Master thesis. Computer Science Center*. University of Geneva.

Khorashadizadeh, H., Amara, F. Z., Ezzabady, M., Ieng, F., Tiwari, S., Mihindukulasooriya, N., Groppe, J., Sahri, S., Benamara, F., & Groppe, S. (2024). Research trends for the interplay between large language models and knowledge graphs. *arXiv*. https://arxiv.org/abs/2406.08223

Liu, Y., Lo, S. K., Lu, Q., Zhu, L., Zhao, D., Xu, X., Harrer, S., & Whittle, J. (2024). Agent design pattern catalogue: A collection of architectural patterns for foundation model based agents. *arXiv*. https://arxiv.org/abs/2405.10467

Métral, C., Daponte, V., Caselli, A., Di Marzo Serugendo, G., & Falquet, G. (2020). Ontology-based rule compliance checking for subsurface objects. International Archives of the Photogrammetry, Remote Sensing and Spatial Information Sciences, *XLIV-4/W1-2020*, 91–94. https://doi.org/10.5194/isprs-archives-XLIV-4-W1-2020-91-2020

North, M. J., & Macal, C. M. (2011). Product design patterns for agent-based modeling. In *Proceedings of the 2011 Winter Simulation Conference (WSC)* (pp. 3085–3097). IEEE. https://doi.org/10.1109/WSC.2011.6148008

Oluyomi, A., Karunasekera, S., & Sterling, L. (2007). A comprehensive view of agent-oriented patterns. *Autonomous Agents and Multi-Agent Systems*, *15*(3), 337–377. https://doi.org/10.1007/s10458-007-9014-9

Peng, B., Zhu, Y., Liu, Y., Bo, X., Shi, H., Hong, C., Zhang, Y., & Tang, S. (2024). Graph retrieval-augmented generation: A survey. *arXiv*. https://arxiv.org/abs/2408.08921

Russel, S., & Norvig, P. (2020). *Artificial intelligence: A modern approach* (4th ed.). Pearson.

Ryś, A., Lima, L., Exelmans, J., Janssens, D., & Vangheluwe, H. (2024). Model management to support systems engineering workflows using ontology-based knowledge graphs. *Journal of Industrial Information Integration*, *42*, 100720. https://doi.org/10.1016/j.jii.2024.100720

Sedoh, A. A. (2023). Analysis, design and development of an ontology-based chatbot for drug interactions. *Master thesis. Computer Science Center*. University of Geneva.

Sengar, S. S., Hasan, A. B., Kumar, S., & Carroll, F. (2024). Generative artificial intelligence: A systematic review and applications. *arXiv*. https://arxiv.org/pdf/2405.11029

Wang, Z., Chu, Z., Doan, T. V., Ni, S., Yang, M., & Zhang, W. (2024). History, development, and principles of large language models introductory survey. *arXiv*. https://arxiv.org/abs/2402.06853

Wooldridge, M. (2009). *An introduction to multi-agent systems* (2nd ed.). Wiley.

Chapter 8

Cooperation Between Artificial Intelligence and Lateral Transshipment: Qualitative Study

Elleuch Fadoi

Independent Researcher, Tunisia

Abstract

Artificial intelligence (AI) is transforming inventory management by leveraging advanced algorithms and machine learning techniques to analyze large data sets quickly and accurately. AI-powered systems can process data at unprecedented scale and speed, unlike traditional methods that rely on manual data entry and analysis.

Transshipment and supply chain management are crucial concepts in modern logistics, often used to optimize the flow of goods between different points in the network. It refers to the process of transferring goods from one means of transport to another during their journey. It can occur at various points in a transportation network, such as ports, warehouses, or distribution hubs. This allows for more efficient redistribution of goods, often for geographical or economic reasons.

Keywords: Transshipment policies; artificial intelligence; Complete-Pooling; Partial-Pooling; supply chain management

Introduction

The use of artificial intelligence for the automation of inventory management firstly brings a gain in precision by producing predictions linked to each point of sale separately. This is possible thanks to the volumes and continuous flows of data that these data science tools can ingest.

AI-Driven Knowledge Management Assets, Volume 2, 153–165

Published under exclusive licence by Emerald Publishing Limited
doi:10.1108/978-1-83662-778-420261008

This qualitative study explores the cooperative dynamics between artificial intelligence (AI) systems and lateral transshipment processes in logistics management. With the rise of complex supply chains requiring efficient and adaptable operations, understanding how AI can enhance transshipment strategies is essential for modern logistics.

The ever-evolving landscape of logistics and supply chain management necessitates innovative approaches to meet the increasing demands for efficiency and responsiveness. Lateral transshipment, which involves transferring cargo between two or more points in a network, offers a flexible solution for inventory management and resource allocation. This study investigates the collaboration between AI technologies and lateral transshipment, aiming to uncover qualitative insights into their synergistic potential.

Supply chain management is an efficient approach to managing the flow of information, goods, and services in fulfillment of customer demand.

Artificial intelligence (AI) and transshipment are two concepts that, when combined, can have a major impact on the efficiency of supply chains and logistics operations.

AI can analyze large amounts of data (weather, traffic, costs, demand, etc.) to optimize transport routes and schedules. For example, in the case of container transshipment between ships, AI can predict the best transfer windows based on real-time conditions, reducing delays and increasing efficiency.

It enables optimized inventory management in the warehouses where transshipment takes place. Using machine learning algorithms, it can predict inventory needs based on demand trends, seasonality, or other external factors. This minimizes the risk of stockouts or overstocking.

In cross-docking facilities, robots and autonomous vehicles can be used to move goods from one location to another without human intervention. AI oversees these systems by optimizing their movements, monitoring operations, and minimizing human error.

AI enables the collection and analysis of real-time data on cross-docking operations, providing continuous feedback that can be used to improve processes. For example, AI can detect inefficiencies in resource utilization and suggest changes.

It can help reduce operating costs by optimizing resource use and improving transportation efficiency. It can also help reduce carbon footprints by enabling more precise route management and reducing unnecessary trips or equipment downtime.

Thumbelina, this paper focuses on lateral transshipment as an alternative and studies transshipment policies at a supplier with two symmetrical retailers.

According to Samtani et al. (2021), integrating artificial intelligence (AI) into your warehouse management could be the innovation you have been waiting for to improve your operational efficiency. And, they explain that in such a complex environment, AI can act as a catalyst to make the system smoother and more efficient. By making better use of every available resource, AI makes the supply chain more connected, leading to better product traceability and increased performance. The result is added value not only for the company but also for consumers. With AI's ability to provide more accurate information, customer trust can only increase.

Landwehr (2015) shows that AI, a cutting-edge technology that has the potential to learn and analyze data in real time, is now an indispensable tool for inventory management and the operation of an efficient supply chain. The positive impact of AI is undeniable, going even beyond automation and robotization to increase time savings, profitability and even customer satisfaction.

Justin and Mizuko (2017) agree that, in the context of inventory management, AI offers undeniable added value, particularly in terms of time savings and profitability. Drawing on a multitude of data, it can, for example, predict the company's future needs based on historical sales data, orders and stock levels.

It can also optimize decisions regarding procurement and storage, even going so far as to recommend adjustments in the physical layout of stocks in the warehouse.

Nakandala et al. (2017) indicate that the role of artificial intelligence in optimizing inventory management by applying Transshipment-Lateral is multifaceted and complex. For example, AI can analyze the sales rate of products and create an inventory management model based on this. It is thus possible to precisely adjust stock levels at retailers to avoid shortages or excess products, which corresponds to Transshipment-Preventive. This contributes not only to better inventory management but also to a significant reduction in costs.

According to the research work of Petousi and Sifaki (2020), Artificial Intelligence has quickly become an essential pillar in supply chain management and optimization. Whether by accelerating the decision-making process, optimizing production, storage, or transport capacities, or updating multiple action scenarios and crisis prevention, AI is capable of improving almost all facets of supply chain management.

This is, for example, the case in an omnichannel warehouse that manages inventory. Located at the heart of all operations, from delivery to online sales, including in-store pickup, an omnichannel warehouse must deal with a delicate mix of different channels and actors, and a multitude of different locations and preparation methods.

Ultimately, whether it's improving inventory management efficiency or increasing customer satisfaction, AI is an asset for any company looking to optimize its supply chain.

According to Ayling and Chapman (2022) and Tahiru (2021), the future of AI in inventory management is here, and it is transforming the way retailers operate. As AI improves at lightning speed and takes over more and more business tasks, its impact is being felt across the retail industry. At the same time, retail itself is reinventing itself in the wake of digital transformation, omnichannel expectations, and changing customer demands post-COVID.

Today, technology is becoming a critical part of business. Artificial intelligence and machine learning are widely expected to reshape businesses. By enabling organizations to automate repetitive tasks and analyze vast data sets, AI will drive faster, more efficient performance across the enterprise and in nearly every industry.

Supply chain is no exception. In fact, AI has already begun to transform manufacturing, from how we build our products to how we source, schedule, manage, and distribute the raw materials that go into them. Particular firms are taking advantage of *AI*. In the next decade.

Danaher (2018) shows that more and more companies with very large supply chains and a large number of orders are now using AI to automate these processes. Indeed, with the amount of data generated by the different links in the supply chain, AI makes it possible to avoid sources of errors and save time and money.

First, we must differentiate between process automation (RPA) and Artificial Intelligence. RPA makes it possible to execute data processes without many possible options by reproducing the mechanical gestures of humans. Artificial Intelligence is capable of analyzing and structuring information (machine learning) and thus reproducing thought processes that humans might have. Of course, these concepts can be used at the same time within a structure.

Process automation is a field where artificial intelligence uses machine learning to learn to identify phenomena or analyze data using algorithms. In this way, the machine will identify patterns and associate answers with questions to understand how certain given situations work.

The research of Jarrahi (2018) focuses on the study of e-commerce where customers want to be able to get their products everywhere, all the time and at the best price, cooperating with AI. This can be extremely useful. Indeed, artificial intelligence has never been as mature and accessible as it is today, especially in logistics, because its environment and its operation allow us to imagine many applications of AI to optimize processes.

Artificial intelligence (AI) collaboration can transform business practices across various sectors by enabling synergies, innovation, and increased efficiency.

First, AI can automate repetitive tasks, analyze massive volumes of data, and make more accurate forecasts. When adopted collaboratively by multiple stakeholders (companies, research institutions, technology startups), it can lead to cost reductions and increased productivity in sectors such as manufacturing, logistics, and financial services.

Second, AI can enable more responsive and intelligent supply chain management. By collaborating with technologies such as blockchain, AI can help track products in real time, improve demand forecasting, and reduce inefficiencies. This allows companies to better respond to market fluctuations and consumer needs.

It also enables a deeper understanding of consumer preferences by analyzing their behaviors and interactions. In sectors such as retail, banking, and healthcare, AI can be used to offer highly personalized products or services. Cooperation between technology and commercial companies can advance this personalization to a level where the customer experience becomes more seamless and satisfying.

AI collaboration allows expertise from different sectors to be combined to develop new products or services. For example, in the automotive sector, partnerships between car manufacturers and technology companies have enabled the development of autonomous vehicles. In the healthcare sector, collaborations between laboratories, pharmaceutical companies, and AI startups have contributed to improved diagnostics and treatments.

It can help better understand and manage risks, particularly in the financial sector, by anticipating fraud or adjusting investment portfolios in real time. Collaboration between financial institutions, technology companies, and regulators makes it possible to create intelligent systems to enhance security and minimize risks.

Furthermore, in sectors such as healthcare, education, and public services, AI can be used to create accessible and inclusive solutions. For example, AI collaborations have led to the development of tools for people with disabilities or populations living in remote areas. AI can also be used to improve online learning services, making education more accessible to a broad population.

Finally, cross-sector cooperation between the public and private sectors, as well as between different commercial actors, is essential to successfully integrate AI on a large scale. By creating innovation ecosystems where companies, governments, and researchers share data, resources, and skills, AI applications can be deployed on a larger scale, thus strengthening collaborations within different industrial sectors.

In short, AI cooperation makes it possible to combine the strengths of different actors to more effectively meet the needs of a constantly evolving market, while fostering smarter, more inclusive, and more sustainable solutions.

Qualitative Study

A qualitative research design was employed, focusing on interviews with industry experts and stakeholders involved in logistics and supply chain management. The participants were selected based on their experience with AI integration and lateral transshipment processes. Thematic analysis was utilized to identify patterns and insights from the data collected. According to the state of the literature, it is likely that the research works that deal with the problem of Lateral-Transshipment combined with Artificial Intelligence, are too rare. For that, in this paper, we study a qualitative study based on this concept.

This collaboration between different retailers at the same level generally takes the form of a "lateral transshipment," presented in Fig. 8.1.

There are two Lateral Transshipment policies, which are:

(1) Complete-Pooling: The retailer agrees to transfer all of its available stock when needed; that is, to pool all of its stock with another site, without any restriction.
(2) Partial-Pooling: Transshipment is performed by preserving a targeted stock level.

We then find the following variants:

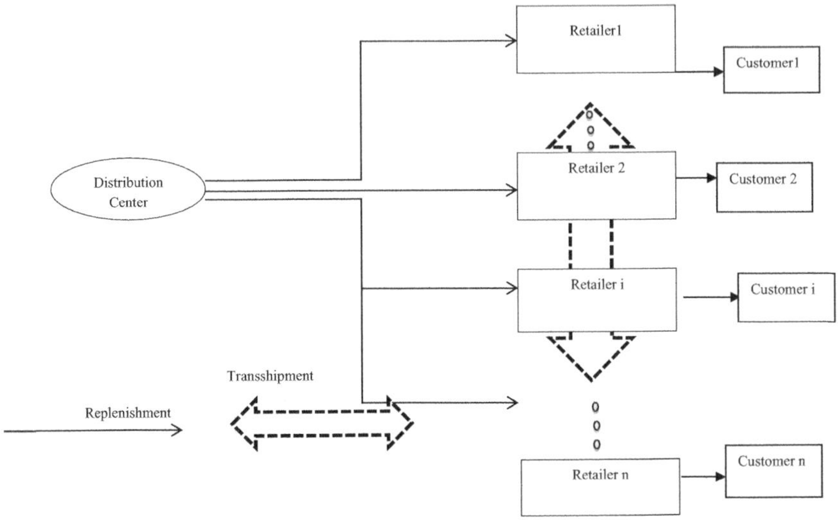

Fig. 8.1. Representation of Transshipment in a Logistics Chain. *Source:* Paterson et al. (2012)

- A retailer accepts transshipment up to the surplus stock at a transshipment threshold equal to the estimated demand for the next period.
- The decision to integrate a transshipment at the level of a retailer depends on the current stock level and the time remaining before the next supply.
- A retailer accepts transshipment up to the excess stock of a threshold equal to its reorder point (Petousi & Sifaki, 2020).
- The retailer applies transshipment up to the excess stock of a threshold equal to its safety stock.

Research Design

In our paper, we seek to study the impact of "Artificial Intelligence" on "Lateral Transshipment."

For this, we conducted an in-depth survey with Tunisian companies.

This sampling is done online, which helps us to better understand the functioning of these companies.

We used thematic analysis to divide the results into categories based on a common divisor.

The data are collected from January 27, 2024 to November 27, 2024 from seven Tunisian companies.

The demographic data collected includes several categories, namely types of activity, sector of activity, company size, etc. (Table 8.1).

Table 8.1. Qualitative Analysis.

Asked Question	Answer
What is the lead time for the initial order from the central warehouse to the retailer?	Constant
What is the quantity of the order to be delivered from the central warehouse to the retailer?	According to the law and the company
What is the distance between Warehouse Central and the retailer?	Longer than that between different retailers of the same level
What is the law of random demand?	$N(\mu, \sigma)$, $P(k)$
What is the number of retailers?	Two or Multi-Retailer

Qualitative Analysis

The main objective is to minimize, as much as possible, the total cost of retailers and the Disservice rate. Delivery represents a cost for companies. As companies increasingly deliver to their customers with multiple delivery options, to limit costs, the company can direct the consumer to the most economically advantageous solution about the available resources. This is where Artificial Intelligence comes in since it allows us to anticipate several things based on delivery times and points.

The integration of AI in lateral transshipment presents significant opportunities for improvement in logistics operations. By fostering cooperation between human expertise and AI capabilities, organizations can achieve greater levels of efficiency and responsiveness. However, it is vital to address challenges such as data privacy, integration complexities, and the need for skilled personnel to manage AI tools effectively.

From the data, AI will be able to anticipate consumers' purchasing intentions based on days, times, but also according to other factors such as weather, events, etc. But also to improve customer satisfaction, by optimizing delivery and return times. For the logistics manager, flow management can quickly become a headache. Artificial intelligence provides an answer to this problem by automatically optimizing the various logistics flows. AI in logistics can help you optimize... Human physical flows in the warehouse.

In warehouses, Artificial Intelligence is profoundly changing the game by managing the complete cycle from stock receipt to customer delivery, including packaging and order preparation.

Based on historical data, Artificial Intelligence detects current orders and stocks, predicts the needs of the entire network, and suggests optimized decisions (purchases, transfers, etc.).

Improving the level of Disservice for customers has become a major concern in the management of distribution systems. For a network made up of two or multiple retailers, the imbalance of quantities stored in these sites due to random demand is a common problem. In the case where one retailer has a surplus of stock while the other is facing a shortage, the collaboration between these retailers, called "Lateral Transshipment," could solve the problem and avoid any shortage.

Artificial intelligence also makes it possible to considerably facilitate the work of order pickers, thanks to automation. In this way, they can save time on their tasks and also gain in productivity.

To achieve this, artificial intelligence guides robots moving alone between the different retailers. It is then possible to optimize the quantity of Transshipment between warehouses for faster picking and a lower error rate.

AI Cooperation in Various Sectors in Tunisia

Artificial intelligence (AI) is playing an increasingly crucial role in many sectors, transforming the way businesses and industries operate. Here's an overview of its importance in various sectors. First, in healthcare, AI is revolutionizing the healthcare sector by enabling faster and more accurate diagnoses through the analysis of medical images (X-rays, MRIs, etc.), disease prediction based on genetic data, and improved personalized treatments. Applications such as virtual patient assistants and the automation of administrative processes are reducing costs and freeing up time for healthcare professionals.

Second, in the financial sector, AI is used for process automation (such as portfolio management or lending), fraud detection through intelligent surveillance systems, and risk management. Machine learning algorithms are also used to predict market trends and assist in investment decision-making. Similarly, autonomous vehicles represent one of the most high-profile applications of AI. However, AI in the transportation sector is not limited to this. It is also used to optimize delivery routes, improve traffic management, and develop smart public transportation systems.

Also, AI is transforming the e-commerce and retail sectors by enabling personalized recommendations based on consumer purchasing behavior, automating customer service with chatbots, and optimizing inventory through predictive analytics. AI also helps create a smoother and more engaging customer experience.

AI offers new opportunities to personalize learning. AI-powered educational tools allow courses to be tailored to the pace and needs of each student. Furthermore, teachers can automate certain administrative tasks, allowing them to devote more time to teaching.

AI is used to improve productivity in the manufacturing sector through predictive machine maintenance, automation of production processes, and optimization of supply chains. Intelligent robots can work alongside humans to improve the efficiency and safety of industrial processes.

In agriculture, AI can analyze real-time data from sensors and drones to optimize irrigation, monitor crops, and detect diseases. It also helps predict crop yields and minimize the use of pesticides and natural resources, contributing to more sustainable agriculture.

Finally, AI plays a key role in cybersecurity by detecting anomalies and anticipating threats in real time. It is also used in video surveillance for facial recognition and tracking suspicious behavior, thus improving public safety.

AI is used to improve energy efficiency, for example, by optimizing power grid management or monitoring energy consumption. It also plays a key role in the development of green technologies and the optimization of renewable energy production systems.

In the entertainment industry, AI enables personalized recommendations for movies, series, and music. It is also used in content creation (for example, to generate special effects or animations), as well as in improving the user experience.

AI is reshaping many sectors by optimizing processes, automating repetitive tasks, and enabling faster and more accurate decision-making. Its impact is widespread and continues to grow in all areas of economic and social life. Companies that adopt these technologies can gain a significant competitive advantage.

The collaboration of AI with logistics in Tunisia represents a significant opportunity to improve the sector's efficiency, profitability, and sustainability. Integrating artificial intelligence (AI) into the supply chain could transform several aspects of operations, from transportation to inventory management to delivery process optimization. Here are some examples of AI applications in the logistics sector in Tunisia:

First, route optimization and transportation management. AI can be used to optimize transportation routes by analyzing traffic conditions, weather, and other external factors in real time. AI systems can help reduce delivery times and save costs by minimizing travel distances. This can particularly benefit Tunisian companies that manage truck fleets for product distribution.

Second, AI systems can improve inventory management by predicting needs based on sales trends, seasons, and special events. This helps minimize stockouts and surpluses. Additionally, AI can optimize warehouse layouts and automate certain inventory management tasks.

Also, the use of autonomous robots and AI systems in warehouses is expanding worldwide. In Tunisia, these technologies can be used to automate sorting, storage, and order preparation, reducing operational costs and improving order processing speed.

AI can predict demand by analyzing historical sales data, consumer trends, and other variables. These forecasts allow Tunisian companies to better anticipate market needs, optimize production, and better plan logistics based on fluctuations in demand.

AI-based technologies can also improve the traceability of goods throughout their journey. Geolocation systems, combined with AI, can track the location of products in real time, ensure their security, and inform customers about the status of their order.

In Tunisia, a significant logistics sector is linked to the import and export of goods. AI can be used to facilitate customs document processing, regulatory compliance, and the optimization of international trade processes. This reduces the risk of human error and speeds up administrative procedures.

Finally, AI can also be used to improve customer relations in the logistics sector. AI-powered chatbots and virtual assistants can instantly answer customer questions, track orders, and resolve issues in real time. This improves the customer experience and reduces staff workload.

AI can also be used to promote more sustainable logistics practices by optimizing resources, reducing CO_2 emissions, and promoting more responsible resource management. For example, AI can help reduce fuel consumption by optimizing routes and improving vehicle fleet management.

Despite these advantages, integrating AI into Tunisian logistics presents some challenges:

First, implementing AI in logistics requires significant investments in infrastructure, software, and employee training.

Also, the lack of specialized talent in AI and advanced logistics may slow the development of these technologies in Tunisia.

Finally, regulations surrounding data use and cybersecurity must be taken into account to ensure the protection of sensitive information in AI systems.

Cooperation between AI and logistics in Tunisia offers significant potential to improve business competitiveness, modernize the sector, and offer faster and more efficient services. However, it requires government support, investments in training, and infrastructure development to overcome current challenges and fully leverage the benefits of AI.

Case Study: Cooperation Between Artificial Intelligence and Transshipment Lateral in the Tunisian Society of Artificial Intelligence (STIA)

The cooperation between artificial intelligence and lateral transshipment is poised to revolutionize logistics management. As this study highlights, leveraging AI's analytical and decision-support capabilities can profoundly impact operational efficiency and risk management in the transshipment process. Future research should explore quantitative measures of success and further investigate the long-term implications of these cooperative strategies.

The application of Lateral Transshipment in the context of the Tunisian Society of Artificial Intelligence (STIA) could refer to the use of advanced technologies, such as artificial intelligence, to optimize and automate transshipment logistics processes, particularly in ports or between different modes of transport. Transshipment is an operation where goods are transferred from one means of transport to another, often in ports, between ships, or between different types of vehicles (train, truck, etc.).

Within the framework of STIA, several applications can be envisaged:

First, the use of AI to predict the best transshipment routes and times to maximize the efficiency of goods flows and minimize costs.

Also, the implementation of AI algorithms to analyze and manage inventories in real time, to better coordinate transshipments and avoid stockouts or overstocks.

The use of AI systems to automate cargo transshipment, including container management at ports, optimization of cargo placement in warehouses, and real-time tracking.

Furthermore, AI can help predict potential failures in equipment used in transshipment operations (such as cranes, trucks, etc.), thereby reducing downtime and improving overall efficiency.

The use of AI-powered data analysis tools to evaluate the performance of transshipment processes, identify bottlenecks, and recommend improvements.

Finally, machine learning algorithms can analyze various parameters (costs, distances, time, etc.) and propose optimal solutions for cargo transshipment, thus reducing logistics costs while improving delivery times. The use of artificial intelligence in these areas could help Tunisian society modernize its logistics infrastructure and improve the country's competitiveness in the areas of transportation and supply chain management.

The collaboration between artificial intelligence (AI) and lateral transshipment within the Tunisian Artificial Intelligence Society (STIA) could play a crucial role in improving logistics processes, particularly in transportation and supply chain management. Lateral transshipment refers to the action of transferring goods from one means of transport to another without having to repackage or completely unload them. This type of process is particularly relevant in ports, logistics hubs, or transit areas.

Artificial intelligence could be used to analyze transport flows in real time and predict optimal routes for lateral transshipment. AI algorithms, such as those based on machine learning, can optimize transport vehicle routes based on various factors, such as road congestion, weather conditions, or loading/unloading schedules. This would reduce costs, improve efficiency, and minimize delays.

AI can be integrated to monitor and predict storage, inventory management, and distribution needs. By using predictive models, AIMS could better manage logistics and reduce costs associated with stockouts or excess product. AI could also be used to detect anomalies in cross-docking processes, thereby improving the management of human and material resources in cross-docking areas.

Robotic technologies combined with AI can automate certain steps in lateral cross-docking. For example, robots or autonomous systems could be used to move containers or cargo from one transport to another, reducing the need for human intervention and increasing operational accuracy. These systems may also be able to adapt to dynamic environments, such as port docks, where conditions change frequently.

AI could also improve the safety of cross-docking operations. By analyzing surveillance camera footage and using image and object recognition systems, AI can detect suspicious behavior, handling errors, or potential safety issues. This can help reduce the risk of incidents and ensure a safer and more reliable work environment.

By analyzing large amounts of data related to transshipment processes, AI can provide valuable insights for STIA managers, enabling them to make more informed decisions. For example, AI systems could anticipate fluctuations in demand, optimize operators' work schedules, and predict specific equipment needs.

By developing AI solutions tailored to transshipment needs, STIA could also enhance its partnerships with other logistics, port, or international organizations. AI could facilitate document management, cargo traceability, and compliance with international standards, making operations smoother and more transparent.

In summary, the collaboration between AI and lateral transshipment within STIA offers significant opportunities to improve the efficiency of logistics operations, safety, profitability, and human and material resource management. Thanks to artificial intelligence, STIA could become a leader in the digital transformation of the logistics sector in Tunisia.

Conclusion

In our research work, we emphasize the importance of cooperating with "Transshipment - Lateral" and "Artificial Intelligence."

Overall, advancements in artificial intelligence and emerging technologies have undoubtedly revolutionized various aspects of the supply chain and transshipment between different retailers. With the clever application of AI, logistics operations have been able to be optimized substantially, leading to significant reductions in costs and processing times.

Furthermore, the integration of autonomous robots and cobots within warehouses has significantly increased the efficiency of the supply chain, freeing up valuable hours for teams.

The power of AI to anticipate maintenance needs, closely monitor suppliers, and improve customer experience has profoundly transformed the face of the industry, thus offering a brighter logistics future.

By wisely adopting these innovations, companies can make the most of the opportunities offered by these technological advancements, for an ever more efficient supply chain and a brighter logistics future.

But, this area is rare. For this, we put as a perspective the integrated cooperation between AI and transshipment in our Tunisian companies.

References

Ayling, J., & Chapman, A. (2022). Putting AI ethics to work: Are the tools fit for purpose? *AI and Ethics*, *2*(3), 405–429. https://doi.org/10.1007/s43681-021-00084-x

Danaher, J. (2018). Toward an ethics of AI assistants: An initial framework. *Philosophy and Technology*, *31*(4), 629–653. https://doi.org/10.1007/s13347-018-0317-3

Jarrahi, M. H. (2018). Artificial intelligence and the future of work: Human-AI symbiosis in organizational decision making. *Business Horizons*, *61*(4), 577–586. https://doi.org/10.1016/j.bushor.2018.03.007

Justin, R., & Mizuko, I. (2017). *From good intentions to real outcomes: Equity by design in.* Digital Media and Learning Research Hub. https://clalliance.org/wp-content/uploads/2017/11/GIROreport_1031.pdf

Landwehr, C. (2015). We need a building code for building code. *Communication ACM*, *58*(2), 24–26. https://doi.org/10.1145/2700341

Nakandala, D., Lau, H., & Shum, P. K. C. (2017). A lateral transshipment model for perishable inventory management. *International Journal of Production Research*, *55*(18), 5341–5354. https://doi.org/10.1080/00207543.2017.1312587

Paterson, C., Teunter, R., & Glazebrook, K. (2012). Enhanced lateral transshipments in a multi-location inventory system. *European Journal of Operational Research*, *221*(2), 317–327.

Pessot, E., Zangiacomi, A., Marchiori, I., & Fornasiero, R. (2023). Empowering supply chains with Industry 4.0 technologies to face megatrends. *Journal of Business Logistics*, *44*(4), 609–640. https://doi.org/10.1111/jbl.12360

Petousi, V., & Sifaki, E. (2020). Contextualizing harm in the framework of research misconduct. Findings from discourse analysis of scientific publications. *International Journal of Sustainable Development*, *23*(3–4), 149–174. https://doi.org/10.1504/IJSD.2020.10037655

Samtani, S., Kantarcioglu, M., & Chen, H. (2021). A multi-disciplinary perspective for conducting artificial intelligence-enabled privacy analytics: Connecting data, algorithms, and systems. *ACM Transactions on Management Information Systems (TMIS)*, *12*(1), 1–18. https://doi.org/10.1145/3447507

Tahiru, F. (2021). AI in education: A systematic literature review. *Journal of Cases on Information Technology (JCIT)*, *23*(1), 1–20. https://doi.org/10.4018/JCIT.2021010101

The Role of AI and KM in Enhancing Employee Relationship and Talent Management

Chapter 9

How Artificial Intelligence Influences Employees' Organisational Behaviour in Workplaces

Mandy Mok Kim Man[a], *Wong Wan Ting*[b], *Lebene Soga*[c] *and Maria Fernandez-Muiños*[d]

[a]University of Reading, UK
[b]University of Reading Malaysia, Malaysia
[c]Leeds Beckett University, UK
[d]University of Salamanca, Spain

Abstract

Artificial intelligence (AI) has become popular for enhancing organisational productivity, with tools available for administration, management, operations, manufacturing, production and decision-making. This chapter uses the case studies of Walmart and Amazon to discuss how the adoption of AI for productivity and inventory management influences contemporary issues faced by employees. It emphasises the importance of employees' acceptance and response, which significantly influences engagement and our understanding of how AI affects employee roles and behaviours, job satisfaction and expectations, and therefore overall performance. While AI saves time and resources, potentially reducing reliance on human resources, employees' acceptance and responses remain core to AI adoption. On the one hand, AI takes over routine tasks, granting employees more time for participative discussions, strategic planning and research, potentially increasing job satisfaction. On the other hand, AI implementation raises concerns about job displacement. These and other interrelated factors are discussed in this chapter.

AI-Driven Knowledge Management Assets, Volume 2, 169–194

doi:10.1108/978-1-83662-778-420261009

Keywords: Artificial intelligence; employees; organisational behaviour; workplaces; productivity; job satisfaction

Introduction

In the digital era, artificial intelligence (AI) has emerged as a transformative force, reshaping workplace dynamics and organisational behaviour. AI is characterised by its ability to emulate human intelligence, enabling the automation of intricate tasks through algorithms, machine learning (ML) and robotics (Mok, 2022). From streamlining data analysis to optimising decision-making processes, AI has become an indispensable component of contemporary businesses. Organisations leverage AI-driven tools to manage vast amounts of data, anticipate trends and enhance operational efficiencies, thereby reducing reliance on human labour while simultaneously increasing productivity and performance. However, the widespread implementation of AI also necessitates a reassessment of its impact on employees' roles, job satisfaction, workplace dynamics and expectations, as research in this domain is still in its nascent stages. This chapter delves into the influence of AI on employees' organisational behaviour, examining its effects on job roles, decision-making processes, knowledge management and workforce adaptability. It critically evaluates the benefits, challenges and ethical considerations associated with AI while providing industry-specific case studies to contextualise its practical applications. By aligning the discussion with the book's overarching theme 'AI-Driven Knowledge Management: Strategies for the Modern Business Landscape', this chapter aims to offer insights into AI's role in shaping the future workplace.

AI in the Modern Workplace

AI has accelerated rapid developments in science and technology, influencing workplaces, impacting manufacturing and service industries and reshaping business models. With AI's widespread adoption, job displacement has occurred. For instance, AI has replaced manpower in manufacturing and production with automated machines, robots and programmed computer systems to enable 24/7 production. AI also enhances the accuracy of complex tasks, leading to greater efficiency and effectiveness. Organisations can save on human resources, time and costs by implementing AI. For instance, Amazon uses AI robots to scan parcel barcodes 24/7, categorizing them for postal addresses so they can be sent to various regions via air freight on time. AI has sped up lead times and workflows, increasing work performance and shifting the reliance on humans to AI for task completion.

AI creates job opportunities for the workforce with critical-thinking, problem-solving, data-analysis and computer-programming skills to monitor and control AI tools in workplaces (World Economic Forum, 2023). For example, in the medical industry, ML is used to diagnose diseases based on patient symptoms and signs (Mok, 2022). Doctors and nurses must therefore have the knowledge and skills to apply ML, make data-driven decisions and identify diseases. AI is also widely applied in the pharmaceutical industry, where companies use chatbots (programmed robots to respond to consumer inquiries) to help customers find the right medicine or products. For instance, Novo Nordisk has a chatbot to answer questions from patients and recommend appropriate medications. This changes how patients consult doctors and obtain medicines. As a result, people need to be equipped with up-to-date knowledge and skills aligned with scientific and technological advancements to adapt to workplace changes.

AI enables workplace automation, with machines and equipment programmed to run processes and complete tasks (Hassan, 2024). This allows humans more time to focus on creative and innovative work, as well as strategic planning for the organisation. For instance, automated machines can be programmed for manufacturing production and repeated for weekly or monthly cycles. While machines can handle routine production, the human workforce can concentrate on research and development (R&D), strategic marketing, creative product marketing and building long-term customer relationships. For example, Alibaba uses AI chatbots on its e-commerce platforms like Taobao, Tmall, AliExpress, Lazada, Hema, Xianyu and Fliggy to serve over a billion customers, reducing the need for workers to answer customer inquiries. These AI chatbots operate 24/7 and communicate in multiple languages, thereby increasing work efficiency and effectiveness. Organisations can save time and costs on routine tasks and focus on strategic planning to achieve long-term goals.

AI is crucial for the development of international businesses and their future direction in coping with globalisation and digitalisation trends (Park, 2018). AI has a profound impact on various aspects of corporate governance, organisational development, international connectivity, workplace human relations, workflow procedures and efficiency, human dependency on machines for multiple tasks and daily routines involving manual recording and face-to-face interactions (Park, 2018). Organisations that adopt AI technologies in their production and operations tend to experience cost savings, streamline workflows, enhance task completion or service provision, achieve higher productivity and demonstrate improved organisational performance (Goodfellow et al., 2016). AI technologies employed in production and manufacturing encompass robotic machines, automated engines and equipment capable of operating continuously and replacing humans for challenging duties. Examples include software programmes for autonomous vehicles, programmed drones, automated inspection of finished goods and virtual receptionists. Similarly, automated systems can provide comprehensive voice or written information, banking services or analytical services. These systems can automate the completion of numerous tasks and resolve various problems that would otherwise require human intervention. Research indicates that AI can directly enhance production output in the manufacturing sector (Alphabet Inc., 2019) and augment overall employee productivity (Buchmeister et al., 2019) through the utilisation of software, tools or machines that facilitate task completion. Furthermore, AI has replaced certain human workers in service industries, such as hotels, fast food delivery and logistics, with 24/7 scanning and tracking services, automated drone photography and automated laundry with washing machines. This transformation of workplaces redefines job roles and responsibilities, displaces some jobs and simultaneously creates new positions that necessitate AI-related knowledge and skills.

Advancements in AI technology have significantly reduced the need for 8-hour workdays, in-person meetings, brick-and-mortar sales and manual inventory checks, boosting productivity, efficiency and effectiveness. The rapid development of AI is largely driven by digital technology that has enabled the collection and storage of vast amounts of data, so-called big data (Byrum, 2018), and the availability of advanced computer hardware and software, including hardware accelerators and tensor processing units (Kapoor, 2019). These data can then be analysed and utilised by various entities such as individuals, organisations, institutions and governments to detect patterns, make decisions, conduct R&D, forecast, plan and more. Additionally, advancements in computer science, cloud computing and quantum computing have propelled AI development by making computer hardware and software more affordable and widely available through mass production to meet the global demand. This has enhanced AI learning and its applications across many sectors. Consequently, AI is now integrated into daily activities such as Internet access via smartphones, app downloads and centralised data management of financial and administrative information among others. Similarly, AI has taken centre stage in industrial production and manufacturing through robotic automation, proactive healthcare management, disease mapping, social media monitoring and many more.

AI Changes Business Practices

The global trend in AI demonstrates that companies within the AI and high-tech sectors are among the most profitable entities, generating substantial annual revenues. For instance, in 2023, Amazon reported an annual revenue of USD 554 billion, Apple USD 383 billion, Volkswagen USD 335 billion, Alphabet USD 297 billion and Toyota USD 296 billion (Dyvik, 2024). These five companies, which collectively generated the highest revenues in 2023, extensively utilise AI across diverse domains, including science and technology, retail, wholesale and automotive. This broad applicability of AI underscores its pivotal role in propelling these sectors into the future. Notably, Volkswagen and Toyota have integrated AI into conventional technologies to develop autonomous driving capabilities. Amazon has implemented robotic technology in its logistics operations, enabling continuous parcel tracking and location. These robots operate autonomously, systematically identifying parcels within specific districts, states and countries, and automating the scanning and tracking of parcels from dispatch to delivery. Furthermore, Samsung has developed smart glasses for virtual communication among surgical team members during operations. These examples collectively illustrate the transformative potential of AI technology in various industries, contributing to the overall enhancement of human well-being.

AI significantly impacts business practices by enhancing production and boosting productivity (Brynjolfsson et al., 2020). It advances numerous technological fields such as science and technology, robotics and automation, data management and analytics and information technology. It allows industries to overcome human working hour limitations by enabling the continuous operation of machines and robots. This improves production efficiency and effectiveness, freeing humans to focus on tasks like building customer relationships, meeting clients and conducting sales activities that require face-to-face interactions. This approach helps retain existing customers, attract new ones and increase company sales. By integrating AI technologies, innovations in science and technology, and robotic and automation technologies into production, organisations can reduce production costs, achieve economies of scale and scope and meet objectives such as producing high-quality products at lower costs. Through such practice, the industry can lower costs and improve quality, achieving customer satisfaction and enhancing the welfare of both customers and employees.

In addition, AI reduces errors and prevents non-compliance by eliminating miscalculations, skill-based errors, transgressions and arguably human biases (Davenport & Ronanki, 2018). Through scientific data management, big data and related information can be collected and analysed with computer software, leading to accurate decision-making. For instance, SAP ERP (enterprise resource planning), developed by the German company SAP SE, aids businesses in resource analysis and strategic planning, ensuring decisions are based on factual data rather than emotions or bias. In vaccine manufacturing, the SAP ERP system enables centralised management, cost identification, resource allocation, streamlined operations and improved efficiency, thereby speeding up decision-making and boosting productivity. AI is used to detect defects in production units, ensuring zero-defect products by the final stage. This improves total quality management and ensures products meet organisational standards while reducing the need for error-prone manual inspections. Additionally, advanced AI-powered scanning systems record production unit data into computer systems for easy retrieval during post-production operations, such as quality inspections and process reviews. AI technology reduces labour-intensive tasks and simplifies complex production processes.

AI Influences Organisational Behaviour

With the advent of AI tools, numerous tasks can be automated and programmed by systems, significantly altering the nature of human interactions within the workplace. In recent times, employees have increasingly relied on virtual meetings, simulations and online demonstrations to complete projects, organise tasks and coordinate projects, replacing traditional face-to-face meetings. The digitalisation facilitated by AI enables synchronous e-meetings, allowing members to join from various locations globally, transcending geographical boundaries and time constraints. Consequently, employees have exhibited a growing preference for virtual communication over face-to-face interactions, leading to a shift in organisational behaviours from in-person interactions to digital communication. This shift may result in employees perceiving a reduction in the personal nature of their working relationships, as communication becomes primarily focused on task completion rather than fostering closer human connections through face-to-face interactions.

AI tools are being implemented to assist workers by automating hazardous tasks, thereby enhancing workplace safety. For instance, at construction sites, automated and programmed AI tools can assist employees in completing tasks such as robotic piling, bricklaying, welding and constructing structures using 3D printing. This reduces risks for employees, allowing them to focus on other tasks that enhance productivity, such as designing workflows to reduce lead time, optimising operations for faster workflows, accessing relevant information through systematic AI channels and completing tasks on time. Consequently, employees primarily interact with colleagues on matters related to their duties, potentially creating echo chambers where they only engage with those in their work circles. This reinforcement of existing biases can lead to the formation of cliques and the exclusion of individuals outside their immediate working groups (Soga, Vogel, et al., 2021; 2021b).

The implementation of AI within organisations directly influences employee motivation by fostering a positive work environment when AI automates repetitive tasks (Hassan, 2024). AI can be utilised to analyse data for precise decision-making, enabling organisations to attain their long-term objectives and goals. For instance, organisations employ diverse algorithms, including ML, deep neural networks, expert systems, decision trees and rule-based systems, for decision-making purposes. These decisions encompass strategic planning, resolving intricate problems that necessitate critical thinking, administrative and management functions, daily control and monitoring and customer relationship management.

Employees in organisations report increased job satisfaction when AI assists them in their workplaces. Research indicates that 59% of employees believe AI has enhanced their job satisfaction (Cawley, 2024). This is attributed to the introduction of new AI tools in the workplace, which ignites employees' curiosity to acquire new knowledge and skills (Dardis, 2023). This fosters an environment of exploration and self-assurance in utilising and applying these tools. Consequently, employees develop confidence in their work, leading to improved performance and credibility in completing challenging tasks. Achieving success in these tasks enhances their career satisfaction and self-esteem. As a result, employees experience career advancement and professional growth within the organisation. Indirectly, this contributes to employee retention and training, reducing turnover rates and alleviating the burden on the human resources department for recruitment (Oginni et al., 2018). This fosters a sense of belonging among employees within the organisation (Drapkin, 2024).

AI significantly influences job expectations within organisations. Job expectations encompass various aspects, including responsibilities, compensation, job satisfaction, rewards and opportunities for advancement (Cambridge Dictionary, 2024). As shown by Oginni et al. (2018), job expectations also include salary, working hours, job duties, protection from workplace hazards and adherence to organisational regulations. While there is a concern among employees that AI tools may lead to job displacement, most organisations report minimal job displacement. Instead, there is a growing demand for employees with AI knowledge and skills to manage AI-related tasks, creating new job opportunities. AI tools in the workplace enhance workflow, increase productivity and improve efficiency. Consequently, employee expectations of their employers have shifted towards safer work environments with reduced responsibilities and increased assistance from AI, leading to enhanced rewards and promotions due to improved organisational performance.

In the following sections, a structured analysis of case studies examining Walmart and Amazon's Smart Inventory Management System and its impact on employee organisational behaviour is conducted to explore the integration of AI into retail operations. AI has revolutionised inventory management, supply chain efficiency and customer satisfaction. Walmart and Amazon, two global retail giants, have adopted distinct yet equally ambitious approaches to integrating AI into their operational ecosystems, particularly in inventory management. Walmart, a leader in brick-and-mortar retail, has been at the forefront of digital transformation by deploying AI-driven systems to enhance inventory accuracy, streamline replenishment and optimise stock distribution across its extensive network of physical stores and distribution centres. Leveraging predictive analytics and real-time data, Walmart aims to minimise stockouts, improve shelf availability and respond promptly to evolving consumer demands. In contrast, Amazon, as the dominant force in e-commerce, has established a highly sophisticated AI ecosystem underpinned by its advanced logistics infrastructure and cloud-based services. Amazon's AI applications extend comprehensively into its fulfilment centres, where intelligent robots and ML algorithms manage inventory movement, automate picking and packing processes and optimise delivery routes. These technologies enable Amazon to achieve exceptional speed, scalability and accuracy in order fulfilments. While both companies utilise AI for inventory optimisation, their approaches reflect their unique business models. Walmart focuses on integrating AI within physical retail operations to enhance in-store efficiency and customer satisfaction. Amazon, on the other hand, leverages AI as the backbone of its digital-first supply chain, enabling seamless automation from warehouse to doorstep. In essence, Walmart and Amazon illustrate two complementary models of AI-driven retail innovation – one grounded in enhancing traditional retail operations, the other redefining commerce through digital automation and logistics excellence.

Case Study One: Walmart

The retail industry has experienced significant technological advancements, with AI playing a pivotal role in transforming traditional operations. Walmart's adoption of AI in its inventory management system serves as a prime example of how technology can enhance efficiency and accuracy. Walmart has implemented an AI-powered inventory management system designed to ensure product availability, optimise restocking processes and reduce waste. By leveraging historical data and predictive analytics, the system strategically positions products across distribution centres and stores, enhancing the overall shopping experience (Walmart Global Tech, 2023). This integration reflects Walmart's commitment to utilizing technology to meet customer needs efficiently. However, the integration of AI also brings challenges, particularly concerning its influence on employees' organisational behaviour.

The deployment of AI within Walmart's operational ecosystem has catalysed a fundamental shift in employee roles, redefining job functions, skill requirements and behavioural expectations across various levels of the organisation. AI is not merely a tool for automation. It is a transformative force that reshapes how employees interact with technology, customers and each other. For instance, AI-powered automation has revolutionised warehouse workflows by minimising the dependency on manual labour for repetitive tasks such as sorting, inventory placement and product retrieval. Advanced robotics and ML systems now execute these processes with greater speed and accuracy. Consequently, employees are transitioning from physically intensive roles to more supervisory and technical positions, where responsibilities include overseeing automated systems, diagnosing operational issues and ensuring performance optimisation (Just Think AI, 2023).

This paradigm shift demands elevated levels of technical literacy and problem-solving aptitude. Employees must now engage in real-time decision-making and system management, driving a culture of proactive maintenance and operational agility. As such, continuous upskilling has become essential to workforce relevance in this increasingly digital warehouse environment. For in-store employees, AI integration serves as an enabler of efficiency and strategic contribution. Tools such as AI-powered shelf-scanning robots and real-time inventory trackers automate routine checks, identify stock discrepancies and alert staff to replenishment needs. This automation liberates associates from repetitive, low-value tasks and empowers them to focus on customer engagement, sales support and problem resolution (SymphonyAI, 2023). As a result, the behavioural shift among associates is marked by increased autonomy, greater emphasis on interpersonal skills and a stronger alignment with customer-centric objectives. These changes contribute positively to job satisfaction, as roles become more purpose-driven and interactive (Laker et al., 2024).

Managers now rely heavily on AI-driven analytics to inform tactical and strategic decisions, particularly in areas like inventory forecasting, promotional planning and workforce scheduling. Access to granular, real-time data allows managers to anticipate demand fluctuations, optimise stock levels and tailor operations to evolving customer behaviours (Walmart Global Tech, 2023). This data-centric management style fosters behavioural traits such as agility, responsiveness and evidence-based decision-making. Managers are expected to integrate cross-functional insights and lead dynamic teams with a heightened awareness of technological capabilities and limitations. AI adoption at Walmart has not occurred in isolation; it has necessitated deliberate structural transformations to ensure alignment between technological innovation and organisational capability.

Changing Managerial and Employee Roles

Walmart has instituted a new cadre of specialised roles – AI engineers, data scientists and automation analysts – that serve as the backbone of its AI infrastructure. These professionals bridge the divide between traditional retail functions and cutting-edge technology, ensuring seamless system integration and operational continuity (Kearney, 2023). The creation of these roles reflects a broader organisational commitment to interdisciplinary collaboration. It also introduces a new behavioural dynamic wherein employees across functions must interact with technical experts, fostering cross-pollination of ideas and greater interdepartmental synergy. To support this transformation, Walmart invests heavily in employee training programs focused on digital fluency, AI literacy and adaptive thinking. These initiatives are designed to cultivate an agile workforce capable of evolving alongside technological advancements (Seek AI, 2023). Such investments not only enhance technical competence but also foster a growth mindset, encouraging employees to view change as an opportunity rather than a threat. Behavioural shifts include increased openness to experimentation, willingness to engage in lifelong learning and resilience in the face of disruption.

AI has driven the reengineering of core business processes to maximise efficiency and operational excellence. Legacy workflows are being streamlined to integrate seamlessly with AI capabilities – reducing redundancies, eliminating bottlenecks and improving throughput (HackerNoon, 2024). Employees are now expected to contribute to process innovation by offering feedback on AI–human interactions and identifying further opportunities for enhancement. This participatory approach instils a sense of ownership and encourages proactive behaviour at all levels of the organisation. At the heart of AI implementation lies the human capacity to adapt. Walmart's success with AI hinges not only on its technical infrastructure but also on the behavioural transformation of its workforce.

Walmart fosters a positive narrative around AI by positioning it as a collaborative asset rather than a replacement for human labour. Employees are encouraged to embrace technological change as a means of augmenting their capabilities and adding value to their roles (Business Insider, 2025). This mindset cultivates psychological safety, reduces resistance to change and promotes a culture of innovation. Employees become more open to experimentation and more willing to engage with new technologies. AI's rapid evolution necessitates a workforce that is perpetually learning. Walmart supports this through structured learning pathways, certifications and on-the-job training programmes focused on emerging technologies and soft skills (Marketingblatt, 2024). This emphasis on continuous development drives behavioural shifts towards self-directed learning, curiosity and intellectual agility. Employees who invest in their growth are more adaptable, engaged and prepared to navigate the evolving AI landscape.

Walmart promotes an integrated model where human intelligence complements AI capabilities. Rather than viewing AI as an isolated entity, employees are trained to interact with it dynamically – interpreting its insights, validating its outputs and enhancing its applications. This human–AI collaboration fosters a workplace culture rooted in partnership, efficiency and co-creation. It enhances employee satisfaction by enabling smarter workflows and reinforcing the strategic value of human oversight.

Case Study Two: Amazon

As a global leader in e-commerce, Amazon continually innovates to maintain operational excellence and customer satisfaction. One of its most transformative initiatives is the integration of AI into inventory management. Faced with the complexities of managing millions of products across vast networks of fulfilment centres, Amazon has implemented an AI-driven inventory management system to enhance efficiency, accuracy and responsiveness. As Drenik (2023) states, AI empowers Amazon to optimise inventory allocation through dynamic, real-time decision-making, thereby minimizing both stockouts and excess inventory. This technological shift signifies more than operational efficiency; it represents a fundamental transformation in the knowledge management landscape, where decision-making is increasingly driven by algorithmic insights rather than traditional human intuition. In this AI-augmented environment, tacit knowledge—once central to inventory planning—is now being codified, automated and continuously refined through ML models that learn from vast datasets in real time. Consequently, employee roles and behaviours are undergoing significant transformation. Instead of serving as primary decision-makers, employees are increasingly positioned as supervisors of intelligent systems, interpreters of AI outputs and strategic collaborators who must adapt to data-centric workflows.

Amazon's inventory management system employs ML algorithms, real-time data analytics and predictive modelling to optimise stock levels, product placement and restocking schedules. By processing vast amounts of data, including customer behaviour, historical sales, regional demand patterns and supply chain fluctuations, the system accurately forecasts inventory needs. As Harvard Business Review (2022) noted, 'Companies like Amazon utilise AI not only for demand forecasting but also for autonomously adjusting supply chains in response to changing signals.' Advanced robotics further contributes to Amazon's inventory management. AI-powered robots assist in locating, transporting and organising inventory, significantly reducing manual handling and error rates. As Forbes (2023) emphasises, Amazon's advanced robotics systems now excel in executing inventory picking and movement tasks with unmatched speed and precision, surpassing human capabilities. The seamless integration of AI software and physical automation enables Amazon to fulfil orders swiftly, minimise operational costs and minimise inventory waste.

The advent of AI has profoundly reshaped the responsibilities of employees within Amazon's warehouse operations. Traditional manual roles are transforming, transitioning into more analytical and supervisory functions. Employees are now required to monitor automated systems, identify and resolve exceptions flagged by AI and manage technical operations. A report by McKinsey & Company (2023) underscores Amazon's strategic investment in AI, which has shifted workforce demands towards higher-skilled employees capable of overseeing and interacting with intelligent machines rather than engaging in routine, repetitive tasks. Consequently, Amazon has made substantial investments in upskilling initiatives, providing training in digital literacy, system diagnostics and robotics management. This evolution not only enhances operational efficiency but also fosters career development opportunities, positioning employees as strategic contributors within a high-tech, AI-augmented work environment.

Amazon's fulfilment centres are the epicentre of its AI-driven transformation. ML systems and robotics, such as Kiva robots, autonomously navigate storage areas to sort, transport and retrieve products. This automation increases operational speed, reduces human error and lowers physical strain on workers. However, it significantly redefines employee roles and behaviour. Instead of manual labour, employees are now expected to monitor automated systems, respond to alerts and troubleshoot technical faults. This shift fosters a behavioural transition from task executors to system supervisors and problem-solvers, requiring higher levels of digital literacy, critical thinking and adaptability. As McAfee and Brynjolfsson (2017) asserted, technological augmentation serves not to replace human labour but to amplify the value of human judgement, positioning it as an indispensable component within digitally enhanced systems. Rather than rendering workers obsolete, such advancements encourage employees to assume more proactive, cognitively engaged roles – acting as strategic stewards of digital workflows rather than passive executors of routine tasks. This shift underscores the evolving nature of work in AI-integrated environments, where human insight and contextual understanding complement algorithmic efficiency to drive more intelligent, adaptive decision-making processes.

With the expansion of Amazon Go and Whole Foods Market, AI has made its presence felt in Amazon's physical retail landscape. Technologies like 'Just Walk Out' and shelf-monitoring sensors have automated repetitive tasks such as scanning items and checking stock. As a result, store associates are transitioning from routine transactions to customer engagement, technical troubleshooting and digital system support. This shift in role expectations fosters a behavioural change towards greater autonomy, interpersonal interaction and adaptive thinking. Employees must interpret system alerts, explain technology to customers and ensure the smooth operation of AI-driven tools. Davenport and Ronanki (2018) highlighted that AI alleviates employees from routine, repetitive tasks, empowering them to focus on functions that require creativity, emotional intelligence and complex problem-solving. This strategic shift in task allocation aligns with Amazon's customer-centric culture, valuing adaptability, innovation and empathetic engagement. From a workforce behaviour perspective, the integration of AI not only redefines job roles but also reshapes employee expectations and interactions within the workplace. Workers are increasingly encouraged to adopt more proactive, collaborative and cognitively intensive roles, transitioning from task executors to problem solvers and innovation enablers.

Changing Managerial and Employee Roles

AI has revolutionised managerial decision-making by providing real-time insights into inventory levels, consumer trends and team productivity through data dashboards and predictive analytics. This increased access to information fosters evidence-based decision-making, strategic foresight and rapid responsiveness. In the context of AI integration, managerial roles are undergoing significant transformation. Managers are no longer solely responsible for overseeing operations; they are now expected to synthesise AI-generated insights, facilitate cross-functional collaboration and lead teams through continuous digital adaptation. This evolution necessitates a shift in behavioural expectations towards greater agility, technological fluency and proficiency in data interpretation. As highlighted by the Harvard Business Review (2022), the successful adoption of AI extends beyond technological implementation; it necessitates leadership capable of cultivating and guiding a data-driven organisational culture. This underscores the importance of developing leadership competencies that align with AI-enabled environments—where success depends not only on technical implementation but also on human adaptability and strategic vision.

To support its AI infrastructure, Amazon created specialised roles like AI engineers, MLOps professionals and robotics specialists within operational teams. This shift promotes cross-functional collaboration and knowledge sharing by encouraging employees to engage with technical colleagues. As Wilson and Daugherty (2018) noted, the integration of AI fundamentally reconfigures organisational relationships and role expectations, leading to the emergence of 'collaborative intelligence' between humans and AI systems. Employees must now collaborate, co-create solutions with AI technologies and adapt to fluid role boundaries. This transformation fosters a workplace environment where collaboration, continuous learning and mutual dependence between human insight and machine intelligence are central to performance. AI enhances operational efficiency and redefines behavioural norms, encouraging an integrative, communicative and innovation-oriented workforce.

Amazon's retraining initiatives align its workforce capabilities with the demands of an AI-driven ecosystem. These initiatives prioritise AI literacy, coding proficiency, data interpretation and cloud infrastructure management—essential skills in digitally transformed organisations. The Career Choice programme exemplifies Amazon's investment in cultivating internal talent pipelines for emerging technological roles. Structured learning pathways enhance technical proficiency and foster behavioural transformation. Employees embrace intellectual agility, self-initiative and lifelong learning in response to rapid technological change. The expectation shifts from static task execution to continuous adaptation and proactive engagement with evolving digital tools. As Davenport and Kirby (2016) noted, AI-augmented success requires continuous, lifelong learning. AI shapes employees' roles, knowledge interaction and career progression in an automated and knowledge-intensive workplace.

Amazon's integration of AI-driven insights has revolutionised legacy workflows, particularly in demand forecasting, inventory management and logistics planning. AI systems augment human roles, creating opportunities for employees to refine and co-evolve AI–human interactions. This participatory approach enhances technological implementation and fosters employee ownership and accountability. Behaviourally, this shift from passive task execution to active process innovation empowers employees as contributors to dynamic workflows shaped by intelligent algorithms and continuous data feedback. Collaboration platforms and iterative feedback loops facilitate real-time learning, cross-functional engagement and rapid response to operational changes. AI cultivates agile mindsets, experimental thinking and a culture of continuous improvement. In Amazon's context, this behavioural transformation reflects a broader organisational strategy: leveraging AI to optimise processes and empower employees as co-designers of efficiency, resilience and innovation in the digital workplace.

At Amazon, AI integration is framed as a tool for enhancing human capabilities and decision-making, rather than replacing human labour. This framing shapes organisational culture, promotes innovation and addresses job displacement concerns. Consistent leadership, transparent communication and employee engagement initiatives foster a psychological safety climate, encouraging employees to embrace change. This fosters experimental thinking, calculated risk-taking and active participation in innovation processes (Huang & Rust, 2021). Employees engage with AI-driven tools, contribute to their improvement and align their efforts with digital transformation goals. This cultural and behavioural alignment sustains agility in high-velocity environments like Amazon, where rapid technological adaptation is crucial. Through comprehensive internal platforms and certification —such as AWS training modules and the Career Choice initiative—employees are encouraged to take proactive ownership of their skill development. By embedding learning opportunities into daily workflows, Amazon cultivates behavioural attributes such as intellectual curiosity, adaptive resilience and collaborative knowledge sharing. These behaviours are critical in a technologically dynamic environment where AI integration continuously reshapes job roles and competencies. Organisations that nurture strong learning cultures 'consistently outperform in adapting to AI integration,' underscoring the direct correlation between employee adaptability and organisational success (Brynjolfsson et al., 2020). At Amazon, this learning-centric approach not only enhances workforce agility but also empowers employees to engage meaningfully with intelligent systems—transforming them into active contributors within a rapidly evolving digital ecosystem.

Workers are not just passive recipients of AI outputs; instead, they actively participate in tasks like validating algorithmic predictions, refining recommendation engines and handling complex or ambiguous edge cases that require human judgement. This approach creates a symbiotic relationship between human expertise and machine intelligence, reinforcing behaviours like trust in technology, collaborative problem-solving and shared accountability in decision-making processes. By positioning employees as co-creators and overseers of AI systems, Amazon fosters a workplace culture where human intuition and machine precision complement each other. As Wilson and Daugherty (2018) argue, 'the future of work hinges on building collaborative intelligence where humans and machines enhance each other's strengths.' Amazon exemplifies this vision by aligning its workforce development strategies with the changing dynamics of AI-augmented organisational performance.

Influence on Employee Roles and Behaviour—an Analysis of Walmart and Amazon

AI has become a cornerstone of contemporary business strategy, especially within the retail sector where complex supply chains and real-time consumer demands necessitate agile, intelligent systems. Among global retail leaders, Walmart and Amazon have emerged as archetypes of AI adoption in inventory management, leveraging data-driven knowledge systems to enhance efficiency, responsiveness and customer satisfaction. However, the true strategic differentiator lies not merely in technological capability but in how AI integration reshapes employee behaviour, knowledge flows and organisational culture. This comparative analysis explores the application of AI in Walmart and Amazon's inventory systems, assessing the behavioural implications for employees and aligning these transformations with the broader theme of AI-driven knowledge management strategies in the modern business environment.

Walmart's warehouse employees are no longer merely handlers of goods; they are overseers of autonomous systems. Their roles demand new cognitive skills such as system monitoring, data interpretation and technical troubleshooting (Just Think AI, 2023). Similarly, Amazon's workforce engages in managing exceptions and optimizing ML feedback loops, transforming them into knowledge stewards who contribute to the refinement of AI logic and performance (McAfee & Brynjolfsson, 2017). This transformation supports Wilson and Daugherty's (2018) notion of 'collaborative intelligence', where AI augments human insight, and humans, in turn, enrich AI through contextual judgement— reshaping the behavioural norm from passive compliance to active co-creation.

Walmart's in-store associates utilise AI-generated insights from shelf scanners and real-time inventory trackers, enabling them to redirect their focus towards high-touch customer service and decision-making. Similarly, Amazon's Just Walk Out technology requires associates to act as digital facilitators, capable of resolving system issues and guiding tech-savvy shopping experiences. These roles reflect a behavioural shift towards interpersonal intelligence, digital proficiency and adaptive learning. The adoption of AI has transformed managerial roles from operational oversight to strategic knowledge management. Walmart managers now rely on data dashboards for tactical planning and inventory forecasting (Walmart Global Tech, 2023). Amazon's managers synthesise AI-driven insights for dynamic workforce scheduling and inventory control, reinforcing the behavioural imperative of agility, cross-functional literacy and data-based reasoning (Harvard Business Review, 2022). Managers assume the role of knowledge brokers who align human capital with AI capabilities, fulfilling Davenport and Kirby's (2016) concept of 'augmentation leaders.'

Both firms have created AI-specific roles—Walmart with data scientists and AI engineers (Kearney, 2023), Amazon with MLOps professionals and robotics specialists—leading to new behavioural dynamics rooted in cross-functional collaboration and interdisciplinary problem-solving (Wilson & Daugherty, 2018). AI adoption requires continuous employee adaptation. Walmart's investments in AI literacy and upskilling have fostered a culture of digital curiosity and learning resilience (Seek AI, 2023). Amazon's Career Choice programme exemplifies self-directed development, promoting employee agency in navigating the digital landscape (Davenport & Kirby, 2016). This cultural shift towards lifelong learning reinforces Brynjolfsson et al.'s (2020) thesis that knowledge-driven adaptability is the linchpin of AI-era competitiveness. Both companies are reengineering business processes to embed human-in-the-loop systems, where employees contribute feedback to AI tools and optimise workflows (HackerNoon, 2024). Behaviourally, this nurtures ownership, experimentation and psychological safety, empowering employees as co-designers of intelligent systems.

AI serves as a dual-purpose entity, simultaneously acting as a knowledge generator and a catalyst for behavioural transformation. Walmart and Amazon serve as illustrative examples of how AI systems must be integrated into human-centred cultures that prioritise emotional intelligence, cognitive agility and digital proficiency. The alignment of AI with human behavioural patterns and knowledge flows is not merely a consequence of technological advancement but rather a strategic imperative for achieving AI maturity in contemporary businesses. When examining Walmart and Amazon through the lens of AI-driven knowledge management, it becomes evident that their success is not solely dependent on technological infrastructure but rather on how human behaviour adapts, integrates and amplifies AI. Warehouse operators, store associates and managers are all transitioning into roles that require analytical judgement, collaborative engagement and adaptive learning. As organisations embark on digital transformation, the cultivation of AI-compatible behaviours rooted in knowledge sharing, emotional intelligence and continuous learning emerges as a decisive advantage. Ultimately, the future of AI in retail lies not solely in the capabilities of machines but rather in the synergistic intelligence of humans and algorithms. Table 9.1 presents a structured comparative analysis of AI-driven inventory management and employee behaviour in the knowledge era, as exemplified by Walmart and Amazon.

Table 9.1. Walmart-Amazon AI Approach in Relation to Employees.

Focal Point	Theme	Walmart	Amazon	Comparative Insights
AI-Driven Inventory Management as Knowledge Infrastructure	AI as a Knowledge System	Utilises predictive analytics and robotics to optimise replenishment; enables real-time knowledge loops and enhances decision-making (Walmart Global Tech, 2023).	Employs autonomous robotics and AI algorithms to dynamically manage global inventory; generates operational intelligence from machine-human interaction (Harvard Business Review, 2022).	Both convert inventory systems into dynamic knowledge infrastructures, positioning AI as a continuous learning and decision-support tool.
Behavioural Shifts in Employee Roles and Responsibilities	Warehouse Operations (Knowledge Stewardship)	Employees supervise AI systems, requiring digital literacy and problem-solving (Just Think AI, 2023).	Employees manage alerts, interpret AI feedback and co-create knowledge loops (McAfee & Brynjolfsson, 2017).	Shift from physical labour to cognitive engagement; both firms support Wilson & Daugherty's (2018) concept of 'collaborative intelligence.'
	In-Store Roles (Human–AI Collaboration)	Associates use AI tools to focus on strategic, customer-facing tasks (SymphonyAI, 2023).	Associates facilitate AI-driven retail (e.g., Just Walk Out), supporting tech interactions and customer service (Davenport & Ronanki, 2018).	AI liberates employees from low-value tasks; roles pivot towards emotional intelligence, adaptability and customer experience.

	Managerial Functions (Data-Driven Leadership)	Managers utilise data dashboards for planning and forecasting (Walmart Global Tech, 2023).	Managers analyze AI insights for real-time scheduling and control (Harvard Business Review, 2022).	Leadership evolves into strategic augmentation, aligning with the 'augmentation leader' concept (Davenport & Kirby, 2016).
Organisational Restructuring and Knowledge-Based Transformation	Specialised Roles (Cross-functional Collaboration)	Introduced AI engineers, data scientists to bridge tech-retail functions (Kearney, 2023).	Employs MLOps experts, robotics professionals to support intelligent infrastructure (Wilson & Daugherty, 2018).	New roles foster interdisciplinary teams, enhancing innovation and system integration.
	Learning Ecosystems (Behavioural Adaptability)	Upskilling in AI fluency and adaptive thinking (Seek AI, 2023).	Career Choice programme promotes lifelong digital learning (Davenport & Kirby, 2016).	Both embed continuous learning to promote curiosity, resilience and agility (Brynjolfsson et al., 2020).
	Process Innovation (Human-in-the-Loop Feedback)	Employees contribute feedback to AI workflows to optimise efficiency (HackerNoon, 2024).	Incorporates user feedback loops into intelligent systems for adaptive improvement.	Encourages experimentation and employee ownership; fosters a co-creative innovation culture.

(Continued)

Table 9.1. *(Continued)*

Focal Point	Theme	Walmart	Amazon	Comparative Insights
AI-Driven Knowledge Management and Behavioural Integration	Strategic Alignment	AI is framed as a knowledge-enhancing partner; it fosters a digitally agile culture emphasizing emotional intelligence and growth (Business Insider, 2025).	AI is embedded in a culture of trust, openness, and shared accountability (Huang & Rust, 2021).	AI success depends on behavioural integration—combining technical systems with human values, cognitive agility and emotional adaptability.

In summary, Walmart and Amazon perceive AI not merely as a tool for enhancing efficiency but as a catalyst for transforming organisational workflows, decision-making processes and employee roles. The adoption of AI introduces new behavioural expectations, encouraging a shift from routine task execution to more proactive problem-solving, digital fluency and emotional intelligence. This transformation is supported by robust learning ecosystems and collaborative AI systems that incorporate human insights into continuous AI feedback loops. In today's knowledge management landscape, organisations must align AI capabilities with human behavioural dynamics to fully unlock AI's strategic potential.

Contemporary Issues Faced by Employees in Adopting AI

AI has both positive and negative impacts on organisational behaviours within workplaces. On the positive side, AI has revolutionised various industries, enabling organisations to enhance their decision-making processes and strategies. This transformation has led to increased effectiveness and efficiency within organisations. However, the integration of AI also presents several contemporary issues for employees, which can be categorised into technological, organisational and ethical dimensions. One of the primary technological challenges is the complexity of AI systems. Unlike traditional software, AI algorithms often require a deep understanding of ML principles, data science and programming languages such as Python, R and SQL. These concepts can be challenging for many employees, particularly those in non-technical roles, resulting in a steep learning curve. Furthermore, the rapid advancement of AI technologies has outpaced the development of necessary skills in the workforce. The accelerated pace of AI development necessitates that even technically trained employees continuously update their skills to keep pace with new advancements. According to a survey conducted by the World Economic Forum (2023), 60% of businesses struggle with local skills gaps, and 53% identify talent acquisition difficulties as the primary barrier to business transformation.

It is imperative to address the issue of a lack of skilled employees, as it can hinder the organisation's AI initiatives if not mitigated appropriately. Furthermore, integrating AI into existing organisational systems and processes can be intricate and challenging. As highlighted by Khan (2023), outdated legacy systems may not be compatible with the latest AI technologies. Integrating AI can be costly and time-consuming, necessitating extensive technical adjustments and potentially disrupting daily operations. For instance, in the financial sector, the rapid growth of fintech has heightened consumer expectations for mobile-based banking services. However, numerous financial services companies still rely on outdated legacy systems. These systems not only restrict the implementation of modern technologies that could enhance the customer experience but also affect the emotional well-being of employees involved. Employees may experience frustration and resistance as they adapt to new technologies and tools, particularly if the new systems are poorly managed or perceived as inefficient.

From an organisational standpoint, one of the most significant challenges is resistance to change. Employees may apprehend that AI could potentially replace their roles, leading to job insecurity and diminished morale. As reported by the Visier Team (2024), a substantial 61% of employees are concerned that their current abilities may become obsolete as AI advances. This sentiment reflects a growing apprehension among employees regarding the potential of AI to supplant their roles, which could result in resistance and impede the effective implementation of AI systems. While these concerns are not unfounded, it is believed that a growing number of tasks currently performed by humans could be automated by AI in the future. However, rather than dwelling on the negative implications, organisations should emphasise the potential of AI to augment human capabilities, enabling employees to concentrate on more strategic and creative aspects of their work. Furthermore, the organisational culture plays a pivotal role in the adoption of AI. In organisations with a strong tradition of manual processes and decision-making, employees may encounter difficulties in adapting to AI-driven processes. This resistance can hinder the integration of AI and negatively impact business growth. As elucidated by Berruti and Morris (2022), innovation can flourish if the organisational culture is receptive to novel approaches, as exemplified by the rapid digitalisation of operations during the COVID-19 pandemic. Additionally, the World Economic Forum underscores the significance of a culture that values diversity, creativity and risk-taking in overcoming challenges posed by traditional processes (Willard, 2023). Such a culture fosters an environment where employees can explore and implement AI without apprehension of failure. Therefore, fostering a culture that embraces change and encourages experimentation is paramount for organisations to successfully integrate AI and maintain competitiveness in the digital era.

Ethical concerns present substantial challenges for employees in adopting AI. Issues such as data privacy, bias in AI algorithms and the ethical use of AI technologies impact the willingness and ability of employees to implement AI within their organisations. Employees developing or implementing AI systems that could negatively impact humans or perpetuate inequities may struggle with the moral implications of their work. Confidence in the accuracy and reliability of AI applications is paramount, as biases can undermine trust. For instance, biases in AI-driven hiring processes have raised concerns about fairness and discrimination. Therefore, ensuring transparency in AI algorithms and involving employees in the development and monitoring of these systems is essential for building trust. Furthermore, integrating AI into the workplace raises ethical and privacy concerns due to the substantial amounts of data required. This increases concerns among employees about how AI systems collect and use personal data. The General Data Protection Regulation (GDPR), effective since 25 May 2018, sets stringent guidelines on data protection (Willard, 2023). This indicates a growing privacy concern related to AI adoption. While employees must ensure that data are collected and used in compliance with privacy regulations and ethical standards, it adds pressure on employees as data breaches and misuse of personal information become more prevalent. Consequently, the ethical implications of AI decision-making, including biases and algorithm transparency, pose significant challenges.

AI and Employee Job Satisfaction

AI has both positive and negative effects on job satisfaction, depending on the specific jobs it affects and how it integrates into workflows. On one hand, AI can enhance job satisfaction by automating tasks, allowing employees to focus on the creative and strategic aspects of their roles. For instance, generative AI tools can assist in drafting content and analysing data, which frees employees to work on more fulfilling and challenging projects (European Commission, 2018). Consequently, job satisfaction among employees may increase as they feel more valued and capable of completing complex tasks, contributing to the goals of their organisations. Furthermore, AI can improve job satisfaction by enhancing work-life balance. AI-driven tools can simplify workflows and reduce the time needed to complete tasks, allowing employees to have more flexible schedules and fewer work hours. Debates around the four-day workweek suggest that companies effectively using AI are more likely to consider and adopt hybrid work patterns (Drapkin, 2024). This approach enables employees to achieve company goals more efficiently without sacrificing personal time, aligning with the growing demand for a healthier work-life balance and boosting job satisfaction.

However, there are two sides to the impacts of AI adoption in the workplace. According to Tiwari et al. (2024), although AI can enhance productivity and job satisfaction in some cases, it can also lead to decreased job satisfaction due to concerns over job security and the fear of being replaced by machines. These concerns are particularly pressing in fields like manufacturing and some service sectors where AI can directly replace human labour. This uncertainty can create a sense of unease among employees and lead to a decline in job satisfaction. Furthermore, the impact of AI on job satisfaction is influenced by the extent to which employees are trained to work with AI technologies. Employees who are proficient with AI tools and view them as opportunities rather than obstacles are more likely to be satisfied in their roles. Cawley (2024) highlights that 59% of senior leaders who use AI agree that it has enhanced their job satisfaction. This suggests that employees with AI-related skills are more satisfied with their jobs and tend to be high performers compared to those who lack these skills. This underscores the importance of continuous learning and development in the era of AI, as the ability of employees to adapt to new technologies is crucial for enhancing job satisfaction.

Despite its positive and negative effects, AI's impact on job satisfaction is complex and situation-specific. While AI can enhance efficiency, creativity and work-life balance, it also poses challenges related to job security and the need for continuous skills development. Organisations must carefully manage the integration of AI to mitigate its potential negative impacts on job satisfaction. This includes providing adequate training, addressing job security concerns and fostering a workplace culture that views AI as a tool for empowerment rather than a threat. In these ways, businesses can maximise the benefits of AI while minimizing its risks, creating a more satisfied and engaged workforce. As AI continues to evolve and become more embedded in everyday work processes, it will significantly influence job satisfaction. Therefore, it should become a top priority for both businesses and employees.

AI and Employee Expectations

As AI tools become more prevalent, they are reshaping employees' expectations in various ways and affecting their attitudes towards work and future career paths. The influence AI has on productivity expectations is multifaceted. According to Hassan (2024), AI can boost productivity and efficiency by automating repetitive tasks. However, executives and decision-makers often set high expectations for AI to significantly improve operational output. Robinson (2024) notes that while 96% of CEOs believe AI will boost production, 77% of workers report that technology has increased their burden, restricted productivity and heightened the risk of burnout. This gap between anticipated and actual productivity improvements can lead to frustration and disappointment among employees. Additionally, AI impacts employees' perceptions of job security. As AI technologies emerge, employees may feel anxious about losing their jobs and their future roles within the organisation (Tiwari et al., 2024). These concerns are exacerbated by current trends in AI adoption, with many employees worrying that AI could render their abilities obsolete. Thus, although AI can enhance human capabilities and offer new job opportunities, employees may feel insecure about their jobs because organisations value AI-driven efficiencies over human labour.

Moreover, AI plays a crucial role in reshaping skill requirements, influencing employees' expectations regarding their professional development. As AI technologies evolve, the demand for new skill sets grows, necessitating continuous learning and adaptation by employees. They need to develop new skills in data analysis and AI techniques in this digital era. For example, employees must have a growth mindset to develop skills in prompt engineering and maximise the use of AI tools to stay competitive in their careers (Dardis, 2023). However, the pressure to constantly update skills can be overwhelming, increasing stress and making employees feel inadequate as they struggle to keep pace with technological advancements. This affects employees' expectations about career development and can create an insecure working environment. Additionally, AI influences employees' expectations of work-life balance because the technology's integration blurs the boundaries between personal and professional time. While AI can streamline work processes and reduce manual labour, it can also increase workload and working hours (Segal, 2024). For instance, although AI-driven tools can help humans communicate and monitor remotely, they can also cause employees to disconnect from work, resulting in less personal time. This shift may affect the work-life balance of employees and raise concerns about their well-being, as AI can lead to burnout and decreased job satisfaction.

In summary, the impact of AI on employee expectations is multifaceted and complex. While AI can enhance productivity and efficiency, actual outcomes often deviate from initial expectations. Employees may encounter increased workloads, heightened job insecurity, escalating demands for skills and challenges to achieving a healthy work-life balance. These factors could compel employees to reevaluate their current positions and career aspirations. Addressing these challenges necessitates that organisations align AI implementations with realistic expectations. It is recommended that organisations provide comprehensive training and support, and foster a work environment that strikes a balance between technological advancements and employee well-being. By addressing these difficulties, organisations can enhance both operational efficiency and employee satisfaction with AI systems.

Recommendations and Conclusion

Based on the analysis provided, integrating AI into the workplace presents both advantages and disadvantages. To ensure that AI effectively enhances business growth and maintains employee satisfaction, organisations must overcome the challenges associated with its integration. Firstly, companies should invest in continuous training and skill development to ensure that employees possess the necessary knowledge and expertise to work with AI technologies. As AI systems become increasingly sophisticated, employees require a comprehensive understanding of ML, data science and programming. According to the World Economic Forum (2023), bridging the skills gap through continuous training opportunities is paramount. This approach not only facilitates employees' adaptation to technological advancements but also enhances their confidence and job performance. Secondly, organisations should effectively manage the integration of AI with legacy systems. Many organisations still rely on outdated systems that may not be compatible with new AI technologies. Integrating AI necessitates infrastructure and workflow modifications, which can be costly and time-consuming. As per Khan (2023), a well-structured integration process can minimise errors and facilitate employees' smoother adoption of AI technologies. It is crucial to provide adequate support and resources during this transition period to address employee frustration and resistance.

Thirdly, addressing resistance to change is crucial for fostering a positive work environment and ensuring the successful implementation of AI systems. Employees often harbour concerns that AI may replace their roles, leading to insecurity about their jobs and decreased morale. To alleviate these apprehensions, organisations should emphasise the advantages of AI and demonstrate how it can augment rather than replace human capabilities. Berruti and Morris (2022) underscore the significance of leadership engagement with employees to overcome their fears and highlight the benefits of AI adoption. Willard (2023) also underscores the importance of cultivating a culture that promotes continuous learning and adaptability as essential strategies to overcome resistance to change. Fourthly, companies should promote ethical AI practices to establish trust and uphold ethical standards within organisations. AI systems must be transparent and devoid of biases to avoid inequities and violations of privacy regulations. The European Commission (2018) emphasises the paramount importance of adhering to data protection regulations, such as the GDPR, to address privacy concerns. Consequently, it is imperative to establish robust mechanisms for monitoring AI algorithms and involve qualified employees in managing AI systems to ensure compliance with ethical guidelines and foster trust among users. Enhancing job satisfaction is crucial for addressing AI implementation issues. AI should support employees' roles, not intensify workloads. Reducing repetitive tasks and allowing focus on strategic aspects enhances job satisfaction. Companies should provide a supportive environment where employees can benefit from AI, maintaining engagement and satisfaction. Leaders should promote collaboration and employee exploration of AI. A comprehensive strategy is needed for successful AI integration. Focus on continuous training, managing legacy systems, addressing change resistance, ethical practices, job satisfaction and a supportive culture. These approaches address concerns and foster long-term success in the AI era. Businesses can grow effectively by responsibly and strategically using AI tools.

References

Alphabet Inc. (2019). *Alphabet announces fourth quarter and fiscal year 2019 results.* https://abc.xyz/investor/static/pdf/2019Q4_alphabet_earnings_release.pdf

Berruti, F., & Morris, A. (2022). *How virtual work is accelerating innovation.* McKinsey & Company. Retrieved 3 August 2024 from https://www.mckinsey.com/capabilities/operations/our-insights/how-virtual-work-is-accelerating-innovation

Brynjolfsson, E., Rock, D. & Syverson, C. (2020). The productivity J-curve: How intangibles complement general purpose technologies. *American Economic Journal: Macroeconomics, 12*(1), 333–372.

Buchmeister, B., Palcic, I., & Ojstersek, R. (2019). Artificial intelligence in manufacturing companies and broader: An overview. In B. Katalinic (Ed.), *DAAAM international scientific book*, 81–98. DAAAM International. https://doi.org/10.2507/daaam.scibook.2019.07

Business Insider (2025). *Walmart's AI strategy: Enhancing jobs, not replacing them.* Available at: https://www.businessinsider.com [Accessed 21 Mar. 2025].

Byrum, J. (2018). Preparing for an AI future. *OR/MS Today, 45*(6), 24–26. https://doi.org/10.1287/orms.2018.06.08

Cambridge Dictionary. (2024). *Job expectations.* https://dictionary.cambridge.org/dictionary/english/job-expectations

Cawley, C. (2024). *Business attitudes towards AI in the workplace 2024.* Marketing VF Ltd. Retrieved 16 July 2024 from https://tech.co/news/business-attitudes-ai-workplace

Dardis, S. (2023). *Preparing employees for generative AI: Skills to consider. Linkedin.* Retrieved 8 August 2024 from https://www.linkedin.com/pulse/preparing-employees-generative-ai-skills-consider-stephanie-dardis

Davenport, T. H. & Kirby, J. (2016). *Only humans need apply: Winners and losers in the age of smart machines.* HarperBusiness.

Davenport, T. H. & Ronanki, R. (2018). Artificial intelligence for the real World. *Harvard Business Review, 96*(1), 108–116.

Drapkin, A. (2024). Does AI improve job satisfaction? Here's what leaders say. *TalentCulture*. Retrieved 5 August 2024 from. https://talentculture.com/blog/does-ai-improve-job-satisfaction-survey-results

Drenik, G. (2023). *How Amazon uses AI to streamline inventory*. Forbes, [online] Available at: https://www.forbes.com [Accessed 21 Mar. 2025].

Dyvik, E. H. (2024). *The 100 largest companies in the World ranked by revenue in 2023*. Statista. Retrieved 23 July 2024 from https://www.statista.com/statistics/263265/top-companies-in-the-world-by-revenue

European Commission (2018). *Data protection in the EU*. https://commission.europa.eu/law/law-topic/data-protection/data-protection-eu_en

Forbes (2023). *Amazon's Robot Army: Faster fulfillment with AI*. Forbes, [online] Available at: https://www.forbes.com [Accessed 21 Mar. 2025].

Goodfellow, I., Bengio, Y., & Courville, A. (2016). *Deep learning*. The MIT Press.

HackerNoon (2024). Walmart's digital transformation through AI. *HackerNoon*, [online] Available at: https://www.hackernoon.com [Accessed 21 Mar. 2025].

Harvard Business Review (2022). Managing inventory with AI: Lessons from Amazon. *Harvard Business Review*, [online] Available at: https://hbr.org [Accessed 21 Mar. 2025].

Hassan, A. O. (2024). The power of AI: Automating repetitive tasks in businesses. *Linkedin*. Retrieved 8 August 2024 from https://www.linkedin.com/pulse/power-ai-automating-repetitive-tasks-businesses-aiman-o-hassan-rggjf

Huang, M. H. & Rust, R. T. (2021). Artificial intelligence in service. *Journal of Service Research, 24*(1), 3–20.

Just Think AI (2023). *AI in retail: Walmart's smart warehousing*. Available at: https://www.justthinkai.com [Accessed 21 Mar. 2025].

Kapoor, A. (2019). *Hands-on artificial intelligence for IoT: Expert machine learning and deep learning techniques for developing smarter IoT systems*. Packt Publishing Ltd.

Kearney (2023). Transforming retail through AI talent. *Kearney Report*, [online] Available at: https://www.kearney.com [Accessed 21 Mar. 2025].

Khan, T. (2023). *Legacy application modernization: A comprehensive approach to modernize your business*. International Business Machines Corporation. Retrieved 2 August 2024 from https://www.ibm.com/think/topics/legacy-application-modernization

Laker, B., Soga, L., Bolade-Ogunfodun, Y., & Adewale, A. (2024). *Job crafting*. MIT Press.

Marketingblatt (2024). *Building a learning culture in retail AI*. Available at: https://www.marketingblatt.com [Accessed 21 Mar. 2025].

McAfee, A. & Brynjolfsson, E. (2017). *Machine, platform, crowd: Harnessing our digital future*. W. W. Norton & Company.

McKinsey n Company (2023). *The future of work: AI's role in warehousing*. Available at: https://www.mckinsey.com [Accessed 21 Mar. 2025].

Mok, K. M. M. (2022). How AI changes the technopreneurship in the business World and its impact on business practices. In P. C. Lai (Ed.), *Handbook of research on social impacts of E-payment and blockchain technology*, 468–483. IGI Global. https://doi.org/10.4018/978-1-7998-9035-5.ch025

Oginni, B. O., Dunmade, E. O., & Ogunwole, A. C. (2018). The role of employees' work expectations in job satisfaction and labour turnover in the service industry: A case of selected organisations in Lagos, Ogun and Oyo states Nigeria, *World Journal of Business and Management, 4*(1), 1-17. https://doi.org/10.5296/wjbm.v4i1.12924

Park, S.-C. (2018). The fourth industrial revolution and implications for innovative cluster policies. *AI & Society, 33*(3), 433–445. https://doi.org/10.1007/s00146-017-0777-5

Robinson, B. (2024). 77% of employees report AI has increased workloads and hampered productivity, study finds. *Forbes*. Retrieved 8 August 2024 from https://www.forbes.com/sites/bryanrobinson/2024/07/23/employees-report-ai-increased-workload

Seek, A. I. (2023). *Digital upskilling at Walmart: A case study*. Available at: https://www.seek.ai [Accessed 21 Mar. 2025].

Segal, E. (2024). AI adds to the workload and stress of employees, report says. *Forbes*. Retrieved 8 August 2024 from https://www.forbes.com/sites/edwardsegal/2024/07/23/ai-adds-to-the-workload-and-stress-of-employees-report-says

Soga, L., Bolade-Ogunfodun, Y., & Laker, B. (2021b). *Design your work environment to manage unintended tech consequences*. MIT Sloan Management Review. https://sloanreview.mit.edu/article/design-your-work-environment-to-manage-unintended-tech-consequences/

Soga, L. R., Vogel, B., Graça, A. M., & Osei-Frimpong, K. (2021a). Web 2.0-enabled team relationships: An actor-network perspective. *European Journal of Work & Organizational Psychology, 30*(5), 639–652. https://doi.org/10.1080/1359432X.2020.1847183

SymphonyAI (2023). *How AI is revolutionizing retail stores*. Available at: https://www.symphonyai.com [Accessed 21 Mar. 2025].

Tiwari, R., Babu T, N. S., Marda, K., Mishra, A., Bhattar, S., & Ahluwalia, A. (2024). The impact of artificial intelligence in the workplace and its effect on the digital wellbeing of employees. *Journal for Studies in Management and Planning, 10*(4). https://doi.org/10.5281/zenodo.10936348

Visier Team. (2024). *New research on AI's impact on jobs, time saved has employees divided.* Retrieved 3 August 2024 from https://www.visier.com/blog/ai-impact-on-jobs-employees-divided/

Walmart Global Tech (2023). *Inventory management reinvented.* Walmart Tech Blog, [online] Available at: https://www.walmartglobaltech.com [Accessed 21 Mar. 2025].

Willard, J. (2023). *From ideas to impact: Cultivating a culture of innovation at work.* World Economic Forum. Retrieved 3 August 2024 from https://www.weforum.org/agenda/2023/05/ideas-impact-foster-culture-of-innovation

Wilson, H. J. & Daugherty, P. R. (2018). Collaborative intelligence: Humans and AI are joining forces. *Harvard Business Review, 96*(4), pp.114–123.

World Economic Forum. (2023). *Future of jobs report 2023.* Available at https://www3.weforum.org/docs/WEF_Future_of_Jobs_2023.pdf

Chapter 10

AI in Action: Decoding the Employee Experience Connection to Boost Engagement

Puneet Kumar[a] *and Nayantara Padhi*[b]

[a]GNCT of Delhi, India
[b]Indira Gandhi National Open University, India

Abstract

Change brings about uncertainty, apprehension, nervousness, and optimism. The recent introduction of artificial intelligence (AI) to the workspace has brought about tremendous change in the workplace, affecting employee experience (EEX) and, hence, their engagement at a professional level. The Banking Industry is no exception to this phenomenon. This chapter attempts to identify and explore the effects of AI on the engagement level of employees through a recently researched construct of "Employee experience" in the banking sector of the Delhi-NCR region of India. This phenomenon in the banking sector is studied by administering an adapted structured questionnaire to 530 public and private sector bank employees using Partial Least Squares Structural Equation Modeling (PLS-SEM). SMART-PLS V4.1 is employed to run the tests and for analysis purposes. Results reveal a strong association between AI and Employee Engagement (EE), partially mediated by EEX, in the banking sector. The chapter taps into the intricate behavior of AI at the workplace, influencing the comprehensive nature of the construct of the EEX, and EE. Understanding this compound relation would help the banking sector plan HR functions strategically to realize maximum results.

Keywords: Artificial intelligence; employee experience; employee engagement; mediation analysis; HR digitization; SMART-PLS

AI-Driven Knowledge Management Assets, Volume 2, 195–219

Published under exclusive licence by Emerald Publishing Limited
doi:10.1108/978-1-83662-778-420261010

1. Introduction

The HR ecosystem has transformed in the recent decade with increased digitization and disruptive technology utilization. The effectiveness and creativity within the HR function are steered by the use of Artificial Intelligence (AI). Organizations are advancing toward enhancing employee experience (EEX) and creating an engaged workforce (Bersin et al., 2017; IBM and Globoforce, 2016) with proper automation of HR functions and AI. The unparalleled digitization and automation in operations and human resource management functions are elevating to a whole new concept marked by seamless automation of HR functions with reduced time, efforts, and manual and intellectual processes. Though the concept of AI has been appealing to many large organizations, this technology has been a challenging and concerning concept in the workplace for HR functions for many small organizations (Budhwar et al., 2022; Charlwood & Guenole, 2022). Previous research and literature in this field have attracted mixed emotions and perceptions toward AI and its impact on HR functions. Where many authors are anxious due to its harmful and adverse impact on employees (Presbitero & Teng-Calleja, 2022; Suseno et al., 2022), positive and constructive outcomes are also advocated by many (Malik et al., 2021a, 2022). The data-driven automation caused by AI is being integrated into the human resource management function within the organization to enhance the effectiveness, efficiency, and impact of HR strategies. This digital assistance of AI in HR strengthens the strategic process concerning employees, using machine learning (ML) and HR analytics to comprehend human natural language and big data. The Talent Survey 2022 by Eightfold reveals that most managers (around 92%) plan to inculcate AI-driven technology in at least one of their HR areas. Many are already using AI technology in some of their HR capabilities.

According to Stanford University's "AI Index 2024" annual report (Maslej et al., 2024).

(1) AI intrusion is felt in many human tasks, but not all human tasks are being replaced by AI. AI lacks complex mathematics, common-sense reasoning, and planning and decision-making.
(2) Academia is behind the industry in generating notable AI models and research in 2023.
(3) The training costs of AI models for employees have been increasing significantly.
(4) Investment in generative AI is skyrocketing, and this vast outlay is reflected in a more productive workforce and high-quality work.
(5) Across the globe, people are aware of the possible impact of AI in the workplace, making them more nervous and anxious.

With the advancement of technology and disorder in the workplace, HRM policies, procedures, and practices are being greatly influenced internally and externally (Lepak & Snell, 1999, 2002; Morris et al., 2016). This is quite conspicuous in adopting AI applications and technology in HR functions (Jaiswal et al., 2022;

Vrontis et al., 2022). The EEX toward HR practices is changing due to the availability of time to concentrate on more rewarding tasks and nonroutine jobs caused by the AI-enabled HR applications and more digitized software streamlining HR jobs (Malik et al., 2020). A limited number of studies in this field advocate the dependency of HR managers on digitization for their legitimacy (Mahadevan & Schmitz, 2020), as this advancement offers more scope for integrating and converging the needs of various stakeholders. Though the intrusion of technology and digitization is tapping into the EEX touchpoints, the involvement of AI-enabled social exchange and cultural and physical aspects of employees is still relatively unmapped (Malik et al., 2020; Malik, De Silva, et al., 2021; Nguyen & Malik, 2021). Fig. 10.1 helps in understanding the concept of AI in brief.

Employee Engagement (EE) and EEX are redefining the rapidly changing digitized work environment (Breidbach et al., 2014; Kim & Gatling, 2018). The AI-enabled EE and EEX platform shows impactful positive results. Studies suggest that AI and ML can be a breakthrough in enhancing EEX by leveraging the capabilities of sentiment analysis, context-specific "career crafting," and

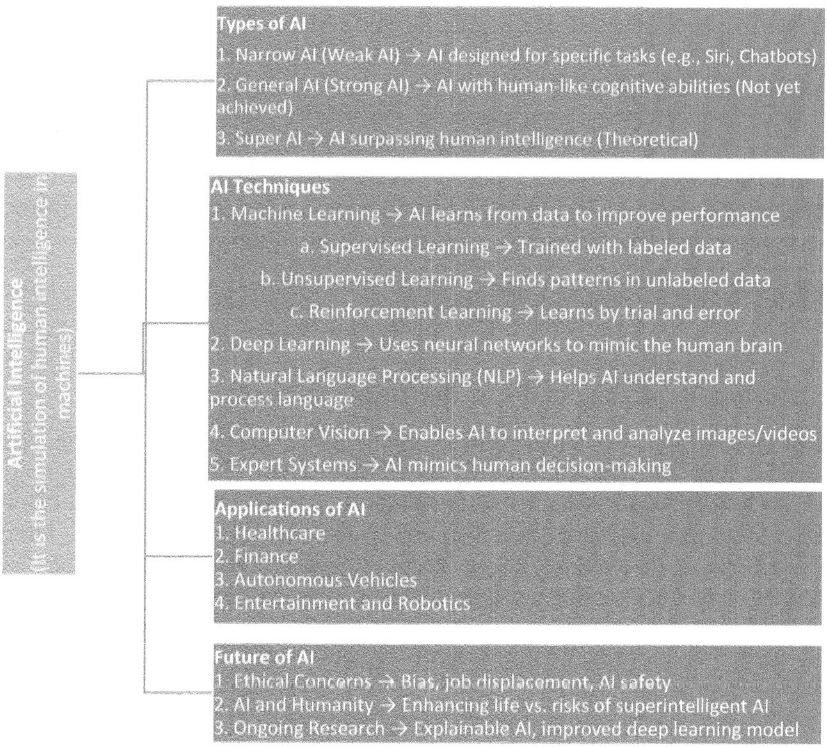

Fig. 10.1. AI Concept and Application. *Source:* Author's own conceptualization.

"augmented mentorship" (Malik et al., 2023; Rodgers et al., 2023). In a successful organization, the success factor is its teams, whose collective efforts are more than the sum of individual members' efforts. Their knowledge, skills, experience, and expertise increase work engagement (Wijayati et al., 2022). Engaged employees are characterized by deep passion, connection, motivation, loyalty, and high organizational satisfaction. Such engaged employees prove to be ambassadors for the company as they spread good words about the company's products and services and show a high level of employee advocacy (Davis & Van der Heijden, 2023; Imam et al., 2022; Parent & Lovelace, 2018). Here, organizational culture plays a significant role. A culture characterized by AI-enabled learning and a supportive culture infuses a sense of accomplishment within employees, encourages teams, and drives toward continuous improvement and adaptability. Such engaged employees who are part of this AI-enabled learning culture tend to be more loyal, committed, and motivated (Kambur & Yildirim, 2023). Owing to the positive impact and influence on EE, it poses the necessity of AI service and AI-assisted HR services (Nguyen & Malik, 2021; Prikshat et al., 2023) to track and monitor the perception, reaction, and experience of employees toward the organizational AI environment. Research has shown that personalized and dedicated AI systems in HR can significantly influence EEX through AI-supported social exchange (Ma & Brown, 2020; Malik et al., 2020, 2021b).

Since the perception and response toward AI are mixed and relatively obscure, it is imperative to investigate whether EEX toward AI influences their engagement level. Moreover, the introduction of AI in HR practices exerts excellent influence on functions like performance management (Basu Mallick, 2019), coaching (Barney, 2018), training and development (Whiteside, 2019), administrative functions (Haak, 2019), and effectiveness (Malik et al., 2020, 2021b), the EE is palpable to be affected.

2. Rationale of the Study in the Banking Sector

Implementing AI technology brings significant advantages by securing vital financial data and providing ready-made solutions to support financial transactions in the banking system. The banking system deals with thousands of daily financial transactions that must be carried out precisely and perfectly. Many transactions in the banking system require constant vigil and involvement of banking employees, making it prone to human error. The various operations, such as equity investments, financial transactions, property management, loans and advances, mutual funds, and investment schemes (Bedford et al., 2018) diversify the banking sector. The involvement of this sophisticated technology in the banking sector is increasing in services like fraud detection using "artificial neural network," portfolio optimization, the use of more plastic money and online transactions, chatbots for customer communication and interactions, reduced customer interaction for credits, quick and easy assessment of eligibility for credits, identification of low- and high-credit-risk applications, more objective decisions rather than subjective strategies, etc. Though AI technology is gradually making the banking system seamless, it will eliminate various repetitive and manual jobs in the banking industry. This destruction will impact the executives of the banking system significantly, as their experience with the technology and engagement level will be impacted. However, this will create space for emphasizing the more extensive value-added activities, which will require more digital upskilling of the employees (Mallah & Boustani, 2020).

3. Literature Review

3.1 Artificial Intelligence

The invasion of AI is visible in various sectors of the economy, including education, banking, and even disaster management. AI technology is characterized by the feature of task automation that typically requires human cognition and interventions. This involvement of AI has led to significant advancements that we all have witnessed during global pandemics like COVID-19. AI assisted in the rapid diagnosis, early detection, and accurate treatment of COVID-19 and aided in predicting the morbidity and mortality caused by the coronavirus (Khabiya et al., 2022). The computerized diagnostic and personalized treatment suggested by AI presence can be felt in the healthcare sector (Karmakar et al., 2024). AI has generated advanced technology backed by learning tools and algorithms, delivering tailor-made solutions to the learner's needs, particularly for children with special needs (CWSN) (Ahmad et al., 2024). The experience of working with AI technology is enriching, as it offers inclusivity and easy access to learning materials (Ahmad et al., 2024). In disaster management, AI is a breakthrough as it aids in prompt decision-making and resource allocation during a disaster (Bohland et al., 2024). The transformation seen in the banking sector in the recent decade is due to the intrusion of AI in primary banking operations. The banking sector is now more enhanced than before in terms of customer service, risk management, streamlined operations, chatbots, and virtual assistance, offering personalized financial advice and facilitating transactions that enhance operational efficiency (Baltgailis et al., 2024; Mucsková, 2024). The involvement of AI in banking operations has significantly reduced money laundering cases by analyzing large data sets of fraud detection, suspicious transactions, and false positives (Hrabariev et al., 2024; Hussain et al., 2024). Furthermore, AI has led to reduced NPAs as it helps in credit risk assessments, analyzing borrower data for better lending decisions and reducing the rate of defaults (Abdulsalam & Tajudeen, 2024; Mucsková, 2024). The "Robotic Process Automation (RPA)" of AI has optimized bank back office operations by automating regular repetitive tasks.

3.2 Employee Engagement

EE has been widely explored and researched due to its advantages for organizations. The proposed concept by Kahn (1990) is "harnessing the organizational members' self with work physically, emotionally and cognitively."

Kahn's proposition of this concept led to devising the construct in various dimensions and concepts. Authors such as Bakker (2011), Wellins and Concelman (2005), Liu (2016), Macey and Schneider (2008), and May et al. (2004) attempted to define the construct as multi-dimensional. EE was observed to be a cognitive construct along with emotional and behavioral application at work (May et al., 2004). Wellins and Concelman (2005) present it as an employee's combination of loyalty, ownership, and commitment toward the organization. Cha (2017) defines the construct as emotional attachment, recognition at work, and a sense of valued work contribution. Macey and Schneider (2008) present an even more comprehensive definition of EE as a combination of "trait," "psychological state," and "behavioral engagement" devised from "proactive personality," "job involvement," and "organizational citizenship behavior," respectively. Bakker (2011) sums it up as an awakened emotional state of employees characterized by energy and task involvement. Liu (2016) described it in five dimensions, namely, "organizational identity," "vigor," "dedication," "absorption," and "pleasant harmony." A study in commercial banks in Ghana revealed that (Puni et al., 2018) the engagement level of employees in terms of job satisfaction is greatly influenced by transformational leadership. A similar study on EE in the banking sector of Bangladesh advocates the relevance of training and development opportunities to inculcate the feeling of being nurtured, committed, fulfilled, and belonging (Afroz, 2018). A similar study in the background of Pakistan's baking sector asserted the effectiveness of training, development opportunities, and communication systems in EE (Ahmed et al., 2017; Sahar & Siddiqui, 2019). Chadha (2018) also asserted that training is relevant to improving the performance of employees in the service sector.

The association of AI and emotional intelligence has been a topic of discussion since its inception. Due to the nature of AI technology, a machine-driven, data-based algorithm, this disruptive technology tends to be emotionless, giving the least priority to human emotion, an indispensable component of human resource management. Fig. 10.2 helps in explaining the comparison between the two in the context of human resource management.

3.3 Link Between AI and Employee Engagement: Employee Experience Decoded

EEX is a recently researched construct that encompasses the employees' journey from pre-hiring to hiring and onboarding to off-boarding. This comprehensive HR concept integrates various dimensions, such as organizational climate and culture, HR practices, emotional intelligence, and other constructs influencing employee satisfaction and performance. In today's dynamic work environment, understanding and practicing EEX is vital for improved EE and retention. In the academic literature, EEX is defined as "the intersection of employee expectations, needs, and wants and the organizational design of those expectations needs and wants" (Morgan, 2017, p. 8). At the same time, Plaskoff (2017) assumes it is "the employee's holistic perceptions of the relationship with his/her employing

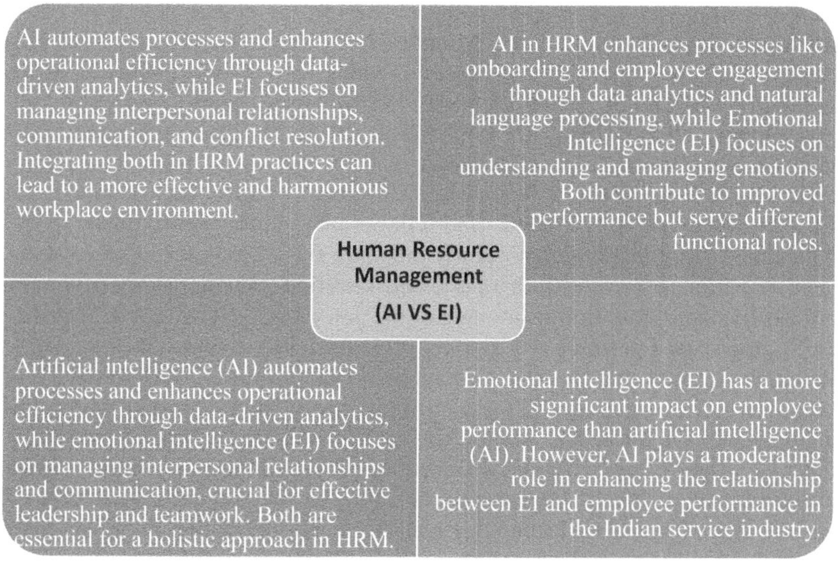

Fig. 10.2. Comparison Between Artificial Intelligence and Emotional Intelligence in HRM. *Source:* Author's own creation.

organization derived from all the encounters at touchpoints along the employee's journey" (p. 137). The extent of literature on this concept characterized this concept on three basic dimensions of the employee life cycle, namely, physical, social, and emotional aspects (Bersin et al., 2017; IBM and Globoforce, 2016; Maylett & Wride, 2017). Morgan (2017) characterized it as the locus of "technological", "physical space", and "cultural experience." According to Basar (2024), emotional engagement in terms of positive affect and emotionally viable culture enhances the EEX within the organization. Additionally, EEX encompasses collaborative management and organizational identification for nurturing engagement Basar (2024). The EEX framework propounded by Batat (2022) advocates personal, cultural, and social factors influencing the well-being of employees that transform the designed experience of employees—organizations practicing adaptability and inclusivity in digital transformation fostering EEX (Kyurova, 2023). Career-driven HR strategies and effective communication play pivotal roles in EEX enhancement (Porkodi et al., 2024).

The intrusion of complex technology in terms of AI is significantly transforming the workplace scenario. AI at the workplace enhances EEX by reorganizing HR processes and practices, nurturing EE, and promoting AI knowledge. Organizations leveraging advanced AI-enabled technology can craft productive and satisfying workplaces. However, this complex relationship between AI and EEX necessitates adopting a balanced approach to amplify the advantages while addressing possible challenges. The available knowledge in the field of EEX suggests the overarching impact on the engagement level of the employees (Itam & Ghosh, 2020; Morgan, 2017; Plaskoff, 2017). The extent of positive EEX in organizational functions tends to positively influence organizational outcomes in terms of better performance, loyalty, retention, and discretionary efforts (IBM and Globoforce, 2016). However, the recent work scenario is witnessing a paradigm shift in EEX and engagement level (Kahn, 1990; Macey & Schneider, 2008) due to the intrusion of advanced technology like AI (Bersin et al., 2017; IBM and Globoforce, 2016; Shivakumar, 2020). AI-enabled HR functions significantly influence the EEX in terms of a streamlined recruitment process with non-biased selection (Zhang, 2024), automatic onboarding, and smooth transitioning of the new entrants (Dwivedi & Mahanty, 2023), need-based personalized training programs (Subramanian & Riya, 2024). Research suggests that positive EEX in terms of "culture," "technology," and "Physical space" intensifies EE levels (Malik et al., 2023). AI applications and digitization have created a vacuum for various administrative and managerial tasks to be performed effectively, freeing employees from monotonous clerical jobs (Malik et al., 2020). AI possesses the ability to integrate the diverse needs of various stakeholders. AI technology has led to more retention, with AI-driven HRD strategies that influence EE and retention (Davis, 2014). However, the conflicting association was also seen in lower retention due to job insecurity and privacy concerns possessed by AI (Brougham & Haar, 2018). The EEX tends to be negatively influenced and thereby detrimental to the engagement level of employees due to serious challenges posed by AI in terms of privacy issues, skill obsolescence, and job loss (Brougham & Haar, 2018). AI-driven HR strategies and functions can accrue many benefits to the organization, such as improved productivity, effective decision-making, and enhanced EEX (Sharma et al., 2024). The capacity of AI assistance helps provide customized EEX, enhanced employee satisfaction, and improved engagement (Agarwal et al., 2023). AI technologies like Augmented Reality, chatbots, and virtual assistance assist employees in real time with operations like customer grievance redressal, employee onboarding, training, and performance evaluation (Sharma et al., 2024).

4. Research Objectives and Hypothesis

The exhaustive literature review on AI, EEX, and EE posed serious concerns and gaps that need to be addressed empirically. Thus, this empirical study seeks to achieve the following research objectives:

RQ1. Relationship between and impact of AI and EEX in the banking sector in India.

H1. "AI has a significant positive relationship with EEX"

RQ2. Relationship between and impact of EEX and EE in the banking sector in India.

H2. "EEX has a significant positive relationship with EE."

RQ3. Relationship between and impact of AI and EE in the banking sector in India.

H3. "AI has a significant positive relationship with EE."

RQ4. Relationship between AI and EE mediated by EEX in the banking sector in India.

H4. "EEX mediates the positive relationship between AI and EE."

5. Research Method and Measures

This empirical study first extensively explores the literature on AI, EEX, and EE to create a strong theoretical foundation for executing quantitative research in the Indian banking sector. This cross-sectional study collects data using a standardized questionnaire to measure the constructs of AI, EEX, and EE among banking sector executives in India (Public and Private Banks of India). A purposive and convenience sampling technique is adopted to randomly fetch required responses from public and private commercial banks in India's Delhi-NCR region. The online web link is used to administer the questionnaire with the explicit prior consent of the respondents. A total of 750 questionnaires were administered, out of which 530 valid responses were obtained to conduct the final analysis (Table 10.1). This study is not a comparative analysis of India's public and private banking sectors but a combined approach to studying this sector's phenomenon. Partial Least Squares (PLS-SEM) is adopted using the SMART PLS 4.1 version (Ringle et al., 2024). The mediation analysis uses Baron and Kenny's (1986) approach with a model proposed by Hair et al. (2017) to assess the mediation role of EEX in the relationship between AI and EE. AAAW (Attitude toward AI application at work) (Park et al., 2024) scale measures AI attitude. EEX is measured using a 13-item scale devised by Acuña-Hurtado et al. (2024). EE is measured using a Techno-work engagement scale of nine items (Balgiu, 2022; Mäkiniemi et al., 2020). All three measurement scales measure the construct on a 5-point Likert scale ranging from 1 (*Strongly Disagree*) to 5 (*Strongly Agree*).

6. Results and Findings

6.1 Measurement Model

- *Reliability and Validity:* In this study, AI, EEX, and EE are assumed to be the "*second-order formative construct.*" The evaluation model here evaluates the factor loading of the variables of the constructs (AI, EEX, and EE), followed by

Table 10.1. Demographic Details of the Participants.

Section		Frequency	Ratio
Gender	Male	336	63.3%
	Female	194	36.7%
Age	20–30	206	38.8%
	31–50	198	37.6%
	50 and above	126	23.6%
Designation	Executive/Junior assistant	256	48.3%
	Probationary officer/Manager	176	33.2
	Specialist officer	98	18.5
Work experience	0–5 years	130	24.5
	6–10 years	106	20.0
	11–15 years	138	26.0
	16–20 years	104	19.6
	20 years and above	52	9.0
Bank type	Public	296	55.9
	Private	234	44.1

Source: Author's own calculation.

their reliability and validity. The following table gives factor loadings, Indicator multi-collinearity, and Construct reliability. Factor loading of all the items of the constructs is more than 0.708 (Table 10.2), representing more than 50% of the variance (Hair et al., 2021, p. 21) except for the items AI15, AI23, and SX3. However, the construct reliability is established due to the "*Average Variance Extracted (AVE)*" of more than 0.50. Therefore, such items need not be removed. The VIF values of less than 3 (Table 10.2) represent the absence of indicator multi-collinearity (Hair et al., 2021, p. 21). The construct reliability for the factors is established using Cronbach's alpha, composite reliability, Rho, and AVE. All the values of these parameters were in an acceptable range of 0.70 and 0.95 (Hair et al., 2021, p. 30), and AVE was more than 0.50; for AVE and HTMT, parameters are used to construct validity. The convergent and discriminant validity are established with AVE (Table 10.2) more than 0.50 and HTMT within the threshold limit of 0.850 (Hair et al., 2021, p. 30).

- *Higher Order Construct (HOC) Validation:* In our study, AI, EEX, and EE are assumed to be the higher-order constructs due to the relevance of each factor that defines the very nature of the construct. Removal of any of the factors may distort the very nature of the construct measured. So, first, redundancy analysis helps establish convergent validity in higher-order formative construct validity. The correlation of the formative construct with reflected measured items should be more than 0.708 (Hair et al., 2022). All the

Table 10.2. Construct Reliability and Validity.

Construct	Factor	Items	Factor Loading	VIF	Cronbach Alpha	Composite Reliability	Rho	AVE
Artificial intelligence (AI)	Human likeness	AI1	0.711	1.336	0.765	0.815	0.723	0.675
		AI2	0.861	1.322				
		AI3	0.844	2.001				
		AI4	0.808	1.453				
	Adaptability	AI5	0.801	1.672	0.801	0.763	0.781	0.591
		AI6	0.709	1.523				
		AI7	0.714	1.632				
		AI8	0.843	1.730				
	Quality	AI9	0.708	1.832	0.834	0.805	0.842	0.592
		AI10	0.752	1.882				
		AI11	0.753	1.934				
		AI12	0.810	1.451				
		AI13	0.819	1.492				
	Anxiety	AI14	0.787	1.792	0.780	0.742	0.732	0.624
		AI15	0.698	1.771				
		AI16	0.881	1.581				
		AI17	0.783	1.889				
	Job insecurity	AI18	0.724	1.088	0.841	0.805	0.798	0.661
		AI19	0.775	1.162				
		AI20	0.907	1.176				
		AI21	0.834	1.370				
	Personal utility	AI22	0.842	1.294	0.759	0.811	0.802	0.582
		AI23	0.560	1.833				

(Continued)

Table 10.2. *(Continued)*

Construct	Factor	Items	Factor Loading	VIF	Cronbach Alpha	Composite Reliability	Rho	AVE
		AI24	0.885	1.448				
		AI25	0.732	2.223				
Employee experience (EEX)	Sensory experience (SX)	SX1	0.901	2.375	0.805	0.841	0.811	0.626
		SX2	0.841	1.320				
		SX3	0.692	1.008				
		SX4	0.711	1.332				
	Intellectual experience (IX)	IX1	0.821	1.873	0.711	0.745	0.741	0.650
		IX2	0.763	1.829				
		IX3	0.756	1.998				
		IX4	0.831	1.723				
		IX5	0.882	1.823				
		IX6	0.775	1.883				
	Emotional experience (EX)	EX1	0.791	1.862	0.742	0.784	0.759	0.673
		EX2	0.908	1.439				
		EX3	0.755	1.309				
Employee engagement (EE)	Techno_Vigor	Techno_VI1	0.743	1.390	0.821	0.811	0.802	0.550
		Techno_VI2	0.761	1.672				
		Techno_VI3	0.721	1.629				
	Techno_Dedication	Techno_DE1	0.801	1.729	0.779	0.795	0.821	0.657
		Techno_DE2	0.821	1.490				

		Techno_DE3	0.811	1.620			
	Techno_Absorption	Techno_AB1	0.762	1.992	0.859	0.825	0.833 0.555
		Techno_AB2	0.751	1.888			
		Techno_AB3	0.722	1.628			

Validating Higher Order Construct

Factors and Construct	Redundancy Analysis (Path Coefficient)	Outer Weights	VIF	*T*-statistics	*p* Values	Outer Loading
Humanlikeness → AI	0.742	0.408	1.016	11.421	0.000	0.612
Adaptability → AI		0.394	2.011	26.832	0.003	0.619
Quality → AI		0.491	1.172	2.877	0.000	0.566
Anxiety → AI		0.581	1.019	3.782	0.000	0.721
Job insecurity → AI		0.602	1.110	11.895	0.000	0.691
Personal utility → AI		0.372	2.007	4.661	0.002	0.588
Sensory experience (SX) → EEX	0.815	0.381	2.012	21.661	0.000	0.891
Intellectual experience (IX) → EEX		0.499	1.092	12.427	0.000	0.766
Emotional experience (EX) → EEX		0.401	1.023	11.672	0.000	0.882
Techno_Vigor → EE	0.744	0.302	1.041	10.221	0.000	0.801
Techno_Dedication → EE		0.411	1.056	9.123	0.000	0.792
Techno_Absorption → EE		0.322	1.071	3.182	0.001	0.885

Source: Author's calculation.

path coefficients are above 0.708 (Table 10.2), confirming the same. Second, the formative model has no collinearity issue, as VIF values are less than 3 (Hair et al., 2021, p. 21). Third, Outer Weights' statistical significance and relevance are assessed, which were significant with $p < 0.05$ (Hair et al., 2021). Finally, each indicator's outer loading and significance of the higher-order formative constructs AI, EEX, and EE are tested. All the outer loading is more than 0.50 and significant (Sarstedt et al., 2019). Hence, HOC validity is established.

6.2 Structural Equation Modeling

- *The goodness of Model Fit:* R^2, Q^2 and the paths' significance are considered relevant for assessing the structural model. The model's goodness is determined by the R^2 value of the dependent variables (i.e., EEX and EE). Since R^2 values are above 0.1(Table 10.3) (Falk & Miller, 1992), the model has predictive capacity. Moreover, our model has predictive relevance, as Q^2 is more than 0 (Table 10.3) (Hair et al., 2013). The model fit is assessed using SRMR, which has a value of 0.063, less than the threshold limit (Hair et al., 2021) (Table 10.3, Fig. 10.3).
- *Hypothesis Testing: H1*, "Artificial Intelligence has a significant positive relationship with Employee experience" is supported ($\beta = 0.522$, $t = 29.772$, $p = 0.000$ ($p < 0.05$)). *H2*, "Employee Experience has a significant positive relationship with Employee engagement" is also supported ($\beta = 0.529$, $t = 13.762$, $p = 0.003$ ($p < 0.05$)). *H3*, "Artificial Intelligence has a significant positive relationship with Employee Engagement" was found to be supported ($\beta = 0.430$, $t = 21.782$, $p = 0.000$ ($p < 0.05$)) (Table 10.3, Fig. 10.3).

Table 10.3. Path Coefficient and Goodness of Fit.

Path Coefficient	***B***	**STDEV**	***t*-Statistics**	***p* Values**	**Confidence Interval**		**Decision**
					2.50%	**97.50%**	
H1: AI → EEX	0.522	0.087	29.772	0.000	0.019	0.187	Supported
H2: EEX → EE	0.529	0.074	13.762	0.003	0.901	0.996	Supported
H3: AI → EE	0.430	0.092	21.782	0.000	0.813	0.911	Supported
	R^2	Q^2					
EEX	0.634	0.449					
EE	0.577	0.677					

Source: Author's calculation.

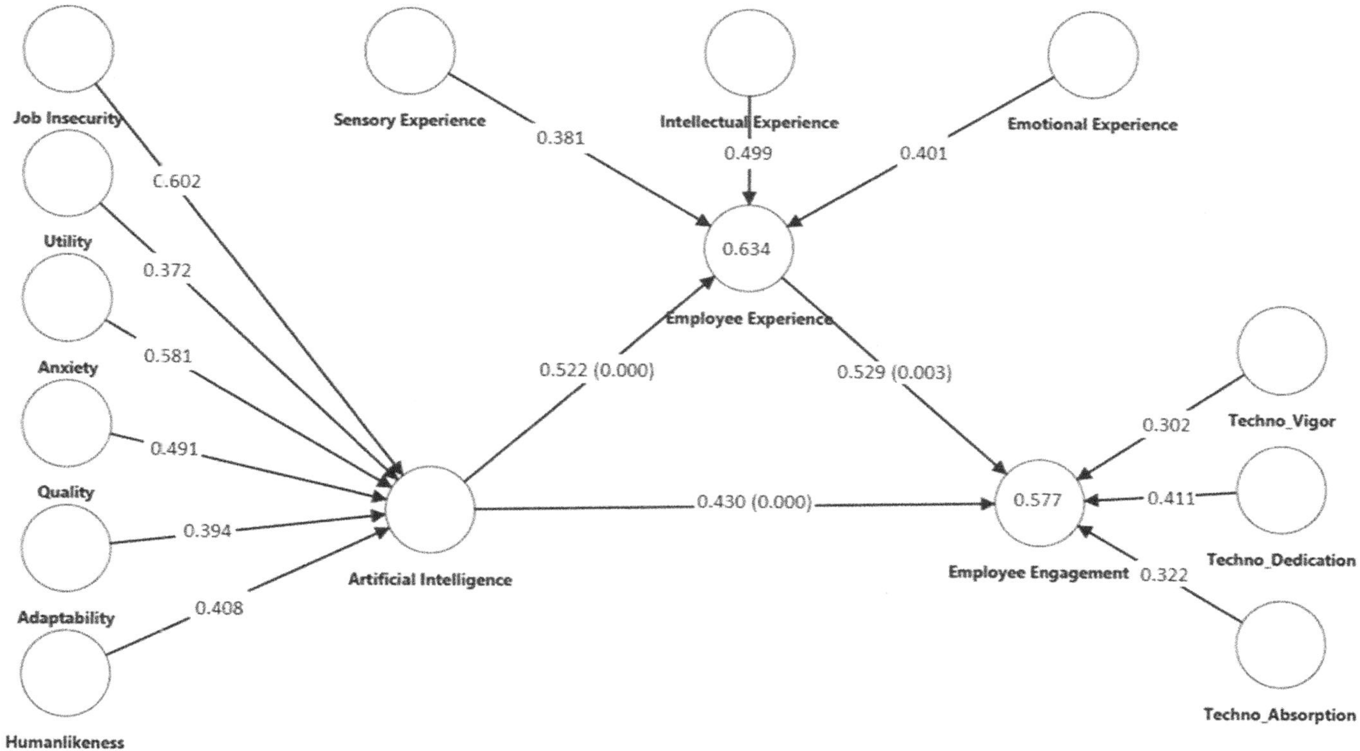

Fig. 10.3. Path Coefficient Model for AI, EEX, and EE. *Source:* Author's own creation and calculation.

6.3 Mediation Analysis

In order to assess *H4*, the "Relationship between Artificial Intelligence and Employee Engagement is mediated by Employee Experience," as well as the direct, indirect, and total effects, is calculated. The results confirm the mediation effect of EEX between AI and EE as the indirect effect is significant ($\beta = 0.484$, $t = 18.219$, $p = 0.02$ ($p < 0.05$)) (Table 10.4). Moreover, this mediation effect is found to be partially mediated due to significant direct ($\beta = 0.430$, $p = 0.00$ ($p < 0.05$)) (Table 10.4) and indirect effects. Additionally, complementary partial mediation exists due to the positive beta (β) (Table 10.4) value of direct and indirect effects (Sheko & Braimllari Spaho, 2018). Hence, *H4* is supported.

7. Discussion and Conclusion

This study was conducted to investigate the impact of the introduction of AI on engagement at work, thereby boosting EEX in the banking industry. The impact of AI is quite influential in various industries, influencing employees' attitudes. The workforce's attitude in the banking industry is multifaceted, depicting mystifying characteristics of optimism and apprehension. While observing it as a boon, many assume it is a bane in India's banking sector. Appreciating its contribution to enhancing efficiency and customer service experiences, its ethical implications, and job displacement are concerning. Our study taps into this issue by analyzing the association between AI, EEX, and EE. The measurement model attempts to identify the crucial factors defining the phenomenon of AI, EEX, and EE in India's banking sector. The outer weights in our measurement model help identify the impactful factors of the construct in the banking industry. Out of six factors measuring the attitude of banking personnel toward AI, "Job Insecurity, Anxiety, and Quality" (Brougham & Haar, 2018; Nam, 2019; Wixom & Todd, 2005) was found to be the most impactful, unlike "Personal Utility" factor, highlighting low weightage for them contrary to previous studies (Park & Woo, 2022; Uziel, 2007). The second construct of this study, i.e. Employee Experience, is studied on three parameters, namely, "Sensory Experience," "Intellectual Experience," and "Emotional Experience." Out of these three factors devised by Acuña-Hurtado et al. (2024), "Intellectual Experience" (Hemment et al., 2023) is observed to be the most influential factor, causing around 50% of the impact, followed by "Sensory Experience" (Bloch et al., 2003; Parsons & Conroy, 2006; Simonson & Schmitt, 1997). For the factors incorporated to measure EE in terms of AI technology, "Techno_Dedication" is found to be most impactful, followed by "Techno_Absorption" with a 41% correlation with EE (Schaufeli et al., 2002).

Our study also asserts various studies' findings that AI significantly impacts the EEX (Bersin et al., 2017; IBM and Globoforce, 2016; Kyurova, 2023; Porkodi et al., 2024). Similarly, EEX exerts a significant positive impact on EE with a beta value of 0.529, showing approximately 53% change in EE due to EEX (Bersin et al., 2017; IBM and Globoforce, 2016; Malik, Budhwar, et al., 2021; Malik et al., 2022). On the contrary, the impact of AI on EE is found to be

Table 10.4. Mediation Analysis.

Total Effect (AI → EE)		**Direct Effect (AI → EE)**		**Indirect Effect of AI on EE**						
B	***p* Value**	***B***	***p* Value**		***B***	**STDEV**	***t*-Statistics**	***p* Values**	**CI [2.5%, 97.5%]**	**Decision**
0.915	0.000	0.430	0.000	H4: AI → EEX → EE	0.484	21.723	18.219	0.028	[0.013,0.194]	Supported

Source: Author's calculation.

relatively low but significant to the tune of 0.430, depicting the relevance of EEX in the relationship between AI and EE. The indirect effect of AI on EE through EEX is found to be significant to the tune of 0.484, concerning the direct effect of AI on EE with a magnitude of 0.430. However, the impact improved marginally yet seems significant, introducing EEX as a catalyst and mediator to enhance the impact of AI on EE (Malik et al., 2020, 2021b). This is contrary to the previous studies advocating the adverse impact of AI on EEX and thereby reducing the engagement of employees (Brougham & Haar, 2018; Makriddakis, 2017). Integrating AI in the financial or banking sector has unlocked various capabilities and potentials. Introducing this radical technology has significantly enhanced the EEX in many sectors. However, the impact is low and apprehensive due to job displacement and anxiety, which has led to significant positive changes in EEX in the banking sector. The positives of AI will lead to cost reduction and free banking staff for more productive and creative jobs in terms of speedy service and service extension for customers. This will enhance not only customer satisfaction but also the number of clients. Though AI poses a concern about job loss, its welcoming response by banking employees proves it to be a support rather than a substitute. Though many routine and clerical jobs will be at stake, it will increase jobs in managerial and administrative functions. The association between AI, EEX, and EE in this study was weak yet significant due to its limited presence in India's banking sector. The full-fledged impact of AI is yet to be seen when significant banking functions get automated and digitized.

The practical implication of AI in enhancing EEX and engagement is overarching. The banking system in India can implement AI technology to supplement the training and development programs to meet the objectives of employee skill enhancement and engagement. This increases job satisfaction and reduces attrition (Kamber & Akar, 2021). In addition to this, the banking system can employ a real-time feedback mechanism to review employees' performance and engagement levels. This addresses employees' concerns and alleviates customer service (Claus, 2019). Leveraging data analysis technology using AI to identify and monitor key performance trends to enhance EEX management can significantly improve decision-making (Nguyen & Malik, 2021; Prikshat et al., 2023). Introducing effective AI-assisted communication channels can facilitate the free flow of communication and quick grievance handling of employees.

References

Abdulsalam, T. A., & Tajudeen, R. B. (2024). Artificial intelligence (AI) in the banking industry: A review of service areas and customer service journeys in emerging economies. *Business and Management Compass*, *68*, 19–43. https://doi.org/10.56065/9hfvrq20

Acuña-Hurtado, N., García-Salirrosas, E. E., Villar-Guevara, M., & Fernández-Mallma, I. (2024). Scale to evaluate employee experience: Evidence of validity and reliability in regular basic education teachers in the Peruvian context. *Behavioral Science*, *14*, 667.

Afroz, N. N. (2018). Effects of training on employee performance – A study on the banking sector, Tangail Bangladesh. *Global Journal of Economics and Business, 4* (1), 111–124.

Agarwal, S., Gupta, A., & Roshani, P. (2023). Redefining HRM with artificial intelligence and machine learning. In *The adoption and effect of artificial intelligence on human resources management* (Vol. Part A, 1–13). https://doi.org/10.1108/978-1-80382-027-920231001

Ahmad, W., Ruchika, S., & Raj, R. (2024). Artificial intelligence. In *Advances in educational technologies and instructional design book series*. https://doi.org/10.4018/979-8-3693-5538-1.ch017

Ahmed, U., Isa, N. M., Majid, A. H. A., Zin, M. L. M., & Amin, B. M. (2017). Towards understanding work engagement: Can HR buffer HR? Test of a moderated model. *International Journal of Economic Research, 14*(20), 1–18.

Bakker, A. B. (2011). An evidence-based model of work engagement. *Current Directions in Psychological Science, 20*(4), 265–269. https://doi.org/10.1177/0963721411414534

Balgiu, B. (2022). The adaptation and validation of the techno-work engagement scale (TechnoWES-9) in the case of Romanian employees. *Psihologia Resurselor Umane, 20*(2), 89–100. https://doi.org/10.24837/pru.v20i2.513

Baltgailis, J., Simakhova, A., & Buka, S. (2024). AI in banking: Socio-economic aspects. *Baltic Journal of Economic Studies*. https://doi.org/10.30525/2256-0742/2024-10-3-26-35

Barney, M. (2018). *Artificially intelligent coaching has arrived*. https://trainingindustry.com/magazine/mayjun-2018/artificially-intelligent-coaching-has-arrived/. Accessed on February 23, 2020.

Baron, R. M., & Kenny, D. A. (1986). The moderator-mediator variable distinction in social psychological research: Conceptual, strategic, and statistical considerations. *Journal of Personality and Social Psychology, 51*, 1173–1182.

Basar, D. (2024). The relationship between employee experience and employee engagement with the moderating role of positive affect in the finance sector. *Borsa Istanbul Review*. https://doi.org/10.1016/j.bir.2024.05.002

Basu Mallick, C. (2019). *How AI-driven performance feedback can make you a better manager*. https://www.spiceworks.com/hr/performance-management/articles/ai-driven-performance-feedback/https://www.hrtechnologist.com/articles/performance-management-hcm/aidriven-performance-feedback/. Accessed on February 23, 2020.

Batat, W. (2022). The employee experience (EMX) framework for well-being: An agenda for the future. *Employee Relations, 44*(5), 993–1013. https://doi.org/10.1108/er-03-2022-0133

Bedford, D., Bellens, J., Meekings, K., & Schlich, B. (2018). *FinTech is disrupting the banking industry, and banks must react to the rapid emergence of these new market players*. Ernst & Young

Bersin, J., Flynn, J., Mazor, A., & Melián, V. (2017). *Rewriting the rules for the digital age – 2017 Deloitte global human capital trends*. Deloitte University Press. https://dair.nps.edu/bitstream/123456789/3432/1/SEC809-AWF-17-0044.pdf. Accessed on July 15, 2021.

Bloch, P. H., Brunel, F. F., & Arnold, T. J. (2003). Individual differences in the centrality of visual product aesthetics: Concept and measurement. *Journal of Consumer Research, 29*(4), 551–565.

Bohland, J. R., Rechkemmer, A., & Rogers, P. (2024). *Artificial intelligence*. https://doi.org/10.1093/oxfordhb/9780190466145.013.13

Boustani, N. M. (2020). *Traditional banks and fintech: Survival, future and threats ICT for an inclusive world*. Springer.

Breidbach, C., Brodie, R., & Hollebeek, L. (2014). Beyond virtuality: From engagement platforms to engagement ecosystems. *Managing Service Quality, 24* (6), 592–611.

Brougham, D., & Haar, J. (2018). Smart technology, artificial intelligence, robotics, and algorithms (STARA): Employees' perceptions of our future workplace. *Journal of Management and Organization, 24*(2), 239–257. https://doi.org/10.1017/jmo.2016.55

Budhwar, P., Malik, A., De Silva, M. T. T., & Thevisuthan, P. (2022). Artificial intelligence – Challenges and opportunities for international HRM: A review and research agenda. *The International Journal of Human Resource Management, 33*(6), 1065–1097. https://doi.org/10.1080/09585192.2022.2035161

Cha, S. C. (2007). *Research on structural modelling of enterprise employee engagement*. Unpublished manuscript. Jinan University.

Chadha, D. (2018). A study of training and development practices in service sector about employee engagement across Delhi and NCR. *International Journal of Human Resource Development and Management, 8*(1), 1–11. https://www.ripublication.com/ijhrdm18/ijhrdmv8n1_01.pdf

Charlwood, A., & Guenole, N. (2022). Can HR adapt to the paradoxes of artificial intelligence? *Human Resource Management Journal, 32*(4), 729–742. https://doi.org/10.1111/1748-8583.12433

Claus, L. (2019). HR disruption—Time already to reinvent talent management. *BRQ Business Research Quarterly, 22*(3), 207–215. https://doi.org/10.1016/j.brq.2019.04.002

Davis, M. C., Challenger, R., Jayewardene, D. N., & Clegg, C. W. (2014). Advancing socio-technical systems thinking: A call for bravery. *Applied Ergonomics, 45*(2), 171–180. https://doi.org/10.1016/j.apergo.2013.02.009

Davis, A. S., & Van der Heijden, B. I. J. M. (2023). Launching the dynamic employee engagement framework: Towards a better understanding of the phenomenon. *Employee Relations: The International Journal, 45*(2), 421–436. https://doi.org/10.1108/ER- 08-2021-0338

Dwivedi, D. N., & Mahanty, G. (2023). AI-powered employee experience. In *Advances in human resources management and organizational development book series*. https://doi.org/10.4018/979-8-3693-0039-8.ch009

Falk, R. F., & Miller, N. B. (1992). *A primer for soft modelling*. University of Akron Press.

Haak, T. (2019). *Personalisation in HR: Some ideas*. https://www.hrtrendinstitute.com/blog/2019/04/29/personalisation-in-hr. Accessed on February.232020 ,

Hair, J. F., Hult, G. T. M., Ringle, C. M., & Sarstedt, M. (2017). *A primer on partial least squares structural equation modeling (PLS-SEM)* (2nd ed.). Sage Publications Inc.

Hair, J., Hult, G. T. M., Ringle, C., & Sarstedt, M. (2022). *A primer on partial least squares structural equation modeling (PLS-SEM)*. Springer.

Hair, J., Hult, G. T. M., Ringle, C., Sarstedt, M., Danks, N., & Ray, S. (2021). *Partial least squares structural equation modeling (PLS-SEM) using R: A workbook*. Springer.

Hair, J. F., Ringle, C. M., & Sarstedt, M. (2013). Partial least squares structural equation modelling: Rigorous applications, better results and higher acceptance. *Long Range Planning*, *46*(1–2), 1–12.

Hemment, D., Simperl, E., Sandler, M., Kennedy, H., Benford, S., & Manghani, S. (2023). A manifesto for intelligent experiences. *Generative AI Arts: A Synthetic Future Foretold*. https://doi.org/10.2218/newreal.9248

Hrabariev, A., Derbentsev, V., Rososhenko, V., Myslynskyi, D., & Fedorenko, O. (2024). AI in banking: Current applications, challenges, and prospects. *Successes and Achievements in Science*, *6*(S6), 658–674. https://doi.org/10.52058/3041-1254-2024-6(6)-658-674

Hussain, A., Khan, M. A., Manoj, B. N., & K, S. (2024). *A study on impact of artificial intelligence in financial services of private banks in Bangalore* (pp. 91–98). QTanalytics Publication. https://doi.org/10.48001/978-81-966500-8-7-9

IBM and Globoforce. (2016). *The employee experience Index: A new global measure of a human workplace and its impact*. https://www.globoforce.com/wpcontent/uploads/2016/10/The_Employee_Experience_Index.pdf. Accessed on December 21, 2020.

Imam, H., Sahi, A., & Farasat, M. (2022). The roles of supervisor support, employee engagement and internal communication in performance: A social exchange perspective. *Corporate Communications: An International Journal*, *28*(3), 489–505. https://doi.org/10.1108/CCIJ-08-2022-0102

Itam, U., & Ghosh, N. (2020). Employee experience management. *International Journal of Human Capital and Information Technology Professionals*, *11*(2), 39–49. https://doi.org/10.4018/IJHCITP.2020040103

Jaiswal, A., Arun, C. J., & Varma, A. (2022). Rebooting employees: Upskilling for artificial intelligence in multinational corporations. *International Journal of Human Resource Management*, *33*(6), 1179–1208.

Kahn, W. A. (1990). Psychological conditions of personal engagement and disengagement at work. *Academy of Management Journal*, *33*(4), 692–724.

Kamber, E., & Akar, C. (2021). Human resource developments with a touch of artificial intelligence: A scale development study. *International Journal of Manpower*, *43*(1), 168–205.

Kambur, E., & Yildirim, T. (2023). From traditional to smart human resources management. *International Journal of Manpower*, *44*(3), 422–452. https://doi.org/10.1108/IJM-10-2021-0622

Karmakar, P., Sinha, S., & Pal, D. (2024). Artificial intelligence. *International Journal of Advanced Research in Science, Communication and Technology*, *4*(2), 79–87. https://doi.org/10.48175/ijarsct-19613

Khabiya, R., Shrivastava, A., Dwivedi, A., Batt, P., Meval, A., Derashri, A., & Darwhekar, G. (2022). Artificial intelligence. *International Journal of Health Sciences (IJHS)*, *6*(S6), 3014–3024. https://doi.org/10.53730/ijhs.v6ns6.9986

Kim, J. S., & Gatling, A. (2018). The impact of using a virtual employee engagement platform (VEEP) on employee engagement and intention to stay. *International Journal of Contemporary Hospitality Management*, *30*(1), 242–259.

Kyurova, A. (2023). The employee experience is a key component of the SME digital transformation strategy. *Economics & Law*, *5*, 91–98. https://doi.org/10.37708/el.swu.v5i2.8

Lepak, D. P., & Snell, S. A. (1999). The human resource architecture: Toward a theory of human capital allocation and development. *Academy of Management Review*, *24*(1), 31–48.

Lepak, D. P., & Snell, S. A. (2002). Examining the human resource architecture: The relationships among human capital, employment, and human resource configurations. *Journal of Management*, *28*(4), 517–543.

Liu, Z. A. (2016). Study the development of a structured model of engagement for knowledge employees. *Business Management*, *11*, 65–69. https://doi.org/10.13395/j.cnki.issn.1009-0061.2016.11.018

Ma, X., & Brown, T. (2020). AI-mediated exchange theory. In *Extended abstracts of the 2020 CHI conference on human factors in computing systems (workshop)*. Association for Computing Machinery.

Macey, W. H., & Schneider, B. (2008). The meaning of employee engagement. *Industrial and Organisational Psychology*, *1*(1), 3–30. https://doi.org/10.1111/j.1754-9434.2007.0002.x

Mahadevan, J., & Schmitz, A. P. (2020). HRM as an ongoing struggle for legitimacy: A critical discourse analysis of HR managers as "employee-experience designers". *Baltic Journal of Management*, *15*(4), 515–532. https://doi.org/10.1108/BJM-10-2018-0368

Mäkiniemi, J. P., Salla, A., & Johanna, J. (2020). A novel construct to measure employees' technology-related experiences of well-being: Empirical validation of the techno-work engagement scale (TechnoWES). *Scandinavian Journal of Work and Organizational Psychology*, *5*(1). https//doi.org/10.16993/sjwop.79

Makriddakis, S. S. (2017). The forthcoming artificial intelligence (AI) revolution: Its impact on society and firms. *Futures*, *90*, 46–60.

Malik, A., Budhwar, P., Mohan, H., & Srikanth, N. R. (2023). Employee experience – The missing link for engaging employees. *Human Resource Management*, *62*(1), 97–115.

Malik, A., Budhwar, P., Patel, C., & Laker, B. (2021). Holistic Indigenous and atomistic modernity: Analysing performance management in two Indian emerging market multinational corporations. *Human Resource Management*, *60*, 803–823. https://doi.org/10.1002/hrm.22057

Malik, A., Budhwar, P., Patel, C., & Srikanth, N. R. (2022). May). The bots be with you! Delivering HR cost-effectiveness and individualised employee experiences in an MNE. *International Journal of HRM*, *33*(6), 1148–1178. https://doi.org/10.1080/09585192.2020.1859582

Malik, A., De Silva, M. T., Budhwar, P., & Srikanth, N. R. (2021). Elevating talents' experience through innovative artificial intelligence-mediated knowledge sharing: Evidence from an IT-multinational enterprise. *Journal of International Management*, *27*(4). https://doi.org/10.1016/j.intman.2021.100871

Malik, A., Pereira, V., & Budhwar, P. (2020). HRM in the global information technology (IT) industry: Towards multivergent configurations in strategic business partnerships. *Human Resource Management Review*, *31*(3), 100743.

Maslej, N., Fattorini, L., Perrault, R., Parli, V., Reuel, A., Brynjolfsson, E., Etchemendy, J., Ligett, K., Lyons, T., Manyika, J., Niebles, J. C., Shoham, Y., Wald, R., & Clark, J. (2024, April). *The AI Index 2024 annual report.* AI Index Steering Committee, Institute for Human-Centered AI, Stanford University.

May, D. R., Gilson, R. L., & Harter, L. M. (2004). The psychological conditions of meaningfulness, safety ava, liability and the engagement of the human spirit at work. *Journal of Occupational and Organisational Psychology, 77*(1), 11–37. https://doi.org/10.1348/096317904322915892

Maylett, T., & Wride, M. (2017). *The employee experience: How to attract talent, retain top performers, and drive results.* John Wiley & Sons.

Morgan, J. (2017). *The employee experience advantage: How to win the war for talent by giving employees the workspaces they want, the tools they need, and a culture they can celebrate.* John Wiley & Sons.

Morris, S., Snell, S., & Björkman, I. (2016). An architectural framework for global talent management. *Journal of International Business Studies, 47*(6), 723–747.

Mucsková, M. (2024). Transforming banking with artificial intelligence. *Trends Economics and Management, 18*(42), 21–37.

Nam, T. (2019). Technology usage, expected job sustainability, and perceived job insecurity. *Technological Forecasting and Social Change, 138*, 155–165. https://doi.org/10.1016/j.techfore.2018.08.017

Nguyen, T. M., & Malik, A. (2021). A two-wave cross-lagged study on AI service quality: The moderating effects of the job level and job role. *British Journal of Management, 33*(3), 1221–1237. https://doi.org/10.1111/1467-8551.12540

Parent, J. D., & Lovelace, K. J. (2018). Employee engagement, positive organisational culture and individual adaptability. *On the Horizon, 26*(3), 206–214.

Park, J., & Woo, S. E. (2022). Who likes artificial intelligence? Personality predictors of attitudes toward artificial intelligence. *Journal of Psychology, 156*(1), 68–94. https://doi.org/10.1080/00223980.2021.2012109

Park, J., Woo, S. E., & Kim, J. (2024). Attitudes towards artificial intelligence at work: Scale development and validation. *Journal of Occupational and Organizational Psychology, 97*, 920–951. https://doi.org/10.1111/joop.12502

Parsons, A., & Conroy, D. (2006). Sensory stimuli and e-tailers. *Journal of Consumer Behaviour: International Research and Review, 5*(1), 69–81.

Plaskoff, J. (2017). Employee experience: The new human resource management approach. *Strategic HR Review, 16*(3), 136–141.

Porkodi, S., Ahmad, A., & Bassam, T. (2024). Employee experience management and its critical impact on the sustainable development of an enterprise – A systematic literature survey with meta-analysis. *Journal of Sustainability Science and Management, 19*, 203–237. https://doi.org/10.46754/jssm.2024.04.015

Presbitero, A., & Teng-Calleja, M. (2023). Job attitudes and career behaviors relating to employees' perceived incorporation of artificial intelligence in the workplace: A career self-management perspective. *Personnel Review, 52*(4), 1169–1187. https://doi.org/10.1108/PR-02-2021-0103

Prikshat, V., Malik, A., & Budhwar, P. (2023). AI-augmented HRM: Antecedents, assimilation and multilevel consequences. *Human Resource Management Review, 33*(1). https://doi.org/10.1016/j.hrmr.2021.100860

Puni, A., Mohammed, I., & Asamoah, E. (2018). Transformational leadership and job satisfaction: The moderating effect of contingent reward. *The Leadership & Organization Development Journal*, *39*(4), 522–537.

Ringle, C. M., Wende, S., & Becker, J.-M. (2024). *SmartPLS 4*. SmartPLS. https://www.smartpls.com

Rodgers, W., Murray, J. M., Stefanidis, A., Degbey, W. Y., & Tarba, S. Y. (2023). An artificial intelligence algorithmic approach to ethical decision-making in human resource management processes. *Human Resource Management Review*, *33* (1). https//doi.org/10.1016/J.HRMR.2022.100925

Sahar, N., & Siddiqui, D. A. (2019). The impact of training & development and communication on employee engagement–A study of banking sector. *Business Management and Strategy*, *10*(1), 23–40.

Sarstedt, M., Hair, J. F., Cheah, J.-H., Becker, J.-M., & Ringle, C. M. (2019). How to specify, estimate, and validate higher-order constructs in PLS-SEM. *Australasian Marketing Journal*, *27*(3), 197–211. https://doi.org/10.1016/j.ausmj.2019.05.003. (Original work published 2019)

Schaufeli, W. B., Salanova, M., González-Romá, V., & Bakker, A. B. (2002). Measuring engagement and burnout: A two sample confirmatory factor analytic approach. *Journal of Happiness Studies*, *3*, 71–92.

Sharma, P., Sharma, V., Diddee, S., & Sandhu, S. (2024). Influence of artificial intelligence on employee performance in banking industry Indian perspective. In N. Pathak et al. (Eds.), *Proceedings of the 2nd international conference on emerging technologies and sustainable business practices-2024 (ICETSBP 2024), advances in economics, business and management research* (p. 296). https://doi.org/10.2991/978-94-6463-544-7_27

Sheko, A., & Spaho, A. (2018). Information technology inhibitors and information quality in supply chain management: A PLS-SEM analysis. *Academic Journal of Interdisciplinary Studies*, *7*, 125–138. https://doi.org/10.2478/ajis-2018-0064

Shivakumar, S. K. (2020). Introduction to employee experience platforms. In *Build a next-generation digital workplace*. Apress. https://doi.org/10.1007/978-1-4842-5512-4_1

Simonson, A., & Schmitt, B. H. (1997). Marketing aesthetics: The strategic management of brands, identity, and image. Simon and Schuster. Social exchange: Towards a conceptual model. *IEEE Transactions on Engineering Management*, 1–30. https://doi.org/10.1109/TEM.2022.3163117

Subramanian, Y. R., & Riya, R. (2024). The transformative role of artificial intelligence in human resource. *International Journal on Recent Trends in Business and Tourism*, *8*(2), 14–25. https://doi.org/10.31674/ijrtbt.2024.v08i02.002

Suseno, Y., Chang, C., Hudik, M., & Fang, E. S. (2022). Beliefs, anxiety and change readiness for artificial intelligence adoption among human resource managers: The moderating role of high-performance work systems. *International Journal of Human Resource Management*, *33*(6), 1209–1236.

Uziel, L. (2007). Individual differences in the social facilitation effect: A review and meta-analysis. *Journal of Research in Personality*, *41*(3), 579–601. https://doi.org/10.1016/j.jrp.2006.06.008

Vrontis, D., Christofi, M., Pereira, V., Tarba, S., Makrides, A., & Trichina, E. (2022). Artificial intelligence, robotics, advanced technologies and human resource management: A systematic review. *International Journal of Human Resource Management*, *33*(6), 1237–1266.

Wellins, R., & Concelman, K. (2005). Creating a culture for engagement. *Workforce Performance Solutions*, *4*, 1–5.

Whiteside, E. (2019). *How AI and machine learning enhance personalised learning in the workplace*. https://elearningindustry.com/ai-machine-enhance-personalized-learning-workplace. Accessed on February 23, 2020.

Wijayati, D. T., Rahman, Z., Fahrullah, A., Rahman, M. F. W., Arifah, I. D. C., & Kautsar, A. (2022). A study of artificial intelligence on employee performance and work engagement: The moderating role of change leadership. *International Journal of Manpower*, *43*(2), 486–512. https://doi.org/10.1108/IJM-07-2021-0423

Wixom, B. H., & Todd, P. A. (2005). A theoretical integration of user satisfaction and technology acceptance. *Information Systems Research*, *16*(1), 85–102. https://doi.org/10.1287/isre.1050.0042

Zhang, H. (2024). Exploring the impact of AI on human resource management: A case study of organizational adaptation and employee dynamics. *IEEE Transactions on Engineering Management*, *71*, 14991–15004.

Chapter 11

Reimagining Talent Management Through the AI-Knowledge Nexus

Unnar Theodorsson

University of Iceland, Iceland

Abstract

In today's competitive and complex business landscape, the integration of artificial intelligence (AI) into knowledge management (KM) systems presents transformative opportunities for enhancing talent management (TM) strategies. This chapter explores the pivotal role of AI-driven KM in optimizing TM through technologies such as machine learning, natural language processing, and predictive analytics. AI enables organizations to make data-driven decisions, uncover workforce patterns, and personalize development programs, thereby fostering adaptability and agility. The chapter addresses four primary objectives: assessing AI's role in knowledge-driven TM, exploring it's impact on skill development and career planning, evaluating its contribution to strategic decision-making, and examining associated ethical considerations. By aligning workforce strategies with business objectives, AI-enhanced KM systems promote responsive, ethical, and resilient approaches to managing talent.

Keywords: Talent management; artificial intelligence; knowledge management; human resource management; organizational behavior

Introduction

The integration of artificial intelligence (AI) into knowledge management (KM) and talent management (TM) is transforming the operational landscape of modern organizations. In an era of rapid technological advancement, the convergence of AI, KM, and TM offers innovative pathways to streamline processes, enhance employee development, and maintain a competitive edge (Mejri

AI-Driven Knowledge Management Assets, Volume 2, 221–235

Published under exclusive licence by Emerald Publishing Limited
doi:10.1108/978-1-83662-778-420261011

& Doghan, 2020; Pichler et al., 2021). Organizations increasingly leverage AI tools such as machine learning algorithms, natural language processing (NLP), and predictive analytics to create dynamic, responsive systems that enhance decision-making and drive continuous innovation (Davenport & Ronanki, 2018; McAfee & Brynjolfsson, 2017; Russell & Norvig, 2016). These technologies enable more precise talent planning, more efficient knowledge dissemination, and more agile workforce development (Huang & Rust, 2018; Upadhyay & Khandelwal, 2018). However, alongside these opportunities come significant challenges—including implementation barriers, ethical dilemmas, and the need for cultural adaptation—that must be addressed to realize the full potential of AI integration (Barocas et al., 2023; Cathey & Prabhakar, 2021).

The term *AI-Knowledge Nexus* refers to the synergistic intersection where artificial intelligence enhances both the creation and strategic utilization of organizational knowledge to inform and drive talent management practices. While traditional AI applications in human resources and KM typically emphasize automation, efficiency, or isolated process improvement, the AI-Knowledge Nexus represents a more holistic, integrated framework (Faqihi & Miah, 2023; Theodorsson et al., 2022).

This framework highlights how AI augments KM by enabling real-time knowledge capture, pattern recognition, and insight generation, and then connects these capabilities directly to TM functions such as recruitment, learning and development, and succession planning (Bersin, 2018; Chen et al., 2012; Levenson, 2018). It supports the development of adaptive systems that evolve with organizational needs—transitioning from static knowledge repositories and HR systems to interconnected, intelligence-augmented ecosystems that are responsive to internal and external change (Gandomi & Haider, 2015; Russ, 2021).

Theoretical Background: Defining the Terms

Artificial Intelligence (AI), at its core, refers to the capability of machines and systems to perform tasks that would typically require human intelligence, including reasoning, learning, problem-solving, and decision-making (Russell & Norvig, 2016; Wang, 2019). AI technologies range from rule-based expert systems to advanced applications of machine learning and deep learning, which enable systems to learn from data and adapt to new information without explicit programming.

Knowledge Management (KM) is defined as the systematic process of creating, sharing, managing, and applying knowledge to achieve organizational goals. KM frameworks focus on making knowledge accessible, actionable, and embedded in organizational routines (Nonaka & Takeuchi, 1995). Talent Management (TM), meanwhile, is the strategic approach to attracting, developing, retaining, and deploying individuals with the skills and potential needed to meet current and future business demands (Collings & Mellahi, 2009; Theodorsson, 2024).

Historically, AI implementations in organizational contexts focused on rule-based systems and expert models. However, with the advent of machine learning and deep learning (LeCun et al., 2015), AI applications have become more autonomous and capable of handling complexity. These advancements have made it possible to apply AI to nuanced challenges in TM and KM—ranging from predictive modeling of workforce behavior to automated knowledge synthesis from vast, unstructured datasets.

Underpinning AI Integration

The integration of AI into KM and TM can be contextualized through several theoretical lenses that emphasize innovation, learning, and adaptability. Two particularly relevant frameworks are the *Resource-Based View (RBV)* and the *Dynamic Capabilities Perspective*. The RBV argues that intangible assets—such as organizational knowledge, intellectual capital, and human talent—are key sources of sustained competitive advantage (Barney, 1991). AI enhances these assets by enabling organizations to derive data-driven insights from large, complex datasets, thus improving their capacity to make strategic decisions (Gandomi & Haider, 2015; Wang, 2019).

The Dynamic Capabilities Perspective further emphasizes an organization's ability to sense, seize, and transform opportunities in fast-changing environments (Teece et al., 1997). AI strengthens these capabilities by supporting real-time analytics, automating knowledge-intensive tasks, and allowing firms to respond rapidly to market signals and internal performance data (Davenport & Ronanki, 2018; McAfee & Brynjolfsson, 2017). Empirical studies underscore these benefits. For instance, Huang and Rust (2018) found that AI-powered predictive analytics can help identify early signs of employee disengagement, improving retention outcomes. Similarly, IBM's Watson demonstrates how AI systems can extract insights from unstructured information to support decision-making in both healthcare and corporate environments (Chen et al., 2012). These findings provide strong support for integrating AI into organizational KM and TM systems.

Applications of AI in KM and TM

AI technologies are revolutionizing how organizations approach knowledge and talent management. Applications span the entire employee lifecycle, from recruitment and onboarding to training, performance analysis, and succession planning.

AI has significantly improved recruitment by enhancing the efficiency and objectivity of candidate evaluation. Machine learning algorithms can parse resumes, analyze applicant data, and rank candidates based on predicted fit and success (Upadhyay & Khandelwal, 2018). Predictive models are also used to forecast skill needs and workforce gaps, enabling more effective workforce planning (Huang & Rust, 2018). During onboarding, AI-driven chatbots offer instant access to organizational knowledge—answering common questions and guiding new hires through company policies, tools, and cultural norms. These systems reduce HR workload and provide personalized support to new employees (Davenport & Ronanki, 2018).

AI has transformed learning and development through adaptive learning platforms that offer personalized training pathways. Platforms like *Coursera* and *Degreed* use AI to recommend content based on individual skill profiles and career goals (Bersin, 2018). These systems identify knowledge gaps, suggest training interventions, and track learning progress over time. By doing so, AI supports continuous professional development while aligning employee growth with organizational capability needs (Levenson, 2018). It also contributes to a culture of lifelong learning—essential for knowledge-intensive sectors.

AI enhances knowledge dissemination by making internal knowledge assets more accessible and useable. NLP-based systems can extract, classify, and summarize unstructured data from documents, emails, and meeting transcripts. For example, tools like IBM Watson allow employees to retrieve key insights from massive knowledge repositories in seconds (Salvi et al., 2017). AI-powered recommendation engines also personalize the delivery of relevant content, enabling employees to receive the right knowledge at the right time (Gandomi & Haider, 2015; Schütze et al., 2008). This has far-reaching implications for collaboration, productivity, and innovation.

AI enables organizations to analyze workforce behavior through real-time analytics, sentiment analysis, and predictive modeling. These tools identify engagement trends, predict turnover risks, and reveal high-potential employees (Cathey & Prabhakar, 2021; McAfee & Brynjolfsson, 2017). Such insights allow leaders to make proactive talent decisions. For example, Google's *Project Oxygen* applied people analytics and machine learning to identify the behaviors of effective managers. Based on performance reviews and feedback data, Google refined its leadership development programs—demonstrating the power of data-driven TM (Davenport & Ronanki, 2018).

AI contributes to succession planning by analyzing historical performance, learning patterns, and behavioral traits to assess leadership potential. Predictive models can evaluate employees' readiness for higher roles and recommend personalized development tracks (Levenson, 2018). These insights reduce the risks of leadership gaps and improve strategic workforce continuity.

Mini Case Example: IBM Watson in Knowledge Management

IBM's Watson platform exemplifies the use of AI in KM. Initially developed for healthcare applications, Watson has been adapted for enterprise use to process and synthesize vast amounts of organizational data. For instance, it can extract relevant knowledge from research databases, policy manuals, and internal reports—improving accessibility and saving valuable time. In this way, Watson supports a dynamic learning environment and enhances knowledge retention (Chen et al., 2012; Salvi et al., 2017).

Mini Case Example: Google's Project Oxygen in Talent Management

Google's Project Oxygen illustrates how AI can support evidence-based leadership development. The company used AI to analyze performance evaluations and employee surveys to identify behaviors linked to effective management. The findings informed the design of targeted leadership training programs and restructured performance criteria, leading to measurable improvements in employee satisfaction and team effectiveness (Davenport & Ronanki, 2018).

The Intersection of AI, KM, and TM

The intersection of artificial intelligence (AI), knowledge management (KM), and talent management (TM) represents a transformative frontier in organizational strategy and performance. As the business environment becomes increasingly data-driven and technology-intensive, organizations must leverage new approaches to manage both intangible assets and human capital in a synchronized, adaptive manner. By integrating AI into KM and TM systems, organizations gain the ability to enhance operational efficiency, drive innovation, and maintain long-term competitiveness (Mejri & Doghan, 2020; Pichler et al., 2021).

KM has traditionally played a vital role in supporting innovation and improving organizational learning by making explicit and tacit knowledge accessible and usable (Nonaka & Takeuchi, 1995). The integration of AI into KM systems enhances the process of capturing, organizing, and disseminating knowledge through tools such as machine learning, natural language processing (NLP), and intelligent recommendation engines (Gandomi & Haider, 2015; Schütze et al., 2008). These tools enable organizations to move beyond static repositories and toward dynamic knowledge ecosystems that evolve in response to both internal needs and external conditions.

Simultaneously, TM focuses on the strategic attraction, development, retention, and utilization of individuals whose skills and potential align with organizational objectives (Collings & Mellahi, 2009). Activities such as recruitment, onboarding, performance management, and succession planning are core to effective TM. AI augments these processes by enabling predictive analytics, automating screening and selection, and facilitating personalized learning and development pathways (Bersin, 2018; Levenson, 2018; Upadhyay & Khandelwal, 2018).

As shown in Fig. 11.1, AI functions as the connective tissue between KM and TM, forming a dynamic, interdependent ecosystem. On the KM side, AI-powered tools support real-time knowledge extraction, indexing, classification, and contextual delivery. On the TM side, AI supports data-informed decision-making across various stages of the employee lifecycle, including hiring, onboarding, development, engagement, and retention (McAfee & Brynjolfsson, 2017; Russell & Norvig, 2016).

Fig. 11.1 illustrates the central role of AI in bridging knowledge management and talent management functions. AI acts as an enabling layer that facilitates seamless data flow between knowledge assets and human resource systems. On the KM side, AI supports knowledge capture, indexing, and accessibility. On the TM side, AI

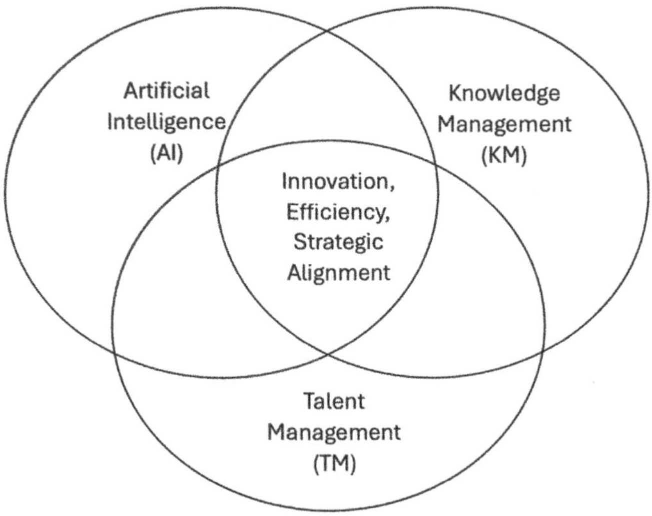

Fig. 11.1. The Intersection of AI, KM, and TM.

informs workforce planning, recruitment, training, and retention strategies. Feedback loops between the two systems allow for adaptive learning and continuous alignment. For example, data from talent analytics may reveal emerging skill gaps, prompting updates to KM content and training modules. Likewise, newly captured organizational knowledge may inform future leadership development initiatives. A comparative overview of traditional versus AI-enhanced practices in KM and TM is presented in Table 11.1 to further illustrate the practical implications of the AI-Knowledge Nexus.

Table 11.1. Comparative Table: Traditional vs AI-Enhanced KM & TM.

Feature	**Traditional KM/TM**	**AI-Enhanced KM/TM (AI-Knowledge Nexus)**
Knowledge capture	Manual documentation, static repositories	NLP for real-time data capture, auto-tagging, dynamic updates
Talent acquisition	Resume screening, human interviews	AI-based predictive analytics skill-matching algorithms
Learning and development	One-size-fits-all training	Adaptive learning platforms, personalized development paths
Decision-making	Manager intuition, historical trends	Data-driven insights, predictive modeling

Table 11.1. *(Continued)*

Feature	**Traditional KM/TM**	**AI-Enhanced KM/TM (AI-Knowledge Nexus)**
Succession planning	Subjective performance reviews	Behavioral trend analysis, leadership potential prediction
Knowledge sharing	Email, meetings	AI-curated knowledge hubs, context aware recommendations

This integrated framework promotes a holistic approach to organizational learning, enabling companies to continuously align workforce capabilities with strategic objectives. By connecting KM and TM through AI, organizations create a feedback-rich, intelligence-augmented environment that supports proactive decision-making and personalized employee experiences (Cathey & Prabhakar, 2021; Davenport & Ronanki, 2018). Moreover, such integration positions knowledge not merely as a static asset, but as a living, strategic resource—deeply embedded in the fabric of talent development and organizational adaptability (Russ, 2021).

Challenges in AI Integration

While AI offers considerable promise in advancing knowledge and talent management, its integration into organizational systems is not without complications. A range of interrelated challenges (technical, organizational, financial, and ethical) must be addressed in order to fully realize AI's transformative potential (Barocas et al., 2023; Bughin et al., 2018).

One of the most pressing technical challenges is the prevalence of fragmented data infrastructures within organizations. Knowledge assets and HR data are often maintained in isolated, incompatible systems, which significantly limits the analytical power of AI. Without well-integrated and high-quality data, even the most advanced AI models can produce incomplete or misleading insights (George, 2024). Addressing this issue requires not only robust data governance policies but also investment in interoperable systems that enable seamless data exchange across departments (Gandomi & Haider, 2015).

Beyond the technical domain, organizational resistance often presents a major obstacle. Many employees perceive AI, especially in performance management or hiring contexts, as intrusive or even threatening to job security. This resistance is commonly rooted in a lack of familiarity with AI's capabilities and an absence of transparent communication about its intended role (Bessen, 2018; Huang & Rust, 2018). Overcoming this barrier requires strategic change management that positions AI as a tool for empowerment and augmentation rather than replacement. Leaders must engage stakeholders early in the adoption process, offer targeted training, and promote a culture of collaboration and innovation (Kotter, 1996).

Even after initial adoption, maintaining and scaling AI systems presents ongoing challenges. AI models must be continually updated to reflect changes in business strategy, workforce behavior, and environmental context. This process is resource-intensive, requiring dedicated technical staff and continuous retraining of models to ensure accuracy and relevance (Goodfellow et al., 2016; LeCun et al., 2015). Without this sustained effort, AI systems can degrade in performance, produce outdated recommendations, or even introduce new forms of bias.

Financial constraints further complicate AI integration, particularly for small and medium-sized enterprises. Implementing AI technologies requires significant upfront investment—not only in software and infrastructure, but also in training, cybersecurity, and change management initiatives. Unlike larger corporations, smaller firms may lack the internal capacity or financial flexibility to absorb these costs (Bughin et al., 2018). Policy interventions such as public-private partnerships or subsidized access to shared AI platforms could help level the playing field and ensure more equitable AI adoption.

Ethical complexity is another major concern, especially in people-related domains such as TM. Biased algorithms, opaque decision-making, and data privacy violations are increasingly the subject of academic scrutiny and regulatory attention (Barocas et al., 2023). For example, AI systems trained on historical HR data may inadvertently reinforce gender or racial disparities in recruitment and promotion. Moreover, compliance with data protection regulations such as the General Data Protection Regulation (GDPR) and the California Consumer Privacy Act (CCPA) is essential when handling sensitive employee information (Voigt & Von dem Bussche, 2017). Organizations must adopt comprehensive ethical AI frameworks, including fairness audits, explainability standards, and transparent accountability structures (Dignum, 2018).

Finally, successful AI integration hinges on thoughtful stakeholder engagement and cross-functional alignment. Too often, AI projects are led by technical teams with little input from HR professionals or end users, resulting in solutions that are misaligned with actual needs. To avoid this disconnect, leadership must ensure that AI initiatives are grounded in a clear understanding of the organization's human dynamics and strategic goals (Shneiderman, 2020). AI should be seen not as a plug-and-play solution, but as an evolving partnership between technology and human expertise.

Ethical Considerations

As artificial intelligence becomes increasingly embedded in knowledge and talent management systems, ethical considerations must take center stage. The promise of AI in improving efficiency, personalization, and strategic alignment is significant, but so too are the risks, particularly when algorithmic decisions influence hiring, performance evaluation, promotion, or access to learning and development resources.

One of the most persistent ethical challenges is bias. AI systems trained on historical organizational data may unintentionally perpetuate existing inequalities. For example, if past hiring decisions favored certain demographics, those patterns may be encoded into recruitment algorithms, resulting in discriminatory outcomes despite the appearance of neutrality (Barocas et al., 2023). The complexity and opacity of many AI systems make these biases difficult to detect, especially when decision-making logic is embedded deep within complex neural networks or ensemble models.

Transparency is closely linked to the problem of bias. The so-called "black box" nature of many AI models erodes stakeholder trust and accountability, particularly when high-stakes decisions about people are involved. Employees and managers alike may be skeptical of decisions generated by systems that do not offer clear rationales. To address this, organizations are increasingly adopting explainable AI (XAI) frameworks such as SHAP (SHapley Additive exPlanations) and LIME (Local Interpretable Model-Agnostic Explanations), which make it possible to interpret the output of complex models in human-understandable terms (Calderon-Monge & Ribeiro-Soriano, 2024). These tools allow decision-makers to evaluate AI recommendations with a critical eye and to identify potential sources of error or bias. A summary of the core ethical challenges associated with AI in KM and TM and potential mitigation strategies, is presented in Table 11.2.

Privacy is another major concern, particularly when AI systems process sensitive employee information. Knowledge and talent management systems often rely on behavioral data, internal communications, feedback scores, and even biometric inputs to generate insights. The ethical use of such data requires strict compliance with legal frameworks such as the General Data Protection

Table 11.2. AI Ethics: Challenges and Solutions.

Ethical Dimension	**Challenges**	**Mitigation Strategies**
Bias and fairness	Discriminatory outcomes in decision-making	Auditing, fairness metrics, diversified datasets
Transparency	Opacity of AI systems undermining trust	Explainable AI techniques (e.g., SHAP, LIME), accountability frameworks
Privacy and compliance	Misuse of sensitive employee data	GDPR/CCPA compliance, anonymization, secure storage
Automation oversight	Over-reliance leading to ethical lapses	Hybrid workflows integrating AI and human judgment

Regulation (GDPR) and the California Consumer Privacy Act (CCPA), both of which mandate informed consent, data minimization, and the right to opt out (Voigt & Von dem Bussche, 2017). In practical terms, this means organizations must clearly articulate what data is being collected, how it will be used, and what rights employees have regarding their digital footprint.

A more nuanced issue is the tension between automation and human oversight. While AI excels at identifying patterns and optimizing routine processes, over-reliance on automation can lead to the dehumanization of decision-making. Delegating too much authority to machines risks undermining empathy, context sensitivity, and organizational judgment, particularly in domains like performance evaluation or leadership development, where human insight is essential. The most ethical and effective systems, therefore, are those that integrate human oversight at key decision points. Hybrid models, in which AI provides recommendations that are ultimately reviewed and refined by humans, are emerging as a best practice for balancing efficiency with ethical responsibility (Dignum, 2018).

Ultimately, ethics must not be viewed as a constraint but as a core design principle in AI development and implementation. Organizations that embed ethical reflection into their AI strategies are better positioned to earn stakeholder trust, comply with regulations, and foster inclusive and equitable workplaces. Moreover, ethically grounded AI systems are more likely to support long-term organizational success by aligning technological innovation with human values and societal expectations (Floridi et al., 2018).

Future Directions

The future of AI in knowledge and talent management is poised to expand the boundaries of what organizations can achieve in terms of learning, engagement, and strategic alignment. As AI technologies continue to evolve, several key developments are likely to redefine how knowledge is captured, shared, and applied—and how talent is recruited, developed, and retained.

One of the most promising advancements lies in generative AI, which enables systems to autonomously produce human-like text, visuals, and even code. Tools such as ChatGPT and DALL·E have already demonstrated significant potential to augment knowledge work by automating tasks like report writing, learning content creation, and employee support (Bommasani et al., 2021). In the KM context, generative AI can be used to synthesize insights from complex datasets, produce internal documentation, and create dynamic learning resources. In TM, it can support the generation of personalized development plans, adaptive training content, and context-specific feedback—thereby enhancing engagement and professional growth.

Another innovation with transformative implications is blockchain technology, particularly its applications in credentialing and data verification. In KM, blockchain offers a secure and tamper-resistant way to track the evolution of knowledge assets, ensuring provenance and accountability. In TM, blockchain could be used to authenticate employee qualifications, training histories, and skill portfolios—streamlining hiring, reducing fraud, and increasing trust between organizations and their workforce (Pilkington, 2016).

In parallel, advances in real-time analytics are driving a shift from reactive to anticipatory decision-making. With the integration of machine learning and IoT, organizations can monitor workplace dynamics continuously and respond proactively. For example, predictive analytics may reveal emerging skill gaps or declining engagement levels, enabling timely interventions through tailored upskilling or leadership coaching (Gandomi & Haider, 2015). These capabilities support agile workforce planning and more resilient knowledge strategies.

Augmented reality (AR) and virtual reality (VR) also offer new possibilities for immersive learning and development. In high-stakes industries such as healthcare, manufacturing, and defense, AR/VR simulations can be used to train employees in complex or hazardous environments—allowing for experiential learning without physical risk. These technologies not only enhance knowledge retention but also make onboarding and professional development more interactive and engaging (Pantelidis, 2010).

A growing area of interest is the development of collaborative AI-human systems, in which AI acts not as a replacement for human judgment but as a partner. For example, AI can support brainstorming sessions, contribute to project management workflows, or even serve as a digital facilitator in hybrid work environments (Shneiderman, 2020). These systems are particularly relevant in KM and TM, where creativity, empathy, and contextual understanding remain essential to effective decision-making.

In addition, AI-driven approaches to employee well-being are likely to become more sophisticated. Tools such as sentiment analysis and AI-powered chatbots can detect early signs of stress, burnout, or disengagement, and provide personalized wellness interventions. By integrating these insights into KM and TM systems, organizations can take a more holistic approach to workforce sustainability and organizational health (Zhang et al., 2020).

From a technical and governance perspective, federated learning represents an emerging method for privacy-preserving AI. This approach allows organizations to build powerful models across decentralized datasets without sharing raw data—thereby enhancing privacy and regulatory compliance (Kairouz et al., 2021). It is particularly promising in sectors where sensitive data cannot be easily centralized, such as healthcare, education, and finance.

Finally, the future of AI in KM and TM will be shaped by the creation of formal governance frameworks that address ethical, legal, and operational challenges. Collaboration among academia, industry, and policymakers will be essential to establishing common standards, ensuring responsible AI use, and protecting stakeholder rights (Cowls et al., 2019; Floridi & Cowls, 2022). Such frameworks will help organizations strike the right balance between innovation and integrity.

Together, these trends signal a shift toward AI systems that are not only more powerful but also more accountable, transparent, and human-centric. The organizations that thrive in this new era will be those that embed emerging technologies into the heart of their knowledge and talent strategies—while also remaining deeply committed to ethics, inclusion, and long-term value creation.

Conclusion

The integration of artificial intelligence into knowledge and talent management systems represents a defining shift in how organizations operate, learn, and evolve. Through the lens of the AI-Knowledge Nexus, it becomes clear that AI is not merely a tool for automation or efficiency, but a catalyst for reimagining how knowledge is captured, shared, and used to empower human potential.

By embedding AI into KM processes, organizations can transform passive repositories into dynamic, responsive knowledge ecosystems. When extended to TM, AI enhances the ability to attract, develop, and retain talent in ways that are both data-driven and deeply personalized. Together, these capabilities enable organizations to align their human capital strategies with evolving business objectives—creating adaptive systems that are more resilient in the face of disruption.

However, this transformation is neither automatic nor without consequence. Technical barriers, ethical dilemmas, and organizational resistance all pose significant challenges. The responsible adoption of AI in these domains requires thoughtful governance, inclusive stakeholder engagement, and an ongoing commitment to transparency, fairness, and accountability. Ethical principles must be embedded not as an afterthought but as a foundation of design and deployment.

Looking ahead, the most successful organizations will be those that treat AI not as a standalone solution but as part of a larger strategy to foster learning, innovation, and human development. As new technologies emerge—from generative AI to federated learning and immersive simulations—the imperative will be to integrate them in ways that enhance, rather than replace, human judgment and collaboration.

Ultimately, the AI-Knowledge Nexus offers not just a new set of tools, but a new mindset—one that views technology and talent as mutually reinforcing drivers of long-term value. For researchers, practitioners, and policymakers alike, the opportunity lies in shaping these systems with purpose, vision, and integrity.

References

Barney, J. (1991). Firm resources and sustained competitive advantage. *Journal of Management*, *17*(1), 99–120.

Barocas, S., Hardt, M., & Narayanan, A. (2023). *Fairness and machine learning: Limitations and opportunities*. MIT Press.

Bersin, J. (2018). A new paradigm for corporate training: Learning in the flow of work. *Deloitte Review*, (22), 48–63. https://www.deloitte.com/us/en/insights/topics/talent/human-capital-trends/2019/reskilling-upskilling-the-future-of-learning-and-development.html

Bessen, J. (2018). *AI and jobs: The role of demand.* Working Paper No. 24235. National Bureau of Economic Research. https://doi.org/10.3386/w24235

Bommasani, R., Hudson, D. A., Adeli, E., Altman, R., Arora, S., von Arx, S., Bernstein, M. S., Bohg, J., Bosselut, A., & Brunskill, E. (2021). On the opportunities and risks of foundation models. *arXiv Preprint.* https://arxiv.org/abs/2108.07258

Bughin, J., Seong, J., Manyika, J., Chui, M., & Joshi, R. (2018). *Notes from the AI frontier: Modeling the impact of AI on the world economy.* McKinsey Global Institute.

Calderon-Monge, E., & Ribeiro-Soriano, D. (2024). The role of digitalization in business and management: A systematic literature review. *Review of Managerial Science, 18*(2), 449–491. https://doi.org/10.1007/s11846-023-00647-8

Cathey, G., & Prabhakar, A. (2021). Ethical AI: A new strategic imperative for recruiting and staffing. *MIT Sloan Management Review.* https://sloanreview.mit.edu/sponsors-content/ethical-ai-a-new-strategic-imperative-for-recruiting-and-staffing/

Chen, H., Chiang, R. H. L., & Storey, V. C. (2012). Business intelligence and analytics: From big data to big impact. *MIS Quarterly, 36*(4), 1165–1188.

Collings, D. G., & Mellahi, K. (2009). Strategic talent management: A review and research agenda. *Human Resource Management Review, 19*(4), 304–313. https://doi.org/10.1016/j.hrmr.2009.04.001

Cowls, J., King, T., Taddeo, M., & Floridi, L. (2019). Designing AI for social good: Seven essential factors. *Social Science Research Network.* https://doi.org/10.2139/ssrn.3388669

Davenport, T. H., & Ronanki, R. (2018). Artificial intelligence for the real world. *Harvard Business Review, 96*(1), 108–116.

Dignum, V. (2018). Ethics in artificial intelligence: Introduction to the special issue. *Ethics and Information Technology, 20*(1), 1–3.

Faqihi, A., & Miah, S. J. (2023). Artificial intelligence-driven talent management system: Exploring the risks and options for constructing a theoretical foundation. *Journal of Risk and Financial Management, 16*(1). Article 31. https://doi.org/10.3390/jrfm16010031

Floridi, L., & Cowls, J. (2022). A unified framework of five principles for AI in society. In *Machine learning and the city* (pp. 535–545). Springer. https://doi.org/10.1002/9781119815075.ch45

Floridi, L., Cowls, J., Beltrametti, M., Chatila, R., Chazerand, P., Dignum, V., Luetge, C., Madelin, R., Pagallo, U., & Rossi, F. (2018). AI4People—An ethical framework for a good AI society: Opportunities, risks, principles, and recommendations. *Minds and Machines, 28*(4), 689–707. https://doi.org/10.1007/s11023-018-9482-5

Gandomi, A., & Haider, M. (2015). Beyond the hype: Big data concepts, methods, and analytics. *International Journal of Information Management, 35*(2), 137–144.

George, J. (2024). Data to AI: Building a solid data foundation for your generative AI applications in the cloud. *International Journal of Science and Research Archive, 11*(1), 2601–2604.

Goodfellow, I., Bengio, Y., & Courville, A. (2016). Convolutional networks. In *Deep learning* (pp. 330–372). MIT Press.

Huang, M.-H., & Rust, R. T. (2018). Artificial intelligence in service. *Journal of Service Research, 21*(2), 155–172.

Kairouz, P., McMahan, H. B., Avent, B., Bellet, A., Bennis, M., Bhagoji, A. N., Bonawitz, K., Charles, Z., Cormode, G., & Cummings, R. (2021). Advances and open problems in federated learning. *Foundations and Trends® in Machine Learning*, *14*(1–2), 1–210. https://doi.org/10.1561/2200000083

Kotter, J. P. (1996). *Leading change*. Harvard Business School Press.

LeCun, Y., Bengio, Y., & Hinton, G. (2015). Deep learning. *Nature*, *521*(7553), 436–444.

Levenson, A. (2018). Using workforce analytics to improve strategy execution. *Human Resource Management*, *57*(3), 685–700.

McAfee, A., & Brynjolfsson, E. (2017). *Machine, platform, crowd: Harnessing our digital future*. W. W. Norton & Company.

Mejri, K., & Doghan, M. (2020). A knowledge management lens to talent management: Towards a framework. In *Proceedings of the European conference on knowledge management (ECKM 2020)*. Academic Conferences and Publishing International Ltd.

Nonaka, I., & Takeuchi, H. (1995). *The knowledge-creating company: How Japanese companies create the dynamics of innovation*. Oxford University Press.

Pantelidis, V. S. (2010). Reasons to use virtual reality in education and training courses and a model to determine when to use virtual reality. *Themes in Science and Technology Education*, *2*(1–2), 59–70.

Pichler, S., Kohli, C., & Granitz, N. (2021). DITTO for Gen Z: A framework for leveraging the uniqueness of the new generation. *Business Horizons*, *64*(5), 599–610. https://doi.org/10.1016/j.bushor.2021.02.021

Pilkington, M. (2016). Blockchain technology: Principles and applications. In *Research handbook on digital transformations* (pp. 225–253). Edward Elgar Publishing. https://ssrn.com/abstract=2662660

Russ, M. (2021). Knowledge management for sustainable development in the era of continuously accelerating technological revolutions: A framework and models. *Sustainability*, *13*(6), 3353. https://doi.org/10.3390/su13063353

Russell, S. J., & Norvig, P. (2016). *Artificial intelligence: A modern approach* (3rd ed.). Pearson.

Salvi, E., Parimbelli, E., Basadonne, A., Viani, N., Cavallini, A., Micieli, G., Quaglini, S., & Sacchi, L. (2017). Exploring IBM Watson to extract meaningful information from the list of references of a clinical practice guideline. In *Artificial intelligence in medicine: Proceedings of the 16th conference (AIME 2017)* (pp. 90–99). Springer. https://doi.org/10.1007/978-3-319-59758-4_12

Schütze, H., Manning, C. D., & Raghavan, P. (2008). *Introduction to information retrieval* (Vol. 39). Cambridge University Press.

Shneiderman, B. (2020). Human-centered artificial intelligence: Reliable, safe & trustworthy. *International Journal of Human-Computer Interaction*, *36*(6), 495–504.

Teece, D. J., Pisano, G., & Shuen, A. (1997). Dynamic capabilities and strategic management. *Strategic Management Journal*, *18*(7), 509–533.

Theodorsson, U. (2024). *Without talent, success may be latent: Talent management practices in commercial banks*. [Manuscript in preparation].

Theodorsson, U., Gudlaugsson, T., & Gudmundsdottir, S. (2022). Talent management in the banking sector: A systematic literature review. *Administrative Sciences*, *12*(2). Article 61. https://doi.org/10.3390/admsci12020061

Upadhyay, A. K., & Khandelwal, K. (2018). Applying artificial intelligence: Implications for recruitment. *Strategic HR Review*, *17*(5), 255–258.

Voigt, P., & Von dem Bussche, A. (2017). *The EU general data protection regulation (GDPR): A practical guide*. Springer International Publishing.

Wang, P. (2019). On defining artificial intelligence. *Journal of Artificial General Intelligence*, *10*(2), 1–37.

Zhang, X., Zhao, Y., Tang, X., Zhu, H., & Xiong, H. (2020). Developing fairness rules for talent intelligence management systems. In *Proceedings of the annual Hawaii international conference on system sciences* (pp. 4731–4740). https://doi.org/10.24251/HICSS.2020.580

The Future of AI in Knowledge Management: Challenges and Opportunities

Chapter 12

The Prospective Developments of Artificial Intelligence in the Domain of Knowledge Management: Challenges and Opportunities

Viraj Dawarka[a], *Alisha Hingun Goolam Gukan*[b] *and Aisha Bibi Idoo*[c]

[a]University of Staffordshire, UK
[b]Nottingham Trent University, UK
[c]Middlesex University, Mauritius

Abstract

As organisations increasingly embrace digital transformation, artificial intelligence (AI) is poised to revolutionise knowledge management (KM). This chapter explores the evolving role of AI in KM, analysing the transformative potential of AI technologies like machine learning, natural language processing and automation in enhancing the creation, sharing and utilisation of knowledge within organisations. The chapter also delves into the challenges businesses face when integrating AI into KM systems, as well as the opportunities that AI presents to streamline processes, drive innovation and enable smarter decision-making. The chapter will address both the technical and human aspects of AI in KM, proposing strategies to maximise AI's benefits while mitigating risks such as data privacy concerns, algorithmic biases and resistance to change. By synthesising current trends and future projections, the chapter will provide insights into how AI can shape the future of KM across industries.

Keywords: Artificial intelligence; knowledge management; machine learning; knowledge sharing; AI ethics

AI-Driven Knowledge Management Assets, Volume 2, 239–263

Published under exclusive licence by Emerald Publishing Limited
doi:10.1108/978-1-83662-778-420261012

Introduction

Knowledge management (KM) can be defined as a systematic way of identifying, capturing and sharing information to enhance the decision-making, innovation and performance of an organisation. KM fosters a learning culture where collaboration is encouraged and organisations can invest in people, avoiding inefficiencies like reinventing the wheel. According to KPMG (2021), organisations that have well-defined KM strategies are reported to have made a 35% improvement in decision-making and a 25% improvement in innovation output, which shows that KM is crucial to organisational success. KM has become more relevant in today's data-rich environment where organisations are expected to manage and use large amounts of organisational knowledge, which is projected to exceed 175 zettabytes by 2025 (IDC, 2024).

The implementation of artificial intelligence (AI) has brought about another revolutionary shift in KM. There are AI tools such as knowledge graphs, machine learning and natural language processing (NLP), which have changed the way that businesses capture, manage and disseminate information (Russell & Norvig, 2016). For instance, AI-enabled semantic search tools can enhance productivity by providing relevant and contextualised information that can help reduce the time and resources wasted on searching for information (Afraz, 2024). However, the integration of AI and KM has some challenges as these include data privacy issues, algorithmic bias and the decline of creativity and human autonomy (Floridi, 2013). Such issues may have a dramatic effect on how we deal with sources of knowledge in organisations and groups.

Therefore, the purpose of this chapter is to examine the opportunities that AI presents for KM and the issues that are likely to be encountered in the process of integration. This chapter discusses in detail how KM, with the help of AI, can help organisations achieve innovation and resilience while ensuring that the practices are responsible and ethical. Through the analysis of real-life examples of business cases and ethical challenges, the discussion emphasises that it is crucial to strike the right balance between human-centred design, ethical oversight and technological progress. We thus begin by examining the core technologies enabling this change.

AI Technologies Transforming Knowledge Management

Machine Learning

To fully appreciate the impact of AI on KM, it is important to examine the specific technologies enabling this transformation. For instance, enterprises use machine learning (ML) to forecast trends, recommend knowledge resources and extract data insights. Actionable insights that inform strategic choices can be obtained by incorporating ML models into enterprise architecture (EA) (Rehman et al., 2024). Computers and other devices can mimic human learning, comprehension, problem-solving, decision-making, creativity and autonomy using AI technology. To glean insightful information from data, contemporary data mining and business intelligence services employ automation technologies, ML algorithms and statistical techniques (Sarker, 2023). Utilising data, knowledge and ML, data science aims to comprehend, forecast and enhance results. With the ability to uncover significant patterns and insights, ML has become an effective tool for big-data analysis. ML algorithms are used in recent developments in text analytics to extract insights, patterns and trends from data.

Data science and ML can be applied to network management to forecast possible faults and collect insightful information from large datasets (Sarker et al., 2020). Additionally, ML methods have been applied to healthcare disaster decision-making. For example, data mining and deep learning pilot experiments have been used to predict the incidence of COVID-19 (Kellner et al., 2023). Extracting insights from data, forecasting trends and suggesting knowledge resources have all been made possible by the incorporation of ML algorithms into a variety of domains, including EA, data mining, business intelligence and healthcare. Better decision-making and performance forecasts across a range of areas can result from utilising knowledge engineering and ML.

Natural Language Processing

Beyond ML, NLP further expands the scope of AI in knowledge systems by enabling a human-like understanding of language. NLP is a type of AI that allows machines to perceive, interpret and synthesise human language. It powers a wide range of applications, including conversational interfaces, which allow users to communicate with systems through natural language. NLP has become essential in applications like sentiment analysis, content automation and conversational knowledge retrieval. As demonstrated by the introduction of the HealthFC dataset by Vladika et al. (2023), fact-checking has used NLP techniques to evaluate the accuracy of assertions. According to Khennouche et al. (2024), chatbots have transformed consumer interactions through a variety of strategies, including rule-based, retrieval-based, generative and hybrid models. NLP improves data analysis by gleaning insights from unstructured text data, including social media and consumer reviews. NLP contributes to automation through chatbots, virtual assistants, content creation, language translation and automated insights and analysis, where, according to Liu (2010), it uses named entity identification and sentiment analysis to automate tasks like content moderation, information retrieval and customer service. Pragmatic analysis in NLP aims to satisfy a range of user demands and preferences by employing contextual prior knowledge to assist users in discovering the intended meaning of the text (Khurana et al., 2023). According to Azure Database for PostgreSQL (2024), Azure AI Language Services offers NLP capabilities like sentiment analysis and real-time translation, supporting more than 100 languages. In conclusion, NLP transforms how we engage with machines by improving information retrieval, enabling intelligent sentiment analysis and automating content analysis for better decision-making and efficiency. In conclusion, NLP transforms how we engage with machines by improving information retrieval, enabling intelligent sentiment analysis and automating content analysis for better decision-making and efficiency.

Robotic Process Automation

While NLP enhances interaction and analysis, robotic process automation (RPA) focuses on improving efficiency through the automation of routine knowledge tasks. RPA enhances knowledge workflows by automating repetitive tasks, especially in accounting and auditing. RPA optimises task execution by combining human and robotic agents, reducing time spent on monotonous tasks and freeing up experts to focus on more complicated decision-making. This integration streamlines operations and improves efficiency (Mahala et al., 2024). Increased efficiency is one of the advantages of RPA in knowledge workflows, as it automates rule-based tasks, resulting in reduced operational costs and speedier completion times (Wewerka & Reichert, 2023). It also improves accuracy by reducing human error in repetitive duties, which is particularly advantageous in audit processes. Furthermore, RPA provides scalability, which enables organisations to effortlessly adjust to evolving business requirements and fluctuating duties.

RPA implementation is not without its difficulties, though. The intricacy of integrating with current systems is a significant obstacle that necessitates meticulous preparation (Plattfaut & Borghoff, 2022). The requirement for qualified staff to create and oversee automation scripts presents another difficulty, meaning that having the appropriate talent is essential for a successful deployment (Agostinelli & Marrella, 2022). Organisations must consider potential disadvantages, such as the initial investment in technology and training, even if RPA offers significant advantages, such as increased productivity and efficiency. These considerations must be balanced against the long-term benefits of RPA, particularly in terms of gradually increasing accuracy and productivity.

AI-Powered Knowledge Graphs

Complementing process automation, knowledge graphs provide structured ways to visualise and connect complex data. AI-powered knowledge graphs are transforming the way businesses handle and utilise huge amounts of data. A knowledge graph is a data structure that reflects the relationships between items such as people, products or concepts in a network, assisting in the organisation of complicated information (Chen et al., 2020). Using AI and ML technology, these graphs can map, connect and visualise knowledge in previously impossible ways and improve knowledge graphs by automating the extraction, classification and organisation of data from a variety of sources, including documents, databases and external APIs. NLP techniques are critical in this process, allowing AI to analyse and interpret unstructured material, such as text, before transforming it into structured representations. Knowledge graphs, using AI's semantic analysis, can capture intricate relationships between concepts, providing a better grasp of how data points relate to one another (Fensel et al., 2020).

One of the primary advantages of AI-powered knowledge graphs is their capacity to connect different information throughout an organisation. With the increasing volume of data, human techniques of organising and linking information frequently fall short. AI can recognise patterns, uncover hidden links and update the knowledge network when new data are supplied (Nemati et al., 2002). This dynamic and changing structure ensures that the organisation's knowledge base is both relevant and complete. Overall, AI-powered knowledge graphs facilitate KM, decision-making and innovation by providing a holistic, interconnected picture of an organisation's data. These tools not only improve operational efficiency but also lay the groundwork for advanced analytics and strategic insights.

Personalised Learning and Adaptive Systems

In addition to managing data relationships, AI also supports personalised learning, adapting content and resources to individual user needs. AI is revolutionising personalised learning by tailoring educational experiences to each student's needs. Technologies like ML and generative artificial intelligence (GAI) make it possible to create personalised learning resources and flexible learning environments that promote ongoing student growth. AI supports personalised learning in a few ways. To increase student engagement and comprehension, GAI creates a variety of educational materials that are suited to their learning preferences (Mittal et al., 2024). Adaptive learning systems assess students' behaviour and knowledge to offer personalised recommendations for materials and activities. ML algorithms optimise the educational process by dynamically identifying and adapting to students' preferred learning styles (Wang et al., 2024).

AI has a lot to offer the educational sector. Student interest and engagement are raised by customisable learning resources, such as those that combine several types such as pop-culture or conventional forms (Pesovski et al., 2024). Learning outcomes are enhanced by adaptive systems that monitor progress and deliver resources and feedback on time. Furthermore, by sustainable development goals, AI-driven personalised learning promotes economic growth and educates citizens, supporting sustainable educational reform (Strielkowski et al., 2024). AI integration necessitates careful management and control due to worries about algorithmic bias and data privacy (Mittal et al., 2024). Significant funding and teacher training are also necessary for the implementation of AI-driven systems. To preserve holistic learning experiences, some educators contend that an over-reliance on AI could reduce the human component of education, highlighting the significance of striking a balance between technology and interpersonal connection. Notwithstanding these obstacles, AI can completely transform personalised learning, which justifies more research and advancement.

AI Integration Issues in Knowledge Management

Data Quality and Accessibility

Despite these technological advancements, the integration of AI in KM presents several challenges that must be addressed. This involves the quality and accessibility of data which are equally important to the implementation of AI within KM. To generate proper insights, enhance creativity and facilitate better decision-making, AI models require large amounts of high-quality data that is easily accessible. Unfortunately, it is still a common occurrence to encounter inadequate datasets, data separation and the lack of variety in information provided by organisations. This limits AI opportunities and may lead to biases or other errors in KM systems (Davenport & Prusak, 2000).

The problem of data silos is one of the biggest obstacles in the implementation of AI in KM as data silos cannot be easily integrated with AI. Silos are specific data stores that are often located in isolation and are not integrated with other systems. Silos are mainly caused by organisational structure or the absence of data-sharing policies. This is raising a major issue as AI has the potential to produce insights from partial data, which may lead to wrong decisions (Russell & Norvig, 2016). Additionally, the problem of incomplete or low-quality data may arise when AI models use large datasets for training and implementation. These data may be outdated, contradictory or missing key information, which can lead to several issues, including the propagation of biases that are inherent to the given datasets (O'Neil, 2017).

Technological Complexity

As observed from the previous section, the integration of AI with legacy KM systems thus creates several technological issues for organisations. The legacy systems may be developed on outdated infrastructure and are not equipped to support the dynamic features offered by the current AI tools such as ML, NLP and knowledge graphs. This incompatibility results in ineffective operations, high costs and slow integration of AI-enabled KM systems (Aldoseri et al., 2023). Legacy systems are designed to store information in isolated ways, and this makes it hard for AI algorithms to easily get and analyse data systematically (Müller & Bodendorf, 2023). Consequently, AI is unable to fully support KM, for instance, through assisting with knowledge curation or search. In the long run, it is the expenses and efforts of upgrading infrastructure that may be the biggest problem. Organisations also run the risk of losing data or may experience upgrading downtime during infrastructure migration. This can be detrimental to businesses and may create a sense of distrust among employees in KM processes (George, 2024).

The rapid evolution of AI technologies introduces further complexities when integrating with legacy KM systems. Many legacy systems are built on outdated architectures that lack the computational power and scalability required to support advanced AI functionalities, such as real-time data processing and complex algorithmic computations (Denton, 2023). Additionally, data within these systems are often stored in proprietary or obsolete formats, creating significant challenges for AI models that rely on structured and accessible data for effective learning and decision-making. The absence of standardised protocols for AI integration exacerbates interoperability issues, leading to fragmented implementations where AI tools operate in isolation from core KM platforms (Uncuta, 2023). Furthermore, the lack of robust governance frameworks for AI deployment in KM processes increases the risk of inconsistent practices and potential ethical concerns, underscoring the need for comprehensive strategies to manage AI integration effectively (Gill, 2024). Addressing these challenges necessitates substantial investments in modernising infrastructure, adopting standardised data formats and establishing clear governance policies to fully leverage the benefits of AI in KM.

Human Factors

So, it can be deduced that the effective implementation of AI in KM systems is not without its issues. These include human factors such as resistance from users, trust issues and the need for the workforce to be reskilled. Paradoxically, the move towards AI adoption may hinder the average employee's productivity. This is being triggered by the fear of losing jobs to AI and a lack of understanding of how AI may help enhance expertise (Brynjolfsson & McAfee, 2017). To make matters worse, employees may lack confidence in using AI systems, further eroding trust. To aggravate matters, employees may not have enough confidence in using AI-powered systems and this is not helping to build trust. This sense of distrust is reinforced by the black-box nature of AI in which the decision-making process is not easily understood (O'Neil, 2017). This implies that employees will not depend on AI-based KM systems if they cannot determine the credibility of the information given by the system.

Moreover, integrating AI into KM systems presents significant human-centric challenges that organisations must address to ensure successful adoption. Beyond the technical hurdles, fostering a culture that embraces AI is crucial. Employees often fear job displacement due to AI integration, leading to resistance and decreased morale. To mitigate these concerns, companies like Colgate-Palmolive have implemented internal AI hubs, empowering employees to develop personalised AI assistants, thereby enhancing acceptance and demonstrating AI's role as a collaborative tool rather than a replacement (Kapadia, 2025). Additionally, the lack of transparency in AI decision-making processes, often referred to as the 'black-box' dilemma, exacerbates trust issues among employees. Implementing explainable AI (XAI) techniques can demystify AI operations, fostering greater trust and facilitating smoother integration into existing KM systems (McKinsey and Company, 2024). Furthermore, comprehensive upskilling and reskilling initiatives are essential to equip the workforce with the necessary competencies to effectively collaborate with AI technologies, ensuring that employees view AI as an augmentation of their capabilities rather than a threat (IBM, 2023).

Ethical and Privacy Concerns

It is therefore clear that the integration of AI in KM systems offers significant benefits but at the same time, raises crucial risks in the areas of data privacy and security. To be more accurate, AI-driven KM systems rely on large datasets, which in turn can include sensitive organisational and personal data. This enhances the chances of data loss, misuse or theft as well as unauthorised access to the data. The central KM repositories may be hacked, and thus, the intellectual property and other knowledge assets may be compromised, as revealed in the cases analysed by Floridi (2013). Also, it can lead to data privacy concerns if organisations do not seek proper consent from the employees or the clients first before processing and storing their data (Schwab, 2018).

Furthermore, with the information easily available using AI and other open AI systems, children and young adults do not feel the need to learn facts and concepts by heart. This shift from information retention to retrieval has been made to enhance efficiency, but at the same time, it poses a threat of eroding critical thinking, creativity and problem-solving skills that can only happen through the understanding of information and interconnecting knowledge (Yan et al., 2024). These changes may lead to a generation that would be good at using technological tools but less apt at coming up with new ideas or being able to apply what they know in different contexts (Luckin, 2018).

The integration of AI into KM systems introduces significant ethical and privacy concerns that organisations must address. AI systems often require access to extensive datasets, which may include sensitive personal and organisational information. The collection, storage and processing of such data raise issues related to user consent, data security and potential misuse. For instance, without robust data governance policies, there is a heightened risk of unauthorised access and data breaches, leading to compromised intellectual property and personal privacy violations (IBM, 2024). Moreover, AI algorithms can inadvertently perpetuate biases present in training data, resulting in unfair or discriminatory outcomes, which pose ethical dilemmas and can erode stakeholder trust (Kirk, 2024). To mitigate these risks, organisations should implement transparent AI systems with explainable decision-making processes, ensure compliance with data protection regulations and establish comprehensive ethical guidelines for AI deployment in KM practices (Bloomfire, 2024).

Bias in AI Models

As mentioned earlier, the ethical considerations of AI decision-making are further heightened since it may simply amplify the biases that are inherent in the historical data that it uses. When algorithms are trained using skewed datasets, they tend to exhibit the same biases that are present in society, thereby perpetuating barriers in places of work, promotions, hiring or resources (O'Neil, 2017). Also, the question of the ethical application of AI tools in such environments only adds more complexity to the problem. AI systems with KM can be run for malicious initiatives like data fraud or surveillance, thus compromising trust and social coherence (Bostrom, 2014).

There are also concerns that AI models pose a threat to KM as they can alter the way knowledge is gathered, organised and shared (O'Neil, 2017). These biases, which are often embedded in the data that AI systems are trained on, have the potential to mislead or exclude certain aspects of information, especially in areas involving cultural storytelling, narrative archetypes and preservation of indigenous knowledge. The role of storytelling in the formation of the global consciousness has been pivotal as it has served as a means of preserving the archetypes including the mother, hero, villain, good and evil, across cultures. These universal patterns can be observed in myths, legends and religious works and have helped nations build and shape societies based on the classical values of each archetype culturally. However, it is still unclear whether the algorithms will distinguish between the classical archetypes and their modern adaptations (Floridi, 2013).

Original data need to be preserved without any form of alteration to protect cultural assets and traditional knowledge. However, there is now a growing use of online backup and management systems, which present several challenges. This means that without human intervention, the changes that may be made to the data by the algorithms could be accidental. It is especially significant to preserve the authentic content as they represent cultural traditions and generational wealth, which are the basic components of society, and define an individual's identity and the society's future (Ofosu-Asare, 2024).

Under this analysis, it can be observed that the integration of AI into KM systems introduces significant challenges related to bias, particularly concerning the preservation of cultural narratives and archetypes. AI models trained predominantly on data from dominant cultures may inadvertently marginalise or misrepresent minority perspectives, leading to a homogenisation of cultural expressions. This bias threatens the richness of diverse storytelling traditions, as AI-generated content may favour mainstream narratives over culturally specific ones, thereby eroding the authenticity of indigenous knowledge systems (Rettberg, 2024). For instance, the AI STORIES project investigates how narrative archetypes influence AI outputs, highlighting concerns that AI may replicate existing biases present in training data, potentially impacting cultural diversity (University of Bergen, 2024).

Moreover, the reliance on AI for knowledge curation and dissemination raises ethical considerations regarding the authenticity and integrity of cultural heritage. AI algorithms might inadvertently perpetuate stereotypes or fail to accurately represent the nuances of diverse cultural practices, leading to the erosion of unique cultural identities. To address these challenges, integrating indigenous epistemologies into AI development has been proposed to counter cognitive imperialism and foster inclusivity (Ofosu-Asare, 2024). By incorporating diverse perspectives and knowledge systems into AI training data, organisations can work towards mitigating biases and ensuring that AI-driven KM systems respect and preserve the cultural heritage they aim to manage.

Opportunities of AI in Knowledge Management

Unquestionably, as documented in the previous sections, despite the challenges, AI offers significant opportunities in KM, mainly, transforming how knowledge is created, accessed and used within organisations. Among the most impactful advancements are improved knowledge discovery, process optimisation, automated knowledge sharing, enhanced collaboration and innovation, predictive analytics and data-driven decision-making.

Improved Knowledge Discovery

For instance, knowledge discovery can be highly improved when AI technologies are leveraged. That is, by enhancing search functions, retrieval systems and tools, these contribute to uncovering insights. Through advanced AI algorithms, large volumes of data can be processed, which allows identification of patterns, trends and connections, which would have been difficult to discover using traditional methods. As discussed by Jarrahi et al. (2023), tools such as knowledge graphs allow the organisation and linking of several data points which makes it much easier to explore the relationships and access the relevant information. Furthermore, by embracing analytics capabilities, which include data analytics and ML, knowledge discovery is further enhanced since structured and unstructured data can be analysed which will then generate actionable insights (Sahoo & Chakraverty, 2022). The discussed systems improve the speed and accuracy of knowledge retrieval as well as allow deeper exploration by unravelling hidden relationships within datasets. As for the search functions, using AI, these are further refined by providing more contextually and relevant results which in turn minimises the time and effort required to get the necessary information. Moreover, since AI systems are designed to adapt to user interactions, they tend to continuously improve to provide more accurate and tailored results. By integrating AI technologies, organisations can enhance their ability to manage knowledge effectively, allowing better decision-making and create opportunities for innovation.

Process Optimisation

Additionally, the use of AI technologies can lead to improvements in KM workflows through the automation of redundant processes and improved process efficiency. Information Systems, which refer to integrated systems designed for collecting, organizing, and filtering data, play a crucial role in supporting AI by managing and structuring the information it relies on. These processes help to reduce human effort and ensure that the information is well-managed and available across teams and departments (Olan et al., 2022). These types of systems minimise both repetitions and errors while standardising tasks such as data entry and classification. These operations allow organisations to ensure that their knowledge base is accurate, up-to-date and accessible whenever required. For example, tools like the Machine Learning Canvas are widely used to standardise workflows, allowing efficient data management and smooth operational processes (de Biase et al., 2022). Moreover, AI technologies are crucial in identifying inefficiencies within workflows, such as bottlenecks, and implementing corrective measures to optimise the flow of information and better allocate resources. These enhancements allow employees to concentrate on more critical and strategic tasks, leaving routine operations to be handled by automated systems. By addressing workflow inefficiencies and ensuring that KM practices are aligned with an organisation's objectives, AI allows for better decision-making and operational outcomes daily. As such, this leads to more effective utilisation of knowledge assets, enhancing daily operations.

Automated Knowledge Sharing

By automating processes which are involved in creating, organising and distributing information, using AI technologies, more efficient knowledge sharing thus is enabled. Through these tools, a smooth flow of knowledge is ensured across different departments, teams and even regions, ensuring that all employees can easily access any required information and that this information is up to date. Also, with AI-driven platforms, knowledge sharing is greatly simplified since the information is categorised and structured. As such, limited manual effort is required to find or distribute the information (Shaikh & Birajdar, 2024). By automating these processes, knowledge sharing is done in a timely and accurate manner, which breaks down the barriers between teams and promotes a more unified understanding of information. Furthermore, these systems provide employees with the required resources without them having to face the challenges associated with the traditional methods of knowledge distribution. These technologies are rather valuable, especially in large organisations with several departments where proper communication is of utmost importance. AI can enhance the consistency and accessibility of shared knowledge.

AI for Collaboration and Innovation

From this perspective, AI technologies are also revolutionising collaboration and innovation by improving problem-solving processes and idea generation through intelligent platforms. Teams are being helped by AI-powered tools to examine complex data, identify patterns and generate insights that guide creative solutions (Kakatkar et al., 2020). Moreover, AI automates routine tasks like data collection and cleansing, freeing up time for innovation. Tools such as clustering algorithms and predictive analytics enable organisations to explore more ideas and identify those with the greatest potential. Furthermore, AI systems are evolving from tools to collaborative teammates, enhancing team dynamics where they offer suggestions, analyse data and assist in decision-making, boosting human problem-solving abilities (Seeber et al., 2020). These systems are especially helpful in cross-disciplinary collaboration, where they can connect different fields by analysing and combining information from various sources. By embedding AI into collaborative workflows, organisations can increase efficiency, foster creativity and achieve better results. While challenges in integrating AI with human teams persist, its transformative potential for collaboration and innovation is clear.

Predictive Analytics

Using AI-driven predictive analytics, organisations can also better anticipate any knowledge gaps, potential risks and emerging trends. Leveraging advanced data analysis techniques and processing datasets using ML and NLP, AI can identify any patterns, trends and relationships, which will provide actionable insights for future planning. ML can identify correlations and predict outcomes, while NPL will extract insights from text such as customer feedback to better understand preferences and customer behaviour. Deep learning improves these processes by detecting more complex patterns within the data (Okeleke et al., 2024). These tools help detect risks like inefficiencies or market shifts early, enabling proactive action. Additionally, with predictive analytics, organisations will be able to know exactly where knowledge or data is missing, which informs them about the areas of improvement in data management practices. By integrating predictive analysis, organisations tend to make more informed decisions and aid in long-term planning.

AI in Decision-Making

Besides, decision-making is considerably improved by AI technologies, which provide actionable insights and enhance strategic processes. Large amounts of data are analysed by AI tools to identify patterns, evaluate options and recommend the best actions to take. Unstructured and complex data are effectively handled using advanced ML and data analytics, enabling more informed business decisions. Uncertainty is reduced, and strategies are grounded in solid evidence through these tools (Kaggwa et al., 2024). In contrast to traditional approaches, outcomes can be predicted by AI, allowing businesses to plan proactively. According to Soori et al. (2024), AI-based decision support systems (DSSs) are a standard architecture, which first involves data acquisition, followed by model learning and then decision inference. These are often integrated with ERP systems. Also, these systems make use of ML algorithms for predictive, perceptive and adaptive AI methods to enable people to make the best decisions with optimal outcomes. As noted by Kaggwa et al. (2024), AI is viewed as more than just a tool since it is considered a strategic asset that complements human intuition by offering refined, practical and innovative options. By integrating AI into decision-making processes, businesses are enabled to adapt to changing conditions, improve efficiency and achieve long-term success.

A Review of AI-Driven Knowledge Management Case Studies

Case Studies of Organisations With AI in KM

To understand how these benefits manifest in real-world scenarios, the following section presents several case studies of AI in KM. Several organisations have adopted AI in KM systems to enhance collaboration, decision-making and innovation. Another example of a company is an IT multinational enterprise (AITECH), which adopted AI-mediated KM tools in its global talent management section. AITECH uses tools such as INTELLIBOT, which identifies employees' skills and matches them with project skills, and QABOT, which helps in managing real-time staffing and deployment queries. The AI systems helped in improving the knowledge transfer within the subsidiaries and improved employee engagement by offering them more personalised and hyper-personalised engagement. In addition, platforms such as HEARME recorded and processed the emotions of employees, which helped the organisation to build collaboration and innovation in its global operations. The use of these tools helped to increase job satisfaction and decrease turnover intention as well as to change the culture of knowledge sharing (Malik et al., 2021).

The MITRE Corporation also demonstrates how AI can transform KM practices. By aggregating data on employee activities and expertise, MITRE's AI-driven systems help connect employees working on similar technical challenges, fostering collaboration and accelerating problem-solving. These systems effectively break down organisational silos, improving access to knowledge and enabling faster decision-making. Such an approach highlights AI's potential to bridge gaps in expertise and facilitate more effective workflows across departments. Similarly, Repsol, a global energy company, leverages AI to optimise crude oil production. Its KM system processes over 100 million data points daily, allowing engineers to reduce nonproductive time by 40–50%. This application of AI has significantly improved operational efficiency and resource allocation within Repsol's operations (Jarrahi et al., 2023).

These examples show how AI can be a powerful tool in managing and sharing knowledge. By performing the basic tasks, improving cooperation and providing the necessary analyses, AI allows organisations to deal with a variety of issues. In addition, the AI-enabled KM systems empower employees by facilitating access to the information they need and, in doing so, fostering a culture of learning and improvement. In talent management, problem-solving or performance improvement, these systems prove how the integration of AI into KM can support innovation, improve decision-making and achieve operational excellence.

Real-World Examples of AI-Powered Knowledge Systems

Across various sectors, AI has been integrated successfully into KM systems, which has shown improvement in knowledge sharing, decision-making and innovation. For instance, in smart cities, AI-powered systems have enhanced e-governance and service delivery by optimising knowledge processes. These cities make use of AI to manage data that are related to public services and therefore enable more efficient e-services such as online passport renewals, tax fillings and vehicle registrations. South Korea and Japan are perfect examples of this approach, making use of strong e-governance frameworks to provide citizen-friendly services and support innovation in governance structures. In contrast, emerging economies like Pakistan and Bangladesh are adopting similar technologies to improve their service delivery models (Bokhari & Myeong, 2022). Another noteworthy example is AI's significant role in knowledge discovery from unstructured data, particularly textual documents and social media posts. Organisations make use of techniques such as NLP, which enables them to extract valuable insights from extensive information sources. Within healthcare, AI-powered algorithms undertake analysis of patient data along with medical records to identify patterns that enhance diagnosis and treatment plans. Similarly, financial institutions employ sentiment analysis of news articles and social media, which assists them in assessing market trends and making well-informed investment decisions (Waykar, 2022).

Retail organisations have experienced substantial benefits through AI-powered recommendation systems. These systems conduct analysis of customer purchase histories, which enables them to provide personalised product suggestions, thereby improving both customer satisfaction and sales figures. Within the manufacturing sector, predictive analytics makes use of historical data, which optimises maintenance schedules, thereby reducing equipment downtime and improving operational efficiency (Waykar, 2022). Such implementations demonstrate how AI not only handles routine tasks but also provides innovative solutions for complex challenges. Furthermore, AI-driven knowledge-sharing tools, particularly virtual assistants and chatbots, have facilitated enhanced collaboration within organisations by providing immediate access to relevant information. Such implementations have promoted a learning environment, which empowers employees to make data-driven decisions. Through the integration of AI into KM practices, organisations have succeeded in bridging knowledge gaps and encouraging innovation through continuous improvement and collaborative efforts (Waykar, 2022).

In the South African mining industry, AI-powered KM systems have been transformative in business-to-business (B2B) marketing. Using these systems, mining companies can generate customer, user and external market knowledge through the analysis of extensive datasets. The insights gained then allow organisations to make more rational decision-making processes, which enhances firm performance and competitiveness, especially in volatile market conditions (Bag et al., 2021). With big data, these organisations were able to address challenges in customer relationship management and operational efficiency. The implementation of AI has demonstrated a significant transformation of KM processes across various industries, which has led to enhanced efficiency and improved decision-making capabilities. Organisations that make use of AI in a considered manner have shown the ability to achieve sustained improvements in their operations and outcomes.

To further emphasise the practical impact that AI-powered knowledge systems have in real-world case applications, an empirical study was used. Using the fuzzy set theoretic approach for organisations that have implemented AI-powered knowledge systems, Olan et al. (2022) showed that using AI alone does not improve performance compared to when it is paired with knowledge-sharing. The AI-powered knowledge sharing gave a consistency threshold above 0.80, which indicated consistent improvements in performance, and the impacts were noted across three performance domains, namely: financial, product competitiveness and employee efficiency.

Additionally, several other companies were able to develop and use AI-powered knowledge systems, which significantly improved operational efficiency. Table 12.1 summarises some real-world scenarios in different industries supported by quantitative outcomes (Radhakrishnan & Gupta, 2020).

Table 12.1. Real-World Applications of AI-Powered Knowledge Systems With Quantifiable Results.

Case Study	Company Name	Industry	Description	Quantitative Impact
Arterys AI for Medical Imaging	Arterys Inc	Health Sector	An AI-based platform for MRI analysis for cardiovascular diagnostics.	• Reduce scan time from 90 minutes to 10 minutes. • Enable an average of 25 minutes saving time per study.
HireVue	Hirevue	Talent Management	Measures the facial expressions and other personality traits ensuring interviews are bias-free.	• Save more than 50,000 recruiter hours within one and a half years of implementation.
Blue River Technology	Blue River Technology	Agriculture	Uses computer vision and AI for precision agriculture.	• Reduce herbicide usage by 90% through their see and spray system.

Lessons Learnt and Practical Insights for Adopting AI in Knowledge Management

Drawing from these lessons, we can now explore how AI is likely to shape the future of KM across industries. The adoption of AI in KM presents many opportunities to enhance knowledge creation, sharing and decision-making. However, critical challenges must be addressed by organisations to unlock their full potential, as highlighted by Leoni et al. (2024) and Chatterjee et al. (2020). One essential lesson is the importance of aligning AI adoption with organisational goals. Tools should be selected based on specific requirements rather than following trends. The use of structured frameworks, such as interpretive structural modelling (ISM), allows the relationships between critical success factors to be analysed and prioritised efforts. This approach ensures that AI implementation remains both effective and practical (Chatterjee et al., 2020).

Support from leaders and top management is crucial for the success of AI-driven KM systems. Resource allocation, motivation and resistance to change are managed effectively through their involvement. Without active participation from leaders, momentum can be lost during challenging periods. To gain organisation-wide support, clear communication about AI's purpose and benefits is necessary (Chatterjee et al., 2020). Employee training and engagement also play a critical role. Resistance to AI often arises from concerns about its implications or unfamiliarity with the tools, and these issues can be minimised by involving employees early in the process and offering proper training. This not only reduces fear but also builds trust and smoothens the transition to new systems (Leoni et al., 2024).

Data security and privacy are other essential aspects that should be considered when adopting AI. Since AI relies on large datasets, strong security measures and clear privacy policies must be implemented. Addressing these concerns early builds stakeholders' confidence and ensures compliance with data protection regulations. Failing to prioritise these aspects can erode trust and slow adoption (Chatterjee et al., 2020). Simplicity and usability are equally important for successful adoption. Complex systems may discourage users and reduce engagement. Intuitive and user-friendly tools minimise the need for extensive training and promote higher adoption rates (Chatterjee et al., 2020).

AI systems offer practical benefits to organisations. Real-time data processing improves decision-making, operational efficiency and risk management. By breaking down silos, AI enhances knowledge sharing across teams and locations, ensuring employees access up-to-date information when required (Leoni et al., 2024). Continuous monitoring and iterative improvements based on feedback also help maintain the relevance and effectiveness of AI systems. Lastly, ethical considerations, including addressing biases in AI algorithms, are critical. Transparent and explainable models build trust and reduce resistance, making them essential for successful adoption. By proactively addressing these challenges, organisations can navigate AI complexities in KM, improving collaboration, efficiency and decision-making (Leoni et al., 2024).

The Future of AI in Knowledge Management

Emerging Trends: The Role of AI in Knowledge Management for Future Industries

KM is critical for organisational success, particularly in industries like healthcare, finance and education. The integration of AI into KM processes is revolutionising how organisations capture, share and utilise knowledge (Olan et al., 2022). AI is enhancing KM systems by improving efficiency, personalisation and decision-making across these sectors.

In healthcare, AI's role in KM is expanding rapidly. AI-powered systems can analyse vast amounts of clinical data, such as patient records and medical imaging, to assist healthcare professionals in diagnosing diseases, predicting outcomes and personalising treatment plans (Esteva et al., 2019). AI-driven knowledge-sharing platforms enable the seamless exchange of research findings and patient data, enhancing collaborative decision-making. A key challenge remains integrating AI with existing electronic health record (EHR) systems and ensuring data privacy. Nonetheless, AI models continue to support informed decision-making through real-time insights from clinical knowledge.

In finance, AI is transforming KM by enhancing risk management, fraud detection and customer service where AI-driven analytics help financial institutions predict market trends, optimise portfolios and improve decision-making (Rane et al., 2023). KM systems powered by AI integrate data from various sources, creating personalised client experiences while ensuring regulatory compliance. NLP and ML are used to automate customer inquiries and provide financial advice, reducing costs and improving information flow.

In education, AI technologies are reshaping KM by enabling personalised learning experiences, automating administrative tasks and offering insights into student performance where the AI tools analyse student data to suggest tailored learning paths, enhancing knowledge transfer (Shoaib et al., 2024). AI also supports teachers by streamlining grading, assessing student progress and identifying areas for improvement. As these industries embrace AI, the future of KM will shift from static systems to dynamic, AI-enhanced frameworks. While challenges related to data privacy, algorithm transparency and ethics remain, responsible deployment of AI in KM systems will be crucial for success.

AI and the Evolving Workforce

AI is reshaping KM across industries, especially in how knowledge professionals, such as knowledge managers and content curators, will perform their roles. As AI systems take on more complex tasks traditionally handled by humans, significant changes are expected in the workforce's roles, skills and responsibilities.

AI's primary impact on KM professionals will be the automation of routine tasks like data entry, content classification and document retrieval through the reduction of time spent on administrative work (Jarrahi et al., 2023). AI allows KM professionals to focus on strategic tasks such as knowledge sharing, decision-making and fostering collaboration. With AI's ability to analyse large datasets and identify trends, knowledge workers will be better equipped to make informed decisions, driving problem-solving and innovation. KM professionals will thus increasingly serve as facilitators, guiding the application of AI-driven insights in alignment with organisational goals.

As AI continues to evolve, the KM profession will demand new technical and strategic skills. Knowledge managers will need to understand AI tools, data analytics and ML algorithms to oversee AI-enhanced KM systems (Chakraborty et al., 2024). They will also need to assess AI outputs, ensuring that human judgement remains integral to decision-making and that biases are avoided. Interpreting AI insights and translating them into actionable strategies will become a crucial skill for future KM professionals.

AI will also encourage cross-disciplinary collaboration, requiring KM workers to work closely with AI specialists, data scientists and IT professionals. These interdisciplinary teams will design, implement and optimise AI systems for KM. Thus, KM professionals will need to enhance their communication and teamwork skills. The integration of AI into KM will transform the profession by automating tasks, demanding new skills and fostering collaboration. While automation will increase efficiency, the human workforce will remain essential for interpreting and strategically applying AI insights.

Impact of AI on Knowledge Democratisation

AI is transforming KM by democratising access to information and reshaping how knowledge is distributed across organisations and communities. One way AI facilitates knowledge democratisation is by improving access to information. Traditionally, knowledge has been siloed within organisations, requiring individuals to navigate complex systems. AI-powered tools such as intelligent search engines, chatbots and content curation systems can break down these barriers, offering instant access to relevant information based on user queries (Casheekar et al., 2024). AI-driven platforms like knowledge graphs and recommendation systems can further personalise content, enabling users to find what they need without specialised training, speeding up decision-making in organisations and also helping make insights more transparent and understandable, where complex data analysis, once requiring expertise, can now be automated with ML algorithms, making data-driven insights accessible to non-experts (Schmitt, 2023). Tools like NLP and data visualisation present complex information in intuitive formats, broadening their reach.

Additionally, AI facilitates collaboration and collective intelligence where AI tools can connect individuals with varying expertise, promoting knowledge sharing and collaborative problem-solving. In sectors like finance or law, AI can analyse large volumes of data, providing insights that can be shared across teams and making specialised knowledge more accessible (Dwivedi et al., 2021).

However, the democratisation of knowledge through AI raises concerns about data privacy, equity and algorithmic bias. Ensuring fairness and transparency in AI models and decision-making is essential to fully realizing the potential of AI-driven knowledge democratization for all stakeholders.

Human–AI Collaboration

AI is rapidly transforming KM practices, not by replacing human workers but by augmenting human capabilities, especially in knowledge-intensive tasks. Human–AI collaboration emphasises the complementary strengths of both, where AI enhances human decision-making, creativity and productivity. In KM, human–AI collaboration is crucial in enhancing decision-making and problem-solving as the AI systems can analyse vast datasets, uncovering trends and insights that are time-consuming for humans to process manually (Hao et al., 2024). For example, AI-powered analytics can identify patterns, offering actionable insights. However, human expertise is necessary to interpret these findings, considering context and applying them strategically. This collaboration improves decision-making in fields like healthcare, finance and law, where complex data analysis is essential.

Additionally, AI can automate repetitive tasks, allowing knowledge workers to focus on higher-level cognitive functions. For instance, in document management, AI tools can categorise, tag and search content, reducing administrative burden which frees up time for employees to engage in strategic thinking, creative problem-solving and innovation (Farooq et al., 2024). In legal and research sectors, AI can summarise documents, highlight key points and suggest resources, enabling professionals to focus on analysis rather than manual review. AI-powered tools can align individuals based on expertise, analyse knowledge gaps and suggest relevant sources, improving collaboration across departments or organisations. In corporate settings, AI can recommend experts for projects or provide teams with the latest research, streamlining knowledge sharing.

Despite AI's significant potential, it cannot replace human intuition, emotional intelligence or ethical judgement. In healthcare, for example, AI can suggest treatments based on patient data, but doctors must use their clinical experience to make final decisions. The future of AI in KM is one of collaboration, where human expertise and AI capabilities work together to achieve outcomes neither can achieve alone (Olan et al., 2022). The future of AI in KM lies in collaboration, where AI enhances human decision-making, creativity and collaboration in knowledge-intensive tasks. The future of AI in KM lies in collaboration, where it supports human decision-making, creativity and productivity in knowledge-intensive tasks. As AI evolves, the key will be designing systems that empower human workers, enabling them to harness AI's potential while preserving the irreplaceable value of human judgement and expertise.

Future Challenges and Considerations

As AI is becoming increasingly embedded in KM systems, several future challenges must be addressed to ensure both responsible and effective adoption of this technology. Some of the key concerns are regulatory compliance, transparency and ethical governance, particularly since organisational decision-making processes now involve AI. Sharma et al. (2023) underlined the importance of building explainable and trustworthy AI systems that would respect data privacy and mitigate algorithmic bias. Also, Rezaei et al. (2024) further reinforced this idea by identifying transparency, data protection, bias and accountability as the most critical ethical challenges which have high empirical significance in their confirmatory factor analysis ($\lambda \geq 0.86$). Mitigating these challenges is essential to ensure that AI development is aligned with the strategic goals of corporate KM.

Conclusion

This chapter has examined the transformative impact of AI in KM, emphasising both the opportunities and problems associated with incorporating AI into organisational knowledge processes. KM has always been critical to ensuring that organisations can use their pooled intellect and data to drive decision-making, creativity and efficiency. However, the incorporation of AI has considerably increased the potential of KM by providing advanced technologies capable of improving information discovery, streamlining procedures and enabling more personalised learning experiences.

AI technologies, including ML, NLP, RPA and AI-powered knowledge graphs, are changing the way businesses store, connect and visualise knowledge. These technologies allow for the extraction of insights from massive datasets, increased workflow efficiency and seamless knowledge sharing across organisational boundaries. Furthermore, AI tools assist organisations in uncovering hidden knowledge, forecasting future trends and fostering cooperation, all of which contribute to more agile and informed decision-making processes.

However, the path to AI-powered KM is not without hurdles. Data quality, technological complexity, human variables and ethical concerns can all be significant impediments to successful AI integration. Ensuring that AI systems are transparent, neutral and ethically sound is critical to building trust and encouraging widespread use. Furthermore, organisations must close the skills gap by reskilling personnel and incorporating AI solutions that supplement, rather than replace, human expertise.

Looking ahead, AI has the potential to further transform KM in a variety of areas, including healthcare and finance, by democratising access to knowledge and encouraging collaboration between humans and intelligent systems. As AI evolves, its role in KM will not only enhance organisational capacities but also shape the future workforce, emphasising human–AI collaboration to produce better results. Finally, the combination of AI and KM provides an intriguing frontier, with the potential to unlock new levels of efficiency, creativity and strategic insight for organisations throughout the world.

References

Afraz, J. (2024). Explore beyond GenAI on the 2024 hype cycle for artificial intelligence. *Gartner*. https://www.gartner.com/en/articles/hype-cycle-for-artificial-intelligence

Agostinelli, S., & Marrella, A. (2022). Intelligent robotic process automation: Generating executable RPA scripts from unsegmented UI logs. In *CEUR Workshop Proceedings* (Vol. 3310, pp. 89–92). CEUR-WS.

Aldoseri, A., Al-Khalifa, K. N., & Hamouda, A. M. (2023). Re-thinking data strategy and integration for artificial intelligence: Concepts, opportunities, and challenges. *Applied Sciences*, *13*(12), 7082.

Azure Database for PostgreSQL. (2024). Azure PostgreSQL with Azure Open AI to innovate banking apps: Unlocking the power of AI extension. *Azure Database for PostgreSQL Blog*. https://techcommunity.microsoft.com/blog/adforpostgresql/azure-postgresql-with-azure-open-ai-to-innovate-banking-apps-unlocking-the-power/4257561

Bag, S., Gupta, S., Kumar, A., & Sivarajah, U. (2021). An integrated artificial intelligence framework for knowledge creation and B2B marketing rational decision-making for improving firm performance. *Industrial Marketing Management*, *92*, 178–189. https://doi.org/10.1016/j.indmarman.2020.12.001

Bloomfire. (2024, May 10). The role of ethical artificial intelligence in knowledge management. *Bloomfire*. https://bloomfire.com/blog/ethical-artificial-intelligence-in-knowledge-management/. Accessed on March, 26, 2025.

Bokhari, S. A., & Myeong, S. (2022). Artificial intelligence-based technological-oriented knowledge management, innovation, and e-service delivery in smart cities: The moderating role of e-governance. *Applied Sciences*, *12*(17), 8732.

Bostrom, N. (2014). *Superintelligence: Paths, dangers, strategies*. Oxford University Press.

Brynjolfsson, E., & McAfee, A. (2017). *Machine, platform, crowd: Harnessing our digital future*. WW Norton & Company. https://www.mintur.gob.es/Publicaciones/Publicacionesperiodicas/EconomiaIndustrial/RevistaEconomiaIndustrial/409/SEGUNDA%20CR%C3%8DTICA%20DE%20LIBROS.pdf. Accessed on April, 03, 2025.

Casheekar, A., Lahiri, A., Rath, K., Prabhakar, K. S., & Srinivasan, K. (2024). A contemporary review on chatbots, AI-powered virtual conversational agents, ChatGPT: Applications, open challenges and future research directions. *Computer Science Review*, *52*, 100632.

Chakraborty, S., Misra, B., & Dey, N. (2024). *AI-empowered knowledge management in education*. Springer.

Chatterjee, S., Ghosh, S. K., & Chaudhuri, R. (2020). Knowledge management in improving the business process: An interpretative framework for successful implementation of AI–CRM–KM system in organisations. *Business Process Management Journal*, *26*(6), 1261–1281.

Chen, X., Jia, S., Ding, L., Shen, H., & Xiang, Y. (2020). SDT: An integrated model for open-world knowledge graph reasoning. *Expert Systems with Applications*, *162*, 113889.

Davenport, T. H., & Prusak, L. (2000). Working knowledge: How organizations manage what they know. In *Survivors' perspectives of organizational downsizing on knowledge sharing in a downsized environment* (pp. 1–7). https://ubiquity.acm.org/article.cfm?id=348775

de Biase, A., Sourlos, N., & van Ooijen, P. M. (2022). Standardization of artificial intelligence development in radiotherapy. *Seminars in Radiation Oncology*, *32*(4), 415–420. https://doi.org/10.1016/j.semradonc.2022.06.010

Denton, J. (2023, March 26). *Integrating AI into legacy systems: Challenges and strategies*. LinkedIn. https://www.linkedin.com/pulse/integrating-ai-legacy-systems-challenges-strategies-josh-denton-pksqe. Accessed on 2025.

Dwivedi, Y. K., Hughes, L., Ismagilova, E., Aarts, G., Coombs, C., Crick, T., & Williams, M. D. (2021). Artificial Intelligence (AI): Multidisciplinary perspectives on emerging challenges, opportunities, and agenda for research, practice and policy. *International Journal of Information Management*, *57*, 101994.

Esteva, A., Kuprel, B., Novoa, R. A., Ko, J., Swetter, S. M., & Blau, H. M. (2019). Dermatologist-level classification of skin cancer with deep neural networks. *Nature*, *542*(7639), 115–118.

Farooq, M., Ramzan, M., & Yen, Y. Y. (2024). AI in management: An overview. In *Transformative impacts of AI in management* (p. 1). https://doi.org/10.4018/979-8-3693-4322-7

Fensel, D., Şimşek, U., Angele, K., Huaman, E., Kärle, E., Panasiuk, O., & Şimşek, U. (2020). Introduction: What is a knowledge graph? In *Knowledge graphs: Methodology, tools and selected use cases* (pp. 1–10). https://doi.org/10.1007/978-3-030-37439-6

Floridi, L. (2013). *The ethics of information*. Oxford University Press.

George, J. (2024). Data to AI: Building a solid data foundation for your generative AI applications in the cloud. *International Journal of Science and Research Archive*, *11*(01), 2601–2604.

Gill, A. (2024, 03 26). UN experts urge United Nations to lay foundations for global governance of artificial intelligence. *AP News*. https://apnews.com/article/f755788da7d5905fcc2d44edf93c4bec. Accessed on 2025.

Hao, X., Demir, E., & Eyers, D. (2024). Exploring collaborative decision-making: A quasi-experimental study of human and generative AI interaction. *Technology in Society*, *78*, 102662.

IBM. (2023, 08 14). *New IBM study reveals how AI is changing work and what HR leaders should do about it*. https://www.ibm.com/think/insights/new-ibm-study-reveals-how-ai-is-changing-work-and-what-hr-leaders-should-do-about-it, IBM Insights.

IBM. (2024, 09 30). *Exploring privacy issues in the age of AI*. IBM Insights. https://www.ibm.com/think/insights/ai-privacy. Accessed on March 26, 2025.

IDC. (2024). *Worldwide IDC Global DataSphere Forecast, 2024–2028: AI everywhere, but upsurge in data will take time*. IDC. https://www.idc.com/getdoc.jsp?containerId=US52076424

Jarrahi, M. H., Askay, D., Eshraghi, A., & Smith, P. (2023). Artificial intelligence and knowledge management: A partnership between human and AI. *Business Horizons*, *66*(1), 87–99.

Kaggwa, S., Eleogu, T. F., Okonkwo, F., Farayola, O. A., Uwaoma, P. U., & Akinoso, A. (2024). AI in decision making: Transforming business strategies. *International Journal of Research and Scientific Innovation*, *10*(12), 423–444.

Kakatkar, C., Bilgram, V., & Füller, J. (2020). Innovation analytics: Leveraging artificial intelligence in the innovation process. *Business Horizons*, *63*(2), 171–181. https://doi.org/10.1016/j.bushor.2019.10.006

Kapadia, S. (2025, March 19). *Companies' biggest barrier to AI isn't tech — It's employee pushback. Here's how to overcome it.* Business Insider. https://www.businessinsider.com/how-to-prevent-employee-skepticism-push-back-gen-ai-2025-3. Accessed on March 26, 2025.

Kellner, D., Lowin, M., & Hinz, O. (2023). Improved healthcare disaster decision-making utilizing information extraction from complementary social media data during the COVID-19 pandemic. *Decision Support Systems*, *172*, 113983.

Khennouche, F., Elmir, Y., Djebari, N., Boubchir, L., Laouid, A., & Bounceur, A. (2024). Comparative analysis and application of large language models on FAQ chatbots. In *2024 International conference on computational intelligence and network systems (CINS)* (pp. 1–6). IEEE.

Khurana, D., Koli, A., Khatter, K., & Singh, S. (2023). Natural language processing: State of the art, current trends and challenges. *Multimedia Tools and Applications*, *82*(3), 3713–3744.

Kirk, S. (2024, March 21). *The ethical dilemmas of AI. USC Annenberg - School for Communication and Journalism.* https://annenberg.usc.edu/research/center-public-relations/usc-annenberg-relevance-report/ethical-dilemmas-ai. Accessed on March 26, 2025.

KPMG. (2021). *Drilling down: Leading in the age of digital determination.* https://assets.kpmg.com/content/dam/kpmg/xx/pdf/2021/02/drilling-down-leading-in-the-age-of-digital-determination.pdf?utm_source=chatgpt.com. Accessed on April 03, 2025.

Leoni, L., Gueli, G., Ardolino, M., Panizzon, M., & Gupta, S. (2024). AI-Empowered KM processes for decision-making: Empirical evidence from worldwide organisations. *Journal of Knowledge Management*, *28*(11), 320–347. https://doi.org/10.1108/JKM-03-2024-0262

Liu, B. (2010). Sentiment analysis and subjectivity. In *Handbook of natural language processing* (Vol. 2, pp. 627–666). https://www.cs.uic.edu/~liub/FBS/NLP-handbook-sentiment-analysis.pdf

Luckin, R. (2018). *Machine learning and human intelligence: The future of education for the 21st century*. UCL Institute of Education Press.

Mahala, G., Sindhgatta, R., Dam, H. K., & Ghose, A. (2024). Multi-objective evolutionary search for optimal Robotic Process Automation architectures. *IEEE Transactions on Services Computing*, *17*, 2654–2671.

Malik, A., De Silva, M. T., Budhwar, P., & Srikanth, N. R. (2021). Elevating talents' experience through innovative artificial intelligence-mediated knowledge sharing: Evidence from an IT-multinational enterprise. *Journal of Business Research*, *131*, 406–417. https://doi.org/10.1016/j.jbusres.2021.03.061

McKinsey and Company. (2024, 11 26). *Building AI trust: The key role of explainability.* McKinsey & Company. https://www.mckinsey.com/capabilities/quantumblack/our-insights/building-ai-trust-the-key-role-of-explainability

Mittal, U., Siva, S., Vinay, C., & Devika, S. (2024). A comprehensive review on generative AI for education. *IEEE Access*, *12*, 142733–142759.

Müller, K., & Bodendorf, F. (2023). Cross-silo federated learning in enterprise networks with cooperative and competing actors. In *The human side of service engineering, AHFE 2023 international conference. San Francisco, USA*.

Nemati, H. R., Steiger, D. M., Iyer, L. S., & Herschel, R. T. (2002). Knowledge warehouse: An architectural integration of knowledge management, decision support, artificial intelligence and data warehousing. *Decision Support Systems*, *33* (2), 143–161.

O'Neil, C. (2017). *Weapons of math destruction: How big data increases inequality and threatens democracy*. Crown.

Ofosu-Asare, Y. (2024). Cognitive imperialism in artificial intelligence: Counteracting bias with indigenous epistemologies. *AI & Society*. https://doi.org/10.1007/s00146-024-02065-0

Okeleke, P. A., Ajiga, D., Folorunsho, S. O., & Ezeigweneme, C. (2024). Predictive analytics for market trends using AI: A study in consumer behavior. *International Journal of Engineering Research Updates*, *7*(1), 36–49. https://doi.org/10.53430/ijeru.2024.7.1.0032

Olan, F., Arakpogun, E. O., Suklan, J., Nakpodia, F., Damij, N., & Jayawickrama, U. (2022). Artificial intelligence and knowledge sharing: Contributing factors to organizational performance. *Journal of Business Research*, *145*, 605–615. https://doi.org/10.1016/j.jbusres.2022.03.008

Pesovski, I., Santos, R., Henriques, R., & Trajkovik, V. (2024). Generative AI for customizable learning experiences. *Sustainability*, *16*(7), 3034.

Plattfaut, R., & Borghoff, V. (2022). Robotic process automation: A literature-based research agenda. *Journal of Information Systems*, *36*(2), 173–191.

Radhakrishnan, J., & Gupta, S. (2020). Artificial intelligence in practice – Real-world examples and emerging business models. In S. Carlsson (Ed.), *Digitalization and big data for resilience and sustainability* (pp. 89–102). https://doi.org/10.1007/978-3-030-64849-7_8

Rane, N., Choudhary, S., & Rane, J. (2023). *Blockchain and artificial intelligence (AI) integration for revolutionizing security and transparency in finance*. SSRN 4644253.

Rehman, Z., Tariq, N., Moqurrab, S. A., Yoo, J., & Srivastava, G. (2024). Machine learning and internet of things applications in enterprise architectures: Solutions, challenges, and open issues. *Expert Systems*, *41*(1), e13467.

Rettberg, J. W. (2024, January 16). How generative AI endangers cultural narratives. *Issues in Science and Technology*. https://issues.org/generative-ai-cultural-narratives-rettberg/. Accessed on March 26, 2025.

Rezaei, M., Pironti, M., & Quaglia, R. (2024). AI in knowledge sharing: Which ethical challenges are raised in decision-making processes for organisations? *Management Decision*. https://doi.org/10.1108/MD-10-2023-2023

Russell, S. J., & Norvig, P. (2016). *Artificial intelligence: A modern approach*. Pearson.

Sahoo, A. K., & Chakraverty, S. (2022). Machine intelligence in dynamical systems: A state of art review. *Wiley Interdisciplinary Reviews: Data Mining and Knowledge Discovery*, *12*(4), e1461.

Sarker, I. H. (2023). Machine learning for intelligent data analysis and automation in cybersecurity: Current and future prospects. *Annals of Data Science*, *10*(6), 1473–1498.

Sarker, I. H., Kayes, A. S., Badsha, S., Alqahtani, H., Watters, P., & Ng, A. (2020). Cybersecurity data science: An overview from machine learning perspective. *Journal of Big Data*, *7*, 1–29.

Schmitt, M. (2023). Automated machine learning: AI-driven decision making in business analytics. *Intelligent Systems with Applications*, *18*, 200188.

Schwab, K. (2018). *Shaping the future of the fourth industrial revolution*. Portfolio Penguin.

Seeber, I. B.-J., Bittner, E., Briggs, R. O., de Vreede, T., de Vreede, G.-J., Elkins, A., Maier, R., Merz, A. B., Oeste-Reiß, S., Randrup, N., Schwabe, G., & Söllner, M. (2020). Machines as teammates: A research agenda on AI in team collaboration. *Information & Management*, *57*(2), 103174.

Shaikh, M., & Birajdar, F. (2024). Artificial intelligence in groundwater management: Innovations, challenges, and future prospects. *International Journal of Science and Research Archive*, *11*(01), 502–512.

Sharma, R., Lakhera, G., & Sharma, M. (2023). Artificial intelligence in KM processes: Emerging trends and challenges. In *2023 1st DMIHER international conference on artificial intelligence in education and industry 4.0 (IDICAIEI)* (pp. 1–6). https://doi.org/10.1109/IDICAIEI58380.2023.10406876

Shoaib, M., Sayed, N., Singh, J., Shafi, J., Khan, S., & Ali, F. (2024). AI student success predictor: Enhancing personalized learning in campus management systems. *Computers in Human Behavior*, *158*, 108301.

Soori, M. K. G. J., Dastres, R., & Arezoo, B. (2024). AI-based decision support systems in industry 4.0: A review. *Journal of Economy and Technology*. https://doi.org/10.1016/j.ject.2024.08.005

Strielkowski, W., Grebennikova, V., Lisovskiy, A., Rakhimova, G., & Vasileva, T. (2024). AI-driven adaptive learning for sustainable educational transformation. *Sustainable Development*. https://doi.org/10.1002/sd.3221

Uncuta, P. (2023). *Integration challenges of AI in businesses: Overcoming hurdles in compatibility*. LinkedIn. https://www.linkedin.com/pulse/integration-challenges-ai-businesses-overcoming-hurdles-pavel-uncuta-fvh6c. Accessed March 26, 2025.

University of Bergen. (2024). *AI Stories*. (J. W. Rettberg, Producer). Center for Digital Narrative. https://www.uib.no/en/cdn/169711/ai-stories. Accessed March 26, 2025.

Vladika, J., Schneider, P., & Matthes, F. (2023). HealthFC: Verifying health claims with evidence-based medical fact-checking. *arXiv*. arXiv:2309.08503.

Wang, X., Xu, X., Zhang, Y., Hao, S., & Jie, W. (2024). Exploring the impact of artificial intelligence application in personalized learning environments: Thematic analysis of undergraduates' perceptions in China. *Humanities and Social Sciences Communications*, *11*(1), 1–10.

Waykar, Y. A. (2022). The role of artificial intelligence in knowledge management. *Journal of Scientific Research in Engineering and Management*, *6*(6).

Wewerka, J., & Reichert, M. (2023). Robotic process automation – A systematic mapping study and classification framework. *Enterprise Information Systems*, *17*(2), 1986862.

Yan, L., Greiff, S., Teuber, Z., & Gašević, D. (2024). Promises and challenges of generative artificial intelligence for human learning. *Nature Human Behaviour*, *8*(10), 1839–1850.

Chapter 13

Artificial Intelligence–Driven Knowledge Management for Development in the Global South: Bridging Digital Divides Through Localized Innovation

Nanette Y. Saes[a], *Bruce W. Watson*[b] *and Liam R. Watson*[c]

[a]XPATTYCAKE, The Netherlands
[b]University of Kwazulu-Natal, South Africa
[c]Watcode AI, Canada

Abstract

This chapter explores the transformative potential of artificial intelligence (AI)-driven knowledge management (AIKM) systems in addressing development challenges in the Global South (GS), particularly in Africa. Traditional KM frameworks often fail to serve the GS due to infrastructural deficits, linguistic diversity and limited technical capacity. However, advances in mobile technology, edge computing and culturally aware AI present a unique opportunity for inclusive innovation. The chapter argues for context-specific AIKM solutions that leverage the GS's demographic strengths – such as its youthful, mobile-savvy population – and proposes strategies to overcome systemic constraints like unreliable internet access, limited power infrastructure and scarce computational resources.

Focusing on localization, the chapter advocates for the development of lightweight, offline-capable AI tools that process knowledge in local languages. It highlights the importance of integrating indigenous knowledge and supporting digital sovereignty through regionally trained AI models. Key application areas include education, financial inclusion, healthcare and entrepreneurship, where AIKM can streamline operations, enhance accessibility and support sustainable development. Emphasis is placed on avoiding reliance on First World AI paradigms, which are often ill-suited to

AI-Driven Knowledge Management Assets, Volume 2, 265–283

doi:10.1108/978-1-83662-778-420261013

GS realities, and instead adopting leapfrogging strategies to build nimble, community-driven systems.

The chapter concludes by calling for ethical, transparent and decentralized governance of AIKM to balance empowerment with safeguards against misuse. Ultimately, it posits that with strategic adaptation, the GS can not only close the digital divide but also lead the next wave of knowledge-based innovation.

Keywords: AI-driven knowledge management (AIKM); Global South (GS); localized AI solutions; edge computing; digital inclusion; indigenous knowledge systems

Introduction

The integration of artificial intelligence (AI) into knowledge management (KM) systems, forming AI-driven knowledge management (AIKM), presents unprecedented opportunities for development in the Global South (GS). Historically, traditional KM systems have struggled to penetrate rural and underserved communities in the GS due to infrastructural limitations, economic constraints and technological barriers. However, the convergence of edge computing, mobile technology and linguistically aware AI is forging new pathways for inclusive development. By leveraging AIKM solutions, the GS can enhance local knowledge ecosystems, facilitate digital transformation and preserve cultural heritage while making information more accessible and actionable for communities (Unwin, 2017).

This chapter explores how AIKM solutions can address the unique needs of the GS by considering local contexts, resource limitations and demographic trends. The discussion will highlight the opportunities and challenges of implementing AI-driven KM systems in emerging markets, particularly in Africa, which represents the fastest-growing and youngest population in the GS. This demographic advantage, coupled with increasing mobile penetration, presents an opportunity to build AIKM solutions tailored to a digitally engaged, yet under-resourced population.

Goals of the Chapter

This chapter aims to:

- elucidate the opportunities and challenges of AI-driven KM in the GS;
- identify the most suitable technologies given regional constraints and trends;
- highlight key socio-economic and technological properties of the GS, with a particular focus on Africa, which make it an ideal candidate for AI-driven KM adoption.

Methodology

To ground the discussion in practical realities, this chapter uses as its foundation an AIKM system currently under development. The system and its ecosystem focus on Africa as a representative example due to its rapid population growth, increasing digital adoption and the pressing need for scalable, localized AIKM solutions. This approach will help illustrate how AIKM can address knowledge accessibility, improve decision-making and support sustainable development in GS communities.

Expected Outcomes

By the end of this chapter, readers will gain:

- a clear understanding of how AI can be effectively used in KM for emerging markets;
- insights into the challenges and obstacles of AI implementation in the GS;
- awareness of the economies of scale associated with Africa's young, digitally literate population of over two billion people;
- an appreciation for why AI solutions developed for the First World (1W) do not align with the needs and realities of GS markets.

Key Claims

The core claims of this chapter emphasize the transformative potential of AIKM for the GS:

- AIKM has the potential to support several sustainable development goals (SDGs) by improving knowledge accessibility, economic participation and digital literacy (Russ, 2018).
- The 1W approach to AI, which assumes stable infrastructure, high digital literacy and abundant computing resources, is not directly transferable to GS contexts (Kwet, 2019). A home-grown AIKM approach is essential to meeting the unique challenges of these markets.
- Global political and economic trends suggest a shift towards protectionism in the 1W, making it increasingly urgent for GS nations to develop their own AIKM solutions to avoid reliance on external technological frameworks.

By addressing these themes, this chapter will contribute to a broader understanding of how AI-driven KM solutions can drive economic and social progress in the GS while ensuring that AI technologies are adapted to local needs and conditions.

Structure of This Chapter

1 Limitations of current AI solutions in the GS

2 Unlocking AI opportunities in emerging markets
3 Designing AIKM tools for local relevance
   - Harnessing the demographic dividend of the GS
   - Language inclusion as a foundation for AI accessibility
   - Leapfrogging legacy systems with home-grown innovation
   - Engineering AIKM within resource-constrained environments
   - Ensuring compliance with local data privacy laws
   - Safeguarding against misinformation and external control
   - Connecting entrepreneurial ecosystems through AI
4 Boosting KM efficiency across key sectors
5 AI for knowledge discovery and cultural preservation
6 Integrating traditional knowledge with future trends
7 Conclusion: Building resilient, inclusive AIKM for the GS

Limitations of Current AI Solutions in the GS

The use of existing AI tools in the GS faces significant challenges due to infrastructural and socio-linguistic barriers. Limited internet access and inadequate technological infrastructure prevent many from fully utilizing AI-driven solutions, exacerbating the digital divide. Additionally, the dominance of English in AI models marginalizes non-English speakers and the numerous local languages and dialects that often lack sufficient linguistic data for AI training. This issue is further compounded by a lack of information and communications technology (ICT) skills among large portions of the population, making it difficult to engage with and adapt AI technologies effectively. Furthermore, AI systems often underrepresent or entirely exclude indigenous cultures and languages, reinforcing biases and limiting the relevance of AI tools to local contexts (Eubanks, 2018). Addressing these challenges requires targeted efforts to develop AI solutions that are inclusive, culturally aware and accessible to diverse populations across the GS.

Unlocking AI Opportunities in Emerging Markets

Despite these challenges, the GS presents immense opportunities for the development of home-grown AI tools tailored to its unique needs. The fastest growing and youngest population of the GS is in Africa, which will serve as an example throughout the chapter. Africa's population is projected to reach 2.5 billion by 2050, of which more than half will be under 25 years old (World Economic Forum, 2023).

A rapidly growing youth population, often more adaptable to new technologies, provides a strong foundation for digital innovation and AI-driven solutions. These tools can address the needs of underserved communities and untapped markets by focusing on local languages, cultural contexts and pressing socio-economic challenges, such as agriculture, healthcare and education. Additionally, fostering an entrepreneurial ecosystem with targeted support –

through funding, policy incentives and AI-focused training programmes – can empower local startups and developers to build AI solutions that bridge accessibility gaps. By leveraging these opportunities, the GS can create more inclusive, relevant and impactful AI technologies that drive sustainable development and economic growth.

Designing AIKM Tools for Local Relevance

The rapid growth and linguistic diversity of Africa, as a key part of the GS, necessitates a fundamental rethinking of AIKM tools. Deploying lightweight language models at the edge of networks offers a powerful solution, allowing AI systems to function effectively in low-bandwidth environments while processing knowledge in local languages without requiring constant internet connectivity. These AI-at-the-Edge solutions are particularly well-suited to the demographic realities of the GS, where a young and fast-growing population represents both a challenge and an opportunity.

Harnessing the Demographic Dividend of the GS

A significant portion of the GS population consists of young people with rudimentary digital skills. While they may not possess deep technical expertise, they are proficient in using mobile devices – a stark contrast to many parts of the 1W, where a smaller proportion of people rely on mobile phones for digital interactions. This presents both challenges and opportunities for AIKM solutions, which must be designed to cater to a population already engaged with mobile technology but without requiring extensive technical training.

The digitally newly skilled and semi-skilled population in GS primarily includes young individuals who are highly adaptable to technology but may lack formal education in AI or advanced computing. Many informal workers use digital tools for commerce and communication but have minimal training in data management or business analytics. Rural populations, who often have limited access to high-speed internet, increasingly rely on mobile devices for connectivity. Additionally, small business owners and entrepreneurs use digital platforms but generally lack deep expertise in AI-driven business intelligence. Given these demographics, AIKM solutions must be intuitive, mobile-friendly and designed with minimal learning curves to enable even those with limited education to benefit from AI tools.

Building for a Young, Mobile-First, Digitally Newly Skilled User Base

Many GS countries have a youth-heavy demographic structure, with a significant percentage of the population under the age of 30. This contrasts with ageing populations in many 1W countries. A young demographic presents unique advantages, including higher adaptability to new technology, faster learning curves with mobile-first interfaces and the potential for greater long-term impact as digital literacy improves over time. However, challenges remain, such as lower levels of formal education, particularly in AI and data-driven fields, and limited access to structured training programmes for digital skills development. By focusing on accessibility, AIKM systems can empower a generation of digital-first users, unlocking new avenues for entrepreneurship, education and economic growth.

While formal technical training is scarce, a large portion of the GS population has basic digital literacy, particularly in mobile technology. Many individuals are accustomed to using smartphones for communication, mobile banking and social media, making mobile devices an ideal platform for AI-driven tools. High mobile penetration rates in the GS mean that most people own at least one mobile device (Aker & Mbiti, 2010), though access to high-performance smartphones and stable internet connectivity remains uneven, with mobile internet penetration in Sub-Saharan Africa reaching only 27% by 2023 despite widespread mobile coverage (GSMA, 2023). This requires AIKM solutions that work on low-end devices and offer offline capabilities where necessary. Despite their familiarity with mobile devices, most users do not have expertise in programming, data science or AI. Therefore, AIKM solutions must be designed with low-code or no-code interfaces that allow users to engage with AI without requiring technical proficiency.

Bridging the AI Gap Between the GS and 1W

AI adoption patterns differ significantly between the GS and 1W due to variations in demographics, digital skills and education systems. While smartphone penetration is high in 1W, mobile-first economies in the GS often exhibit greater total engagement with mobile technology compared to traditional desktop-based digital interactions in 1W. Additionally, the 1W has a higher concentration of professionals with advanced KM skills, particularly in corporate and academic settings. This is largely due to well-established education systems that emphasize data literacy, analytics and formal knowledge organization. Businesses in 1W also have stronger infrastructures that integrate AI for decision-making and automation, along with greater access to enterprise AI tools designed for a highly skilled workforce.

In contrast, AIKM adoption in the GS must focus on accessibility, informal learning and mobile-friendly solutions to serve populations without deep technical expertise. AIKM solutions in the GS should prioritize mobile accessibility, simplified interfaces and language support to effectively serve a digitally newly skilled and semi-skilled population. By designing AI tools that accommodate a young, mobile savvy, yet under-trained user base, GS countries can bridge knowledge gaps and drive economic participation. With strategic adaptation, AI has the potential to democratize access to information, enhancing business opportunities, education and innovation across the region.

Language Inclusion as a Foundation for AI Accessibility

The GS cannot rely on the 1W to develop adequate language support for its thousands of local languages and dialects. Even when 1W institutions attempt to include these languages in AI models, the results often lack contextual depth and linguistic accuracy due to a shortage of native fluency and cultural understanding. Many AI systems trained outside the GS treat language as a technical problem rather than a socio-cultural one, leading to inaccuracies in meaning, tone and nuance. Furthermore, commercial AI models from the 1W prioritize languages with the highest economic return, leaving many GS languages unsupported or poorly represented. To build AIKM systems that are truly accessible and equitable, the GS must take ownership of language model development, ensuring that its linguistic diversity is accurately reflected in AI applications.

GS-specific datasets are invaluable resources for training AI models that can understand and process local languages in ways that international models cannot (Marivate et al., 2020). Many African, South Asian and Latin American languages have rich oral traditions and unique linguistic structures that do not always translate well using conventional AI approaches. Without high-quality training datasets sourced from native speakers, AI models risk perpetuating errors, bias and loss of meaning. Additionally, language diversity in the GS extends beyond national languages to include thousands of regional dialects, each with distinct grammatical rules and vocabulary. The ability to train AI models on these dialects has significant implications for business, education and governance, enabling AI systems to reach rural and underserved populations more effectively.

Human involvement in AI training is essential to maintaining quality and ensuring that language models accurately capture the complexities of GS languages. Automated scraping of text from the internet, a common approach used by 1W models, is insufficient because many GS languages lack a substantial digital footprint. Instead, AI training must incorporate direct input from linguists, educators and native speakers who can refine the model outputs for accuracy and cultural appropriateness. This collaborative, community-driven approach strengthens the credibility of AIKM systems, making them more usable for everyday communication, commerce and knowledge dissemination. By investing in locally trained AI systems, the GS can safeguard its linguistic heritage while simultaneously expanding digital access in a way that is both inclusive and representative of its diverse populations.

Leapfrogging Legacy Systems With Home-Grown Innovation

Historically, the GS has successfully leapfrogged traditional infrastructure by bypassing outdated technologies and adopting more advanced solutions suited to its unique challenges. For example, many GS countries skipped extensive landline telephone networks and moved directly to mobile communications, leading to widespread connectivity at a fraction of the cost and time required for traditional infrastructure. Similarly, mobile banking and fintech solutions emerged in the GS (Aker & Mbiti, 2010) long before they became mainstream in the 1W, largely because traditional banking infrastructure was either insufficient or inaccessible to large portions of the population. AI presents a similar opportunity: rather than investing in the costly development of foundational AI models from scratch, the GS can strategically adopt, modify and optimize existing AI advancements to create systems that cater specifically to its linguistic, cultural and economic realities.

The fundamental research, computational heavy-lifting and development of large AI models have largely been undertaken by 1W institutions, requiring extensive financial, technical and infrastructural resources that the GS currently lacks. Developing AI from the ground up demands high-performance graphics processing units (GPUs), vast amounts of power and highly specialized expertise – elements that are either scarce or prohibitively expensive in many GS nations. However, this limitation can be turned into an advantage. Since the GS has not invested heavily in legacy AIKM infrastructure, it is not constrained by sunk costs or outdated systems. This provides an opportunity to build more agile, localized AI solutions that are tailored to the specific needs of GS populations, without the burden of maintaining expensive legacy architectures.

The example of DeepSeek – a project that leveraged existing AI advancements to develop a regionally optimized language model – demonstrates that the GS can adopt a similar strategy. By building upon 1W research and adapting AI systems to local needs, the GS can create more efficient, cost-effective AIKM solutions that work within its constraints. This approach enables AI models to be fine-tuned with local datasets, improving accuracy, cultural relevance and accessibility. Instead of attempting to replicate 1W AI infrastructure, the GS can focus on creating lightweight, decentralized AI solutions that function effectively in environments with limited computational power and connectivity. By strategically leveraging existing AI breakthroughs, the GS can rapidly develop AIKM systems that empower local communities, drive economic growth and enhance digital inclusion without the prohibitive costs of starting from scratch.

Engineering AIKM Within Resource-Constrained Environments

AIKM solutions must be designed with the infrastructural and economic constraints of the GS in mind. Unlike the 1W, which has abundant computational power, AI-ready data centres and reliable infrastructure, GS countries face significant challenges in power availability, capital investment and network bandwidth. Therefore, AIKM systems must be tailored to operate efficiently in environments with limited resources.

Factors Affecting AIKM Solutions

The AIKM pipeline consists of two major phases: training and inferencing. Each phase has distinct computational, power and connectivity requirements.

Table 13.1. Trade-offs From Scratch-Building a Model Versus Incrementally Building Upon an Existing One.

Training Approach	Computational Needs	Power Consumption	Latency Considerations	Reliability Needs
From scratch (e.g., ChatGPT, etc.)	Massive (NVIDIA GPUs)	Extremely high	Latency irrelevant (weeks-long process)	Medium (restart possible)
Building upon an existing model (e.g., DeepSeek)	Huge (NVIDIA GPUs)	High	Latency irrelevant (dependent on pre-trained model)	Low (restart possible)

Training Phase. Training AI models is one of the most resource-intensive aspects of AIKM implementation. The approach taken – whether training a model from scratch or building upon an existing system – significantly impacts computational needs, power consumption and infrastructure requirements. See Table 13.1 for an outline of the key differences.

Training from scratch demands immense resources, making it infeasible for GS regions with limited access to high-performance GPUs and power infrastructure. Building upon existing models mitigates these challenges but still requires a strong foundational infrastructure to fine-tune AI solutions. Given the high cost and power demands of AI training, GS nations must focus on optimizing existing models and leveraging transfer learning techniques.

Inferencing Phase. Unlike training, inferencing is the process of deploying AI models for real-time decision-making. This phase is more interactive and demands low latency and high throughput to support user engagement. Table 13.2 outlines the core requirements of AI inferencing.

For AIKM to be effective in the GS, inferencing solutions should prioritize localized AI deployments, reducing dependence on remote servers and enhancing system responsiveness. This is particularly important given the limited bandwidth and high latency often experienced in many GS regions.

Characteristics of the 1W Affecting AIKM

The infrastructure and technological environment of the 1W have shaped AI development in ways that may not be directly transferable to GS contexts. Table 13.3 summarizes key characteristics that influence AIKM implementation in 1W.

Table 13.2. Requirements Arising From AI Inferencing.

Factor	**Requirement**
Computational needs	Modest but continuous
Interactivity	High (millions of requests per second)
Throughput	Critical for performance
Latency	Must be low for real-time responses
Connectivity	If model calls a remote server, high bandwidth is required. Local models reduce dependency.
Reliability	High (except in non-critical applications)

Table 13.3. Aspects of the First World (1W) Which Interact With AIKM Implementation Trade-offs.

Factor	**1W Characteristics**
Computational power	NVIDIA GPUs are widely available and affordable.
Power availability	Medium; sufficient for AI training and inferencing.
Power reliability	Medium; stable but not unlimited.
Capital investment	Readily available for AI infrastructure.
AIKM data centres	Established and AI-ready.
Network bandwidth	High in cities; lower and costly in rural areas.
Wireless traffic cost	Expensive (requires verification).
Technical expertise	Skilled workforce is abundant.

The availability of capital and infrastructure in 1W has allowed AI to flourish with significant investments in data centres, computational resources and high-speed networks. However, these conditions do not hold in the GS, necessitating a different approach to AIKM development.

Characteristics of the GS Affecting AIKM

The GS faces numerous structural limitations that impact AIKM implementation. These factors must be considered when designing AI solutions for the region. See Table 13.4 for an overview of these factors and their characteristics.

Given these limitations, AIKM development in the GS must focus on cost-effective solutions that minimize computational requirements and reduce

Table 13.4. Aspects of the Global South (GS) Which Interact With AIKM Implementation Trade-offs.

Factor	GS Characteristics
Computational power	NVIDIA GPUs are too expensive and may face export restrictions.
Power availability	Very low or in deficit.
Power reliability	Low to medium.
Capital investment	Limited, especially for AI data centres.
AIKM data centres	Non-existent or in early stages.
Network bandwidth	High in cities (intra-GS traffic) but limited to 1W; rural areas have low wired bandwidth.
Wireless traffic cost	Cheap and widely used.
Technical expertise	Scarce and expensive.

dependency on scarce resources. In particular, power shortages and unreliable internet connectivity present major barriers that must be addressed through localized AI solutions.

Adaptation Strategies: Pre-Trained Models and Local Layers

To successfully deploy AIKM systems in the GS, adaptations must be made to overcome the challenges of limited computational resources, high-power costs and inadequate AI infrastructure.

Leveraging Pre-Trained Models. Building AI models from scratch is computationally intensive and impractical for most GS regions. Instead, solutions can be built upon existing systems, similar to DeepSeek, to reduce dependency on scarce resources. Table 13.5 gives an overview of the benefits and their respective impact.

Implementing Local AI Layers. Instead of relying entirely on cloud-based AI hosted in 1W, GS nations can implement local AI layers that process data natively. These can be:

- *Second-layer AI models:* Lighter-weight models adapted for local languages and contexts.

Table 13.5. Impact of Using Models That Are Pre-Trained Elsewhere.

Benefit	Impact
Avoids need for NVIDIA GPUs	Reduces reliance on unavailable or restricted hardware.
Reduces power requirements	Training is offloaded to 1W, making AI adoption feasible.
Minimizes capital investment	No need for expensive AI-specific data centres.

- *Retrieval-Augmented Generation (RAG) models:* AI assistants that enhance responses by integrating local knowledge bases.

Table 13.6 gives an overview of the respective benefits and their impact.

Edge Computing: Powering AIKM Without Connectivity. AIKM solutions in the GS should prioritize *edge computing* – processing data on local devices instead of relying on remote servers. This helps address infrastructure limitations while ensuring reliable AIKM. Table 13.7 gives an overview of the advantages of this approach and their impact.

Conclusion

The GS can capitalize on AIKM advancements without developing models from scratch, thereby overcoming limitations in power, capital and infrastructure. By leveraging pre-trained models, building local AI layers and adopting edge computing, AI solutions can be made more accessible and functional within the GS constraints. With strategic adaptation, AIKM has the potential to drive economic and knowledge-based development across the region.

Table 13.6. Impact of Using a Local GS-Based Layer for AI Processing.

Benefit	Impact
Supports local languages	Enhances AI understanding of indigenous and GS-specific dialects.
Reduces bandwidth costs	Less data need to be transmitted internationally.
Improves latency	Faster response times by reducing reliance on offshore servers.
Requires less expertise	Easier to implement than full AI training.

Table 13.7. Impact of Using Edge, or Local Device, Computing.

Advantage	Impact
Works without internet	Essential for remote, low-connectivity regions.
Minimizes latency	Faster responses for interactive applications.
Reduces server load	Limits dependency on expensive cloud infrastructure.

Ensuring Compliance With Local Data Privacy Laws

Data privacy is a growing concern worldwide, and AI systems in the GS must be designed to comply with local regulations, such as South Africa's POPI Act. Unlike AI systems developed in the 1W, which often prioritize compliance with GDPR or US privacy laws, AI solutions for the GS need to address specific local concerns, ensuring that user data remain sovereign and protected from external misuse (Kushwaha et al., 2020).

Safeguarding Against Misinformation and External Control

AI-driven KM systems must also play a role in safeguarding digital spaces from misinformation, election manipulation and external control (Watson-Saes, 2024). By decentralizing knowledge verification and empowering local fact-checking networks, AI can help prevent the spread of disinformation campaigns that exploit digital vulnerabilities in emerging economies. Locally trained AI models that integrate community-driven validation processes can further enhance trust and digital resilience.

However, one of the biggest emerging risks is the outsourcing – particularly offshoring – of AIKM control, which creates a prime vector for external influence over a nation's information ecosystem. Currently, most AIKM innovation remains concentrated in the 1W, leading to an asymmetrical power dynamic where external entities can shape narratives, manipulate public opinion and even influence political outcomes in the GS (Kwet, 2019). The reliance on foreign-controlled AI systems for KM increases the risk of biased messaging, eroding national sovereignty over information flows and enabling covert foreign interference, particularly in sensitive areas like elections and governance.

Developing AIKM systems within the GS would help mitigate these risks, providing nations with more direct control over their digital information spaces. By keeping AI-driven knowledge tools locally governed, countries can work to maintain unbiased messaging, curtail election manipulation and strengthen the integrity of their digital ecosystems. However, this also introduces the risk that the same mechanisms designed to prevent external manipulation could be repurposed by governments to suppress dissent, control populations and entrench authoritarian regimes. Without proper safeguards, state-controlled AIKM systems could become tools for censorship and digital repression rather than instruments of truth and transparency.

To strike a balance, AI-driven KM solutions in the GS must be designed with robust accountability measures, transparency protocols and decentralized governance structures. Community-driven verification processes and independent oversight mechanisms can help ensure that these AI tools serve the public good rather than becoming instruments of political control. By prioritizing open-source AIKM models, collaborative governance and international ethical standards, the GS can develop resilient KM ecosystems that both protect against external manipulation and safeguard against domestic authoritarian misuse.

Connecting Entrepreneurial Ecosystems Through AI

One of the persistent challenges in the GS's economic landscape is the fragmentation of entrepreneurial networks. AI-driven KM systems can help bridge these gaps by facilitating targeted and topic-driven networking, connecting innovators, investors and mentors across different regions. AI-powered matchmaking tools can identify synergies, reducing the inefficiencies caused by isolated business ecosystems and fostering cross-sector collaboration.

By addressing these critical areas, AIKM systems in the GS cannot only overcome existing challenges but also establish a foundation for long-term digital sovereignty, economic resilience and inclusive growth.

Boosting KM Efficiency Across Key Sectors

The implementation of AIKM systems is revolutionizing three critical development pillars in the GS, enhancing efficiency, inclusivity and economic growth. Given the unique challenges faced by businesses in the GS – such as fragmented markets, inefficiencies in supply chains and underdeveloped infrastructure – AI-driven KM solutions can significantly mitigate operational inefficiencies and drive measurable improvements across cost, time and accuracy.

Financial inclusion initiatives are leveraging AI to create sophisticated mentorship networks that not only match entrepreneurs with advisors but also analyze business plans in local languages using natural language processing. This allows for customized guidance tailored to specific market conditions and cultural contexts. Additionally, AI can expand access to credit by integrating informal lending systems, such as rotating savings and credit associations (ROSCAs) into digital platforms. By pooling resources digitally, AI makes informal financial behaviours visible to formal lenders, enabling the creation of alternative credit scoring models based on indigenous lending practices. This, in turn, stimulates formal lending, supporting small businesses that might otherwise be excluded from traditional banking. AI-driven business process automation further enhances efficiency by reducing administrative burdens, improving transaction accuracy and streamlining operations.

Education and skills development can be democratized through AI-powered learning platforms that not only translate but also reconstruct educational materials to reflect local examples, cultural contexts and adaptive learning approaches. These systems improve efficiency by personalizing content to individual learning styles, reducing time wasted on ineffective learning methods. Additionally, AI can ensure better representation of underrepresented communities by incorporating indigenous knowledge, historical perspectives and regional dialects into educational materials, thereby making learning more relevant and accessible. However, for AI-driven knowledge processes to be effective, there must be a capable and willing workforce. The success of AIKM hinges on three key factors: (1) a skilled AIKM implementation force, (2) a workforce that can collaborate with AI in knowledge processes and (3) a workforce that does not feel disempowered or threatened by AI integration.

To achieve these success factors, AIKM systems must be designed specifically for the GS, embedding local languages, business processes and unique workflows by default. Unlike off-the-shelf solutions from the 1W, GS-native AIKM models can integrate seamlessly into existing business structures, making change management significantly easier and driving higher adoption rates. Moreover, AI-driven innovation in the GS should focus on creating new job categories that align with local economic transitions – moving from largely manual or industrial labour markets towards knowledge-based economies. In Africa, for instance, AIKM could enable a leapfrogging effect similar to the mobile banking revolution, bypassing traditional inefficiencies and accelerating the shift towards data-driven economic growth.

Healthcare knowledge distribution is being transformed through AI-powered health advisors that merge codified medical knowledge with localized health insights. These systems create hybrid knowledge bases that respect traditional healing practices while integrating evidence-based medicine, ensuring a culturally sensitive approach to healthcare. AI-driven health assistants can improve accuracy in diagnosis, reduce the burden on overworked healthcare systems and provide timely medical advice, even in remote areas with limited access to healthcare professionals. Furthermore, AI-powered decision-making systems can improve hospital and clinic efficiency by optimizing resource allocation, reducing diagnostic errors and automating administrative processes.

By enhancing efficiency in business operations, improving the accuracy of decision-making processes and better representing diverse groups in AI systems, these AI-driven KM solutions are fostering sustainable development. They provide a pathway for small businesses to thrive, for individuals to access personalized education and for communities to receive more effective healthcare – all while respecting the unique socio-economic and cultural dynamics of the GS.

AI for Knowledge Discovery and Cultural Preservation

The fusion of classical AI models with modern large language models (LLMs) is unlocking unprecedented approaches to knowledge discovery, particularly in the GS. By training AI systems on African datasets, we are uncovering patterns and insights that might otherwise remain hidden, allowing for more accurate and locally relevant AI applications. These hybrid AI systems are especially powerful in identifying and documenting tacit knowledge – the unwritten wisdom that forms the foundation of many African communities. Through natural language processing of recorded oral histories, analysis of traditional practices and pattern recognition in community behaviours, AI is playing a crucial role in preserving and propagating cultural knowledge that is at risk of being lost due to urbanization and modernization.

A key advancement in this AI-driven knowledge discovery is the expansion of broader language support for the GS. By training AI models on diverse linguistic datasets, including indigenous and underrepresented languages, we can develop systems that serve a far greater population, ensuring digital inclusivity. Unlike conventional AI models that primarily cater to dominant global languages, these locally trained models can process and generate content in a wide range of dialects, bridging linguistic gaps and fostering digital literacy.

Furthermore, these AI advancements allow the GS to leapfrog existing AI systems that were not designed with its unique needs in mind. Instead of retrofitting Western-centric AI models, developing homegrown AI solutions enables a direct leap into more advanced, culturally attuned AI applications. By integrating oral traditions and indigenous knowledge into AI frameworks, the GS can build a competitive and sovereign AI ecosystem that serves its people while also contributing novel insights to global AI research. This approach not only preserves cultural heritage but also empowers communities with AI tools that are both relevant and transformative, positioning the GS at the forefront of the next wave of AI-driven innovation.

Integrating Traditional Knowledge With Future Trends

The future of AIKM in the GS lies in seamlessly integrating modern technology with traditional knowledge systems while safeguarding and building upon indigenous knowledge. By leveraging AI to document, preserve and enhance community-driven knowledge, we can create systems that not only recognize but also empower local wisdom. Crowd-sourced KM platforms enable communities to validate and enrich AI-generated insights, ensuring that knowledge remains rooted in local realities rather than being imposed from external perspectives. These systems are particularly effective when combined with distributed KM architectures, which guarantee accessibility even in low-connectivity environments, allowing knowledge to remain decentralized and within community control.

A crucial aspect of this shift is the diminished dominance of Western-centric KM models, fostering a more decolonized, locally relevant AI ecosystem

(Mohamed et al., 2020). By prioritizing the development of AI models trained on African, Latin American and other GS datasets, these technologies reflect local cultures, languages and socio-economic realities rather than being filtered through Western frameworks. This not only strengthens digital sovereignty but also builds trust and identity systems that are grounded in regional contexts. AI-driven trust frameworks can help formalize indigenous knowledge-sharing networks while also creating secure digital identities that empower individuals and businesses within their local economies.

Additionally, AI-driven KM systems have a vital role to play in immunizing the GS against misinformation, election manipulation and external digital control. By enabling decentralized verification processes and ensuring that information is cross validated by local communities, AI can help kerb the spread of disinformation campaigns that often exploit digital vulnerabilities in developing regions. AI coaching networks further enhance this by blending customized AI insights with human networking, ensuring that knowledge transfer remains authentic, community-driven and resistant to external manipulation. By developing AI systems that respect and uplift indigenous knowledge while protecting digital spaces from exploitation, the GS can create a more sovereign, resilient and culturally attuned AI landscape.

Conclusion: Building Resilient, Inclusive AIKM for the GS

The integration of AIKM solutions in the GS presents a transformative opportunity to bridge knowledge gaps, enhance efficiency and foster sustainable development. Throughout this chapter, we have explored how AIKM can address key challenges in financial inclusion, education, healthcare and business operations by tailoring AI solutions to the unique socio-economic and infrastructural realities of the region.

AI-driven KM solutions have the potential to *improve efficiency across multiple sectors* by reducing operational costs, optimizing decision-making processes and streamlining workflows. In business, AIKM can minimize inefficiencies that often result from fragmented markets, underdeveloped infrastructure and limited access to expert knowledge. By automating critical tasks, improving accuracy in business processes, and supporting a more data-driven approach, AIKM helps organizations in the GS enhance productivity and competitiveness. Additionally, AI-powered mentorship and financial inclusion systems, particularly through microlending and alternative credit scoring, can support small businesses and entrepreneurs in securing the resources needed for growth.

A central theme of this chapter has been the *importance of building AI solutions that are contextually relevant* and designed for the GS rather than relying on 1W AI models that fail to address local linguistic, cultural and technological challenges. AIKM systems must be developed using training data that accurately reflect the diversity of the region, ensuring that AI solutions are not only accessible but also inclusive. The ability to process and generate knowledge in local languages, integrate indigenous knowledge systems and accommodate informal business practices will be key to making AIKM widely effective.

Additionally, AIKM must be designed to *work within the limitations of the GS's infrastructure,* ensuring functionality in low-bandwidth environments, optimizing power consumption and leveraging decentralized models to reduce dependence on external cloud computing resources. As demonstrated in previous sections, AIKM solutions that adopt lightweight, edge-computing models will be best positioned to serve communities with intermittent connectivity while ensuring that knowledge remains locally controlled and not subject to external digital manipulation.

Beyond operational efficiency, AIKM systems have the power to *safeguard digital ecosystems and protect against misinformation and external influence.* By decentralizing knowledge verification and integrating community-driven validation processes, AIKM can play a crucial role in maintaining the integrity of information networks. However, this must be balanced carefully to prevent AI from becoming a tool for state control or censorship. Ensuring that AI-driven KM systems remain transparent, decentralized and governed by ethical frameworks will be critical to their long-term success in supporting democratic knowledge access.

Looking ahead, *the future of AIKM in the GS will depend on how effectively these systems integrate with traditional knowledge frameworks* while driving forward economic and technological progress. The ability to harness AI for financial inclusion, education, healthcare and business development will require continued innovation, investment and a focus on local capacity-building. Governments, businesses and AI developers must work together to ensure that AIKM is designed and implemented in a way that empowers communities, strengthens digital sovereignty and contributes to equitable, long-term development.

By embracing a *home-grown, context-aware approach to AIKM,* the GS can not only overcome the challenges of AI adoption but also position itself as a leader in knowledge-driven innovation. Through strategic implementation, AIKM can serve as a powerful catalyst for economic transformation, enabling the GS to leapfrog traditional development models and build a more inclusive, efficient and sustainable future.

References

Aker, J. C., & Mbiti, I. M. (2010). Mobile phones and economic development in Africa. *The Journal of Economic Perspectives*, *24*(3), 207–232.

Eubanks, V. (2018). *Automating inequality: How high-tech tools profile, police, and punish the poor*. St. Martin's Press.

GSMA. (2023). *The mobile economy: Sub-Saharan Africa 2023*. GSMA Intelligence.

Kushwaha, N., Roguski, P., & Watson, B. W. (2020). Up in the air: Ensuring government data sovereignty in the cloud. In *Proceedings of the 12th international conference on cyber conflict*. NATO CCDCOE Publications.

Kwet, M. (2019). Digital colonialism: US empire and the new imperialism in the Global South. *Race & Class*, *60*(4), 3–26.

Marivate, V., Sefara, T., Chabalala, V., Makhaya, K., Mokgonyane, T., Mokoena, R., & Abubakar, A. (2020). Investigating an approach for low resource language dataset creation, curation and classification: Setswana and Sepedi. In *Proceedings of the first workshop on resources for African indigenous languages* (pp. 15–20). https://doi.org/10.48550/arXiv.2003.04986

Mohamed, S., Png, M. T., & Isaac, W. (2020). Decolonial AI: Decolonial theory as sociotechnical foresight in artificial intelligence. *Philosophy & Technology*, *33*, 659–684.

Russ, M. (2018). Knowledge management for sustainable development in the era of continuously accelerating technological revolutions. *Journal of the Knowledge Economy*, *9*(4), 1124–1149.

Unwin, T. (2017). *Reclaiming information and communication technologies for development*. Oxford University Press.

Watson-Saes, N. Y. (2024). THREAT2023 conference: Navigating cyber threats and AI opportunities for a brighter digital future. *Quest. Opening AI*, *20*(1), 11–13.

World Economic Forum. (2023). How Africa's youth will drive global growth. https://www.weforum.org/stories/2023/08/africa-youth-global-growth-digital-economy/

Chapter 14

Artificial Intelligence and Knowledge Management Systems: Transforming the Future of Business Operations in the Fourth Industrial Revolution

Rashmi Kumari, Sujata Priyambada Dash and Rajeshwari Chatterjee

Birla Institute of Technology, India

Abstract

The world is undergoing significant transformations due to the Fourth Industrial Revolution (4IR). At the heart of this revolution is artificial intelligence (AI), which is rapidly becoming an integral component in business operations, decision-making, and knowledge management (KM). This chapter aims to delve into how AI is revolutionizing business knowledge management systems (KMS) by enhancing data processing, decision-making capabilities, and overall organizational competitiveness. Thise chapter will explore the emerging and distinctive features of AI's role in improving and advancing KMS within corporate organizations. It will address the potential benefits and challenges of integrating AI into KMS, focusing on how businesses can leverage this technology to make informed decisions, secure competitive advantages, and navigate the evolving landscape of digital commerce. This research is grounded in a Systematic Literature Review (SLR), conducted using the Preferred Reporting Items for Systematic Reviews and Meta-Analyses (PRISMA) approach. By selecting 21 key research papers from databases like Scopus, Web of Science, and ScienceDirect, the chapter examines the role of AI in KM over the past decade (2014–2024). The focus areas include AI applications in KMS, the implications of these technologies on business processes, and ethical considerations such as data privacy and security. The findings emphasize AI's transformative role in knowledge management by enhancing information

AI-Driven Knowledge Management Assets, Volume 2, 285–303

Published under exclusive licence by Emerald Publishing Limited
doi:10.1108/978-1-83662-778-420261014

processing and enabling real-time decision-making. Moreover they highlight AI's potential to improve organizational agility, adaptability, and competitiveness through data-driven insights, while also underscoring the importance of data privacy and ethical considerations.

Keywords: Artificial intelligence; knowledge management systems; fourth industrial revolution; business operations; data security; ethical AI; systematic literature review; PRISMA

Introduction

The world is set to undergo a major shift due to the fourth industrial revolution, which will affect the way people connect, work, and live. AI remains in an evolving stage, requiring further advancements to reach its full potential in the current technological landscape. Similar to the introduction of electricity in the Second Industrial Revolution, the Fourth Industrial Revolution is expected to be driven by the rise of intelligent technologies (Leoni et al., 2022).

There are numerous applications involving AI (Brynjolfsson & Mcafee, 2017). By exchanging information, the objective is to provide intelligent goods, services, and experiences in order to provide the optimal and long-term value (Gretzel et al., 2015). However, since AI is still in its infancy, it is difficult to precisely forecast what will happen. AI's demands and expectations such as ensuring equity, generating employment, upholding moral principles, educating the public, encouraging cooperation, and evolving over time, must be taken into account in order to fully understand and effectively use it (Kaplan & Haenlein, 2019a, 2019b).

In contrast, KM originated in the management domain before gradually expanding to other domains such as healthcare and information technology. Over time, this idea has been interpreted and adapted distinctly by various sectors. KM, according to the American Productivity & Quality Center (APQC), is the process of imparting the appropriate knowledge to the appropriate individuals at the appropriate time in order to enhance their output and services. According to Wiig (1997), it is a novel approach to enhancing the inventiveness and resilience of companies.

People, technology, and processes are the three main components of KM (Geisler & Wickramasinghe, 2015). Seventy percent of KM success can be attributed to the people or the human factor. This is due to the fact that knowledge is created and disseminated by humans. Creating, storing, sharing, transferring, and using knowledge are all practical components of KM that are governed by processes, which account for 20% of the total. The other component, technology, makes it possible for people to complete these procedures and guarantees that knowledge is accessible whenever and wherever it is required.

Since KM and AI include the creation, organization, and use of information to foster creativity, produce insights, and gain a competitive advantage, they can be considered types of knowledge. Combining AI and KM systems has the potential to work in concert, increasing the effectiveness of knowledge acquisition, organization, and dissemination (Liebowitz, 2000; Mårtensson, 2000). AI gives computers and other devices the ability to acquire, comprehend, and utilize knowledge to carry out tasks, which aids in improved decision-making processes. While KM guarantees that knowledge is well understood, AI enables information to grow, be used, be created, and uncover knowledge in ways that may not even be conceivable (Goncharova & Murach, 2020). Artificial intelligence is an essential component of creating and enhancing knowledge management, despite the fact that some people may not give it enough thought (Wu & Hu, 2018).

This chapter explores the transformative role of AI in Knowledge Management Systems (KMS) by comparing AI-driven KMS with traditional knowledge management frameworks. Traditional KMS rely on manual data entry, rule-based systems, and human-driven decision-making, often leading to inefficiencies in processing large volumes of information. In contrast, AI-powered KMS leverages machine learning, natural language processing, and automation to enhance data analysis, retrieval, and decision-making. By integrating AI, organizations can streamline knowledge-sharing, improve accuracy, and drive innovation. This comparison highlights AI's potential to revolutionize knowledge management, making businesses more agile, adaptive, and competitive in the digital era. The chapter will also examine the new and unique aspects of AI's contribution to the development and enhancement of KMS in business settings. It will discuss the possible advantages and difficulties of incorporating AI into KMS, with an emphasis on how companies may use this technology to secure competitive advantages, make well-informed decisions, and negotiate the changing terrain of online commerce.

Research Gap

Despite the growing body of literature on AI-driven Knowledge Management Systems (KMS), significant gaps remain in understanding their full impact on business organizations. Existing research has primarily focused on AI's technical capabilities in enhancing knowledge retrieval, automation, and decision-making. However, several critical areas require further exploration.

One major gap is the strategic integration of AI in KMS. While AI applications in KM have been explored, there is limited research on how businesses can strategically integrate AI into existing KMS frameworks to maximize efficiency and innovation. A systematic approach to implementation, adoption challenges, and best practices remains underexplored. Businesses need clear strategies for incorporating AI into their KM practices to enhance organizational learning and knowledge-sharing. Another overlooked area is AI's role in real-time knowledge processing. Most studies focus on AI's ability to store, retrieve, and organize knowledge, but few have analyzed its impact on real-time decision-making and knowledge evolution in dynamic business environments. Organizations increasingly require AI-driven KMS that can process and analyze vast amounts of data in real time, yet research on this topic remains scarce.

Ethical and governance challenges in AI-driven KMS also need more in-depth investigation. While ethical concerns such as bias, algorithmic transparency, and accountability are widely discussed, specific guidelines and frameworks for ensuring responsible AI adoption are still underdeveloped. There is a pressing need for research on how organizations can implement responsible AI policies without compromising efficiency or trustworthiness.

Additionally, there is a lack of empirical studies assessing the effectiveness of AI in KMS. Many discussions around AI's impact on knowledge management remain theoretical, with limited quantitative or qualitative evidence to measure improvements in decision-making speed, organizational agility, and competitive advantage. Metrics for evaluating AI's role in KM processes are ambiguous, making it difficult for businesses to assess the return on investment in AI-driven KMS. The long-term implications of AI-driven KMS on workforce dynamics and KM practices also remain underexplored. While AI automates many knowledge-intensive tasks, its effect on human roles, reskilling needs, and human-AI collaboration in decision-making is still unclear. More research is needed to understand how businesses can prepare employees to work effectively alongside AI-driven KM tools. Finally, security and data privacy concerns in AI-enabled KMS require further investigation. While data privacy and security are recognized challenges, research has yet to provide clear methodologies for balancing AI-powered knowledge access with stringent data protection regulations and ethical AI usage. Businesses need more guidance on how to safeguard sensitive information while leveraging AI to enhance KM processes.

This chapter aims to bridge these research gaps by conducting a systematic literature review (SLR) that not only consolidates existing knowledge but also highlights emerging trends, best practices, and potential future directions for AI-driven KMS in businesses.

Research Question

The chapter will be structured around four key research questions:

RQ1. How has AI contributed to enhancing business KM systems?

RQ2. In what ways can AI help organizations make more informed and strategic decisions?

RQ3. What are the major benefits of integrating AI into KMS for corporate organizations, particularly in the context of maintaining competitiveness in a rapidly changing business environment?

RQ4. What are the ethical concerns and vulnerabilities associated with AI-driven KMS, especially in terms of data security and responsible AI practices?

Methodology

Data Extraction

A thorough SLR that adheres to the exacting Preferred Reporting Items for Systematic Reviews and Meta-Analyses (PRISMA) methodology served as the foundation for this study. After a rigorous selection process that included 21 key research papers from credible databases such as Scopus, Web of Science, and ScienceDirect, the chapter explores how AI is changing in the field of KM over the specified period of 2014–2024. The investigation includes a detailed examination of the different aspects of integrating AI into KMS, illuminating its diverse applications, the revolutionary impact these technologies have on organizational operations and workflows, and the crucial ethical issues that come with this digital revolution, with a particular emphasis on data security and privacy concerns.

Keyword Selection

To conduct this detailed search, a specific set of keywords was meticulously curated to yield precise results. This entailed utilizing terms like "AI," "artificial intelligence," "decision support system," and "business intelligence" in combination with operators to refine the search. Concurrently, the search criteria encompassed phrases such as "knowledge management system," "KMS," and "organizational knowledge management system" to capture the essence of organizational knowledge management within the context of business or enterprise settings. Importantly, the temporal scope of the search spanned from 2014 to 2024, providing a decade-long horizon to gather a contemporary and relevant assortment of articles and studies for analysis and synthesis.

Search Strategy

The following three databases were the initial focus of the search: Web of Science provided 34 entries, Scopus produced 808 entries, and ScienceDirect produced 272 records. Duplicates were eliminated from the original 1,114 elements to ensure the validity of the dataset to be used. Following a methodical processing of the items, articles published prior to 2014 or beyond 2024 were eliminated first, followed by the removal of other things that did not align with the research goal. 876 items were eliminated after looking at more recent publications and removing different genres like reviews, conference papers, book chapters, case reports, and discussions. It was decided to keep only freely accessible items, and those that weren't in English were removed.

Search Criteria

Using the inclusion and exclusion criteria listed in Table 14.1, 162 records were meticulously examined at this stage. Of them, 82 papers were identified as

Table 14.1. Inclusion and Exclusion Criteria.

Criteria Type	Criteria
Inclusion	• Studies based on empirical research • Research on business and knowledge management systems • Peer-reviewed publications • Articles with open access • Studies from 2014 to 2024 period • Written in English
Exclusion	• Studies before 2014 • Papers with unmatched keywords • Work-in-progress papers • Book chapters

pertinent to the study's objective and subjected to a comprehensive review. After this assessment, 21 publications were selected for the systematic literature review from 61 articles that did not sufficiently address the study themes. Fig. 14.1 also illustrates the review process.

Results

The number of publications published between 2014 and 2024 is displayed in Fig. 14.2. The quantity of articles shows a distinct upward and downward trend. In

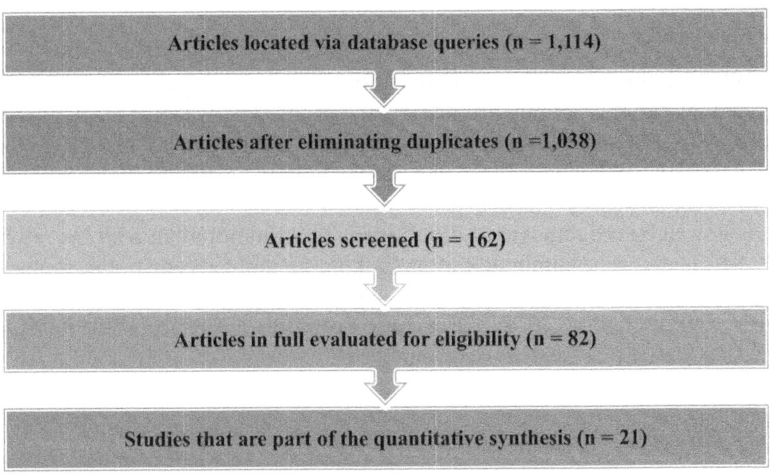

Fig. 14.1. PRISMA Workflow Diagram.

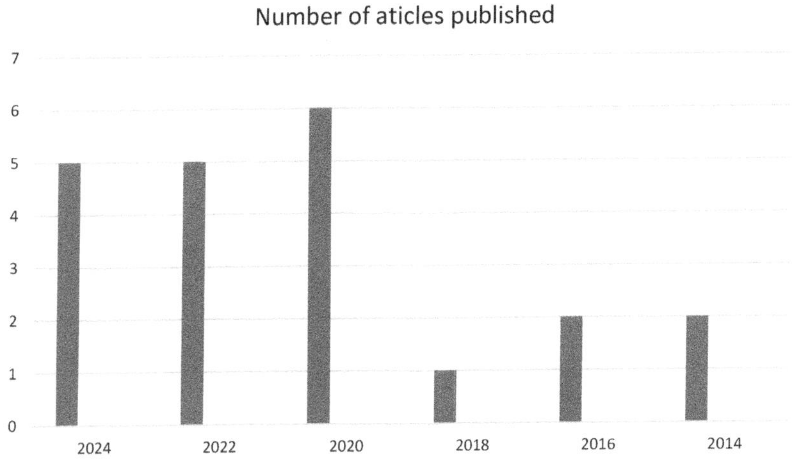

Fig. 14.2. Articles Published Each Year From 2014 to 2024.

2018, the year with the fewest publications on the combination of AI and KM in business, the review of the papers started. However, the quantity of papers on this subject has been rising year after year. 2020 saw a huge shift, most likely as a result of the COVID-19 pandemic's profound effects and all of its ramifications. Even though many organizations were having difficulties, more study was conducted on how AI and KM might be crucial in improving businesses, and that year had the highest number of articles. Following that, the number of articles continued to rise, primarily due to the fact that more companies including smaller ones, began using AI to streamline their operations, particularly in the face of interruptions like the pandemic. This continuous rise in articles indicates that companies are realizing the benefits of the AI-KM synergy for their operations.

The overall number of contributions made by researchers worldwide, the majority of whom are headquartered in the United Kingdom, is depicted in Fig. 14.3. This suggests that several studies were carried out all across the world. It's also noteworthy that authors from Europe expressed a great deal of interest, followed by those from Australia, India, and the United States. This could be because the UK is a significant economic force that is impacted by technology advancement and AI initiatives, along with the USA, India, and European nations.

Fig. 14.4 graph illustrates the data that researchers gathered regarding the impact of AI on KMS in enterprises. Each bar denotes a distinct method used by the researcher to collect data, such as data analysis, qualitative analysis, conceptual/model templates, literature reviews, or quantitative approaches. As can be seen from the graph, the researchers employed a range of techniques to investigate the function of AI in KMS for business. This demonstrates the

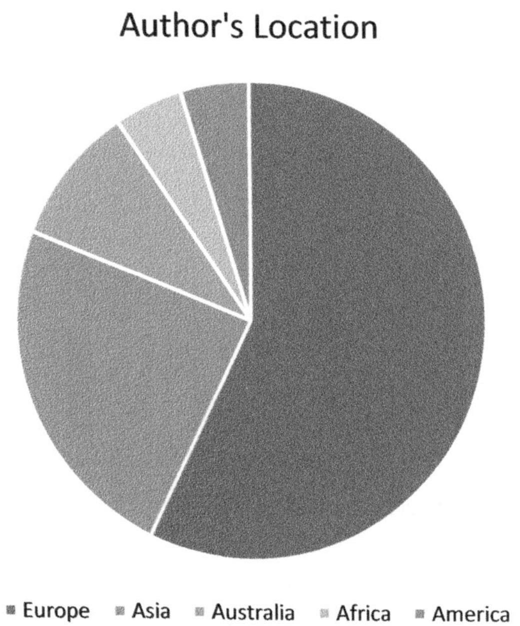

Fig. 14.3. Authors' Nationalities and Demographic Representation.

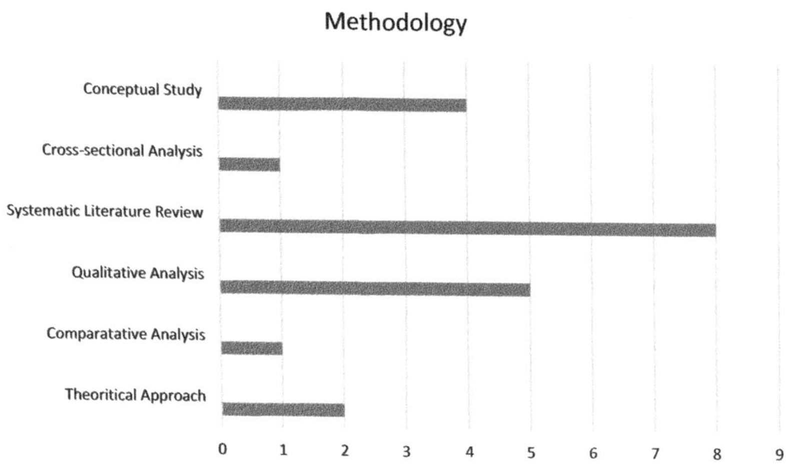

Fig. 14.4. Articles Methodologies Representation.

study's complexity and the need to employ a variety of research techniques in order to fully comprehend the various ways AI affects corporate KMS.

Advantages of AI on KMS in Businesses

Knowledge serves as the core foundation for both KM and AI. Machine learning (ML), knowledge acquisition, and the application of knowledge in a variety of processes for job completion are all made possible by AI. It opens up knowledge, making it accessible to people and improving decision-making. In essence, KM and AI are entwined parts of the same idea. According to Haenlein and Kaplan (2019), KM makes it possible to understand what is known, but AI makes it possible to apply, expand, and create new information in previously unheard-of ways. The need for systems that facilitate the creation and use of knowledge is highlighted by the recognition that knowledge is the most important strategic resource. The authors point out that general organizational process management is intrinsically linked to knowledge management in organizations (Bitkowska, 2020; Criado-García et al., 2020; Moreno et al., 2015).

The studies highlight the importance of AI across a range of industry areas. By encouraging competition and making it easier to adopt innovations and learning systems, the integration of AI systems is especially important in the service sector. Chen and Chen (2013) present a suggested decision support system that may be applied to a number of different industries and is intended to smoothly integrate ideas that foster innovation in the service sector. Either enhancing human talents or completely systematizing corporate processes might improve their performance. For instance, robotic process automation (RPA) automates repetitive administrative operations with a wide range of uses, such as creating energy bills, verifying insurance premiums, and keeping personnel records, by doing away with the need for humans to perform tedious data entry work (Lacity & Willcocks, 2016). Online information sharing has a mediating role in the relationship between leadership and employee outcomes, according to earlier research (Choi et al., 2016; Ma et al., 2013). Online information sharing is advantageous because it helps workers with work-related problems, stimulates their minds, and promotes innovative problem-solving (Singh et al., 2021). According to Gupta and Polonsky (2014), employees who actively participate in online information sharing are also exposed to beneficial organizational learning possibilities.

Our knowledge of how these technologies benefit businesses and workers and impact digital competitiveness is expanded by the junction of AI-KS (Eslami et al., 2019; Gupta & Polonsky, 2014; Ma & Brown, 2020; Russell & Norvig, 2016, Turner & Kuczynski, 2019). In this context, AI refers to intelligent assistance systems that use algorithms, natural language processing, ML, and human intelligence to assist human tasks and decision-making (Akkiraju et al., 2006; De Boeck et al., 2018). These systems provide crucial information from the company and its environment.

Disadvantages of AI on KMS in Businesses

Considering its sole focus on Vietnamese business-to-business (B2B) enterprises, the study by Nguyen et al. (2024) admits its limits in terms of generalizability. Additionally, it acknowledges the limitations of convenience and cross-sectional sampling and suggests more varied and long-term research. The study also emphasizes how online knowledge-sharing can foster employee innovation. Last but not least, it highlights the significance of different leadership philosophies, stressing that in addition to transformational and transactional leadership, creative leadership plays a major role in encouraging a variety of knowledge-sharing activities.

In spite of the wealth of studies on AI and personal management, there are still several areas that may require more investigation. Future research could examine the ideal demand-source balance for AI deployment, based on the work demands-resources model (Bakker & Demerouti, 2007). Investigating the best time and method to introduce AI to managers whether through internal training or incorporation into current performance development review (PDR) procedures is part of this. Researchers can also look into the need for businesses to hire AI experts to work with managers on performance management procedures and policies. If hiring AI experts is thought to be appropriate, it is important to investigate whether their responsibilities could conflict with managers' decision-making. Future research attempts by scholars are urged to address these topics.

Thorough consideration is necessary for the successful implementation of AI, and managers are responsible for learning about AI and understanding its real-world applications. As noted by Rousseau (1989) and George (2009), it is important to deploy AI in a way that actively engages employees rather than making them feel threatened in order to preserve a healthy psychological relationship with them. When discussing AI's limitations in business KMS, it's critical to acknowledge that AI depends on human expertise to solve some problems. Its incapacity to independently enhance this knowledge via practical experiences without human intervention is a significant drawback, though. As highlighted by Mallach (2000), the technology is purposefully made to support humans rather than to replace them. According to observations by Alavi and Leidner (2001), it is a useful tool for professionals to obtain organizational knowledge for resolving business issues or locating internal expertise, but it is insufficient for putting decisions into action. According to Xiao and Benbasat (2007), the human component is still important because AI recommendations still need to be assessed and decisions about their use must be made.

Implementation of AI in Business

In terms of strategies, one of the most unusual and creative contributions made by AI tools and technology is the capacity to affect consumer attitudes and behavior. Social media platforms allow access to a wealth of information on customer preferences and decisions about particular goods and services offered by the company. By analyzing such data with sophisticated algorithms like machine learning and deep learning, businesses may enhance their results and develop successful consumer interaction strategies. Stated differently, it improves the capacity to develop a variety of tactics to effectively engage customers. AI's increasing strategic importance contributes subtly to the improvement of goods and services. AI supports the ongoing process in which customer interactions actively contribute to the formation of new perceptions through dynamic social media knowledge-sharing systems, supporting an approach to continuous development (Olan et al., 2022).

AI has many applications, and its strategic application is not just restricted to customer-focused areas. Organizations use AI in the fields of innovation and KM to solve problems with job security and knowledge sharing. In actuality, AI significantly contributes to improving leadership practices by fostering organizational innovation, bridging the gap between various leadership philosophies, and utilizing the contemporary setting of online knowledge-sharing (Nguyen et al., 2024). The effectiveness and efficiency of operations are greatly impacted by the strategic use of AI. The organization's performance improves when AI-powered processes, tools, and HRM strategies are implemented. This comprehensive approach, driven by AI, impacts not just employee engagement, cognitive growth, and behavior, but also the company's social elements (Olan et al., 2024).

As a key player in business process management, AI is recognized by software developers for its strategic significance. A further indication of industry-wide awareness of AI's potential to transform management practices is the financial services sector's strong interest in the technology (Bitkowska et al., 2022). The use of AI in knowledge production, exchange, and usage is one crucial strategic necessity. Its function extends beyond altering system behavior; it also involves enhancing problem-solving efficiency and offering intricate assistance for cooperative robots. This strategic partnership with AI demonstrates how AI has shaped the contemporary business environment and significantly influences a range of knowledge-related jobs in enterprises (Bencsik, 2021). By encouraging knowledge application, sharing, and learning, AI demonstrates its strategic value in the manufacturing industry. AI's tactical integration into operational processes is demonstrated by the way that its deployment enhances industrial performance and supply chain management (Leoni et al., 2022).

In conclusion, the deliberate incorporation of AI into contemporary business practices is poised to usher in a transformational era. Whether it is used for knowledge management, innovation, operational efficiency, or customer interaction initiatives, artificial intelligence (AI) is a vital component that propels enterprises toward a dynamic and resilient future in the marketplace.

Discussion

Researchers were able to methodically choose and gain access to a collection of 21 scholarly articles by using a particular and stringent review technique. Each article was chosen for its unique viewpoint and its unique scientific methodology. Creating a polyhedric image of the prospective effects of AI on KMS in businesses and the numerous associated reflection prompts has been the main objective of this work. Coombs et al. (2020) draw attention to AI's contribution to improving security and compliance, which is comparable to the findings of other researchers like Rodrigues (2020), who debate the difficulties AI encounters in ever-changing security environments or the difficulties in guaranteeing data protection across jurisdictions. Concerns regarding the necessity for transparent algorithms, cybersecurity risks, potential unfairness and bias, the challenges of challenging findings, and issues with AI's legal status are raised when implementing AI in legal and human rights situations.

The impact of AI on process quality, overall effectiveness, and customer satisfaction in the Polish market is the focus of Bitkowska (2020), which may be compared to studies conducted in other markets or sectors where the impact of AI may be less noticeable or may present different challenges when it comes to data privacy, security, and ethical considerations (Elendu et al., 2023). It is possible to compare Bencsik's (2021) technique with earlier research in the field because it deviates from conventional theory-based methodologies and prioritizes empirical, case-based research in AI-driven business innovation with KM. However, Haidar (2024) emphasizes how theoretical frameworks are still useful for comprehending the intricacies of integrating AI and KM.

According to other research in the field, Olan et al. (2022) expressed concerns regarding AI in KM, namely resource constraints for continuous learning, integration issues, and data quality needs, as well as ethical concerns like privacy and data security. For instance, some research might highlight how new ethical frameworks and privacy laws are reducing the risks associated with AI in KM, or how contemporary AI technologies are better addressing integration and data quality issues. In addition to highlighting the significance of ethical frameworks and privacy legislation in reducing the hazards associated with AI, Mohammad et al. (2023) offer insights into the possible advantages and difficulties of adopting AI in KM. However, in spite of the many benefits, the authors recognized that the use of AI in KMS may have certain drawbacks, difficulties, and issues. The use of human knowledge in decision-making and the necessity of cautious integration to prevent employee resistance are major concerns. The study also emphasizes how critical it is to address the constraints of AI's capacity for self-directed learning in the absence of human intervention. According to research by Jain et al. (2024), the fascinating role of AI in organizations can therefore be linked to a wide range of strategic contributions, from influencing consumer attitudes and behavior to improving goods and services. The authors have demonstrated how AI's influence on KM, innovation, and organizational leadership techniques improves a company's overall social elements as well as its operational success.

The systematic review's conclusion focuses on how companies plan to investigate this new area, where artificial intelligence is becoming a crucial tool for innovation in the KMS process. Implementing suggested techniques that take ethical concerns regarding a positive and productive adoption of AI in the changing business environment into consideration would directly improve the cycle of production, creativity, and market competitiveness.

Managerial Implications

Managers must take a structured approach when integrating AI into Knowledge Management Systems (KMS). AI should not be viewed as a standalone tool but as a strategic asset that aligns with business objectives to enhance efficiency and innovation. Without a clear integration strategy, AI adoption may result in fragmented systems that fail to maximize organizational knowledge-sharing. AI-driven KMS significantly improves decision-making and provides a competitive advantage by enabling real-time data analysis and predictive analytics. Organizations that effectively leverage AI for intelligent automation and decision support can improve operational agility and maintain a strong position in dynamic markets. However, managers must ensure that AI tools are reliable, accurate, and tailored to business needs.

Another critical managerial consideration is ethical AI governance. Business leaders must establish robust frameworks to ensure AI operates transparently and responsibly. Addressing concerns such as data privacy, bias, and algorithmic transparency is crucial for regulatory compliance and maintaining trust among stakeholders. Without proper governance, AI-driven knowledge systems may inadvertently reinforce biases or compromise sensitive information. Workforce adaptation and AI literacy are essential for successful AI adoption in KMS. AI should complement human expertise rather than replace it, and organizations must invest in employee training and AI literacy programs. Encouraging AI-human collaboration will help employees adapt to new knowledge management processes and optimize the use of AI-powered tools. A cross-functional implementation approach is necessary for an AI-driven KMS to be effective across an organization. While IT departments often lead AI integration, other business functions, including HR, marketing, and customer service, should also be involved. A collaborative, interdisciplinary approach ensures that AI enhances various business processes, making knowledge more accessible and actionable.

Finally, organizations should establish key performance indicators (KPIs) to continuously monitor AI's impact on knowledge management. Regular evaluations will help businesses optimize AI applications, ensuring sustained improvements in decision-making, efficiency, and knowledge-sharing practices. Without proper monitoring, AI implementation may not yield the expected long-term benefits.

Practical Implications

AI-driven KMS improves knowledge accessibility by streamlining information retrieval. Employees spend less time searching for data, which enhances productivity and collaboration across departments. AI tools such as chatbots, recommendation systems, and semantic search engines make it easier for users to find relevant knowledge in real time, improving workflow efficiency. Data security and compliance are crucial when implementing AI in knowledge management. Businesses must ensure that AI-enabled KMS adhere to data protection regulations, such as GDPR or CCPA. Implementing cybersecurity measures, encryption protocols, and strict access controls is essential to safeguard sensitive knowledge assets and prevent data breaches.

AI's ability to scale knowledge management processes is another practical advantage. AI-driven KMS can adapt to evolving business needs by continuously learning from data inputs. Organizations should invest in AI solutions that can expand as business operations grow, ensuring long-term innovation and efficiency in knowledge-sharing practices. Customer-centric applications of AI-powered KMS offer businesses valuable insights into consumer behavior. AI can analyze vast amounts of customer data, enabling businesses to personalize products, services, and marketing strategies. By leveraging AI in customer relationship management, organizations can enhance customer satisfaction and retention. Automation of repetitive tasks is another key benefit of AI in KMS. AI can handle routine knowledge management functions such as document categorization, data tagging, and content summarization. This automation frees employees to focus on strategic initiatives, fostering innovation and improving overall business performance.

However, businesses must also address potential employee resistance to AI adoption. Many employees fear that AI will replace human roles, leading to reluctance in embracing AI-driven KMS. To mitigate this resistance, organizations should actively involve employees in the AI integration process, provide training, and demonstrate how AI enhances rather than eliminates their roles.

Conclusion

According to the SLR on how AI affects corporate KMS, firms may pursue a number of strategic initiatives to optimize the advantages of this integration and the effects of AI on KMS. AI's revolutionary role in improving the entire process of creating, sharing, and using knowledge within businesses is what makes it so important in this field. The study's most notable finding is the recognition of AI's significant contribution to well-informed decision-making and the creation of valuable products. These findings are beneficial to both organizations and researchers since they offer fresh perspectives on how to use AI in KM strategies, which is essential for further developments in this area. In order to prevent data breaches that could result in a loss of consumer confidence and legal ramifications, the study also emphasizes the necessity of ethical frameworks and strong data security models while integrating AI in KMS.

However, it is important to note that this study has certain limitations, most of which are related to its methodological scope. In the first case, this review was limited to specific databases and relevant studies from other sources may have been omitted. In the second case, it should be remembered that by choosing particular keywords, relevant literature may be left out. Last but not least, imposing a deadline may have prevented the majority of the latest developments and ideas about AI and KMS in businesses from being included.

Recommendations

Regarding these boundaries, the following conclusions can be made, especially for companies and researchers who are interested in AI and KMS in the commercial world.

Businesses are urged to take a more open stance when integrating AI into their KMS with regard to data and knowledge sources. The ramifications of this procedure include taking into account emerging or unconventional sources of knowledge in addition to standard databases. Businesses seem to have an obligation to stay up to date with the latest developments in AI and KMS, either by leapfrogging or simply modifying their plans and policies to capitalize on emerging technologies and approaches.

For future studies researchers should concentrate on investigating the area more broadly, which means taking into account a greater variety of databases and keywords. This could reveal more varied perspectives and inclinations regarding the topic. In order to better understand and characterize the developing nature of AI and its inventive and disruptive impact on KMS, transversal studies may also be considered. Additionally, interdisciplinary methods are strongly encouraged as they constitute the foundation for exploring new boundaries in the field of AI integration in KM.

The overview of 21 papers covers research from several nations that examines various facets of AI in relation to information exchange, business process control, customer behavior, and HRM strategies. The application of AI in marketing and customer service, knowledge management issues, and how AI is enhancing goods and services were among the main subjects covered. These studies show how AI affects KMS, both positively and negatively. The authors also stress the importance of continuing studies on ethical conundrums, integration challenges, and how AI affects customer perceptions and corporate operations.

References

Akkiraju, R., Srivastava, B., Ivan, A. A., Goodwin, R., & Syeda-Mahmood, T. (2006, September). Semaplan: Combining planning with semantic matching to achieve web service composition. In *2006 IEEE international conference on web services (ICWS'06)* (pp. 37–44). IEEE. https://doi.org/10.1109/ICWS.2006.119

Alavi, M., & Leidner, D. E. (2001). Knowledge management and knowledge management systems: Conceptual foundations and research issues. *MIS Quarterly*, *25*(1), 107–136. https://doi.org/10.2307/3250961

Bakker, A. B., & Demerouti, E. (2007). The job demands-resources model: State of the art. *Journal of Managerial Psychology*, *22*(3), 309–328. https://doi.org/10.1108/02683940710733115

Bencsik, A. (2021). The sixth generation of knowledge management–The headway of artificial intelligence. *Journal of International Studies*, *14*(2), 84–101. https://doi.org/10.14254/2071-8330.2021/14-2/6

Bitkowska, A. (2020). The relationship between business process management and knowledge management-selected aspects from a study of companies in Poland. *Journal of Entrepreneurship, Management and Innovation*, *16*(1), 169–193. https://doi.org/10.7341/20201616

Bitkowska, A., Detyna, B., & Detyna, J. (2022). Importance of IT systems in integration of knowledge and business process management. *Issues in Information Systems*, *23*(1). https://doi.org/10.48009/1_iis_2022_109

Brynjolfsson, E., & Mcafee, A. (2017). The business of artificial intelligence. *Harvard Business Review*, *7*(1), 1–2. https://hbr.org/2017/07/the-business-of-artificial-intelligence

Chen, J. K., & Chen, I. S. (2013). A theory of innovation resource synergy. *Innovation*, *15*(3), 368–392. https://doi.org/10.5172/impp.2013.15.3.368

Choi, S. B., Kim, K., Ullah, S. E., & Kang, S. W. (2016). How transformational leadership facilitates innovative behavior of Korean workers: Examining mediating and moderating processes. *Personnel Review*, *45*(3), 459–479. https://doi.org/10.1108/PR-03-2014-0058

Coombs, C., Hislop, D., Taneva, S. K., & Barnard, S. (2020). The strategic impacts of intelligent automation for knowledge and service work: An interdisciplinary review. *The Journal of Strategic Information Systems*, *29*(4), 101600. https://doi.org/10.1016/j.jsis.2020.101600

Criado-García, F., Calvo-Mora, A., & Martelo-Landroguez, S. (2020). Knowledge management issues in the EFQM excellence model framework. *International Journal of Quality & Reliability Management*, *37*(5), 781–800. https://doi.org/10.1108/IJQRM-11-2018-0317

De Boeck, G., Meyers, M. C., & Dries, N. (2018). Employee reactions to talent management: Assumptions versus evidence. *Journal of Organizational Behavior*, *39*(2), 199–213. https://doi.org/10.1002/JOB.2254

Elendu, C., Amaechi, D. C., Elendu, T. C., Jingwa, K. A., Okoye, O. K., Okah, M. J., & Alimi, H. A. (2023). Ethical implications of AI and robotics in healthcare: A review. *Medicine*, *102*(50), e36671. https://doi.org/10.1097/MD.0000000000036671

Eslami, M., Vaccaro, K., Lee, M. K., Elazari Bar On, A., Gilbert, E., & Karahalios, K. (2019, May). User attitudes towards algorithmic opacity and transparency in online reviewing platforms. In *Proceedings of the 2019 CHI conference on human factors in computing systems* (pp. 1–14). https://doi.org/10.1145/3290605.3300724

Geisler, E., & Wickramasinghe, N. (2015). *Principles of knowledge management: Theory, practice, and cases*. Routledge. https://doi.org/10.4324/9781315686448

George, C. (2009). *The psychological contract: Managing and developing professional groups*. McGraw-Hill. https://books.google.co.in/books?id=uClFBgAAQBAJ

Goncharova, A., & Murach, D. (2020). Artificial intelligence as a subject of civil law. *Knowledge, Education, Law, Management*, *1*(3), 153–159. https://doi.org/10.51647/kelm.2020.3.1.26

Gretzel, U., Sigala, M., Xiang, Z., & Koo, C. (2015). Smart tourism: Foundations and developments. *Electronic Markets*, *25*, 179–188. https://doi.org/10.1007/s12525-015-0196-8

Gupta, S., & Polonsky, M. (2014). Inter-firm learning and knowledge-sharing in multinational networks: An outsourced organization's perspective. *Journal of Business Research*, *67*(4), 615–622. https://doi.org/10.1016/j.jbusres.2013.02.043

Haenlein, M., & Kaplan, A. (2019). A brief history of artificial intelligence: On the past, present, and future of artificial intelligence. *California Management Review*, *61*(4), 5–14. https://doi.org/10.1177/0008125619864925

Haidar, A. (2024). An integrative theoretical framework for responsible artificial intelligence. *International Journal of Digital Strategy, Governance, and Business Transformation*, *13*(1), 1–23. https://doi.org/10.4018/IJDSGBT.334844

Jain, V., Wadhwani, K., & Eastman, J. K. (2024). Artificial intelligence consumer behavior: A hybrid review and research agenda. *Journal of Consumer Behaviour*, *23*(2), 676–697. https://doi.org/10.1002/cb.2233

Kaplan, A., & Haenlein, M. (2019a). Digital transformation and disruption: On big data, blockchain, artificial intelligence, and other things. *Business Horizons*, *62*(6), 679–681. https://doi.org/10.1016/j.bushor.2019.07.001

Kaplan, A., & Haenlein, M. (2019b). Siri, Siri, in my hand: Who's the fairest in the land? On the interpretations, illustrations, and implications of artificial intelligence. *Business Horizons*, *62*(1), 15–25. https://doi.org/10.1016/j.bushor.2018.08.004

Lacity, M. C., & Willcocks, L. P. (2016). A new approach to automating services. *MIT Sloan Management Review*, *58*(1), 41–49. https://doi.org/10.7551/mitpress/11633.003.0015

Leoni, L., Ardolino, M., El Baz, J., Gueli, G., & Bacchetti, A. (2022). The mediating role of knowledge management processes in the effective use of artificial intelligence in manufacturing firms. *International Journal of Operations & Production Management*, *42*(13), 411–437. https://doi.org/10.1108/IJOPM-05-2022-0282

Liebowitz, J. (2000). Knowledge management receptivity at a major pharmaceutical company. *Journal of Knowledge Management*, *4*(3), 252–258. https://doi.org/10.1108/13673270010350057

Ma, X., & Brown, T. W. (2020). AI-mediated exchange theory. *arXiv:2003.02093*. https://arxiv.org/pdf/2003.02093.pdf

Ma, Y., Cheng, W., Ribbens, B. A., & Zhou, J. (2013). Linking ethical leadership to employee creativity: Knowledge sharing and self-efficacy as mediators. *Social Behavior and Personality: An International Journal*, *41*(9), 1409–1419. https://doi.org/10.2224/sbp.2013.41.9.1409

Mallach, E. G. (2000). *Decision support and data warehouse systems*. Irwin/McGraw-Hill. https://www.researchgate.net/profile/EfremMallach/publication/234799082_Decision_Support_and_Data_Warehouse_Systems/links/562fb88508ae02b5739a1c12/Decision-Support-and-Data-Warehouse-Systems.pdf

Mårtensson, M. (2000). A critical review of knowledge management as a management tool. *Journal of Knowledge Management*, *4*(3), 204–216. https://doi.org/10.1108/13673270010350002

Mohammad, M. F. N., Abdullah, R., Jabar, M. A., Nor, R. N. H., & Nur, N. M. (2024). A theoretical framework of knowledge management systems on quality management systems. *JOIV: International Journal on Informatics Visualization*, *8*(4), 2163–2172.

Moreno, V., Cavazotte, F., & Lapa, E. (2015). Integrating knowledge management practices and business processes: A case study. *Academy of Management Proceedings*, *2015*(1), 18915. https://doi.org/10.5465/ambpp.2015.18915abstract

Nguyen, M., Sharma, P., & Malik, A. (2024). Leadership styles and employee creativity: The interactive impact of online knowledge sharing and organizational innovation. *Journal of Knowledge Management*, *28*(3), 631–650. https://doi.org/10.1108/JKM-01-2023-0014

Olan, F., Arakpogun, E. O., Suklan, J., Nakpodia, F., Damij, N., & Jayawickrama, U. (2022). Artificial intelligence and knowledge sharing: Contributing factors to organizational performance. *Journal of Business Research*, *145*, 605–615. https://doi.org/10.1016/j.jbusres.2022.03.008

Olan, F., Nyuur, R. B., & Arakpogun, E. O. (2024). AI: A knowledge sharing tool for improving employees' performance. *Journal of Decision Systems*, *33*(4), 700–720. https://doi.org/10.1080/12460125.2023.2263687

Rodrigues, R. (2020). Legal and human rights issues of AI: Gaps, challenges and vulnerabilities. *Journal of Responsible Technology*, *4*, 100005. https://doi.org/10.1016/j.jrt.2020.100005

Rousseau, D. M. (1989). Psychological and implied contracts in organizations. *Employee Responsibilities and Rights Journal*, *2*, 121–139. https://doi.org/10.1007/BF01384942

Russell, S. J., & Norvig, P. (2016). *Artificial intelligence: A modern approach*. Pearson.

Singh, S. K., Gupta, S., Busso, D., & Kamboj, S. (2021). Top management knowledge value, knowledge sharing practices, open innovation and organizational performance. *Journal of Business Research*, *128*, 788–798. https://doi.org/10.1016/j.jbusres.2019.04.040

Turner, A. J., & Kuczynski, J. (2019, December). Impacts of behavioral modeling assumptions for complex adaptive systems: An evaluation of an online dating model. In *2019 winter simulation conference (WSC)* (pp. 668–679). IEEE. https://doi.org/10.1109/WSC40007.2019.9004665

Wiig, K. M. (1997). Knowledge management: An introduction and perspective. *Journal of Knowledge Management*, *1*(1), 6–14. https://doi.org/10.1108/13673279710800682

Wu, I. L., & Hu, Y. P. (2018). Open innovation-based knowledge management implementation: A mediating role of knowledge management design. *Journal of*

Knowledge Management, *22*(8), 1736–1756. https://doi.org/10.1108/JKM-06-2016-0238

Xiao, B., & Benbasat, I. (2007). E-commerce product recommendation agents: Use, characteristics, and impact. *MIS Quarterly*, 137–209. https://doi.org/10.2307/25148784

Conclusion

Chapter 15

Safeguarding the Future: Addressing Fraud, Misuse, and Ethical Vulnerabilities in AI-Driven Knowledge Management

Meir Russ[a] *and Miltiadis D. Lytras*[b]

[a]University of Wisconsin - Green Bay, USA; Stellenbosch University, South Africa
[b]The American College of Greece, Greece

Abstract

While the integration of artificial intelligence into knowledge management holds transformative potential for businesses, it also introduces a range of *ethical risks, security vulnerabilities, and opportunities for misuse.* As AI-generated knowledge becomes an asset, it also becomes a target—susceptible to manipulation, misinformation, and bias. This chapter offers a sobering yet constructive analysis of what can go wrong in the evolution of AI-driven KM, including fraud, opacity, misuse of organizational data, and algorithmic bias. It also explores safeguards—technical, human, and institutional—that can protect enterprises. Emphasis is placed on the pivotal role of knowledge managers, AI governance boards, ethical design practices, and regulatory compliance in maintaining trust and integrity in AI-powered knowledge ecosystems.

Keywords: Artificial intelligence; knowledge management; AI-driven decision-making; analytics; ethical AI; ethics; regulatory frameworks; AI fraud

Introduction: The Double-Edged Sword of Intelligent Knowledge

Artificial Intelligence (AI) has ushered in a new frontier in knowledge management—one where machines not only process information but increasingly *generate, recommend, and reshape* what constitutes organizational knowledge

AI-Driven Knowledge Management Assets, Volume 2, 307–320

Published under exclusive licence by Emerald Publishing Limited
doi:10.1108/978-1-83662-778-420261015

(Ranjan et al., 2024; Thakuri et al., 2024; Zhao et al., 2025). In fact this new era is expanding classical foundations of Knowledge management as has been covered by various research works (Chui et al., 2020; Chui et al., 2021; Lytras et al., 2020; Lytras, Lytra, & Lytras, 2021; Lytras et al. 2021; Lytras & Pouloudi, 2006; Naeve, Sicilia, & Lytras, 2008; Naeve et al., 2008; Russ, 2014, 2016; Sarirete et al., 2022; Visvizi et al., 2020).

As businesses transition toward AI-driven knowledge assets, the potential benefits are immense: real-time insights, intelligent search and retrieval, predictive knowledge applications, and scalable personalization (Berman et al., 2024; Booyse & Scheepers, 2024; Dwivedi et al., 2023; Rezaei et al., 2024). These capabilities are transforming not only how knowledge is captured and shared, but also how it is created and trusted. However, with great promise comes profound responsibility. The same algorithms that generate productivity-enhancing reports, recommend strategic actions, or structure learning content can also be leveraged—intentionally or inadvertently—for manipulation, deception, or discrimination. In the absence of *ethical design and oversight*, AI-generated knowledge may reinforce biases, spread misinformation, or even be used to create fraudulent documents with convincing language and formatting. Knowledge, once seen as a source of enlightenment, can become a vector for influence, control, or harm.

Unlike traditional knowledge, which has clear provenance and often human accountability, AI-generated knowledge is dynamic, probabilistic, and frequently *opaque in origin* (Naeve et al., 2008). This presents unique challenges to trust, governance, and verification. When AI starts making decisions about what knowledge is relevant, credible, or useful—especially in contexts such as healthcare, legal services, finance, or human resources—the stakes are significantly higher. Misjudgments in such environments can lead to *reputational damage, regulatory penalties, or irreversible harm to individuals and communities.*

Compounding these risks is the accelerating speed of AI evolution. In a matter of months, businesses have gone from piloting large language models (LLMs) for summarization tasks to integrating AI copilots in strategic decision systems. The rapidity of change has outpaced not only regulatory response but also *internal corporate readiness*, creating a gap between technical capability and ethical application.

In this closing chapter of the volume, we offer a critical perspective on what may go wrong as AI becomes further entrenched in KM systems and practices. We begin by outlining the *most pressing risks*, including fraud, data misuse, bias, and untraceable decision-making. Then, we turn to the *human role*—particularly that of knowledge managers and ethical leaders—in actively safeguarding the organization. Finally, we propose a set of *organizational structures and regulatory considerations* that support long-term integrity, accountability, and human-centered design in AI-driven KM.

This is not a cautionary tale meant to discourage innovation. Rather, it is a guide to ensure that *as we evolve toward autonomous, AI-augmented knowledge systems, we do so with wisdom, discipline, and inclusiveness.* In short, we must recognize that the management of knowledge is no longer merely a technical process—it is a matter of strategic, ethical, and societal importance.

In this final chapter, we explore:

- The core ethical vulnerabilities in AI-KM,
- Types of fraud or manipulation that may emerge,
- The role of humans in safeguarding systems,
- Structural and regulatory solutions to support responsible deployment.

What Could Go Wrong? Emerging Ethical Risks and Vulnerabilities

Artificial Intelligence has fundamentally altered the landscape of organizational knowledge. Its ability to synthesize, summarize, generate, and recommend content has unlocked extraordinary efficiencies. However, this evolution brings a *new class of ethical risks and vulnerabilities*—ones that challenge long-standing assumptions about knowledge credibility, authorship, fairness, and control.

In AI-enhanced knowledge management systems, the dangers are not just speculative—they are immediate, multifaceted, and deeply embedded in the very mechanisms that make AI powerful. As AI systems influence decision-making, corporate narratives, and strategic direction, organizations must reckon with the possibility that *not all knowledge generated by AI is accurate, ethical, or fair.*

Below, we unpack the key risk domains that businesses must anticipate and actively mitigate.

Algorithmic Bias and Hallucinated Knowledge

One of the most well-documented problems with AI systems is *algorithmic bias*—the tendency of AI models to reinforce existing inequalities or perpetuate inaccurate assumptions based on skewed training data. In the context of knowledge management, this means AI tools might:

- Prioritize dominant narratives while excluding marginalized perspectives,
- Misinterpret context or tone, leading to inappropriate suggestions or summaries,
- Produce *hallucinated facts*—fabricated information that appears credible.

For example, an AI-powered KM system used for HR decision support might generate onboarding materials or performance evaluations based on past records that carry *gender or cultural biases*, thereby institutionalizing unfair treatment without human realization. Worse still, generative tools might produce knowledge that is factually incorrect but presented with such fluency and detail that it *misleads users into false certainty*.

Such hallucinations are particularly dangerous in compliance, risk management, healthcare, and legal domains, where decisions based on false knowledge can have *severe operational and legal consequences.*

Fraud and Intellectual Property Violations

AI-driven content generation can be a *double-edged sword.* On one hand, it empowers organizations to produce reports, responses, and proposals at unprecedented speed. On the other hand, it introduces new risks of:

- *Plagiarism*, where outputs resemble copyrighted materials without attribution,
- *Fraudulent documentation*, where entire reports or policy briefs are fabricated using AI prompts,
- *Misuse of proprietary datasets*, where confidential or sensitive information is inadvertently exposed through AI training or inference.

Such issues raise significant concerns in sectors that rely on *auditability and originality*, such as academia, consulting, finance, and scientific R&D. The question of "who authored this content?" becomes ambiguous when machine-generated material is indistinguishable from human writing.

The misuse of GenAI to produce fabricated citations, manipulated case studies, or synthesized research claims may *undermine the credibility of organizational knowledge systems* and erode trust among stakeholders, clients, and regulators.

Data Exploitation and Surveillance

Many AI-KM systems learn from internal employee data—emails, chat logs, knowledge base contributions, and task histories. While this can enhance personalization and contextual intelligence, it also introduces *surveillance risks* and *data exploitation*:

- Employees may feel monitored or assessed without consent,
- AI models might infer psychological traits or behavioral tendencies,
- Personal communications can be used as training data for future outputs.

This dynamic creates a tension between personalization and privacy, between AI's hunger for data and individuals' right to digital dignity. If unregulated, such practices could *erode organizational culture*, increase burnout, or lead to legal challenges under emerging data protection laws.

Moreover, the more AI systems are trained on internal knowledge, the more they may inadvertently *expose trade secrets or confidential strategies* in outputs meant for broader audiences—especially when generative outputs are stored or shared on cloud platforms.

Erosion of Accountability and Explainability

As organizations rely more heavily on AI-generated insights to guide decisions, the risk of *accountability diffusion* grows. When something goes wrong—whether it's a flawed product launch, a discriminatory policy, or a failed customer strategy—stakeholders may struggle to determine:

- Who made the decision?
- Was it based on AI-generated knowledge?
- Was human oversight applied?

This lack of transparency—what some call the "*black box problem*"—can lead to ethical and legal gray zones. Explainability is crucial: *How did the system reach this conclusion? On what data? Using what logic?* Yet most AI models, particularly deep learning systems, do not offer this level of introspection.

As AI increasingly becomes an actor in organizational knowledge generation and decision-making, businesses risk creating environments where *actions are taken without responsibility*, decisions are accepted without question, and errors are blamed on machines.

Weaponization of Knowledge Systems

A final risk—often overlooked—is the *intentional misuse of AI-KM systems for manipulation, disinformation, or internal control.* For example:

- Leaders could suppress dissenting internal knowledge by training AI to reinforce preferred narratives,
- Misinformation could be amplified through automated content curation systems,
- AI insights could be selectively filtered to mislead shareholders or regulators.

While such abuses may seem extreme, they mirror real-world cases of *AI-enabled misinformation campaigns*, biased algorithmic news feeds, and data manipulation in political or financial contexts.

In the business world, *knowledge is power*—and AI, if left unchecked, becomes a powerful tool to distort reality. This makes *ethical governance*, transparency mechanisms, and human oversight not just best practices—but imperatives.

The Role of Human Judgment and Knowledge Leadership

As AI becomes more deeply embedded in enterprise knowledge ecosystems, it is easy to fall into the trap of believing that technology alone can manage knowledge. But knowledge, by its nature, is *contextual, cultural, and value-laden*—it cannot be fully automated without *human judgment*. Technology may accelerate information flows and generate insights at scale, but without human intervention, these outputs risk being misaligned with strategy, ethics, or reality.

In this regard, the *human role in AI-driven KM is not diminishing—it is being redefined and elevated.* It is no longer enough for humans to consume knowledge. They must also *curate, critique, validate, and safeguard* it. Below, we outline the three core dimensions of human-centered knowledge governance in the AI era.

Knowledge Officers as Ethical Gatekeepers

As the volume and velocity of AI-generated knowledge increases, the role of knowledge professionals must evolve from custodians of static repositories to *strategic enablers and ethical overseers* of machine-generated assets. Chief Knowledge Officers (CKOs), Knowledge Management Directors, and Information Governance leaders should:

- *Develop quality control frameworks* for AI outputs, ensuring content is accurate, relevant, and aligned with organizational objectives.
- *Design internal protocols* for reviewing, approving, or flagging AI-generated knowledge artifacts before they are shared or implemented.
- *Champion ethical AI use* across departments, encouraging practices that reduce hallucinations, bias, and misuse of sensitive knowledge.
- Serve as *liaisons with AI developers* to align model training with domain-specific knowledge needs and compliance standards.

These leaders play a pivotal role in *bridging technical capabilities with organizational accountability*. Their responsibilities should include not only taxonomy and content governance, but also *guiding principles for responsible knowledge generation*. As such, it is imperative that the officers are *skilled* and *well-trained* for the roles listed above.

Embedding Human-in-the-Loop (HITL) Protocols

Human-in-the-loop (HITL) mechanisms ensure that AI-generated knowledge is not blindly trusted but is subject to *human oversight, context validation, and ethical reflection*. In practice, HITL should not be a one-off intervention but a *systematic layer woven into the knowledge lifecycle*.

Key implementations include:

- *Review Layers*: Before AI-generated content is published (e.g., reports, FAQs, onboarding guides), human reviewers assess it for factual consistency, tone, and cultural relevance.
- *Decision Escalation*: High-risk decisions, such as hiring recommendations or compliance interpretations, are automatically escalated for human validation.
- *Feedback Loops*: Users provide structured feedback on the accuracy, relevance, and usefulness of AI outputs, which is then fed back into fine-tuning or prompt optimization processes.

- *Contextual Annotation*: Human experts enrich AI outputs with organizational context or disclaimers, clarifying what decisions can or cannot be made based on the AI's suggestion.

By embedding HITL into AI-KM workflows, organizations preserve a *critical balance between automation and accountability*, ensuring that knowledge systems serve business goals without compromising integrity.

Cultivating AI Literacy and Ethical Awareness

Even with technical safeguards and executive oversight, *ethical risks in AI-KM can only be addressed if knowledge users are empowered* with the skills to critically engage with machine-generated content. This requires a shift in organizational learning: *from passive compliance training to active ethical engagement.*

Core elements of effective AI-KM capacity building include:

AI Literacy for all Knowledge Workers (at Any Organizational Level)

Employees interacting with AI-driven platforms—whether sales reps using recommendation systems or analysts interpreting AI-generated insights—must understand:

- How these systems work,
- What their limitations are,
- When human verification is needed.

Training should include real-world case studies of AI failure, best practices for prompt engineering, and techniques to detect hallucinated or biased outputs.

Role-Specific Ethical Responsibilities

Different roles require tailored understanding. For instance:

- *Managers* should be trained in interpreting AI dashboards responsibly and knowing when to challenge automated conclusions.
- *Legal and Compliance teams* must understand where AI-KM intersects with data privacy, intellectual property, and regulatory risk.
- *Developers and data scientists* need guidelines for ensuring ethical dataset curation, model transparency, and explainability.

Organizational Culture of Critical Thinking

Perhaps most important is the development of a *culture that encourages questioning, learning, and shared responsibility.* When employees feel empowered to flag suspicious AI behavior or suggest alternative interpretations, the system becomes more robust, inclusive, and accountable.

Structural and Regulatory Safeguards: Embedding Integrity by Design

In the face of rising complexity, scale, and autonomy of AI systems in knowledge management, individual judgment and ad hoc ethical awareness are not enough. Organizations must *institutionalize trust* by embedding safeguards into their architecture, decision-making structures, and compliance strategies. This is about more than avoiding reputational damage or legal fines—it's about *future-proofing the organization's knowledge ecosystem.* To improve agility and sustainability, such ecosystems must also be diverse (see *Homo Sustainabiliticus* in Russ, 2014, 2016).

This section presents four critical domains of action: (a) internal governance structures, (b) transparency and explainability standards, (c) alignment with regulatory frameworks, and (d) the creation of trusted knowledge ecosystems.

Ethical AI Governance Boards

To ensure that AI-KM systems are developed and deployed responsibly, organizations must create *cross-functional governance boards* that combine expertise from knowledge management, data science, ethics, legal affairs, and operations.

These boards should be tasked with:

- *Reviewing AI-KM tools and vendor systems* for alignment with ethical principles, privacy laws, and organizational values.
- *Auditing algorithmic decision processes* related to knowledge generation, especially when they impact customer experience, employee performance, or strategic planning.
- *Setting risk thresholds* for different knowledge domains (e.g., operational content may have lower oversight than legal guidance or public reports).
- *Establishing escalation paths* for ethical incidents, including protocols for reporting, investigation, and resolution.

By integrating these boards into organizational governance, companies create a *systemic layer of accountability* that prevents ethical and operational blind spots from becoming crises.

Explainability and Transparency Standards

A core challenge in AI-driven KM is the *opacity of machine-generated knowledge.* When employees or customers are presented with recommendations or insights, they must be able to understand *how the system reached that conclusion*—not just what the result is.

To address this, organizations should adopt *explainability standards*:

- *Model transparency*: Provide users with insights into what data or patterns influenced the AI's output. For example, when a knowledge chatbot generates a strategic recommendation, the system should indicate whether the basis was customer sentiment analysis, internal reports, or industry data.
- *Content provenance tags*: Label AI-generated knowledge artifacts with timestamps, version history, and source indicators. This builds trust and allows users to assess reliability.
- *Confidence scores*: For sensitive or complex outputs, display confidence levels or probabilistic indicators so users can determine when human validation is necessary.
- *Interface prompts for ethical use*: Reminders, disclaimers, or contextual notes that help users interpret AI-generated content responsibly, especially in decision support contexts.

Such transparency measures not only *improve user trust and engagement* but also help fulfill emerging legal obligations in jurisdictions that are enacting "right to explanation" regulations.

Regulatory Alignment and Legal Compliance

The landscape of AI regulation is evolving rapidly. Organizations must ensure their knowledge systems comply not only with internal ethics but also with *national and international legal frameworks*. Key instruments to consider include:

EU AI Act

Expected to become a global benchmark, the EU AI Act classifies AI systems based on risk and imposes obligations on high-risk applications (including employment, critical infrastructure, and education). Knowledge management systems influencing hiring, promotion, or training must meet:

- Transparency standards,
- Human oversight requirements,
- Documentation and traceability protocols.

ISO/IEC 42001

This international standard outlines *management systems for responsible AI*, emphasizing risk assessment, lifecycle controls, and stakeholder inclusion. It offers a framework for AI-KM integration at scale.

Data Protection Regulations (e.g., GDPR, CCPA)

AI-KM platforms often process personal data to customize content or generate insights. Organizations must:

- Ensure consent and purpose limitation,
- Avoid over-personalization that infringes on privacy,
- Implement robust anonymization and data governance controls.

Intellectual Property Law

AI-generated content challenges traditional notions of authorship. Organizations should adopt *clear policies on content ownership*, licensing, and attribution, especially when AI is used to remix or repurpose internal or third-party knowledge.

By staying aligned with these frameworks, companies not only reduce legal exposure but also *signal maturity and trustworthiness* to stakeholders and the market.

Trusted Knowledge Ecosystems

A final structural safeguard is the development of *ecosystems that enable integrity, traceability, and collaboration* across the knowledge value chain.

Blockchain for Knowledge Provenance

Distributed ledger technologies can ensure that knowledge artifacts—whether AI-generated reports, training modules, or research summaries—have immutable records of:

- Creation and modification,
- Source datasets,
- Authorship and access history.

This is particularly useful in regulated industries (e.g., pharmaceuticals, finance, defense), where audit trails and version control are essential.

Secure AI Sandboxes

Before full-scale deployment, organizations can test AI-KM tools in sandbox environments where outputs are:

- Reviewed by domain experts,
- Stress-tested for bias, security, or hallucination risks,
- Evaluated for ethical and cultural implications.

Inter-Organizational Ethics Collaboratives

Given the cross-cutting nature of knowledge and AI, businesses should join sector-specific or multi-stakeholder collaboratives to:

- Share best practices,
- Align on ethical standards,
- Engage with regulators and civil society.

Examples include the *Partnership on AI*, *AI4People*, and the *OECD AI Principles* initiatives.

Conclusion: Designing for Trust, Empowerment, and Long-Term Value in AI-Driven Knowledge Management

The journey explored throughout this chapter—and indeed, throughout this volume—has illustrated a profound paradox: while AI unlocks unprecedented opportunities for advancing knowledge management in business, it simultaneously introduces profound ethical, operational, and governance challenges.

AI is not just another tool in the knowledge management arsenal; it is a transformative force that *reshapes how knowledge is created, validated, disseminated, and trusted.* It alters roles, blurs boundaries between authorship and automation, and forces a rethinking of what it means to "know" something within a business context. In this sense, knowledge no longer flows linearly from expert to user but is now co-produced, probabilistically assembled, and continuously regenerated by intelligent systems. While this presents enormous possibilities, it also creates *vulnerabilities that must be proactively addressed.*

The risks explored in this chapter—from algorithmic bias and hallucinated outputs to surveillance threats and erosion of accountability—are not theoretical. They are already manifesting in operational settings. Moreover, these risks do not stem from malice or incompetence, but from *misalignment between technical capability and ethical oversight.* Without purposeful design and critical engagement, AI can easily amplify inequalities, mislead decision-makers, and diminish organizational integrity.

The response, as argued, must be multifaceted. It begins with *human agency*—knowledge officers who evolve from gatekeepers to ethical curators, business leaders who understand AI's limitations as well as its promise, and employees who are trained not just to use AI but to *challenge and refine its outputs.* It continues through *structural design*—governance boards, explainability standards, and regulatory alignment—ensuring that AI systems are accountable by design, not just by intention.

But perhaps most crucially, businesses must *cultivate a culture of responsible innovation.* This means not shying away from experimentation, but embedding experimentation within a framework of trust, transparency, and collective responsibility. It means treating knowledge as a *strategic asset and a moral artifact*, whose value lies not only in its utility but in its truthfulness, inclusiveness, and ethical grounding.

Looking forward, the successful organizations will not be those who adopt AI the fastest—but those who adopt it *most wisely*. This involves developing long-term strategies for:

- Ensuring equity and inclusion in AI-generated knowledge,
- Preserving human creativity and intuition amid automation,
- Establishing clear ethical baselines for AI-KM applications,
- Leveraging cross-sector collaboration to align business needs with societal values.

This book concludes with a clear call to action: *the future of AI-driven knowledge management must be built on a foundation of ethical foresight, human empowerment, and organizational accountability*. We are entering an era where the architecture of knowledge is increasingly digital, adaptive, and intelligent. The risks of a society driven by *Homo Technologicus* (Longo, 2005; Russ, 2016) toward Autonomous Businesses (Drenik, 2025; Flor, 2003) at this point are too high. It is up to us—as knowledge leaders, researchers, innovators, and practitioners—to ensure that this architecture is also just, transparent, and human-centered.

If we succeed, AI will not replace knowledge workers—it will *amplify their potential*. It will not obscure the truth—it will *make truth more accessible*. And it will not fragment our shared understanding—it will *help us build new, inclusive, and enduring knowledge ecosystems* for a better business future.

References

Berman, A., de Fine Licht, K., & Carlsson, V. (2024). Trustworthy AI in the public sector: An empirical analysis of a Swedish labor market decision-support system. *Technology in Society*, *76*. https://doi.org/10.1016/j.techsoc.2024.102471

Booyse, D., & Scheepers, C. B. (2024). Barriers to adopting automated organisational decision-making through the use of artificial intelligence. *Management Research Review*, *47*(1), 64–85. https://doi.org/10.1108/MRR-09-2021-0701

Chui, K. T., Lytras, D. M., & Vasant, P. (2020). Combined generative adversarial network and fuzzy C-means clustering for multi-class voice disorder detection with an imbalanced dataset. *Applied Sciences*, *10*(13). https://doi.org/10.3390/app10134571

Chui, K. T., Lytras, D. M., Visvizi, A., & Sarirete, A. (2021). An overview of artificial intelligence and big data analytics for smart healthcare: Requirements, applications, and challenges. In *Artificial intelligence and big data analytics for smart healthcare* (pp. 243–254). https://doi.org/10.1016/B978-0-12-822060-3.00015-2

Drenik, G. (2025, May 13). The rise of autonomous businesses: How AI is redefining startup growth. *Forbes*. https://www.forbes.com/sites/garydrenik/2025/05/13/the-rise-of-autonomous-businesses-how-ai-is-redefining-startup-growth/?utm_source="'flipboard&utm_content=user/forbes

Dwivedi, Y. K., Kshetri, N., Hughes, L., Slade, E. L., Jeyaraj, A., Kar, A. K., Baabdullah, A. M., Koohang, A., Raghavan, V., Ahuja, M., Albanna, H., Albashrawi, M. A., Al-Busaidi, A. S., Balakrishnan, J., Barlette, Y., Basu, S., Bose, I., Brooks, L., Buhalis, D., … Wright, R. (2023). "So what if ChatGPT wrote it?" Multidisciplinary perspectives on opportunities, challenges, and implications of generative conversational AI for research, practice, and policy. *International Journal of Information Management*, *71*. https://doi.org/10.1016/j.ijinfomgt.2023.102642

Flor, N. V. (2003). An analysis of the design of a programmable autonomous business. *Journal of Systems and Information Technology*, *7*(1/2), 111–128.

Longo, G. O. (2005). *Homo technologicus* (Vol. 33). Meltemi Editore srl.

Lytras, M. D., Visvizi, A., & Jussila, J. (2020). Social media mining for smart cities and smart villages research. *Soft Computing*, *24*(15), 10983–10987.

Lytras, D. M., Lytra, H., & Lytras, D. (2021). Healthcare in the times of artificial intelligence: Setting a value-based context. In *Artificial intelligence and big data analytics for smart healthcare* (pp. 1–9). https://doi.org/10.1016/B978-0-12-822060-3.00011-5

Lytras, M. D., & Pouloudi, A. (2006). Towards the development of a novel taxonomy of knowledge management systems from a learning perspective: An integrated approach to learning and knowledge infrastructures. *Journal of Knowledge Management*, *10*(6), 64–80.

Lytras, M. D., Visvizi, A., Chopdar, P. K., Sarirete, A., & Alhalabi, W. (2021). Information management in smart cities: Turning end users' views into multi-item scale development, validation, and policy-making recommendations. *International Journal of Information Management*, *56*, 102146.

Naeve, A., Sicilia, M., & Lytras, M. D. (2008). Learning processes and processing learning: From organizational needs to learning designs. *Journal of Knowledge Management*, *12*(6), 5–14.

Naeve, A., Yli-Luoma, P., Kravcik, M., & Lytras, M. D. (2008). A modelling approach to study learning processes with a focus on knowledge creation. *International Journal of Technology Enhanced Learning*, *1*(1–2), 1–34.

Ranjan, S., Joshith, V. P., Kavitha, K., & Chittakath, S. (2024). The AI-knowledge management nexus for sustainable learning: A PLS-SEM study. *Knowledge Management and E-Learning*, *16*(4), 811–837. https://doi.org/10.34105/j.kmel.2024.16.037

Rezaei, M., Pironti, M., & Quaglia, R. (2024). AI in knowledge sharing, which ethical challenges are raised in decision-making processes for organisations? *Management Decision*. https://doi.org/10.1108/MD-10-2023-2023

Russ, M. (2014). Homo sustainabiliticus and the "new gold". In *Value creation, reporting, and signaling for human capital and human assets: Building the foundation for a multi-disciplinary, multi-level theory* (pp. 1–16). Palgrave Macmillan US.

Russ, M. (2016). The probable foundations of sustainabilism: Information, energy and entropy based definition of capital, Homo Sustainabiliticus and the need for a "new gold". *Ecological Economics*, *130*, 328–338.

Sarirete, A., Balfagih, Z., Brahimi, T., Lytras, M. D., & Visvizi, A. (2022). Artificial intelligence and machine learning research: Towards digital transformation at a global scale. *Journal of Ambient Intelligence and Humanized Computing*, *13*(7), 3319–3321. https://doi.org/10.1007/s12652-021-03168-y

Thakuri, S., Bon, M., Cavus, N., & Sancar, N. (2024). Artificial intelligence on knowledge management systems for businesses: A systematic literature review. *TEM Journal*, *13*(3), 2146–2155. https://doi.org/10.18421/TEM133-42

Visvizi, A., Jussila, J., Lytras, M. D., & Ijäs, M. (2020). Tweeting and mining OECD-related microcontent in the post-truth era: A cloud-based app. *Computers in Human Behavior*, *107*, 105958.

Zhao, W., Rachwalski, A., Berndt-Goke, M., & Jin, Y. (2025). An examination of management of AI-triggered organisational threats from communication practitioners' perspective. *Journal of Contingencies and Crisis Management*, *33*(1). https://doi.org/10.1111/1468-5973.70031

Printed and bound by CPI Group (UK) Ltd, Croydon, CR0 4YY

13/09/2026

14961028-0005